D1564038

THE WEHRMACHT WAR CRIMES BUREAU, 1939–1945

THE WEHRMACHT WAR CRIMES BUREAU, 1939–1945

Alfred M. de Zayas

With the collaboration of Walter Rabus   Foreword by Howard Levie

UNIVERSITY OF NEBRASKA PRESS   LINCOLN AND LONDON

Originally published by Universitas/Langen Müller as *Die Wehrmacht-Untersuchungsstelle*, © 1979 by Alfred M. de Zayas

© 1989 by the University of Nebraska Press   All rights reserved

Manufactured in the United States of America

The paper in this book meets the minimum requirements of American National Standard for Information Sciences—Permanence of Paper for Printed Library Materials, ANSI Z39.48–1984.

Library of Congress Cataloging-in-Publication Data

De Zayas, Alfred M.

[Wehrmacht-Untersuchungsstelle. English]

The Wehrmacht War Crimes Bureau, 1939–1945 / Alfred M. de Zayas.

p.   cm.

Translation of: Die Wehrmacht-Untersuchungsstelle.

Bibliography: p.

Includes index.

ISBN 0-8032-1680-7 (alk. paper)

ISBN 0-8032-9908-7 (pbk.)

1. War crimes.   2. Germany. Wehrmacht-Untersuchungsstelle.

3. World War, 1939–1945—Atrocities.   I. Title.

JX5419.5D4913   1989

341.6'9—dc19   88-31596 CIP

CONTENTS

Individuals of every nation commit violations of the laws and custom of war; and well-disciplined armed forces try their own members for such acts. Although these individuals are usually tried by a court-martial for a violation of the law of their own country and the matter receives little publicity (unless it is a My Lai!), they are actually being tried for war crimes. Perhaps because of this lack of publicity, as well as a general lack of understanding on the part of the public, there is a tendency to believe that only members of the enemy armed forces commit war crimes. The writer's personal library contains approximately one hundred items on various aspects of the World War II war crimes problem and only a very small handful of those items discusses the problem from the German or Japanese point of view. For this reason alone, *The Wehrmacht War Crimes Bureau, 1939–1945*, originally written in German and published in Germany and now translated into English by the author for publication in the United States, is a welcome addition to the literature on the subject, particularly for those of us who are not familiar with the German language.

The research for this book, which extended over a number of years, included the review of several hundred volumes of official records of the investigations of war crimes by the Wehrmacht War Crimes Bureau, the existence of which was hitherto unknown to researchers, the review of other original documents (including many in Russian, one of the author's several languages) and hundreds of interviews and correspondence with Germans who were involved in various capacities in the Bureau and in various aspects of these investigations by or on behalf of the Bureau during the course of World War II, as well as with witnesses to the events described.

The first half of the text is concerned with the work of the Bureau's

World War I predecessor, and the background and World War II activities of the Bureau as well as of other organizations, mostly military, which were engaged in parallel activities. This portion includes an analysis of the Bureau's personnel and method of operation, the uses to which its product was put, examples of investigations of reported violations of the laws and customs of war by members of the German armed forces, etc. It is important to bear in mind that the Bureau was purely an investigatory body, with no power to indict and no prosecutorial functions; however, the Bureau's files had been used as evidence in war crimes trials of Allied (Russian, Polish, and French) prisoners of war which the Germans had conducted during the course of World War II. Of particular interest is the chapter setting forth the manner in which during 1940 a group of German lawyers, including those of the Wehrmacht, met to plan a new codification of international law, one which would more closely meet the requirements of German interests, one which Nazi Germany would be able to impose upon other nations when the then anticipated *Pax Germanica* came into being.

The second half of the text goes into detail with respect to a number of specific cases investigated by the Bureau, investigations of violations of the laws and customs of war allegedly committed by members of the forces in conflict with Germany, primarily, but not exclusively, those of the Soviet Union. Parallel offenses committed by members of the Nazi SS and SD in occupied countries are occasionally referred to during these discussions. The records of the Bureau, as well as information in the public domain, leave little doubt that atrocities were committed by the Russians against Germans, Poles, Ukrainians, etc. It will be the task of some other researcher to present us with a study in depth of the atrocities that were, with equal lack of doubt, committed by those two Nazi organizations, as well as by the *Einsatzgruppen*. (The case of *United States vs. Otto Ohlendorf et al* is only a beginning for such a study.)

One of the author's stated self-imposed tasks was "to draw the line between historical events and mere propaganda." The main impression that this book left with the writer was the professional, non-propagandistic, and uncharacteristic-of-the-Nazis, manner in which the Wehrmacht War Crimes Bureau performed its mission. The author ascribes this in part to the fact that most of the members of the Bureau, and many of the Army judges who performed much of the field work, were jurists of the "old school", neither fanatics nor members of the Nazi Party (for this reason some had actually sought refuge in the military legal department). According to the author, another explanation may have been the comparative freedom of the Wehrmacht from Nazi influence, unlike all other aspects of life in Germany during the period under review. It is somewhat difficult to accept the thesis that, with Nazi Germany being as thoroughly organized as it was, the Bureau could have eluded the grasp of Hitler, von Ribbentrop, Goebbels and Himmler. But while we may thus have some reservations with respect to the author's conclusion in this regard, particularly in view of the positions occupied by and the activities of Keitel and Jodl, he has certainly set forth a well-documented and convincing presentation to support it.

It can be said without fear of contradiction that this book opens a new dimension in the study of the war crimes committed during World War II. It should generate much discussion and encourage other students of that period to further research, not only into the legal and historical, but also into the sociological and psychological, aspects of this facet of that conflict.

Howard S. Levie
Professor Emeritus of Law
Saint Louis University Law School

ACKNOWLEDGMENTS

Many persons have assisted me in the preparation of this book. I am particularly grateful to the archivists of the Bundesarchiv Koblenz and Bundesarchiv-Militärarchiv in Freiburg, of the National Archives at Washington, D.C., and Suitland, Maryland, of the Public Record Office in London and of the Bundesarchiv in Bern. Above all I must thank my colleague Dr. Walter Rabus of the University of Amsterdam in the Netherlands, who in 1976 and 1977 shared the task of research and interviewing when I was in charge of the "working group on the laws of war" at the Institute of International Law of the University of Göttingen in West Germany. His perceptive criticism accompanied my work throughout the project and we subsequently discussed my original German manuscript and this abridged translation into English. His great expertise in international law proved invaluable in shaping our own ideas about the German Army Bureau, its methodology and the weight to be given to its files.

I should also like to thank Professors Andreas Hillgruber (Cologne), Dietrich Rauschning (Göttingen), and Ignaz Seidl-Hohenveldern (Vienna) for their advice while writing this book, and Professor Howard Levie (Newport, R.I.) for his foreword to the American edition.

INTRODUCTION

The military and diplomatic files of the Third Reich have been the object of innumerable scholarly investigations over the past forty years. By contrast, and surprisingly enough, the records of the legal department of the High Command of the Wehrmacht, as well as those of the legal offices of the war-time German army, navy, and air force, have remained practically untouched.

These records are not, of course, complete. The files of the German armed forces and most of their bureaus, many of which had been deposited in the military archives at Potsdam, were largely destroyed during World War II, especially in the great fire following the Allied air bombardment of 14–15 April 1945. Those documents that escaped, including whatever current files the Germans themselves failed to destroy, were seized by Allied troops. How much military documentation fell into Soviet hands is not known (relatively few records have been released by the Soviet Union to the military archives of the German Democratic Republic), but a considerable bulk of official records was subsequently transported to the United States.

Among these, an important record group that has until recently escaped attention is that of the *Wehrmacht-Untersuchungsstelle für Verletzungen des Völkerrechts*, Germany's Bureau for the Investigation of War Crimes. Owing to the frequent air bombardment of Berlin, this Bureau moved its offices in August 1943 to the town of Torgau on the Elbe River, some seventy miles to the south. With the advance of the Soviet army in 1945, it moved again, west to Langensalza in Thuringia. There, before the American troops arrived early in April 1945, some government files were thrown into the courtyard of the military barracks and set on fire.[1] Shortly before the American forces linked up with the Red Army on April 25, the files that remained in Langensalza and Torgau were captured by the U.S. Army's records collecting team and eventually sent to Washington, where they were stored for many years as "classified" documents, out of the reach of scholars.[2] Not until their declassification in 1965 were the files microfilmed and thus made available to researchers at the Modern Military Branch of the National Archives.[3] The documents themselves were shipped back to the Federal Republic of Germany in 1968–69. They are now housed in the military archives (*Bundesarchiv-Militärarchiv*) in Freiburg, where they have been provisionally bound in 226 volumes of 100 to 500 pages each. Their use is unrestricted.

The task assigned to the *Wehrmacht-Untersuchungsstelle* was to investigate reports of alleged violations of the laws and customs of war, whether committed by members of the Allied or the Axis armed forces; however, the extant files of the Bureau—estimated to be perhaps half of its total records—include no investigations of Axis war crimes apart from a thin volume concerning the killing of British prisoners of war in North Africa in 1942. The remaining 225 volumes deal with alleged Allied violations, primarily by the Soviet Union. The bulk of these available records is made up of witness testimony sworn to before German military judges; military intelligence reports and captured Allied documents add valuable information.

The War Crimes Bureau was not a special invention of Nazi Germany, but rather the direct successor to the Prussian Military Bureau of Investigation of Violations of the Laws of War (see Chapter 1), which had operated during World War I as an organ of the Reich War Ministry. Only a minor portion of that agency's records remain (see Note on the Sources preceding the Bibliography). But a notable continuity between the two agencies was maintained in the person of Johannes Goldsche, a military judge who, having been deputy chief of the Prussian bureau, was reactivated upon the outbreak of hostilities in 1939 and headed the War Crimes Bureau for the duration of World War II. The old and new bureaus had the same task of documenting Allied offenses and submitting reports to the German Foreign Office, which used these reports to lodge diplomatic protests against Allied powers. The members of both bureaus were military judges, who either personally questioned the witnesses—mostly members of the armed forces—or delegated the taking of depositions to the competent military or civilian courts in the areas where the witnesses were stationed, hospitalized, or in residence.

In the light of the corrupted court system of the Third Reich, extensively documented in the Nuremberg trials (particularly in the so-called "Justice Trial" before the American Military Tribunal),[4] a serious question as to the credibility of the judicial findings of the War Crimes Bureau is inescapable. Did the judges let ideology influence the depositions on alleged Allied war crimes? To what extent *can* a belligerent state, party to an armed conflict, carry out an objective investigation of reported violations of the laws of war? The answers are not facilitated by the fact that atrocity propaganda is part and parcel of the "artillery" of modern warfare. It is well known that the Nazi regime considered propaganda—whether true or false—an essential weapon of government. As Hitler said in briefing senior military personnel on the forthcoming campaign in Poland: "The outbreak of the conflict shall be launched through appropriate propaganda. Credibility is not so important, since victory creates its own right."[5]

Certainly, the Nazis did not hesitate to fabricate incidents with which to defame their opponents. We know, for instance, that on the eve of the German attack on Poland, the *Schutzstaffel* (Himmler's notorious ss) simulated a Polish takeover of the German radio station at Gleiwitz, Upper Silesia, which lay close to the Polish-German frontier.[6] And for some weeks preceding the attack on Poland, the Nazi press, notably the *Völkischer Beobachter* and *Das Reich*, published real and fictitious reports of abuses and killings committed by the Poles upon the resident German minority. These and subsequent episodes illustrate the extent to which unscrupulous Nazi politicians were prepared to go in order to discredit their enemies. As a result, international public opinion both during and after the war tended to reject German allegations of Allied war crimes out of hand.

Judge Hans Boetticher, one of several military judges sent by the War Crimes Bureau to investigate reported abuses in Poland, remembers the skepticism of foreign journalists with whom he discussed the results of his work at Bromberg (see Chapter 13): "I told them that the depositions . . . clearly established cases of Polish atrocities. . . . But the Polish atrocities that Goebbels had invented had had their effect, so that no one believed anything else that sounded similar. Each time Adolf Hitler wanted to invade a country, all sorts of atrocities were reported. This had been the case with Czechoslovakia as it was also in Poland: a justification . . . had to be found, to wit, that atrocities had been committed on Germans by non-Germans. The journalists therefore took these accusations for propaganda."[7]

According to the evidence collected by the War Crimes Bureau, however, countless excesses were indeed perpetrated upon the German minority in Poland—more than Polish authorities have admitted, though not nearly so many as Goebbels maintained. The German Propaganda Ministry stated that "Polish terror" had taken the lives of "58,000 Germans missing or dead," and a telegram from Berlin dated February 1940 instructed the Central Bureau for the graves of murdered *Volksdeutsche* at Posen—whose register contains only 5,495 names of dead and missing persons—that "the number of 58,000 . . . must be taken as the only official figure."[8]

In some instances of foreign reluctance to believe German allegations, the evidence is still incomplete. When mass graves containing thousands of Polish dead were found at Katyn in 1943 (see Chapter 21), the German and Soviet authorities issued mutual accusations, but the German white book on the matter was generally dismissed as mere Goebbels-style propaganda, and Katyn was incorporated into the Nazi indictment at Nuremberg: "In September 1941, 11,000 Polish officers who were prisoners of war were killed in the Katyn Forest near Smolensk."[9] The German defense was so strong against this point, however, that eventually the accusation was quietly dropped.

Allied reaction to German reports on Soviet excesses in Nemmersdorf and other locations in East Prussia in October 1944 similarly reflects the degree of skepticism prevalent in British and American official circles, regardless of photographic evidence, depositions of witnesses, and even firsthand reports from neutral journalists.[10]

It is understandable that Nazi propaganda tactics—fabrication of incidents, multiplication of the number of victims, and the like—led to an atmosphere of complete mistrust, and this lack of confidence in German sources necessarily extends also to the reliability of the investigations carried out by the War Crimes Bureau, an agency that operated within a highly unscrupulous system. Did Josef Goebbels order the faking of reports and photographs? Did the witnesses and judges who are mentioned in the files and whose signatures are on the reports actually exist? What credibility, if any, can be attributed to the 226 volumes of records left by the *Wehrmacht-Untersuchungsstelle*?

It is the task of this book to evaluate these records, to examine the establishment, function, and methods of this German bureau of investigation, and to try to draw the line between historical events and mere propaganda. In order to do so, the author first attempted to determine whether the files gave the impression of genuine investigations, whether the documents showed the various stages of every case, whether contradictions arose, whether there was any indication that evidence might have been fabricated or documents doctored for propaganda purposes.

The next step was to establish whether the persons named in the documents—judges, witnesses, and victims—really existed, whether they were actually involved in the cases described, and whether they testified of their own volition or were forced to sign prepared statements. The author interviewed more than 300 judges, witnesses, and victims, and in every case they confirmed the correctness of the protocols. Frequently they were able to provide additional information, carbon copies of the same or other depositions, and sometimes even pertinent snapshots taken by themselves or their comrades. Valuable information was added by numerous other witnesses who had not given wartime depositions but could confirm the events described in the documents.

The final effort consisted in verifying the events dealt with in the Bureau's documents by consulting other German record groups and also the relevant American, British, French, and Swiss files. In the Political Archives (German Foreign Office) in Bonn, in the Public Record Office (Foreign Office, War Office, Air Ministry, Admiralty) in London, in the National Archives (State Department, War Department, SHAEF, Judge Advocate General) in Washington, and in the Swiss Federal Archives (Protecting Power papers) in Bern there are many documents that helped to complete the picture (see Note on the Sources).

All in all, the coherency of the War Crimes Bureau files, the confirmation of persons involved, and the comparison with other historical sources justify the conclusion that the Bureau did function in a trustworthy manner, that its investigations were authentic and its documentation reliable. Though there is no guarantee that the depositions are correct in every detail, and though the files of course contain only the German view of the events, it is nevertheless evident that the Bureau was not a propaganda arm of the Nazi regime but a military investigative agency much like those that exist in the legal offices of the armed forces of many other nations. Its sober procedures were surely influenced by its chief, Johannes Goldsche. This old lawyer and judge had no sympathy for the Nazis or their methods; indeed, it is important—and surprising—to note that in spite of his high position, Goldsche was never a member of the National Socialist Party, as was generally expected of senior civil servants under Hitler.

This study of the War Crimes Bureau is in the first place historical. It attempts to contribute to a better understanding of a special aspect of the structure of the Third Reich by elucidating the manner in which a little-known agency functioned and by providing a general view of those of its records that survived the war. This study is also legal, since it analyzes German legal documents on alleged Allied war crimes. The documentation shows that soldiers in many armies committed grave offenses against the laws of war; unfortunately, the files do not reveal whether or to what extent those violations became the subject of court-martial proceedings by the armies involved.

The historical and legal scope of this book has determined its arrangement into two parts: a history of the Bureau itself, and a selection of case studies. In Part I, a description of the origin, task, and organization of the Bureau is followed by an examination of how it functioned in practice and the uses to which its results were put—by the German Foreign Office and other agencies. Part II illustrates the Bureau's work by presenting a number of concrete examples representing investigations carried out during the various phases of the war and in all its theaters.

The selection of cases presented some difficulty, since the goal was to show a cross-section of the Bureau's work and at the same time to examine events of particular historical importance. From the legal point of view, however, it is worthwhile to analyze even those individual cases that carry little historical weight; indeed, the latter best demonstrate the need to strengthen the arm of military justice so that every soldier expects violations of the laws of war to be prosecuted.

It was the horror of World War II that gave rise to the new Geneva Conventions—signed on 12 August 1949, confirmed and extended in the 1977 Geneva Protocols—in which the signatory powers pledged "to enact any legislation necessary to provide effective penal sanctions"[11] against persons who commit or order grave violations of the Conventions; to prosecute offenders before their own courts; "in time of peace as in time of war, to disseminate the text of the present Convention as widely as possible in their respective countries"; and "to include the study thereof in their programs of military and, if possible, civil instruction."[12] It is in the spirit of these humanitarian treaties that this study should be understood: as an appeal for their implementation by all belligerent parties.

In reading about violations of international law on the part of those who were fighting against the Nazi regime, one cannot help remembering the enormity of the crimes committed by Nazi Germany itself. The gas chambers of Auschwitz-Birkenau, the systematic mass murder of Jews and Gypsies, the killing of hostages, and the draconian reprisals taken by the Wehrmacht in occupied Europe belong in a different dimension: they are not just war crimes but crimes against humanity. The events discussed in the following pages must be understood in their proper historical context—chiefly as excesses of individual soldiers fighting an aggressor nation. But certainly crimes on one side do not excuse crimes on the other. All victims are equal in death.

PART I / HISTORY, METHODS, AND USES

OF THE WAR CRIMES BUREAU

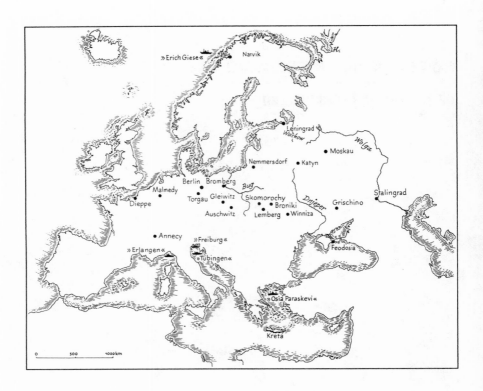

The activity of the German War Crimes Bureau must be seen in the context of the gradual development of the laws of war since the end of the nineteenth century and the emergence of national and international commissions to monitor their implementation.

At the Peace Conferences at The Hague in 1899 and 1907 the laws and customs of war were scrutinized, part of them being codified in the form of regulations annexed to the Hague Convention IV respecting the Laws and Customs of War on Land.[1] On the basis of these regulations military lawyers developed criteria according to which the legality of the behavior of soldiers on the field could be tested. Although inspired by humanitarian considerations,[2] these regulations also reflect the political realities of state interests.[3]

The violation of the laws of war may have manifold consequences. The perpetrator can be held personally responsible and court-martialed by his own military or brought before an enemy tribunal. The state whose citizens become victims of a violation may take such diplomatic steps as official protest via the institution of the Protecting Power.[4] There is a general obligation on the part of the offending state to provide compensation.[5] Moreover, war crimes accusations constitute an important part of modern war propaganda.

In both world wars the belligerent parties established, for judicial and political reasons, special commissions to investigate reported instances of war crimes by the enemy forces.

Allied Investigations of German War Crimes in World War I

Scarcely a week after the outbreak of hostilities in 1914, a special Belgian commission was set up on 8 August, which quickly produced a number of accusations, a report dated 16 September 1914, and a Belgian "Gray Book."[6] These documents concerned the killing of hostages, arson, the destruction of cities (such as Louvain), instances of rape, and the alleged mutilation of children's hands by German invaders.[7]

In December 1914 Great Britain set up a commission under Lord James Bryce[8] to investigate reports of war crimes committed by the German Army in Belgium and the north of France. In the course of the war Great Britain protested a number of events, in particular those involving German submarine warfare, such as the sinking of the hospital ship *Llandovery Castle* on 27 June 1918 by the German submarine U-86 under the command of Helmut Patzig. Survivors reported that they were shot at and many were killed following the sinking.[9] French protests accused Germany of damaging the Cathedral of Reims and of ill-treating French prisoners of war.[10]

After the armistice in November 1918 the victorious Allies pooled their reports on German violations of the laws of war; a special Allied commission compiled a joint list of German war crimes and demanded the extradition of some 900 persons. The commission's report provided the legal basis for the extradition lists[11] and for Articles 228 and 229 of the Treaty of Versailles (signed by Germany on 28 June 1919), by which the German government recognized the right of the Allied and Associated Powers to bring before military tribunals German officers and soldiers accused of having committed acts in violation of the laws and customs of war.

Because the idea of extraditing German soldiers for prosecution in Paris or London proved extremely unpopular in Germany, however, the German government negotiated with the Allies to modify the prosecution requirement by allowing the accused Germans to be tried by the German Supreme Court (*Reichsgericht*) at Leipzig.[12]

In the *Llandovery Castle* case, Commander Helmut Patzig was at large, and First Boatswain's Mate Meissner—who was reported to have shot at the shipwrecked—had died before the trial opened. This is why only Lieutenants Ludwig Dithmar and John Boldt, who were reported to have been on deck at the time of the firing, appeared before the court in Leipzig. They were found guilty of manslaughter and on 16 July 1921 sentenced to four years' imprisonment (Patzig's orders were regarded as mitigating circumstances).[13]

On 26 May 1921 the court sentenced Sergeant Karl Heynen, in charge of a prisoner-of-war camp in Herne, to six months' imprisonment for ill-treatment of prisoners. On 2 June 1921 the court sentenced Private Robert

Neumann and Captain Emil Müller—commander of the prison camp Flavy le Martel—to six months' imprisonment, also for ill-treatment of prisoners. Major Benno Crusius was convicted of having passed down an order of General Karl Stenger not to take any French prisoners and thus to have been responsible for the killing of French soldiers; on 21 August 1921 the court sentenced him to two years' imprisonment.[14] By Nuremberg standards this would appear very lenient, but again the court considered that superior orders constituted mitigating circumstances.

Generally speaking, the German population took exception to these trials, especially because the Allies were not similarly bringing their own soldiers to justice.

German Investigation of Allied War Crimes in World War I

The Allies were not alone in compiling lists of enemy excesses. On 19 October 1914 the *Militäruntersuchungsstelle für Verletzungen des Kriegsrechts* was established in the Prussian War Ministry "to determine violations of the laws and customs of war which enemy military and civilian persons have committed against the Prussian troops and to investigate whatever accusations of this nature are made by the enemy against members of the Prussian Army."[15] This Military Bureau of Investigation of Violations of the Laws of War had wide competence to establish facts in a judicial manner and to secure the evidence necessary for legal analysis of each case. Witnesses were interrogated and their sworn depositions taken by military judges; lists of suspected war criminals were compiled, which would probably have led to criminal proceedings if Germany had won the war. The material remained largely secret, though some excerpts from witness depositions were used in German white books.

One of the first activites of the Prussian bureau was the investigation of alleged *franc-tireur* activity on the part of Belgian civilians. As early as September 1914—even before the investigative agency was established—German military judges had taken the depositions of many witnesses. More were taken in October, November, and December 1914, mainly in Louvain and Brussels, by seven military judges accompanied by eight court officers. In addition, a number of German witnesses who were no longer in Belgium were interrogated by local courts in their home districts in Germany. After due examination of all the material collected, an internal report on the Belgian resistance in Louvain, dated 15 January 1915, was prepared by the Prussian Bureau of Investigation.[16] Belgian accusations of German war crimes in Louvain were countered by seventy-three witness depositions, primarily from German officers and soldiers. According to this testimony, the occupying Germans were suddenly attacked by civilians on 25 August 1914, losing some 30 men and 95 horses. When houses were searched for suspects, "some of these persons were shot in the ensuing struggle. A number of them were made prisoner while still bearing arms." General Max von Boehn stated, "Among those who were caught in the act and immediately shot were a number of persons in very disorderly work attire . . . residents of the town claimed not to know these persons and never to have seen them in Louvain"; further, 300 rifles had been found in a Louvain church, and the chief medical officer Dr. Georg Berghausen testified that a number of wounded German soldiers had been shot with hunting guns.[17]

On 10 May 1915 the German Foreign Office produced a white book titled "The Illegal Belgian Civilian Warfare,"[18] based almost exclusively on the report prepared by the Prussian bureau. Because the judicial depositions were shortened and some "adjustments" made to make the evidence appear more convincing, however, the white book is a far less reliable source than the original protocols.

In 1917 the Belgian government-in-exile published another gray book contradicting the German white book, and the British government published the 1915 Bryce report.[19] By way of reaction the Prussian Bureau of Investigation produced a second report on civilian warfare in Belgium, critically analyzing the Belgian gray book and rejecting atrocity propaganda against German soldiers.[20]

The Prussian bureau also devoted considerable time to the investigation of reported abuses by British and French soldiers. In 1915, upon request of the German Foreign Office, it prepared a special "Response to Accusations Made by the French Government," which rebutted French accusations and presented 128 judicial depositions documenting French violations of the laws of war.[21]

Also in 1915 the bureau published "The Bombardment of the Cathedral of Reims,"[22] contending that the French Army had provoked German fire by using the towers of the cathedral for military purposes.[23] The brochure contains excerpts from French and British newspapers which report the use of church towers for military surveillance purposes.

Another volume, "France and the Laws of War: Atrocities on the Front,"[24] includes 157 reported cases of the killing of prisoners of war and other defenseless persons; wounding, ill-treatment, and robbing of prisoners; endangerment of prisoners by using them as a protecting shield against enemy forces; shackling and chaining of prisoners; mutilation of corpses; threats for the purpose of obtaining information, and so on. The treatment of German prisoners of war in French camps was detailed in a 1918 report, "France and the Geneva Convention."[25]

Part of a report titled "British Violations of the Laws of War in Belgium and France" (prepared but never printed) was incorporated into "British Violations of the Laws of War against Members of the German Armed Forces at the Front," which comprises 355 cases through the summer of 1918. The preface to this volume focuses on the validity of its evidence: "The German investigation rests preponderantly on the sworn testimony of credible witnesses. Only where in some exceptional cases a sworn deposition could not be taken by a competent judicial officer owing to war conditions did the *Untersuchungsstelle* dispense with the requirement. The documents annexed as substantiation are true and unabridged transcriptions of the originals of these documents, which are kept in a special dossier. . . . Impartial observers will not fail to notice that the testimony also contains positive comments made by the witnesses with regard to the behavior of enemy soldiers."[26]

It is interesting to note that in some investigations the Prussian bureau was able to incorporate evidence from non-German sources, as it did with regard to the *Baralong* case. On 19 August 1915 the British steamer *Nicosian* was on its way from New Orleans to Avonmouth, laden with 350 mules, when it was intercepted by a German submarine 70 nautical miles south of Queenstown, Ireland. The submarine allowed the whole crew to take to the lifeboats before bombarding the ship. At this time another ship arrived on the scene, which later turned out to be the British auxiliary cruiser *Baralong*. It flew the colors of the United States (not then at war with Germany), however, and signaled the German submarine that at the request of the crew of the *Nicosian*, it would grant assistance. Shortly thereafter it opened fire on the German submarine and sank it, the American flag being lowered only after the *Baralong* had launched its attack. Five of the shipwrecked German crew were able to seek refuge in the *Nicosian* but were killed under orders of British Captain McBride; others who were holding on to the *Nicosian*'s ropes were shot by the crew of the *Baralong*. The German captain, who while swimming signaled his surrender by raising his hands, suffered the same fate.[27]

Since there were no German survivors, the Prussian bureau first learned of the incident through the testimony of American sailors from the *Nicosian* to the American consul in Liverpool upon their arrival there,[28] information which subsequently reached Germany by way of German consulates in the United States. The consulates made arrangements to take the sworn depositions of those American sailors who wished to testify and sent the documents to the German Foreign Office, which on 28 November 1915 issued a white book in English and German: "Memorandum from the German Government concerning the Murder of the Crew of a German Submarine by the Commander of the British Auxiliary Cruiser *Baralong*."[29]

Long before the white book's publication the U.S. State Department had received the text of the testimony of the American sailors at Liverpool, and on 18 October 1915 Secretary of State Robert Lansing telegraphed the American ambassador in London, Walter Page, asking him to inquire of British Foreign Minister Sir Edward Grey whether the British ship *Baralong* had in fact flown the American flag. On 22 October Page answered that the sailors' affidavits sent to the State Department on 26 and 29 August "are of course authentic; in all essential points they agree; they were made by American citizens before our Consul at Liverpool, Mr. Washington; and I assume that they are such conclusive evidence of what happened that any representations that you may wish to make regarding the use of our flag may be made without asking Sir Edward Grey to verify or to deny the fact of its use. That fact is established."[30]

On 28 November 1915 the German government officially presented to James Gerard, the American ambassador in Berlin, the German *Baralong* memorandum with the request that it be transmitted to the British government. Gerard forwarded the document to his colleague Page, who on 6 December 1915 transmitted it, without commentary, to Sir Edward Grey. Grey responded in a note dated 14 December 1915: "His Majesty's Government do not think it necessary to make any reply to the suggestion that the British navy has been guilty of inhumanity. According to the latest figures available, the number of German sailors rescued from drowning, often in circumstances of great difficulty and peril, amounts to 1,150. The German navy can show no such record—perhaps through want of opportunity."[31] The Prussian bureau nevertheless included the name of the *Baralong*'s Captain McBride in its "Black List of Englishmen who are guilty of violations of the laws of war vis-à-vis members of the German Armed Forces."[32]

German Investigation after World War I

The Prussian Bureau of Investigation did not cease to exist in November 1918 but continued to collect evidence, which it used in several memoranda issued in 1919 during and after the Versailles Conference.[33] Even before the Allies agreed to have war crimes tried in Leipzig, the German parliament established a "Central Bureau for the Defense of Germans Accused of War Crimes." At an early meeting of this bureau in Berlin on 4 October 1919, Johannes Goldsche spoke on behalf of the Prussian Bureau of Investigation. He reported that his office had prepared some 5,000 dossiers on Allied war crimes, consisting of depositions of witnesses and supporting material, which were properly indexed and immediately available to German defense counsel in case of trials against German soldiers. There were also records of investigations of Allied allegations of German war crimes; that material, however, had not been published because the German government feared possible repercussions in Allied countries.[34]

The democratic government of the Weimar Republic, touched to the quick by Allied accusations of German war crimes, repeatedly proposed that an international commission be established to examine mutual allegations of violations of the laws of war. Even the International Committee of the Red Cross (ICRC) at its tenth international conference in Geneva in 1921, resolved that an international investigation of the violations of the Geneva Conventions during the war should be carried out. The Allied powers, however, declined to give any reply to the proposal, and the Red Cross resolution was never implemented.[35]

The Weimar Republic, pursuant to Article 34 of its constitution[36] and in accordance with a motion of the 8th Constitutional Committee of the German Parliament on 20 August 1919, established a special committee with twenty-eight members assigned to determine whether on the German side military or economic methods of warfare had been employed or tolerated which violated the provisions of international law or were unnecessarily cruel and unjust, and also whether other belligerent parties had used such methods.

On 30 September 1919 the committee delegated its task to four subcommittees; the third—chaired by several distinguished members of the Weimar parliament, including ex-minister Johannes Bell (of the Center Party)—was entrusted with the most delicate task: determining what war crimes had in fact been committed and by whom. So as not to interfere with the proceedings then pending before the Supreme Court at Leipzig, the subcommittee first focused on the question whether appropriate measures had been taken by the German authorities in time of peace to instruct German officers and men in the relevant provisions of the Hague and Geneva Conventions.[37] Only later did it turn to its main task, relying primarily on the work of the Prussian Bureau of Investigation and the Central Committee of the German Red Cross, including the special report "Violations of the Geneva Convention by States Hostile to Germany during the Last War."[38]

These materials were carefully weighed in the reports submitted by Christian Meurer (professor of international law at the University of Wurzburg): "Violations of the Geneva Convention" and "Violations of the Law on Prisoners of War."[39] While recognizing that "even sworn testimony may not stand examination in adversary proceedings," the committee was nevertheless of the opinion, "in the light of the statistics kept by Germany's former enemies with regard to the very high death toll among German prisoners of war, that their life and health was not protected to the extent provided for in international law."[40] Meurer's reports describe, for instance, the conditions in which German POWs were kept in Russia (where over 39 percent of them perished).[41] Considerable attention is also focused on testimony regarding the methods of warfare employed by colonial soldiers in the French and British armed forces.

After seven years of methodical investigations, the subcommittee presented its findings in five volumes titled "International Law during the World War."[42] The report was never translated, however, and thus had practically no impact outside of Germany.

Parallel Agencies during World War II

As direct successor to the Prussian bureau, the German government established on 4 September 1939, barely three days after the German invasion of Poland, the new War Crimes Bureau—this time not as a bureau in the War Ministry as such but as a special section within the legal department of the military High Command (*Oberkommando der Wehrmacht*, or OKW).

As could be expected, similar agencies were set up by the Allied governments. In the British Foreign Office, Roger Allen was responsible for the collection of all reports concerning German violations of the laws of war. Very early in the war he started producing internal papers on German war crimes, the monthly "Atrocities Summary."[43] And since British warfare against Germany took place primarily on the high seas, the Royal Navy was principally involved in examining German methods of warfare and systematically interrogated all survivors of sunken merchant ships in order to discover possible violations by the German Navy.[44]

The Soviet Union was also active in collecting evidence of German abuses. On 25 July 1941, shortly after the German invasion, the Soviet government instructed the chief medical officer of the Red Army as follows: "In order to reveal the plundering nature of the fascist conqueror in the eyes of world public opinion, it is necessary to publish in detail all bestial war methods employed by the fascists. All instances of fascist atrocities against medical personnel must be carefully noted and documented with photographs, protocols, organization reports, individual or collective descriptions by soldiers and civilians involved."[45]

On 25 February 1942 specific "guidelines for collecting, evaluating, and keeping documents on atrocities, destructions, plunder, and rape committed by Germans in occupied Soviet areas" were issued by Major Nikitinskij, chief of administration of the state archives of the NKVD.[46] On 4 November 1942 the Moscow radio and press announced the formation of a state commission for the investigation of war crimes.[47]

Meanwhile inter-Allied talks were taking place on the issue of prosecuting German atrocities. At St. James's Palace in London on 13 January 1942, the Inter-Allied Commission on the Punishment of War Crimes was established.[48] And on 20 October 1943 representatives of Australia, Belgium, China, Czechoslovakia, France, Greece, Great Britain, India, the Netherlands, Norway, Poland, Yugoslavia, and the United States signed an agreement setting up the United Nations War Crimes Commission; each country agreed to establish its own investigatory agencies and to make its documentation available to the commission.[49]

President Franklin D. Roosevelt, as early as the summer of 1942, had advocated the establishment of such an international commission,[50] but not until 6 October 1944 did the United States set up its own War Crimes Office under the aegis of the Judge Advocate General.[51] Throughout the war American commanders had heard of Axis violations of international law, but such reports were not being systematically collected. On 28 August and again on 6 October 1944 the 12th U.S. Army Group instructed the other armies on the necessity of collecting such material, and a further instruction was dated 7 November 1944: "Supreme Headquarters, Allied Expeditionary

Forces [SHAEF] has established a standing Court of Inquiry for the purpose of investigating cases involving the alleged violations by the enemy of the provisions of the Geneva Conventions and the laws and usages of war. The purpose of the investigation of these violations is two-fold: (a) to furnish a report of cases to United Nations War Crimes Commission as a basis for inclusion of the names of the perpetrators on a list for later apprehension, and (b) to furnish the State Department evidence of such violations as a basis for protest to the enemy through diplomatic channels, with appropriate publicity in proper cases. The Commanding General, Twelfth Army Group, has been charged with the initial responsibility of assembling the evidence of these violations which occur in the Army Group area."[52] Guidelines for the interrogation of witnesses were included and a model questionnaire enclosed.

Clearly, the Wehrmacht War Crimes Bureau was neither a particularly sinister nor typically German invention; similar bureaucratic institutions existed in most belligerent nations during both world wars. It is important, however, that the Germans set up their Bureau very early and that this agency did collect and evaluate a considerable body of witness depositions and other evidentiary material.

At the Nuremberg Trial No. 12—the so-called OKW Trial—the wartime director of the legal department of the Wehrmacht, Rudolf Lehmann[1] explained the establishment of the War Crimes Bureau within his department:

> When the first murders and cases of ill-treatment against German prisoners of war in Poland were reported, the Bureau was set up with the task of investigating such reports, since we believed at first that they were exaggerations or false reports from the troops. The news about these excesses against German soldiers were so gross that the leadership hesitated to believe them, and this is why only experienced judges were entrusted with the task of ascertaining the facts by taking the sworn deposition of witnesses. The material . . . was systematically ordered and made available to the Foreign Office for the purpose of safeguarding our interests. . . . The bureau ascertained the occurrence of such abhorrent atrocities and excesses that the results of the investigations could only be read with horror.[2]

Mandate and Membership

Given the incompleteness of the records, it is not possible to pinpoint one particular originator of the War Crimes Bureau. Probably the older judges in the legal department of the Wehrmacht, especially those who had investigated war crimes during World War I, proposed that a similar agency be established. In any case, the Bureau was entrusted with the task of collecting and evaluating all material concerning enemy violations of the laws of war. To facilitate the cooperation of other agencies, its establishment and a description of its assignment were publicized in the *Heeresverordnungsblatt*,

Luftwaffenverordnungsblatt, and *Marineverordnungsblatt*, the official publications of the army, air force, and navy. General (later, Field Marshal) Wilhelm Keitel signed the decree, dated 4 September 1939:

> In the High Command of the Wehrmacht (Legal Department) a *Wehrmacht-Untersuchungsstelle* on violations of the laws of war has been established with the task of ascertaining violations of international law committed by enemy military and civilian persons against members of the German armed forces, and at the same time to investigate whatever accusations foreign countries should make against the German armed forces. The Wehrmacht courts are requested to cooperate . . . in establishing the facts, particularly by taking the depositions of witnesses and experts and by their attestation under oath. In the proceedings reference to other documents (entries, messages, reports, earlier statements, etc.) should be avoided; instead, all relevant events should be described in detail.[3]

Pursuant to this decree, German military judges in the field investigated reports of enemy violations—or, at the Bureau's request, took the depositions of specific witnesses—and sent the results to Berlin for evaluation. Further, by a decree of 10 October 1939 issued by Minister of Justice Franz Gürtner, civilian courts (*Amtsgerichte*) also cooperated with the Bureau in the investigation of enemy war crimes, particularly by taking the deposition of witnesses within their jurisdiction.[4] Local courts were frequently requested by the Bureau to interrogate certain witnesses, especially German soldiers who had been prisoners of war and had been released in the course of POW exchanges arranged by the International Committee of the Red Cross.

That the Bureau was the direct successor of its World War I counterpart in the Prussian War Ministry was explained at a meeting of the German Association for Military Policy and Military Science[5] on 28 January 1941 by Bureau head Johannes Goldsche: "In keeping with the tradition of the *Militäruntersuchungsstelle* in the World War and pursuant to its current mandate, the new *Wehrmacht-Untersuchungsstelle* has the responsibility of objectively establishing the facts and the applicable law in cases involving the laws and customs of war; in doing so the Bureau itself, through its members, takes depositions of witnesses or instructs the competent military or civilian courts to take the necessary depositions; it also evaluates official documents and other reliable evidence."[6]

Although the task was not specifically provided for in the decree of 4 September 1939, the Bureau was also responsible for investigating accusations of war crimes committed by enemy forces against non-Germans. In a letter dated 2 August 1940, addressed to the High Command of the Army, Field Marshal Keitel observed: "According to news reports and certain information received by the High Command of the Wehrmacht, British and French troops have committed a variety of abuses against the Belgian and French civilian population, in particular, killings, ill-treatment, plunder, arson, and other war crimes. The High Command of the Wehrmacht considers it necessary to proceed to a thorough investigation of these events in view of the constant accusations that the enemy is wont to make against the German methods of warfare. At the same time, reliable documentary material should be collected for future peace negotiations and beyond this for the eventual claims for compensation which the population of occupied countries may raise vis-à-vis the Reich. The Bureau ought to obtain sworn testimony from the witnesses concerned."[7] Similarly, a memorandum of 7 May 1942 from the Bureau to the intelligence branch of the Wehrmacht High Command declared: "Evidence of violations of the laws of war by enemy armies against members of the armed forces of other Axis States is also being collected, as well as instances of brutality by enemy troops against the Dutch, Belgian, and French civilian population and against ethnic minorities in enemy states, because evidence of such events may yet prove of importance upon the end of the war and in connection with negotiations for the development of new norms of international law."[8]

Although the decree of 4 September 1939 also gave the Bureau authority to investigate allegations of German war crimes when foreign countries made specific accusations, in practice that task was assumed by the legal department of the German Foreign Office in collaboration with the military units concerned; only occasionally did the Bureau receive requests from the Foreign Office in that connection.[9] Sometimes, however, the operations staff of the Wehrmacht (*Wehrmachtführungsstab*) asked for lists of similar cases of enemy war crimes for the purpose of using them in the propaganda war by way of *tu quoque*. But the primary task of the Bureau remained that of collecting material on enemy war crimes. It was not a public prosecutor's office, charged with indicting violators of the laws of war; nor was it an agency of the German Foreign Office with the mandate to draft and publish white books or to lodge diplomatic protests. What it did was to investigate a multitude of alleged abuses and make the documentation available to a variety of governmental offices, which were then independently responsible for its use.

Enough official correspondence and memoranda have survived to present a fairly clear picture of the Bureau's functions. For instance, in a letter dated 27 November 1942 to the 2d Armored Army with regard to Soviet prisoners of war who were suspected of perpetrating specific war crimes, the Bureau observed: "It is expected that courts-martial will be instituted there against the persons charged."[10] In other words, the Bureau itself did not institute criminal proceedings but did make documentary evidence available for any eventual court-martial. Subsequently, upon conclusion of a court-martial, it was customary for the military court to forward a copy of its judgment and sentence to the Bureau to complete its files. Similarly, the German Foreign Office forwarded copies of the diplomatic protest notes sent to various belligerent states of all white books dealing with war crimes.

The apparent ultimate purpose of the Bureau's documentation is revealed in a 1942 internal memorandum: "Our enemies in the World War earnestly endeavored to collect our alleged wartime misdeeds, classify them, and make an indictment out of them so as to brand the Germans as outlaws for all time and thus to disqualify them in the arena of world politics. Because of their inexhaustible propaganda methods, their concerted political pressure, and the weakened stance of postwar German governments, they were largely successful. There is no doubt that upon the conclusion of peace after this war, this disgrace ought to be wiped out. One of the means to this end, which the Wehrmacht should provide for, is the preparation of a catalogue of war crimes and crimes against humanity perpetrated by our enemies on land, sea, and in the air."[11]

As Rudolf Lehmann testified at Nuremberg, only older, experienced judges were selected to serve in the Bureau. Three permanent members were disabled veterans from World War I; another was unfit for field service because of a hernia. Organizationally, the Bureau was attached to the international law section (Group 3) of the legal department of the Wehrmacht, whose chief was an old privy councilor and Prussian Army judge, Maximilian Wagner; he too had been involved in the investigation of war crimes during World War I and actively participated in the work of the Bureau until his death in October 1943.

Johannes Goldsche (1881–1953), who headed the Bureau from its inception until its dismantling at the end of the war, was a prominent Berlin lawyer during the Weimar Republic, a noted expert and patron of the arts, and an accomplished amateur musician who occasionally performed at concerts together with the leading German actor Otto Gebühr and museum director Günther Arnolds;[12] during World War I he had been deputy director of the *Militäruntersuchungsstelle* in the Prussian War Ministry. The other permanent members were Martin Heinemann (1889–1964), judge in the Prussian supreme court (*Kammergericht*) in Berlin; Hermann Huvendick (1895–1966), judge in the district court (*Landgericht*) in Bielefeld; and Lothar Schöne (1899–1965), judge in Berlin.[13]

The Bureau also recruited temporary members who assisted in investigating specific complexes. For instance, when it became necessary after the French campaign in the summer of 1940 to increase the staff, Karl Hofmann (1903–), a public prosecutor from Giessen, was recruited on 7 August via the legal department of the air force, to which he had been drafted upon the outbreak of the war. His main activities consisted in traveling throughout Germany, visiting army hospitals, and interrogating convalescent German soldiers with regard to reported instances of enemy war crimes. With the escalation of the war, however, it became necessary to send most ablebodied men to the field; thus Hofmann was transferred from the Bureau to the Russian Front on 1 February 1944.[14] Another temporary recruit was Judge Eugen Dorfmüller (born 1897), who carried out many investigations in 1941 and 1942, notably for the Yugoslavian dossiers.[15] He also took the sworn depositions of many convalescent German soldiers in hospitals throughout the Reich. Among others called upon to participate were Alfons Waltzog, air force judge and expert in international law questions in the legal department of the Wehrmacht; Ulrich Schattenberg, navy judge; and army judges Bruno Kleiss, Joachim Schölz, and Horst Reger (subsequently personal assistant to Rudolf Lehmann).

Although they were sometimes sent to the front to carry out certain investigations on the spot, Bureau members spent most of their time at headquarters, evaluating the evidence collected by military judges in the field. The Bureau's offices were originally in Berlin at Blumeshof 17,[16] across from the building of the War Ministry (which was located at Tirpitzufer 72/76, today Reichpietsch-Ufer in West Berlin). It was because of the increasing intensity of Allied air bombardment of Berlin that the Bureau moved on 18 August 1943 to Torgau and established new quarters in the military barracks next to the Supreme Military Court (*Reichskriegsgericht*), at the Ziethen-Kaserne, Block VI. After moving again in February 1945 to Langensalza in Thuringia, it continued its activities for several more weeks until it was informally dismantled in April 1945; a few days before the arrival of American troops, the members of the Bureau were transferred to Freising in Bavaria, where no further operations were possible—or, in light of the complete collapse of the Reich, even thinkable.

The Performance of German Military Judges

In most countries the armed forces require the services of and therefore recruit a certain number of legal specialists and judges. The German military was no exception; in World War II it employed some 2,000 judges in its sea, air, and field branches, some of whom were required to investigate enemy war crimes.

The primary responsibility of military judges, of course, is to ensure discipline among the troops by various means, including courts-martial. Their daily tasks include the investigation and punishment of cases of theft, disobedience, absence without leave, crimes committed during leave, and—in wartime—cases of cowardice, desertion, and self-mutilation. Maintaining discipline among the troops also made it necessary for German military judges to prosecute German soldiers who had committed crimes against the civilian population of occupied countries. Precisely this activity vis-à-vis German soldiers sharpened the military judge's eye for violations of the laws of war, whether committed by German or by enemy soldiers, thus providing experience in investigating and perspective in evaluating such abuses. Although it is difficult to determine whether the same or different criteria were employed in judging German and enemy war crimes, the following examples are representative of hundreds of cases that can be consulted in the German archives.

It is a matter of general knowledge that German soldiers committed a variety of crimes against the Polish civilian population. For instance, on 13 September 1939 in the town of Bromberg, near Posen, two German soldiers, named Pothmann and Taefler killed a Polish store owner and then raped his wife. On 15 September 1939 a German court-martial presided over by Alfons Waltzog sentenced both soldiers to die by hanging.[17] Taefler was executed in Bromberg on 9 October 1939; Pothmann's sentence, in the course of a clemency plea, was changed to life imprisonment.[18]

During the French campaign in May–June 1940, German army judges systematically prosecuted abuses against the French civilian population perpetrated by members of the Wehrmacht. The young soldier Willi Knobloch, lawyer by profession and subsequently military judge, remembers an incident in which a German soldier in his regiment had forced a French woman at gun-point to have sex with him. A German court-martial sentenced him to death. The German commander gave the French mayor of the town copies of the judgment so that it could be posted in public places.[19]

After the collapse of the French Army, Hitler issued a decree (*Führererlass*) of 7 July 1940:

> All members of the Wehrmacht must exercise restraint in their relations with the civilian population of occupied territory, as is proper and fitting for a German soldier. Inordinate consumption of alcohol is unbecoming to a soldier and frequently lies at the root of acts of violence and other outrages. Self-induced drunkenness is not an extenuating circumstance in determining the degree of punishment. I expect that every member of the Wehrmacht who as a result of drunkenness commits a crime— also vis-à-vis the civilian population—shall be brought to justice and severely punished. In serious cases the law provides for the death penalty. I declare it to be the official duty of superiors to set an example and to ensure the high level of German discipline by appropriate instructions.[20]

The record shows that the majority of the trials and judgments ensuing from this decree were based on the testimony of French witnesses. And since French local police assisted the German military courts in establishing the evidence, convictions could be obtained in 60 to 70 percent of the cases. Evidence of these German courts-martial presented at Nuremberg included the case of two French women who were raped in November 1943 by two drunken German soldiers; both were sentenced to death by hanging. When two German soldiers, together with French criminals, intimidated French Jews in Nice and forced them to hand over money and jewels, the German court-martial sentenced one of them to death and the other to twelve years' imprisonment. The judgment, dated 11 April 1944, declared: "The fact that the violence in question was directed against Jews in no way excuses the perpetrators . . . the German reputation has thereby suffered."[21]

German military courts in other occupied countries prosecuted German soldiers in similar fashion. In Norway a German court sentenced a German soldier on 15 June 1940 to three years' imprisonment for plundering.[22] On 5 January 1945 a German military court in Denmark sentenced a German soldier to five years imprisonment for theft committed against a Danish woman.[23] On 23 September 1943 a German military court in Greece sentenced to death a German soldier who had raped a sixteen-year-old Greek girl and also assaulted the girl's mother.[24]

The situation on the Eastern Front was somewhat different because Hitler's "Barbarossa Decree" of 13 May 1941 limited the jurisdiction of military courts by removing the automatic requirement to prosecute in cases where soldiers committed arbitrary acts of violence against the local civilian population.[25] The military courts, however, did retain their power to prosecute German soldiers in cases involving the discipline or safety of the troops.[26] Precisely in this connection Field Marshal Walter von Brauchitsch issued his own decree of 24 May 1941 requiring each military commander and his military court to determine on a case-by-case basis whether court-martial proceedings were necessary to ensure the troops' discipline.[27] And, since arbitrary and illegal conduct always endangers the discipline of the troops, commanders could order courts-martial based on the Brauchitsch order. Thus, Hitler's original plan to treat the Russians differently and to ignore the crimes of German soldiers against the Russian population was frequently circumvented by old-school commanders who did not believe in total war and who insisted on the observance of the laws of war by their troops. The following cases illustrate the schizophrenic nature of the Nazi system, whereby Hitler could order crimes against humanity while many of his commanders continued to demand strict discipline and respect for the civilian population of occupied territories.[28]

Gotthard Heinrici, commander-in-chief of the German 4th Army, simply sat on Hitler's decree and did not pass it down to his field commanders. Instead, he ordered that "offenses against the Russian civilian population shall be punished by disciplinary sanctions or by court-martial." As the supreme legal authority he was also responsible for confirming death sentences and did so in the course of the Barbarossa campaign, including those of three members of the 25th Armored Division for killing five women (request for clemency was denied), two members of the 267th Division for plundering, two members of the 260th Division for the rape and murder of a woman.[29]

Georg Lindemann, commander-in-chief of the 18th Army, also confirmed death sentences of German soldiers,[30] as did Eberhard von Mackensen, commander-in-chief of the 14th Army, who similarly ignored Hitler's Barbarossa Decree and preferred to keep his own house in order to the extent possible; he ordered his chief judge, Adolf Block, to prosecute every crime of a German soldier against the civilian population or against prisoners of war. In April 1943 Judge Block sentenced to death a German soldier who had killed a Russian woman in a village fifteen kilometers east of Gorlowka. The court-martial took place one day after the crime; the execution was carried out one day after the judgment; and General von Mackensen ordered that the judgment be posted on placards in the village and brought to the attention of the troops.[31]

Otto Dessloch, commander-in-chief of the 1st and 2nd Artillery Corps and later of the 4th Air Fleet, stated in an affidavit prepared for the defense of the Wehrmacht at the Nuremberg Trial: "In the spring of 1944 a German artillery battery had been moved to Budapest and quartered there in the former homes of Jewish families. Upon orders of a young lieutenant, jewels and radios were arbitrarily confiscated, and a Jewish woman who wanted to report the thefts was killed. The lieutenant was sentenced to death, and several noncommissioned officers were sentenced to long terms of imprisonment."[32] Dessloch confirmed the sentence, and the lieutenant was executed.

Georg von Küchler, commander-in-chief of the Army Group North, also prosecuted German soldiers under his jurisdiction for abuses committed against the civilian population. In one case two German soldiers were attempting to rape a Russian woman when they were surprised by a Russian man; one of the soldiers shot the Russian, and a court-martial convicted him of murder.[33] Another case is described by Army Judge Erich Kuhr: "A German soldier had a sexual encounter with a Russian girl. The mother, however, was in the way, and he simply killed her. The girl even had to dig the grave for her mother. The soldier was sentenced to death and executed. I was the judge."[34] Army Judge Horst Reger's diary notes the case of a drunken German officer in Russia who killed a whole family. He was sentenced to death, and the execution took place outside the house of the victims.[35] The killing of Soviet prisoners of war was also subject to court-martial proceedings. A German sergeant who had killed Soviet POWs and policemen was sentenced to death on 26 February 1943; a plea of clemency was rejected, and the execution was carried out.[36]

As these examples indicate, the principal responsibility of German military judges was to watch over the discipline of the troops, to investigate and if necessary punish by court-martial any violations of military law and the laws of war. Only as a secondary activity did they undertake investigations of reported cases of war crimes committed by enemy soldiers.[37]

The Wehrmacht Legal Department and National Socialism

It may appear surprising that military judges could continue functioning more or less normally in spite of the pressures imposed by a totalitarian dictatorship in total war. Several factors, however, were responsible for the relative independence of the judges of the Wehrmacht, beginning with the organizational structure of the German state, which by law separated the armed forces from political parties. This made it difficult for the Nazis to influence Wehrmacht commanders directly (a *Gauleiter,* or district party leader, could not simply order a Wehrmacht officer around), and even less the Wehrmacht judges, who were imbued with Prussian traditions and many of whom had already served as military judges during World War I.

Former Army Judge Walter Hoffmann describes the situation as follows: "I became an army judge on 1 May 1937 and at no time did I receive any orders or instructions from a party official, neither in peacetime . . . nor during the war. Even in one case where I had to sit as a judge in court-martial proceedings against a high functionary of the Nazi Party in occupied Russia, no attempt was made by the party to influence the proceedings. Army courts in the field were entirely free from such pressures."[38]

A similar view was expressed by Wilhelm Weber, former army judge and subsequently member of the Supreme Court of the Federal Republic of Germany: "During my entire career as an army judge until the end of the war . . . I was never subjected to any influence from the party, nor for that matter from the commanders. . . . I functioned under five commanders-in-chief and it was off limits for the party. . . . Army judges were . . . independent."[39]

It is also interesting to note that at the top of the Wehrmacht legal office there were no National Socialist (NSDAP) party members. Rudolf Lehmann, chief of the legal department of the armed forces; Christian Freiherr von Hammerstein, chief of the legal department of the air force;[40] Karl Sack, chief of the legal department of the army; Johannes Rudolphi, chief of the legal department of the navy; Maximilian Wagner, chief of the section for international law; and Johannes Goldsche, chief of the War Crimes Bureau, all kept clear of the party.[41] This particular constellation explains how it was possible for many jurists who had had trouble with the Nazi Party, or who feared persecution because of their political opinions, to find refuge in the legal department of the Wehrmacht.[42] Former Supreme Court Justice Wilhelm Weber described how he became an army judge:

> I was a county judge [*Amtsrichter*] when Hitler came to power in 1933. I had intended to join the Ministry of Justice, but I was unable to obtain my transfer there because I had had a negative encounter with the Nazi party leader [*Gauleiter*] competent for Saxonia. I thus remained longer than usual an assistant judge in the High Court [*Oberlandesgericht*] of Dresden. There I was relieved of my responsibilities as instructor of junior barristers, since I was "unreliable" and not a party member. Thus, I gradually realized that I had no chance of career development in the *Oberlandesgericht*, and since I was in the army reserve as a former cavalry officer [*Rittmeister*], I decided to request my transfer to the legal department of the army. There I was questioned on the reasons for my wanting to reenter the army. I explained that I had had friction with the party, that I was not a party member, and that I was effectively blocked. Thereupon I was accepted. . . . I know of a whole series . . . of persons who sought an escape from the party by joining the military.[43]

Another former judge in the Supreme Court of the Federal Republic of Germany, Otto Grünewald, became a civil servant with the Hessian Ministry of Justice in Darmstadt in 1933 and was fired without explanation during a vacation in 1935. He then turned to Karl Sack (later head of the legal department of the army), who himself had left the Hessian Ministry of Justice and gone to the military in 1934. The result was that Sack immediately hired him as legal expert. During the war Grünewald was chief judge of the 3d Army and then chief of the section on military justice in the field, directly under Sack.[44]

Yet another example is that of the senior Army Judge Adolf Block: "After completion of my legal studies I became a judge. Since I did not want to join the NSDAP and its influence was increasingly felt in the courts, I decided to seek admission in the legal department of the Wehrmacht. From 1938 until the end of the war I was a judge with the Supreme Military Court. In between, from December 1942 to the end of July 1943, I was chief judge of the 1st Armored Army in Russia."[45]

Understandably, however, the legal department of the Wehrmacht could hardly have survived in Nazi Germany without accepting some party members into its ranks. Moreover, it became increasingly difficult to find young jurists without links—at least *pro forma*—to some party agency or branch. Indeed, a decree of the Minister of Justice dated 11 May 1934 practically forced all students of law into a party organization.[46] Those who did not join were not only ostracized but frequently unable to continue their studies. The Wehrmacht did accept some party members but only after careful scrutiny; moreover, by an established rule of the military, party membership was deemed to be suspended during military service.[47]

The question still remains whether in the course of time military justice gradually embraced or adjusted to the tenets of National Socialism. Certainly there were individuals who did so. Judge Otto Schweinsberger, for instance, refused to prosecute a German civilian administrator in Russia who had murdered seventy-five Jews in the town of Balabanowka; in a written statement against the indictment for murder he explained that he felt himself equally responsible as a National Socialist and as a judge. His attitude was highly disapproved of by his superiors, and he was removed from the case. (In the criminal proceedings that followed, however, the indictment was changed from murder to manslaughter and the new judge sentenced Inspector Weisheit only to a demotion and two years' imprisonment. Shortly thereafter Weisheit was sent to the front as a private and fell in combat.)[48]

Schweinsberger cannot be considered typical of German military judges; even a cursory study of the personnel records of the military legal departments reveals a great many opponents of National Socialism. Helmuth James Graf von Moltke,[49] chief of a section of Wehrmacht intelligence and a close collaborator of Johannes Goldsche, was the founder of the Kreisauer Kreis, one of the most courageous anti-Hitler groups; he was executed in Berlin on 23 January 1945. Karl Sack was involved in the conspiracy to assassinate Hitler on 20 July 1944 and was executed on 9 April 1945 at the Flossenbürg concentration camp.[50] So too Rudolf Schleicher, chief of the legal department of the air force (1934–39), who was executed in April 1945.

It was precisely because of such men that Hitler did not allow the treason proceedings following the assassination attempt to be held before military courts. In fact, his decree of 20 September 1944 ordered that *no* proceedings against soldiers for political offenses should be brought before military courts; instead, he called into being the extraordinary courts and at the top the infamous People's Court under the fanatical Roland Freisler.

But Hitler's hate and mistrust of the Wehrmacht lawyers had surfaced well before the events of 20 July 1944. As early as 1939, shortly after the successful campaign in Poland, he had created a separate, more "reliable," and more political system of justice, establishing special ss and police courts. Illustrative of his contempt for traditional military justice is the fact that during the entire war he avoided any direct contact with Wehrmacht lawyers and never conferred with either Rudolf Lehmann or Johannes Goldsche.

Although the War Crimes Bureau was set up early in the war as the central collecting center and investigating bureau for violations of the laws of war, a number of other official institutions carried out their own independent investigations and usually made their results available to the Bureau.

Ausland-Abwehr

After the political crisis of February 1938 when the Reich Minister of War, General Werner von Blomberg, took his leave and the High Command of the Wehrmacht assumed the responsibilities of the former War Ministry, the old department of military intelligence (counterespionage) was renamed *Ausland-Abwehr* ("foreign affairs" and "defense") and restructured in three divisions. One of these, the section called *Ausland*, ensured the liaison between the High Command of the Wehrmacht and the German Foreign Office and was also responsible for matters of war regulations and the evaluation of intelligence material collected by other secret service agencies.

From 1939 on, *Ausland-Abwehr* had its headquarters in the main building of the High Command of the Wehrmacht in Berlin, across from the offices of the War Crimes Bureau. Fourteen days after Hitler's invasion of Poland, Count Helmuth James von Moltke, a promising young Berlin lawyer who was also a barrister in England and member of the Inner Temple, was recruited to serve in this substantive department. Moltke's activities overlapped to a certain extent with those of the legal department of the Wehrmacht, especially with those of Group 3 (dealing with international law) and those of the War Crimes Bureau; thus he had regular contact with Maximilian Wagner, Alfons Waltzog, and Johannes Goldsche.[1]

Moltke's superior, Colonel Werner Oxé, granted Moltke complete latitude and as a matter of course approved and signed all his memoranda.[2] Both men worked closely with Goldsche until the Bureau moved to Torgau in the summer of 1943, and even then the official exchange of documents and information continued as before. A more serious interruption of contact between the two agencies occurred after Moltke's arrest by the SD (the security service of the SS) on 19 January 1944 for his anti-Hitler activities as head of the conspiratorial Kreisauer Kreis; Colonel Oxé, however, reestablished relations with Goldsche in Torgau and continued Moltke's work.[3] As late as 10 January 1945 he forwarded forty-six reports, supported by sworn depositions, of Anglo-American air attacks on medical transports and hospitals: "The first twelve reports have already been used by the Foreign Office in lodging official protest with the Anglo-Americans. All the other cases are prior to the 10th of December 1944 and are therefore not appropriate for new protest measures."[4] On 1 February 1945 Oxé sent Goldsche eight more reports on attacks by Anglo-American fighter pilots.[5]

Some of the correspondence between the two agencies concerned the disposition of the originals of reports and depositions. On 23 May 1942, for instance, *Ausland-Abwehr* received a captured order issued by Chief of the Soviet General Staff Boris Shaposhnikov concerning the treatment of German prisoners of war. Having been sent only a transcript in German translation of the document, Goldsche wrote back requesting the transmittal of the original order in Russian, "since all documents concerning the conduct of enemy powers toward members of the Wehrmacht, to the extent that they are relevant from the point of view of international law, must be collected and catalogued in the original by the Bureau."[6] *Ausland-Abwehr* promptly complied.

Of course, *Ausland-Abwehr* itself very often received only short reports, so that it was necessary for the Bureau to address a number of other agencies and military commands in order to secure the originals and to request the sworn depositions of specific witnesses. On 29 September 1944, for instance, the Bureau addressed a request to the intelligence section of the Wehrmacht commander-in-chief in the Netherlands, and on 15 November 1944 the chief army judge in the Netherlands forwarded the requested sworn deposition of two witnesses.[7]

The *Wehrmachtführungsstab*

The operations staff of the High Command of the Wehrmacht was another reservoir for documents concerning violations of the laws of war, since it worked with the German Foreign Office for the purpose of lodging diplomatic protests against enemy powers. Because the purpose of diplomatic protests was to demand immediate investigation by the adversary, the *Wehrmachtführungsstab* frequently bypassed the War Crimes Bureau and sent its documentation on reported cases of Allied war crimes to the German Foreign Office with the request that an official protest be transmitted to the Protecting Power. Sometimes the Bureau learned of such a transmittal directly, but when its information came from the German Foreign Office, it had to address a request to the operations staff for the complete documentation.

One such request was formulated on 23 December 1944: "Twelve cases of attacks upon medical installations have been the subject of a protest note of the Foreign Office, dated 30 November 1944. Of these cases only Nos. 3, 7, and 8 are known to this office. In order for the Bureau to carry out its assignment of collecting all documentary evidence on violations of international law, it requests the prompt transmittal of whatever documents you have concerning cases 1, 2, 4 to 6, and 9 to 12, especially the originals of all official reports and any available witness depositions."[8]

In order to facilitate expeditious and uniform use of the many reports reaching the various Wehrmacht offices, the deputy chief of operations, General Walter Warlimont, ordered on 18 August 1944 that all reports of enemy violations of the laws of war should be directed to the *Ausland* section of the operations office, which should evaluate their content and forward the originals as fast as possible to the War Crimes Bureau to be catalogued and filed. Transcripts of the reports, if appropriate, should be sent to other offices and agencies. The *Ausland* section was to maintain constant contact with the War Crimes Bureau, with the Wehrmacht propaganda office, and with the Foreign Office: "In every case it must be ensured that appropriate measures are taken by the Foreign Office."[9]

Wehrmacht-Propagandaamt

On 1 April 1939 a department of propaganda was established in the High Command of the Wehrmacht; Lieutenant Colonel (later Major General) Hasso von Wedel was appointed chief.[10] The department was responsible for all questions of propaganda falling within the scope of activity of the High Command of the Wehrmacht and having relevance to the troops. Subordinate to the central bureau in Berlin were army, navy, air force, and ss propaganda companies, plus a variety of smaller military units made up of soldiers with journalistic and psychological training. The department was not only concerned with the psychological war in shoring up the morale of the troops; it also collected documents, captured enemy papers, diaries, depositions, and photographic evidence of enemy violations of the laws of war. Every corps was equipped with a propaganda unit, every army with a propaganda company. These were immediately sent on assignment when reports of the killing, mutilation, or mistreatment of German prisoners of war reached any army headquarters (for instance, in Feodosia, Grischino, or Lvov).[11] Documentary photographs and motion pictures were made on the spot and forwarded to Berlin for further evaluation.

Heeresfeldjustizabteilung

Shortly after the outbreak of the war the High Command of the Army also ordered the investigation of all enemy violations of international law. On 16 September 1939 Quartermaster of the Army Eugen Müller so instructed the commanders-in-chief of Armies 1, 3, 4, 5, 7, 8, 10, and 14, as well as the commanders-in-chief at Posen, Danzig-Westpreussen, and Krakau:

> According to numerous reports serious violations of international law committed against members of the German army have occurred during the German operations against Poland, e.g., *franc-tireur* activity, misuse of the sign of the red cross, attacks against German medical personnel, mistreatment or killing of wounded soldiers, use of dumdum ammunition, etc. To the extent that it is still possible, serious cases . . . should be established through official investigation. . . . future violations . . . regardless in which theater of war they occur . . . shall be investigated as a matter of course, if at all possible with the participation of army judges. Sworn depositions of the most important witnesses shall be taken. . . . [and] the files shall be forwarded to the High Command of the Army.[12]

Reports and court records collected on the basis of this order were transmitted to the *Heeresfeldjustizabteilung,* the department of military justice in the field—headed by Erich Lattmann until 31 October 1942 and thereafter by Otto Grünewald[13]—which took note of the events and forwarded the documents to the War Crimes Bureau.

Thus it was not always necessary for the Bureau to send special requests from Berlin; the chief judge of the 17th Army on 1 July 1941 instructed all division judges as a matter of course to take sworn depositions of all witnesses of violations of the laws of war. So, for instance, the military court of the 4th Mountain Division ordered on 25 July 1941 that the medical officer Dr. Erich Koch should be interrogated as forensic expert and that his sworn deposition regarding the mutilations of six fallen German soldiers should be sent to the Bureau.[14]

Sonderkommando Buhtz

Because many cases of mutilations of wounded and dead German soldiers were being reported on the Eastern Front, a special detachment for the "investigation of Bolshevist atrocities and violations of international law"[15] was established by the High Command of the Wehrmacht in the summer of 1941. It was headed by Gerhard Buhtz, director of the department of forensic medicine at the University of Breslau, Silesia. As early as 4 December 1941 Buhtz presented an extensive "Provisional Report on the Results of the Forensic and Criminal Investigations of Bolshevist Violations of International Law in the Area Controlled by the Army Group North (High Command of the 16th and 18th Armies) in the Period from 28 August until 21 November 1941."[16] The report referred to the autopsies of 115 corpses—45 German soldiers, 18 members of the German ethnic minority, and 52 Balts—and included the depositions of survivors and the results of the inspection of prisons of the Soviet political police. On the basis of these investigations in the field, Buhtz delivered a technical paper in Berlin on 19 February 1942, "Determination of Bolshevist Atrocities through Forensic Medicine."[17] Following his lecture Buhtz had a special meeting with War Crimes Bureau member Hermann Huvendick in order to coordinate the activities of his group with those of the Bureau. In August 1942 Buhtz's investigations into the apparent murder of a number of officers of the Luftwaffe led to friction with the Bureau, but cooperation between the two agencies was restored, and in April 1943 Buhtz was entrusted with the disinterment and autopsy of the corpses of the ill-fated Polish officers whose mass graves were discovered at Katyn.[18]

Army Medical Office

Beginning with the Polish campaign in September 1939, the Medical Office of the High Command of the Army, under the direction of Dr. Anton Waldmann, was involved in the examination and analysis of the corpses of victims of enemy war crimes, but not until the campaign in France did this office fully deploy its forensic resources. Pursuant to a directive of 24 June 1940 from the Army Medical Inspector, all senior medical officers in military hospitals were obliged to interrogate witnesses of war crimes.[19] The directive also assigned disciplinary jurisdiction over all wounded and sick soldiers in military hospitals to senior medical officers. As a result, though interrogations in hospitals were carried out with the same formality as those before military courts, the depositions could not be sworn to because senior medical officers were not empowered to take the oath of witnesses.

The deposition of Private Erich Lange, dated 16 February 1942, taken at the reserve hospital in Bielefeld, may be quoted by way of illustration: "On 8 July 1941, near Bialystok, I saw three Russians wielding knives put out the eyes of the noncommissioned officer of our assault detatchment. After our assault 26 of our men suffered mutilations."[20] This unsworn statement was sent to the Army Medical Inspector in Berlin, who passed it on to the War Crimes Bureau. On 9 April 1942 the Bureau requested the military court of Division 166 at Bielefeld to take the sworn deposition of Private Lange. In the meantime Lange had been released from the hospital and transferred to Potsdam, where the military court of Division 153 took the deposition and sent it on to the Bureau.[21]

The Army Medical Office was not obliged to forward such reports; indeed, the hospital interrogations were made in the first place for the internal purposes of the Army Medical Office, and the reports were frequently shown first to the forensic medicine expert[22] for his opinion. On 15 November 1942, for instance, one such expert noted:

It is not known here whether on the basis of the directive . . . dated 24 June 1940 the reports received from the chief medical officers of military districts XII and VIII have already been sent to the War Crimes Bureau. . . . the documents here are originals, and there is no indication that copies have been made. In view of the common purpose of our work, it would be sensible to offer these documents to the Bureau. This is all the more important since the Bureau requires that all statements be sworn to, and here it must be given the opportunity to make the necessary arrangements for the deposition under oath of the witnesses. For the time being, the following opinion may be communicated to the Bureau with regard to the content of the depositions: . . . Corporal Keilwagen stated on 23 October 1942 that he had been subjected to ill-treatment and scourged with a multiple whip with lead studs at the tip of the leather straps. The numerous, irregular scars on the legs and back observed in the medical examination would seem to confirm the truth of his allegations.[23]

Similarly, the witness Franz Schifflhuber, interrogated by the senior medical officer of the reserve hospital at Vöcklabruck on 28 October 1942, stated: "I was able to observe from our bandaging bunker as some of the wounded were placed on stretchers. At that moment a number of Russian soldiers assaulted the defenseless wounded Germans and mutilated them in indescribable fashion. In spite of my wounds I dragged myself out of the place with my last strength so as to escape the bestial massacre."[24] This statement was submitted to the forensic medicine expert, and on 16 November 1942 he noted in a memorandum to the Army Medical Office: "Transmittal to the War Crimes Bureau of the text of the interrogation of Corporal Franz Schifflhuber . . . appears in this case to be worth considering. This is particularly so because the deposition . . . describes the mutilation of defenseless German wounded by the Bolshevists with the vague expression 'in indescribable fashion.' The Bureau will presumably want to take a new deposition of the witness in order to determine what precisely were the indescribable mutilations he mentioned." Accordingly, on 30 November 1942 Schifflhuber's testimony was sent to the Bureau, and on 4 December 1942 Goldsche responded that the Bureau "has kept the original of the protocol on the interrogation of Corporal Franz Schifflhuber . . . and sends a transcript of it to you. . . . a further deposition of Corporal Schifflhuber shall be taken."[25]

In a telephone conversation shortly thereafter, Goldsche and the forensic medicine expert agreed that in the future the Bureau would as a matter of course keep the originals of all depositions it received and would prepare transcripts to be sent back to the Army Medical Office. On 21 December 1942 the Army Medical Inspector approved this agreement in writing, noting that "the requirements of documentary authenticity of these records on the part of the Bureau are greater than on the part of our own archives."[26]

This relatively unimportant case illustrates the cooperation between the Bureau and the Army Medical Office, which continued at least through 1944. The records contain numerous other examples of statements from wounded soldiers which resulted in further investigations on the part of the Bureau in order to ascertain the facts and secure the deposition under oath of all witnesses involved. On 26 April 1944 the Chief Medical Officer Geyer of the reserve hospital in Troppau forwarded the long and detailed deposition of Corporal Josef Kuhn to the Army Medical Inspector. The witness described the killing of some thirty German prisoners of war on the evening of 26 March 1944 in the area of Kamenz-Podolsk: "The Soviet guards . . . suddenly started to shoot at us with their machine guns. I . . . dropped to the ground at the same time as the comrade next to me was fatally shot and fell over me and bled to death. His blood so impregnated my coat that the Bolshevists evidently thought that I too was dead. Three to four times the Bolshevists moved up and down the rows of dead and wounded and again shot those who moved."[27]

Sometimes the statements of wounded soldiers questioned by the medical officer were not put in writing. When noncommissioned officer Kurt Heyer was interrogated in the reserve hospital in Vienna, only his name was noted down. Not until several weeks later, when the witness was in Hildesheim, did the local court there take his sworn deposition. On 2 August 1943 he described a corpse that had "already taken that color of death . . . in each eye a wooden picket had been pressed in. I left the body there and did not tell anyone about my experience."[28]

The Army Medical Office also received photographs, undeveloped film, and sometimes even more concrete evidence. On 23 July 1941 the military intelligence section of the 29th Army Corps received a jar containing two human fingers: "Since the jar is closed with the cover of a package of German field-dressings, it is supposed that Russians mutilated a German soldier. The jar was discovered . . . in a cupboard at the provisions office in Shitomir. The locality of this distribution center had previously been a Communist establishment." On 12 August 1941 the Army Medical Inspector transmitted the jar to the legal department of the Wehrmacht with the following opinion:

> The material enclosed consists of finger parts which were cut approximately in the middle of the center joint. The forced separation may have occurred through the use of a sharp instrument (ax, sidearm, bayonet) or a machine. The finger joints do not show any other traces of injury or evidence of pathological changes. Thus it is unlikely that the fingers were removed in the course of a medical operation. . . . It cannot be determined whether the fingers were detached after death or while the person was alive. . . . It is recommended that in the future such cases

should be brought to the attention of the senior medical officer at command headquarters, because a clear opinion can be formulated only on the basis of special medical investigation.[29]

German Foreign Office

Besides the various Wehrmacht offices described above, the German Foreign Office was also engaged in evaluating reports of enemy violations of the laws of war. The legal department of the Foreign Office under Assistant Secretary Friedrich Gaus maintained the German government's liaison with the Protecting Power, and his deputy Erich Albrecht in turn maintained liaison with the War Crimes Bureau. The Foreign Office also had a so-called archive commission under Kurt Jagow, who compiled the reports and captured enemy documents used in the preparation of white books.

Jagow routinely sent copies of his material to the Bureau, some of it already known from other sources but some entirely new to the Bureau. On 3 November 1941, for instance, Jagow forwarded six protocols concerning reported violations of the laws of war by British troops in Crete. Shortly thereafter the archive commission received new material from Crete, including the diary of the British vice-consul in Candia, one Captain Pendlebury, and receipts handwritten in Greek by Cretan civilians evidencing the deliveries of weapons and ammunition. Jagow forwarded photocopies to the Bureau on 4 March 1942.[30] Two days later he sent material concerning the campaign in Russia, including two reports of the military intelligence section of the 6th Army, dated 31 January and 2 February 1942, which the archive commission had received from its liaison officer at the Army High Command.[31]

The German Foreign Office relied on a variety of sources for its reports on enemy violations of international law. For example, in 1940 the German Embassy in Brussels compiled a forty-page list of British and French violations in Belgium. A reference in a letter from the commander-in-chief for Belgium and northern France to the Army High Command on 5 December 1940 alerted the War Crimes Bureau—which was on the list of recipients of copies of such correspondence—to the existence of these interesting materials, which had hitherto escaped its attention. Accordingly, on 4 February 1941, Goldsche requested the Foreign Office to transmit the documentation. The Foreign Office complied on 7 March 1941.[32]

Of course, the Foreign Office did not depend merely on such occasional information. It was precisely the function of sixteen liaison officers to the armies in the field and of additional liaison officers to the High Commands of Army, Navy and Air Force to keep the Foreign Office abreast of developments. These officers were known as VAAs (*Vertreter des Auswärtigen Amtes*) or representatives of the Foreign Office.[33] Among many other things, they regularly reported on apparent enemy violations of international law, transmitting copies of sworn depositions and the originals of captured enemy documents and enemy propaganda.

Sometimes the War Crimes Bureau learned indirectly about independent inquiries and investigations in which VAAs had been involved. For instance, on 3 September 1941 the head of the army's department of military justice in the field, Erich Lattmann, informed the Bureau that it could request from the VAA at the Army High Command the text of the testimony of a Soviet prisoner of war known as T, who had confirmed that German soldiers had been subjected to mutilations. On 15 September 1941 the Bureau requested that the VAA "promptly transmit the *original* of the statement of T. If your office so desires, the Bureau will make a photocopy of the testimony and forward it to you as replacement for the original." On 11 October 1941 the VAA, in accordance with the routine cooperation between the Bureau and the German Foreign Office, complied with the request.[34]

Russian-German Commissions of Investigation

Shortly after the German Army occupied the Crimean Peninsula on the Black Sea in December 1941, many German military headquarters were approached by prominent Ukrainian citizens who reported the killing of their relatives by the NKVD (the Soviet political police) and other atrocities allegedly committed by the Soviet troops against the Ukrainian civilian population and against German wounded and prisoners of war. On the initiative of Werner Otto von Hentig, the VAA at the High Command of the Eleventh Army (then under Field Marshal Erich von Manstein), a "Russian-German Committee for the Investigation of Soviet-Russian Atrocities against German and Russian Soldiers" was founded in April of 1942 at Simferopol. The costs were borne by the German Foreign Office's information department. At the committee's meeting on 27 May 1942 in Simferopol the Ukrainian Buldejew was elected chairman, and the Ukrainian Wischnjankow principal rapporteur. Von Hentig and another VAA named Rimscha participated in the discussions leading to a program of action that provided for the investigation of the following complexes: (1) the execution of detainees in the prisons and NKVD headquarters at Simferopol; (2) the blowing up of a train full of wounded Red Army soldiers at the Simferopol train station; (3) the arson of a hospital in Simferopol; (4) the execution of 250 men in Aluschta; and (5) the execution of fifteen Red Army recruits at Manut-Sultan.[35]

On 6 July 1942 von Hentig transmitted to the High Command of the Wehrmacht two dossiers of depositions and the committee's conclusions, underlining the thoroughness of the inquiry into the arson of the hospital, which had caused the death of some twelve victims.[36] In the summer of 1942 the committee focused on the investigation of the execution of German prisoners of war and also of some two hundred non-German detainees at the Sevastopol prison.

Other German commanders-in-chief followed the example of von Manstein in establishing Russian-German commissions to study reports of Soviet abuses, particularly against non-Communist Russians and Ukrainians. One such commission was established in the summer of 1942 at Smolensk. Composed of distinguished lawyers and scholars, this "Russian Commission for the Investigation of Soviet Atrocities and other Illegal Acts" on 14 July 1942 visited the place of execution used by the former NKVD administration for the district: "On the left wall there are two wooden posts, each about 1¼ meters high, and on their side of the wall 3 stretchers of sackcloth. One of the stretchers is full of blackened blood . . . the floor along the wall with the backstop is covered with sawdust some 5 cm deep and 1¼ m wide. The sawdust was saturated with blood." The report was signed by Russian Professor Jefimov, Judge Fisikov, lawyer Meshagin, and editors Dolgonenkow and Repuchow. On 2 September 1942 another member of the Smolensk Commission, Professor Kolessnikow, took the deposition of a Russian priest, Nikolai Domuchowski from Smolensk, who described his arrest in 1930 by the OGPU (predecessor to the NKVD), the attempts to extract a false confession from him, his ill-treatment both before and after conviction, and his imprisonment under inhumane conditions for ten years. On 14 September 1942 Professor Jefimov took the deposition of the archeologist Ilia Morosow, who declared that he had been arrested in 1931, forced to make a false confession, and sentenced to ten years' imprisonment in a Soviet concentration camp.[37]

All these investigatory commissions and committees gradually ceased their activities and dispersed as the fortunes of war turned against the Germans and the Wehrmacht retreated toward the Reich. But although these additional sources of information dried up, the War Crimes Bureau pursued its investigatory work and indeed continued receiving new material through the last weeks of the war in Europe.

Demobilization Office

It is an interesting arabesque of history that even after the Wehrmacht's unconditional surrender in May 1945, the government of the Reich under Admiral Karl Dönitz quite seriously endeavored to continue documenting Allied violations of international law. On 21 May 1945 General Alfred Jodl issued the following order: "All violations of the provisions of international law shall be uniformly evaluated by the Demobilization Office. All relevant materials shall therefore be transmitted to this office immediately. In the compilation and evaluation of documents the Demobilization Office shall call upon the assistance of the competent departments. The High Command of the Navy and of the Luftwaffe shall compile and evaluate cases arising within their field of competence and, if necessary, will take steps to lodge protest with the responsible authorities of the Occupying Power."[38]

There is little doubt that the bureaucratic German machinery for collecting and cataloguing reports of Allied violations of international law would have rolled on indefinitely had the Allies not put an end to the Dönitz government by arresting him and his cabinet on 23 May 1945.[39]

The War Crimes Bureau received material on enemy violations of international law—dispatches, reports, expert opinions, military records, captured enemy documents, protocols, interrogations of prisoners of war, sworn deposition of witnesses—from a variety of sources. It may be estimated, however, that the material received from the parallel institutions described in the preceding chapter made up only some 15 percent of its documentation. The bulk of its records consisted of the sworn testimony of tens of thousands of witnesses whose depositions had been taken directly by members of the Bureau, by military judges in the field, or by local courts at the Bureau's request.

Special Commissions and Hospital Interrogations

It became routine practice for the Bureau to assign an individual judge or a small group of judges to a particular case or complex of cases. Frequently the judges were members of the Bureau staff or of the legal department of the Wehrmacht; sometimes they were so-called "flying judges" who did not belong to any specific unit.

The Bureau's first task consisted of documenting events reported from Poland. Eleven military judges, together with their respective judicial clerks and secretaries, were sent to the many towns and villages where members of the German minority (*Volksdeutsche*) were said to have been killed or where wounded German soldiers or prisoners of war were liquidated by members of the Polish Army or militia.[1] One such investigator was Alfons Waltzog, subsequently specialist for international legal matters at the legal department of the Wehrmacht. His orders read: "Luftwaffe Judge Dr. Waltzog, with the approval of the commander-in-chief of the Luftwaffe, has been commissioned by the Wehrmacht to carry out investigations in matters relating to international law in his capacity as military judicial officer, assigned primarily to the Bromberg area. To this end he will collaborate with Navy Judge Dr. Schattenberg, from the High Command of the Wehrmacht, who has been similarly commissioned."[2] In the course of the war many military judges were similarly commissioned to fact-finding missions in Belgium, Holland, France (especially Alsace), Crete, Yugoslavia, and Russia.

Preliminary investigations frequently showed that the witnesses were convalescing in military hospitals throughout the Reich. The fact that they were physically closer to Berlin facilitated the task of taking their depositions, and the Bureau frequently commissioned its own members or other judges from the legal department of the Wehrmacht to visit military hospitals in Berlin, Vienna, Prague, Frankfurt, Trier, Marienbad, Würzburg, Nuremberg, Kassel, Darmstadt, Celle, Marburg, Göttingen, and other locations. Depositions were taken on preprinted forms with the letterhead of the High Command of the Wehrmacht and the War Crimes Bureau. The deposition form also bore subtitles: "About the Person" (*Zur Person*) was to be filled in with date and place of birth, civilian occupation, date of recruitment into the armed forces (if applicable), rank, military unit, and so on; "Events" (*Zur Sache*) required the date and place of the occurrences in question, description of the military events surrounding the alleged violation, and a complete account of the heart of the matter.

Among the military lawyers who routinely visited the military hospitals were Bureau members Lothar Schöne, Hermann Huvendick, Martin Heinemann, Eugen Dorfmüller, and Karl Hofmann, who explained: "The High Command of the Wehrmacht notified us of the hospitals to be visited. The hospitals had already been informed through a circular letter from the Bureau and asked whether among the wounded soldiers there were any who . . . could give testimony about . . . violations of international law . . . more or less rapidly we received answers from the hospitals listing names of possible witnesses. . . . The protocols of the depositions were written down by me personally during the interrogation of a witness. Upon my return to headquarters I delivered the originals of the depositions."[3] Frequently the traveling judge obtained additional pieces of evidence from the witnesses, including photographs or rolls of undeveloped film. On 7 November 1942 Karl Hofmann received from Josef Rötzer, a wounded noncommissioned officer whom he interrogated at the military hospital in Nuremberg, a roll of undeveloped black and white film containing eight photographs of members of Rötzer's company who had fallen into Russian hands on 3 April 1942 and whose corpses were subsequently found; twenty-one of the bodies had been mutilated.[4]

Military Judges in the Field

A considerable if not a preponderant proportion of the material collected came from the approximately 2,000 army, navy, and air force judges in the field.[5] Whenever the Bureau learned that a witness of war crimes was in a certain division at the front, it made use of its authority—granted by the decree of 4 September 1939[6]—to call upon the assistance of the division's judge to have the sworn testimony of the witness taken.

Of course, many military judges carried out independent inquiries and took depositions without waiting for a specific request from the Bureau, because it belonged to a judge's responsibilities to ascertain facts and locate witnesses (and possibly perpetrators) whenever he learned of violations of military or international law.[7] Many judges thus acted on their own initiative, especially when their intelligence officers reported enemy war crimes and when the witnesses were readily available. The protocols of these depositions bear a different identification from those of depositions taken at the request of the Bureau: the former are labeled AL (*Allgemeine Liste*, "general list"); the latter, RHL (*Rechtshilfeliste*, "judicial assistance list").

Intelligence Reports

Every division in the German Army (or in any army) had a section for military intelligence. This Ic section, as it was known in the Wehrmacht, was also responsible for reporting on enemy violations of the laws of war. It collected dispatches, reports, witness testimony, captured enemy records, diaries, bulletins, photographs—anything having to do with enemy war crimes—and sent them along the normal chain of command from Division Ic to Corps Ic to Army Ic to Army Group Ic to High Command of the Army Ic and from there to the so-called "Fourth Department," also known as *Fremde Heere* (enemy armies), which was divided into *Fremde Heere West* (Western Front) and *Fremde Heere Ost* (Eastern Front).[8]

After the German invasion of the Soviet Union, the High Command of the Army focused increased attention on enemy war crimes. On 9 July 1941 a special circular issued within the jurisdiction of the High Command of the 6th Army[9] gave the following instruction: "It is of great importance for the Office of the General z.b.V.[10] at the High Command of the Army that all occurrences of this type (ill-treatment of wounded and prisoners of war) be immediately reported together with official documentation. The sworn deposition of witnesses shall be taken. The Ic of each division shall first report such occurrences via the Ic channels and immediately inform the division judge, who shall ascertain the facts and interrogate the witnesses under oath and transmit this material through the chain of command."[11]

Pursuant to an established distribution list, the Ic section of the 16th Army communicated its material on enemy violations of international law to the following agencies: (1) the War Crimes Bureau (originals); (2) the High Command of the Army, General z.b.V.; (3) the Ic of the High Command of the Army Group; (4) the Foreign Office liaison officer (VAA) at the Army High Command; (5) the Sonderkommando Buhtz (see Chapter 3).[12]

The procedure followed by the War Crimes Bureau in working with intelligence sections may be illustrated by a case that arose in the first days of the German invasion of the Soviet Union. It began with the discovery by German soldiers of the mutilated bodies of their comrades near the town of Skomorochy in the western Ukraine, northeast of Lvov. Lieutenant Heinze of the Ic section of the 6th Army High Command telegraphed the following message on 1 July 1941: "In Skomorochy we found the mutilated bodies of a German major, a first lieutenant, a staff sergeant, and other soldiers. The major's name is Söhnke, and he belonged to the 7th Infantry Regiment. Further reports will follow."[13]

Dr. Emil Stankeit, medical officer of the 208th Infantry Regiment, examined the corpses and prepared a two-page expert opinion.[14] On 3 July 1941 the intelligence officer transmitted Stankeit's original report to the High Command of the Army; of the six copies made, one was sent to the Army Group South and another to the Foreign Office's liaison officer with the 6th Army, VAA Hellenthal.[15] On 10 July 1941 General z.b.V. Eugen Müller sent the original of Stankeit's report to the War Crimes Bureau. A few days later Maximilian Wagner, Goldsche's immediate superior, signed a letter addressed to the legal department of the Army High Command requesting that the competent military court in the field be instructed to "take the deposition of the senior medical officer of Infantry Regiment 208, Dr. Stankeit, in his capacity as witness and medical expert, of the junior medical officer Wendler and of the medical orderly Müller, both from the First Battalion of Infantry Regiment 208, in their capacity as witnesses of the events; to proceed to establish the facts in detail; and to send the originals of the depositions to this office." [16]

On 23 July 1941 the senior judge at the Army High Command, Erich Lattmann, acting on Wagner's request, instructed the judge of the 83rd Infantry Division "to comply with the request . . . and to forward the originals of the depositions to be taken to the legal department of the Wehrmacht." But since the 208th Infantry Regiment did not belong to the 83rd Infantry Division, the judge returned the matter to Lattmann on 2 August 1941. On 9 August 1941, Rudolph von Schönfeld, representing Lattmann, sent the request to the 79th Infantry Division; [17] on 15 August 1941 that division's Judge Erich Kuhr interrogated the three witnesses and on the same day sent their sworn statements to the War Crimes Bureau. [18] On 29 August 1941 copies of the transcripts of these depositions were incorporated into "Special Dossier Russia A2" and "Special Dossier Russia A7." [19]

There were hundreds if not thousands of similar cases in which the Ic report was followed by judicial investigation. Sometimes, however, an intelligence report could not be corroborated by witness testimony—if, for example, the witnesses were civilians outside the operational zone of the division involved. This was the situation when Lattmann had to write back to the Bureau on 19 August 1941: "The town of Slobodka, as far as I can determine, lies outside the operational zone of the army. I should like to bring to your attention quite generally that because of the great distances of the areas behind the front, it will hardly be possible to comply with requests for the depositions of civilians. Military courts have been set up in only a few central points behind the front." [20]

Newspaper Reports

In addition to relying on official reports for the initial evidence of war crimes, the Bureau staff systematically perused the newspapers for relevant information. News articles themselves were not deemed to possess any evidentiary value, but they did lead to a number of successful investigations. One such inquiry concerned the events in Narvik in April 1940. [21] On 25 June 1940 Maximilian Wagner wrote to the High Command of the Navy: "According to reports in the press and on the radio, British forces shot at defenseless German sailors who were shipwrecked in the waters off Narvik in April of 1940. . . . Now that hostilities have ended in Narvik, the High Command of the Wehrmacht requests that all navy personnel who were eyewitnesses of the criminal conduct of the British should be interrogated and their *sworn* depositions taken by military judicial officers."[22] Shortly thereafter, Navy Judge Helmut Sieber was given the task of taking the depositions of approximately twenty witnesses, and two other navy judges were called upon to interrogate navy personnel stationed at other ports.

In the summer of 1941 another examination was opened as a result of a press report. Bureau chief Johannes Goldsche wrote to the legal department of the navy: "According to an account in the 25 August 1941 issue of the newspaper *Monday*, a British submarine attacked a German hospital ship on 23 August 1941 along the coast of Norway. . . . The Bureau requests that the matter be investigated . . . particularly by the sworn interrogation of eyewitnesses through the competent navy judge."[23] And it was following a press bulletin on the bombardment of the hospital ship *Freiburg* in Venice[24] that the Bureau requested the Navy High Command to transmit "the original of the report of the chief medical officer and . . . any depositions of witnesses." On 13 September 1944 the Navy High Command complied, and the case became the subject of an official diplomatic protest to the governments of the United States and Great Britain.[25]

Interrogation of Exchanged POWs

Former German prisoners of war who returned to Germany after being exchanged through the good offices of the International Committee of the Red Cross[26] frequently alleged that they had suffered abuses and irregularities during detention. The War Crimes Bureau was quick to tap this source of information and systematically circulated special questionnaires among former POWs; many were then asked to give their statements under oath. Among the questions posed were these: (1) Were you subjected to pressure to force you to give information on the situation in the Wehrmacht or at home? (2) Were you shackled during your transport, and if yes, how? (3) Were items of personal property (money, valuables) or pieces of equipment (helmet, gas mask) taken away from you? (4) Were identification papers, badges of rank, decorations, or stripes taken away from you? (5) Were you assigned work that was directly connected with the enemy conduct of war (e.g., transport of ammunition)?[27]

The first two questions were mostly answered in the negative; positive answers were more frequently given to questions 3, 4, and 5. The complaints primarily involved violations of the Geneva Prisoner of War Convention of

1929, mostly cases of arbitrariness or unjustified denial of certain rights; only seldom did they concern such serious violations as ill-treatment or killing of German pilots after an emergency landing,[28] confiscation of private property,[29] shackling,[30] and—especially in French POW camps—the use of German prisoners of war for the removal of land mines.[31] And relatively few reports referred to violations of international law on the field of battle prior to detention.[32]

In July 1944 the Bureau compiled an internal dossier, "Sworn Testimony of Returned German Prisoners of War about Their Treatment in Contravention of International Law during British or North American Detention."[33] Unlike its practice in many other cases, the German Foreign Office did not publish a white book on the basis of this material, though it is probable that the Protecting Power was informed of the content of the study.

In October 1944 numerous former prisoners of war returned to Germany after being released from French detention in an exchange of seriously ill POWs. Upon questioning, a number of them mentioned the shooting eighty German prisoners of war by French partisans in Savoy on 2 September 1944.[34] German authorities were already aware of the killings because the International Committee of the Red Cross had acted as mediator between the German government and the Forces Françaises de l'Intérieur (FFI), the French partisans, also known as *maquisards*. The FFI, which held great numbers of German POWs, insisted upon recognition of the partisans as combatants[35] and tried to force the issue by threatening to shoot German prisoners unless the German government changed its policy. The ICRC attempted to persuade Berlin to agree, but six days after the FFI's ultimatum, in the absence of any response from Berlin, forty men were shot at Annecy and forty at St. Pierre de Rumilly.[36]

In this case, then, the Bureau's reports merely confirmed what the German Foreign Office already knew. On 3 November 1944, Master Sergeant Georg Fackler testified that "in all 80 prisoners of war (mostly policemen) were shot as hostages ten days after they had been taken prisoner, 40 in Annecy, the rest in Bonneville." Private Rudolf Diepold's testimony differed slightly: "40 officers and 35 men were shot at the prisoner of war camp in Annecy."[37]

This kind of questioning was not limited to routine questionnaires. The War Crimes Bureau carefully studied and compared the POWs' statements with information already in its files, trying to piece the cases together; former

POWs were frequently interrogated again, even months after their return, and local courts were asked for assistance. One form letter read as follows: "The Bureau has the task of investigating all violations of international law committed by enemy soldiers and civilians against members of the German armed forces and medical personnel. The former German prisoners of war and members of the army medical service _____(names)_____, who on __(date)__ returned home from British and American detention pursuant to the provisions of the Prisoner of War Convention, should be interrogated about their treatment during captivity, and if they were witnesses of substantial violations of international law by the enemy, their sworn depositions should be taken."[38] Using specific questions formulated for the witnesses, the local courts took the depositions and forwarded them as requested, pursuant to the decree of the Ministry of Justice of 10 October 1939, requiring local courts to cooperate with the War Crimes Bureau.[39]

Among many such depositions is one taken in Hindenburg, Upper Silesia, on 9 January 1945. The former POW who had returned from American captivity recalled that the Americans had asked him about his equipment, weapons, and the morale of his company: "When I refused to give any such information, the interrogator told me that if I persisted in not answering questions, I would be turned over to the Soviets."[40] Indeed, it seems to have been a widespread American practice to threaten German prisoners with transfer to a French or a Soviet POW camp if they refused to cooperate with American interrogators.

Communications from the Protecting Power

The War Crimes Bureau not only sent reports to the German Foreign Office but also received information from it, including copies of all relevant communications to and from the Protecting Power. On 25 May 1944, for example, the Swiss Federal Political Department transmitted to the German legation in Bern the text of a protest from Master Sergeant Willi Reimann, a medical orderly who at the time was at American POW Camp 131 in Oran, North Africa.

On 31 January 1944 I was taken prisoner by the Americans near Isola Bella (Anzio Bridgehead, Italy). I was in a trench about 30 cm deep. Before me lay noncommissioned officer Klug, who had suffered a bullet wound through the hip. I was about to bandage him when an American soldier . . . ordered me to go back some 300 yards to a farmhouse. I obeyed without any resistance, and as I arrived at the farmhouse an American soldier who was already there signaled me with his hands to go against the wall, some five yards down. Hardly had I done so when a shot rang out from the gun that he held at the hip and hit me in my right thigh. I fell and lost consciousness. He must have shot two more times, since I was grazed on the right thigh and left side of my chest and had a shot through my helmet, which only grazed the skin of my head. . . .

After regaining consciousness I saw that my wallet and my paybook and identification as medical orderly and my watch were missing. When I was taken prisoner I was wearing a red cross armband around the left upper arm of my parachutist uniform, which was clearly visible. I reported this incident on 1 February 1944 to a certain American captain N.C., whom I did not know, at the . . . "56th Evac. Hospital" at the bridgehead, and the Captain told me that in the moment of combat that sort of thing can happen, since it was do or die.[41]

The document had been given to the representative of the Protecting Power by the American authorities, indicating that the American Provost Marshal had ordered an inquiry into the complaint.

The German Foreign Office transmitted a copy of Reimann's statement to the War Crimes Bureau, which sought further confirmation through the interrogation of other possible witnesses. On 15 September 1944 the court of the garrison headquarters of the Wehrmacht in Berlin took the sworn deposition of Dr. Peter Edmund Schenkel, a medical officer who in March 1944 had seen Reimann at POW Camp 131 and had recognized him because they belonged to the same division. Schenkel confirmed that Reimann's description of the events at the time coincided with the text of his complaint.[42]

War Diaries

On the recommendation of *Ausland-Abwehr* in 1942, the War Crimes Bureau considered the possibility of supplementing its files by carrying out a systematic review of the war diaries (official logs) of all army groups, armies, divisions, regiments, and battalions in order to document "enemy violations of international law and crimes against humanity on land, in the sea, and in the air."[43] War diaries had played a role in the Leipzig trials conducted after World War I by the German Supreme Court; they had been extensively used by both the prosecution and the defense. There is no indication, however, that the Bureau did in fact implement its projected review of war diaries. Most probably it did not, considering the small size of its staff and the intensity of its active role in taking depositions throughout the Reich and undertaking special missions into occupied territory.

Because an examination of the methods employed in obtaining witness testimony is essential in assessing the degree of credibility that may be assigned to the protocols found in the records of the War Crimes Bureau, this chapter attempts to test the reliability of the protocols in three ways: (1) How did the definitive text of the depositions emerge? (2) Did the questions of the examining judge contribute to increased precision and relevancy, or did they influence the testimony in a particular direction? (3) According to what criteria did the judges themselves evaluate the credibility of the witnesses?

The author has interviewed some three hundred former military judges and witnesses and given them copies of the depositions taken more than forty years ago. These persons almost invariably remembered the events and could describe the proceedings. From their statements it appears that the method of taking depositions was uniform throughout the war. One former judge, Rudolf Albrecht, explained it as follows: "First of all I let the witness describe the events. Then I dictated his statement in his presence to the clerk. After finishing dictation I read the protocol to the witness and asked him whether his statement had been correctly recorded. . . . If he confirmed it, I then asked him whether he consented to the content of the protocol. If so, the protocol was then submitted to him for his signature."[1] Former Army Judge Otto Mackel described the sequence in greater detail.

> Depositions of witnesses were carried out in a very exhaustive and cautious manner. The witness was questioned a first time before giving his statement to protocol and only after he said, "This is correct, so I can swear to it" would the attestation proceed. . . . A deposition took in the typical case about two hours. The clerk was present during the depo-

sition and sat at his typewriter ready, so that the protocol was dictated to him in presence of the witness, who at all times could speak out. The witnesses could make corrections throughout. Then the protocol was read to him another time, and he signed it under "v.g.u,"[2] that is, read, approved, and signed, and then followed the oath, all of this in the presence of all the persons involved in the deposition. Thereupon the examining judge and the clerk also signed the protocol."[3]

Interrogation and Administration of the Oath

As in every legal system, it was prohibited for judges to influence the witnesses or to manipulate the testimony in a particular direction. Still, as every lawyer knows, precise questions on legally relevant facts must be posed to ensure that tangential or unimportant information is not also recorded. In order to determine which facts or events are relevant to the investigation, the judge must hear the witness out and let him describe in detail the course and circumstances of the occurence, but the judge must also probe for those key facts the legal significance of which only he can appreciate. Many German parachutists, for instance, complained of Allied violations of the laws of war in Crete 1941; they alleged that they had been shot at while still in the air and "defenseless." Judge Steigmeier had to explain to them that shooting at parachuting soldiers is a legitimate act of war.[4] Moreover, many of the parachutists were not at all "defenseless" but were already shooting at the ground forces during their descent.

The Bureau, endeavoring to avoid a flood of protocols, pursued a policy of having only those witnesses questioned who reported genuine violations and who could deliver legally relevant evidence. This is why the military judges were requested to pose very precise questions so as to ferret out the legally significant facts.

Many reports from the Italian theater of war accused Anglo-American fliers of bombarding or machine-gunning German hospitals and hospital trains. On 28 April 1944 the commander of Army Group C forwarded a list of reported cases to the High Command's operations staff and commented: "In spite of the general rise in the number of air attacks in the month of April, it appears that attacks on medical facilities and ambulances have increased at a greater pace than the prevailing proportion would have led us to expect."[5] The Bureau asked the military courts to pursue specific aspects of these reports: "For the intended documentary evaluation of the deposition it is important to know the degree of visibility, the height from which the bombardment took place, [the position and size of] the red cross markings, and, most importantly, whether the medical facilities at the time of the attack were clearly and recognizably separated from military objectives."[6] Following these guidelines, the military judges were able to sort out the reports and to reject a number of them as unjustified: "No violation of the Geneva Convention is discernible in the case of 20 March 1944 . . . because both vehicles had just been turned over to the unit and owing to lack of red paint had not yet been marked with red crosses. The vehicles were on the way to Perugia for repairs, where the red cross markings would have been painted on them."[7]

In other cases the Bureau's own research revealed that some allegations did not in fact involve violations. These cases were sorted out and not used either in official white papers or in diplomatic notes of protest. On 12 December 1944, for instance, the Bureau communicated to the Navy High Command, that "the attack of U.S. bombers on the hospital ship *Stuttgart* at Gotenhafen on 9 September 1943 was not included in the enclosed list because the *Stuttgart*, as indicated by the Naval War Staff on 23 October 1943, was camouflaged on the seaside with sackcloth and therefore did not enjoy the protection of the Hague Convention of 18 October 1907, even though there were red cross markings on deck."[8] The Bureau showed itself similarly skeptical about the relatively frequent allegations of the shooting at shipwrecked crews and always pursued the question of whether the shooting had actually been directed at the survivors and whether there was any other military objective nearby that would have justified the shelling.[9]

In order to test the credibility of witnesses, some military judges resorted to posing trick questions. One such judge was Gerhard Wulle: "I still remember quite well my depositions of Private Haase and noncommissioned officer Kirchner on 26 August 1940 and 7 January 1942, because the events they described very much affected me. . . . Quite importantly, I did not have the impression that either of them was giving a black-and-white picture of the events . . . they had been simply too deeply shocked. Furthermore I tested their credibility (as I usually do) by posing special questions, for instance with respect to the use of particular instruments for maltreatment or torture. These questions were answered by the witnesses objectively and not indiscriminately in the affirmative."[10]

Leading questions may, of course, suggest answers to the witnesses and thereby falsify their testimony, but the possibility of misconduct by examining officers does not necessarily cast doubt on the entire interrogation and its results. In the case of expert witnesses the danger of leading questions hardly existed, since the examining judges lacked the necessary specialized knowledge and therefore left the formulation of the protocols to the witnesses themselves. As Erich Kuhr said of the deposition of Dr. Emil Stankeit, a medical officer:

> This was obviously dictated by the medical officer directly to the clerk, since I could not pose many questions. . . . From the use of technical language it is clear that the doctor dictated it. The purpose of the deposition is that the doctor does not simply report his findings but that he writes them down in the form of a legal document so as to give them more weight in subsequent investigations, particularly because of the oath. At the bottom of the deposition you read that he took the oath both as witness and as expert, pursuant to paragraph 32 of the Regulations for Criminal Procedure in Wartime, because he gave testimony not only as witness but also as medical expert who was able to determine the nature of the wounds examined, especially whether they were mutilations.[11]

It was the practice of military judges to advise and instruct witnesses before each deposition "of the subject matter of the questioning, of their duty to tell the truth, on the meaning of the oath, and on the criminal consequences of making false or reckless statements."[12] Otto Mackel, a former judge, elucidated the steps in administering the oath as follows: "As far as I remember the oath ran thus: 'I swear by God the Almighty and Omniscient, that I have said the pure truth and withheld nothing. So help me God.'[13] This formula was recited while raising the right hand with the three oath fingers. Thus it is a genuine oath that was spoken after an admonition on the consequences of perjury. For this reason I have no doubt whatever about the authenticity of this protocol that bears my signature and also no doubt about the truth of the testimony of this lieutenant."[14]

In cases where a witness could report only hearsay, usually no oath was administered: "The deponent was not sworn because he did not himself witness the events."[15] Judges did administer the oath in cases where the testimony contained personal observations as well as hearsay. More important, judges emphasized that they had only those witnesses take the oath whose testimony appeared truthful in every detail. In the course of verifying a deposition made thirty-six years before, Judge Wilhelm Landwehr explained:

"I would not have administered the oath to the witnesses if I had had the impression that they were not telling the truth."[16]

When the judge was familiar with the character of the witnesses—as was frequently the case with officers and doctors—it was unnecessary for him to take additional steps to verify their testimony. In all cases, however, military judges followed the rule that if the testimony was not plausible in every detail, the witness should not be sworn. Judge Geier commented on a 1944 report sent to the Bureau: "I have refrained from swearing the witness because additional investigations appear to be necessary and the testimony is not entirely plausible, in particular with respect to the destruction of the tank. Bschorr [the deponent] actually makes a good impression. He seems quite intelligent and is an alert and clearly thinking person. He did not contradict himself in any way in the course of testifying and his statement was in all details understandable. Still, his judgment may be impulsive. He is also too convinced of his own importance. In judging his statement one should take into account that he is only 17 years old."[17]

Verification through Multiple Witnesses

Because the administration of the oath cannot offer an absolute guarantee of the truth of the testimony, German military judges made an effort to question more than one witness for every case. In investigating the massacre of German prisoners in Broniki,[18] four judges interrogated a total of twelve survivors and witnesses. Their testimony presented a complete picture of the events; there were only minor differences with respect to the estimated number of victims.

This method of multiple depositions was also followed when the monitoring of enemy wireless transmission picked up information about enemy violations of the laws of war: both the wireless operator and an interpreter or two operators were interrogated about the contents of the message. On 15 July 1943, for example, Judge Ernst Hartke took the deposition of wireless operator Robert Bilinski: "On 7 July 1943 I was assigned to the communications unit 282 with the duty to listen to enemy transmissions with a B-wireless set. I have full command of the Russian language and I translated the intercepted messages into German and sent them on." In order to check the accuracy of Bilinski's statement, a Russian prisoner of war who had been employed in radio transmission was also interrogated: "I was with Corporal Bilinski on 7 July 1943 and heard the intercepted messages. I wrote them down in Russian independently of Bilinski. Then they were translated into German. The content of the three messages has been read to me. It is correct. In all three messages Red Army soldiers reported that they had liquidated German prisoners of war." The oath was administered to both witnesses.[19]

In a similar case Judge Jancke of the 28th Army Corps interrogated a number of witnesses on 30 July 1944. Noncommissioned officer Eduard Sandner stated: "On 27 July 1944 at 8:20 A.M. I heard . . . part of a communication between two Russian officers: 'I have a prisoner of war from Infantry Regiment 68 of the 23rd Infantry Division.' The superior officer answered: 'Don't make me any reports on prisoners of war. They should all be shot.' I immediately wrote this statement down in Russian and gave it to our company commander . . . who also serves as translator. I have myself passed the translator's examination and certify that I correctly heard this transmission." Ludwig Kob, Sandner's superior, confirmed the testimony: "On 27 July 1944 at 8:30 noncommissioned officer Sandner handed me an intercepted wireless message which he had written down in Russian. . . . 'I have a prisoner of war from Infantry Regiment 68 of the 23rd Infantry Division.' . . . Answer: 'Don't make me any reports on prisoners of war. They should all be shot.'"[20]

Multiple depositions also helped discover errors and exaggerations. On 3 September 1941 Sergeant Gerhard Steingrüber stated: "I did not see our wounded comrades . . . burned with petroleum. I also never gave such a description to Sergeant Thonig. I did speak with Thonig after being wounded, but I know I did not tell him anything about the burning of our wounded by the Russians. There must be some sort of error or misunderstanding here. I may have been confused with another sergeant."[21]

On-the-Spot Verification

One case that illustrates the care with which testimony was investigated is that of the medical orderly Herbert Dietzel, whose testimony was taken by Judge Heinrich Arnold before the court of the 10th Armored Division on 14 January 1944. The examining judge noted at the end of the thirteen-page deposition:

The person of Dietzel as well as his statements have not left an impression of credibility or plausibility in all points. His former disciplinary superior, First Lieutenant Scherdel, was asked today for an evaluation of Dietzel, which he formulated as follows: "versatile, skillful, has a desire to dominate, deceiver, evasive under interrogation, always falling on all fours, tendency to exaggerate and falsify, lacking passion for truth, can organize well, adaptable; easily irritable; tendency to make up stories which his comrades do not believe, they rather laugh at his alleged experiences; cunning; not a bad medical orderly; would not desert." First Lieutenant Scherdel gave this opinion before he was informed in detail of the matter under investigation; he also knew from hearsay that Dietzel had returned from Russian imprisonment. Dietzel's testimony was communicated to him subsequently. First Lieutenant Scherdel has expressed doubts with respect to the accuracy of Dietzel's statements.[22]

In view of these doubts, Dietzel's deposition together with the judge's comments were submitted to the division's intelligence department with the request that its personnel try to determine whether Dietzel had been taken prisoner by the Russians, whether he was witness to the shooting of German POWs, and whether he had been separated from his troop without being guilty of a punishable offense. The intelligence department was asked to specify whether the results of its investigations supported Dietzel's allegations that five German POWs had been executed by the Russians: "We can only make a report on this matter if it is absolutely certain that the five soldiers were shot as prisoners of war."[23]

The intelligence department interrogated a number of German soldiers and Russian prisoners of war, and visited the village where the alleged shooting had taken place. Its report was then submitted to Judge Arnold, who forwarded the entire file to the War Crimes Bureau together with his comments:

The statements made by Captain Schiele, Commander of the Reserve Battalion 10, on 16 and 17 January clearly establish that Dietzel had in fact been taken prisoner . . . that Dietzel was the first man to come in contact with the Russians. Subsequent investigations eliminate the suspicion that Dietzel may have removed himself from his troop, so no military offense was committed. The reservations expressed in points 1 and 3 of my comment of 15 January 1944 with respect to Dietzel's credibility are therefore dropped. On 21 January 1944 Dietzel was sent for questioning by the intelligence officer of the 47th Armored Corps at his request. The Russian tank offensive was then reconstructed on location at Malyje-Wiski with the help of Dietzel and in my presence. . . .

[He] was able to discard any doubt by positively identifying the location where the shootings had taken place. . . . Dietzel further remembered a house where he had been treated humanely and kindly by Russian civilians. Dietzel pointed out several civilians who were then interrogated by our interpreter . . . and who confirmed that they knew Dietzel . . . and they also made expressions of sincere joy upon Dietzel's entering their house wholly unexpectedly and upon their realizing that he had been liberated. . . . The general impression emerging from the results of the investigations at Malyje-Wiski is that we can conclude that Dietzel appears to have spoken the truth not only in substance but also in all secondary details in his testimony of 14 January 1944.[24]

The Dietzel case was one of many in which an investigation was carried out on the spot. Of course, no such investigation was possible if witnesses and their troop contingent had been redeployed. Nevertheless, besides interrogating witnesses, many judges tried to see the evidence for themselves. Alfons Waltzog had the opportunity to see a number of corpses of executed ethnic Germans in Poland in 1939: "I even went to a Catholic monastery near Bromberg where Polish Catholic nuns live, interrogated several persons and they showed me mutilated children's hands. I also saw mutilated corpses. As a judge I had to take judicial view of corpses from time to time."[25] Judge Ulrich Schattenberg, inspected a cellar with rubber-covered walls, where reportedly people had been beaten; outside in the courtyard he saw fingernails that had been pulled off.[26]

Follow-up Verification

Even though its outcome remains unknown, the Donkels case illustrates the care exercised by the War Crimes Bureau in pursuing the truth of allegations contained in the witness protocols it received. On 15 June 1942 a member of the Bureau's staff in Berlin, Karl Hofmann, was sent to carry out routine interrogations at the army hospital in Frankfurt am Main. One of the witnesses he questioned was Corporal Hugo Donkels, who was convalescing from a serious grenade injury to his left shoulder. After Hofmann delivered the depositions, the Bureau found further checking necessary in a number of cases, including the Donkels statement. Therefore Johannes Goldsche wrote on 26 June 1942 to the Army Medical Inspector: "Enclosed for your information is a transcript of sworn witness testimony on a raid by Russian partisans on

1

2

3

4

6

5

7

1. Bureau headquarters in Torgau, 1943–45 (Zayas Archive)
2. Judge Johannes Goldsche (1881–1953), deputy chief of the Prussian War Crimes Bureau, 1917–19, chief of the Wehrmacht War Crimes Bureau, 1939–45 (Zayas Archive)
3. Judge Martin Heinemann (1889–1964), member of the War Crimes Bureau (Zayas Archive)
4. Judge Lothar Schöne (1899–1965), member of the War Crimes Bureau (Zayas Archive)
5. Judge Karl Hofmann (1903–87), member of the War Crimes Bureau (Zayas Archive)
6. Judge Hermann Huvendick (1895–1971), member of the War Crimes Bureau (Zayas Archive)
7. Building that housed the Wehrmacht High Command in Berlin, today the Reichpietschufer in West Berlin (Zayas Archive)
8. Palace of Justice in Nuremberg, site of the Nuremberg trials, 1945–46 (U.S. Army)

8

58

9

9. Judge Rudolf Lehmann, chief
of the legal department of the
Wehrmacht, testifying at the
Nuremberg trials (U.S. Army)
10. Victim of mutilation: medical
examination determined that the
eyes of Corporal Hans Muth had
been deliberately put out
(Bundesarchiv)

10

59

11–12. GIs shot at Malmédy
(U.S. Army)

11

12

60

13

14

13. The Malmédy trial opened in
July 1946 (U.S. Army)
14. Colonel Joachim Peiper
testifying at Malmédy trial (U.S.
Army)

a German field hospital in Roslawl in December of 1941 during which some 120 wounded German soldiers, two doctors, and several nurses were allegedly killed. According to the sworn statement, the doctors and the nurses were Swiss citizens. Do you know of this raid and do you have any proceedings that you could send us?" On 6 July 1942 the Army Medical Inspector replied that he knew nothing about the raid.[27]

Meanwhile, the chief Army doctor in the High Command pursued the matter further and in late July received through channels a report of the chief medical officer of the 4th Army: "In December of 1941 Roslawl lay in the rear zone of operations. . . . No raids were made by either regular troops or partisans. The team of Swiss surgeons assigned to the 4th Army (under Captain Nicole) was in Juchnow . . . through 19 December 1941. They then moved on 20 December 1941 to Smolensk and arrived without suffering any loss. . . . we find that the events described in the report are false and must be characterized as simply made up. Other army commands had no field hospitals at Roslawl during the time in question."

The chief Army doctor thereupon returned the file to the Army Medical Inspector on 30 July 1942 with the comment: "Corporal Donkels is apparently a psychopath inclined to confabulation and *pseudologia phantastica*."[28]

The Bureau was not yet satisfied. On 16 August 1942 Maximilian Wagner turned to the court of Division 159 at Frankfurt am Main asking that Donkels be confronted with these statements and that the head doctor of the hospital in Frankfurt be asked for his opinion "whether Donkels is a psychopath or whether he could have imagined the happenings about which he reported as a result of delirium induced by his very severe wounds." But since Donkels had been transferred to Army Hospital Oberhof in Thuringia, it was not until 28 September 1942 that he was interrogated a second time, by Judge Baetz of the court of Division 179 in Erfurt. Donkels was adamant: "What I reported in my statement of 15 June 1942 . . . corresponds to the events. I am convinced that there must be other witnesses who were there with me and who could confirm my testimony. Unfortunately, I cannot name any of these comrades because I never learned their names. . . . I can only think that maybe I made a mistake in locating the events at Roslawl, since I went through quite a few hospitals and I was gravely wounded. As you may see from my paybook, I was in Army Hospitals III/605 and II/1, to which I was admitted on 10 December 1941. I was treated by a Swiss doctor. He was a captain and of small stature. It is out of the question that because of my wounds I might have been in such a state of mind as to relate the experiences of other comrades as my own."[29]

Notwithstanding, the court of the 179th Division sent a request to Army Hospital Oberhof for an expert opinion on Donkels's mental condition and received a reply on 5 October 1942. It appears that Donkels had lost much blood before arriving at the hospital but was not suffering a high fever. Dr. Erich Koch, the physician treating Donkels at Oberhof, reported: "Retrospectively, I exclude the possibility of mental illness during the period in question. Organic injury of the brain such as could have led to delirium or erroneous sense perception must also be excluded, because otherwise Donkels could not remember so clearly the events he described. . . . During his ambulant treatment nothing occurred that would either support or detract from Donkels's credibility."[30]

On 6 October 1942 the chief medical officer of Army Hospital Oberhof endorsed Dr. Koch's opinion:

> During his hospital treatment from 27 July 1942 to today Donkels has never given reason to believe he is . . . mentally ill. . . . according to Donkels's hospital record he was transferred from the dressing station to field hospital 664 on 27 November 1941. He was then transferred on 29 November 1941 by ambulance to field hospital 651. From there, on 8 December 1941, to Army Hospital 3/605. In his testimony Donkels asserted that he had been transferred from the dressing station to field hospital 651. Since Donkels is not mentally ill, it must be determined whether the reported raid did not take place in field hospital 664, considering that Donkels stated in his deposition of 15 June 1942 that the raid had been at a field hospital. Furthermore, in the report of the chief medical officer of the 4th Army dated 20 July 1942, field hospital 664 is not mentioned but only field hospitals 622 and the hospital for the not seriously wounded 4/591.[31]

But in the meantime a criminal investigation for perjury had been initiated by the court of the 409th Division in Frankfurt am Main; it turned for information to the court of the 179th Division in Erfurt, which on 9 October 1942 forwarded a transcript of Donkels's deposition together with the medical opinions. On 13 October the court of the 409th Division sent the file to the Army High Command in Berlin. On the basis of these documents, the Bureau again requested the Army Medical Inspector on 21 October to recheck whether there had been any raids on field hospitals 664 or 651.[32]

Field hospital 664 responded on 15 November 1942 that it had suffered no raid since its establishment, but that field hospital 260 in Ugodsky Savod had undergone a surprise attack on 24 November 1941. The records indicated that Donkels had not been under treatment in field hospital 260 at the time of the raid, but that several survivors of the raid on field hospital 260 had been accepted at field hospital 651. The suspicion thus emerged "that Donkels heard descriptions of the raid, which he later repeated as his own, without himself having been there."[33]

The War Crimes Bureau, however, in the course of evaluating all this material, encountered a number of contradictions, which it communicated to the Army Medical Inspector on 5 February 1943. For example, the chief medical officers of the 4th Army and the High Command had reported that the team of Swiss surgeons had never been employed in Roslawl, yet field hospital 664 asserted that the Swiss surgeons had been in Roslawl from 3 November 1941 to 18 January 1942 in Army Hospital 3/605. "It appears possible that Corporal Donkels . . . was briefly accommodated in Army Hospital 3/605, which was set up in November 1941. Should this be the case, it would be necessary to determine whether this hospital was raided by Russian partisans in November or December 1941."[34]

On 26 March 1943 the overburdened Army Medical Inspector replied: "The reports of the chief medical officer of the High Command and of the chief medical officer of the 4th Army indicate that neither Army Hospital 3/605 nor any other hospital in Roslawl has been attacked. The Army Medical Inspector therefore declines to pursue this case further."[35]

In the meantime Donkels, incapacitated by his grenade injuries, had received a medical discharge on 6 March 1943.[36] His name then disappears from the available files, so that the case remains a mystery.[37] Still, the persistence shown by the Bureau in pursuing this investigation (a persistence which, as other files demonstrate, was not unique) throws light on its concern neither to take witness testimony on face value nor to dismiss it without making every effort to verify it through other sources.

Many injuries can occur in battle which a lay observer might erroneously assume to be deliberate mutilation: for example, wounds resulting from hand-to-hand combat, or truncations caused by fragmentation bombs or heavy shells. For this reason the War Crimes Bureau required wherever possible that allegations of the torture or mutilation of German soldiers be investigated by the army doctors who accompanied the fighting troops.

Medical Investigations in the Field

Reports of mutilations were extremely rare in France, Belgium, and North Africa, but after the invasion of the Soviet Union on 22 June 1941, such reports arrived almost daily. As a result, the army decreed on 27 August 1941 that additional experts in forensic medicine would be assigned to the Eastern Front "to examine whatever wounds or injuries are caused by the Bolsheviks as are outside the scope of legal warfare." A few weeks later, on 19 September 1941, General Kurt Weckmann, chief of staff of the German 9th Army, also ordered that experts in forensic medicine investigate all reports originating in his area of command: "A brief description of the facts and precise location are imperative. . . . Examination of corpses and autopsies have evidentiary value only as long as the corpses are fresh. The decomposition of the body may confuse the medical evidence and give rise to doubts and objections in foreign countries about what actually happened."[1]

Similarly, for the area under the 18th Army, the chief medical officer issued a "Basic Instruction" dated 19 April 1942: "The examination of corpses [by medical officers] must first determine whether the injuries in battle were deadly, whether mutilations were caused by means of military weapons or by other means such as blunt instruments, and whether they were perpetrated on living persons or on corpses. For this it is necessary to know the effect of the various weapons and munitions. Consideration must also be given to weather effects, damage caused by animals feeding on the corpse, and also decomposition."[2]

According to the available files, it is evident that German soldiers and doctors did not think first of mutilations when they encountered a wounded soldier or a heavily damaged corpse. In those areas where hand-to-hand combat was frequent, the observer usually explained wounds and mutilations as legitimate combat injuries. Dr. Walter Muellerhof, reporting on the examination of twenty corpses stated:

> All injuries had one thing in common, namely that they were received in hand-to-hand combat. The bullets had partially burst open the scalp so that brain chunks had been spread around; some bodies had been stabbed with the bayonet after death, as evidenced by the fact that no blood issued out of the wounds. Some bodies still had a knife stuck on the back. One corpse had stab wounds under both cheekbones under the eyes; the eyes themselves were not injured. Sergeant von Buelow's clothing was ripped by shots and stabs around the abdomen. I saw no cut testicles or poked-out eyes.[3]

Many witness depositions described wounds similarly. On 19 September 1942 noncommissioned officer Guenther Blob testified: "I do not believe that the members of the patrol were deliberately mutilated by the Russians. The patrol was probably attacked with grenades and shot at. The men were wounded and attempted a retreat during which a hand-to-hand struggle developed in which they were stabbed. This is how I explain the stab wounds."[4]

In many other cases, however, medical examination excluded that possibility. For instance, Dr. Sebastian Wittmann reported on 13 August 1941:

> In my opinion the injuries to these two corpses in the area of the face and forehead come from deliberate mutilation, because (1) there are no indications that these wounds . . . could have been caused by shrapnel or other shells—the other head bones and skin are totally undamaged; (2) the derma was hardly torn but showed sharp edges indicating the use of sharp instruments; (3) there were no traces of gunpowder burns in the adjacent skin areas. . . .
>
> I consider it out of the question that these injuries were the result of

hand-to-hand combat, since such injuries run irregularly on the body. In my opinion, the bullet wounds I found had not been deadly; hence, the wounded soldiers were subsequently mutilated when they were defenseless.

[With respect to a third corpse], the injuries of the tongue cannot be explained otherwise than as deliberate mutilation. Judging by the saturation of blood at the cuts, they were inflicted at the time when the soldier was still alive. There is no doubt about this.[5]

Injuries to the Eyes

It is difficult to determine whether eyes have been deliberately put out or whether the damage is attributable to decomposition, to drying up by the sun, or to the gnawing of rats or birds. An effort was made to have medical experts examine all such cases, but even doctors were not always able to tell. For instance, Dr. Richard Eckl and Dr. Herbert Siegmund were given the task of examining the corpses of three German Air Force officers who had been found shot to death at the military hospital in Lvov in the Ukraine. On 4 July 1941 Dr. Eckl reported: "It was impossible to prove whether the eyes of the German pilots had been poked out, since the corpses were so covered with worms that the loss of the eyes could also be explained as destruction caused by worms."[6] But sometimes the victim did not die and could still be saved by the doctor who treated his eye injuries. On 13 August 1941 Judge Hans-Georg Jeremias took the sworn deposition of medical officer and eye specialist Dr. Lothar Wetzlich:

> On 22 July 1941 in the afternoon I was called to the dressing station at Newel . . . to treat a number of soldiers with eye injuries, among them Corporal Hans Muth. As he had explained upon delivery at the dressing station, he had fallen into Russian hands around 9:00 A.M.. He told me that he evidently had been dealt a blow to the head and that when he woke up he could not see any more. He was very emotionally shaken and could not give me further details. The medical examination of the eyes rendered these findings. Right eye: A wound about one inch long could be seen on the lower rim of the eye socket going through the lid. Upon opening the eyelids I discovered that the cornea and part of the lower derma evidently had been cut with a sharp instrument. The lens and the vitreous humor had flowed out. Left eye: The lids were undamaged.

Upon opening the eyelids I saw that the lower half of the derma as well as the cornea had been cut, apparently with a sharp instrument, and hung to the eyeball only at the top. Lens and vitreous humor had flowed out; the choroid membrane was exposed. In order to prevent infection and great pain I removed the remains of the eyes. In my opinion the injuries were inflicted with a shaving blade, or a fragment from his shattered eyeglasses. . . . Since the eyelids of the left eye were undamaged, they must have been held apart while cutting inside. Thus it is impossible that this wound could have occurred in combat.[7]

In another case Judge Erich Kuhr took the deposition of Dr. Emil Stankeit on 15 August 1941:

On 1 July 1941 at 5 A.M. I received an order from Regiment 208 to examine bodies of German soldiers said to be mutilated. Together with Dr. Wendler and with the medical orderly Mueller I went to the fortress Skomorocchy and made there in the early hours the following examinations: Major Peter Soehngen . . . left eye socket empty, wound edges sharply cut. The jaw has been skinned from ear to ear with an even cut; the bones of the upper and lower mandibles are exposed. . . . Sergeant-major Pelzer . . . right eye put out, left eye heavily damaged, cause undetermined. Half of left ear separated by a semicircular cut from below . . . wood splinters in the right eye indicate that the eye was poked out with a piece of wood. Corporal Clemens Schlägers . . . the corpse wears around the head level with the nose an eight-cm-wide bandage without immediately evident reason (possibly an eye bandage that slipped). The left eye socket is empty. Cause undetermined, probably poked out. Sergeant-major Ernst Wegner . . . around the right eye a wound with sharp edges the size of the palm of the hand; the eye is missing, the bony eye socket is exposed. Noncommissioned officer Lange . . . both eye sockets surrounded by even-edged cuts; the eyes hang out stalked and in shreds. . . . It could not be determined with certainty whether the mutilations were inflicted before or after death. The fact that in all cases heavy bleeding out of the eye sockets had occurred tends to support the supposition that the mutilations were inflicted before death.[8]

In an interview on 31 August 1976 Dr. Stankeit further explained: "A bullet causes a more or less ragged wound, whereas if the eyes are cut out this leaves more even edges. Explosives cause damage in all directions; a knife cuts a circle sharply and evenly through. To this extent it is possible to discern by what means a wound has been inflicted." Injuries caused by mice or birds, he added, "look entirely different."[9]

In another case a Dr. S. described in a deposition dated 22 November 1941 the condition of the corpse of Dr. Guenther Reichardt: "Although the body had already started to decompose, I could identify it as that of Dr. Reichardt. . . . I found the following injuries, which I believe were inflicted by the Russians before his death, since traces of blood were found on the body: both eyes were poked out, the nose was cut off, genitals were cut off."[10] In a letter dated 7 April 1978 Dr. S. gave further details:

I was assigned together with Dr. Reichardt . . . near Koroston. A patrol was sent out to reconnoiter the strength of the Russian defenses. Dr. Reichardt joined the patrol. As the patrol leader later informed me, Dr. Reichardt went far ahead of the patrol on the road to K. Suddenly Russians sprang out of the ditch on the left side of the road, grabbed Dr. Reichardt, and were gone before they could be effectively shot at. It was not possible to free Dr. Reichardt, since the enemy was very strong but also because they quickly disappeared. On 24 August 1941 an army information officer . . . mentioned in passing that a dead German officer had been found and buried by his troop in the area of Koroston. . . . The regiment put a vehicle at my disposal. At the spot described . . . I found the grave and had it opened. It was the late Dr. Guenther Reichardt. I recognized his thin reddish blond hair, the light army fatigues with the ribbon of the Iron Cross, second class, and the unmistakable riding breeches with leather trimming. Boots were missing. The damage to the eyes, nose, and genitals was not a result of the process of decomposition. . . . I found blood residue in all these parts. This explains the findings of my autopsy report.

At the end of May 1942, during the battle of Charkov, a military orderly named Taschen belonged to an antiaircraft unit. About four hundred yards from his position a German fighter plane made an emergency landing in an area that was still in Russian hands. When Taschen was able to get to the plane a day later, he found the bodies of the five-man crew:

All bodies were naked with the exception of one that still wore the blue bathing trunks of our fliers. . . . Their eyes had been put out. Quite evidently this was a case of deliberate blinding, since there were no other facial injuries around the eyes. . . . Four of the bodies were missing feet and in some cases hands. . . . The places where separation had taken place were sharp, so that the members must have been severed with a sharp instrument such as an ax. In my opinion and the opinion of all comrades, these mutilations can only be attributable to the human hand. By no means could they have arisen as a result of the landing. . . . Another corpse had a gaping wound in the abdomen around the groin and the genitals had been cut off. I did not see any bullet wounds.[11]

Some witnesses testified to having seen Russians carry out mutilations. On 25 June 1942 Judge Lothar Schöne took the deposition of Corporal Ernst Gottschalk: "We had to cover part of the forest and saw a wounded Russian soldier lying on a field. The medical orderly of the neighboring company went up to tend him. From a distance of about 300 meters I saw the Russian suddenly take out his pistol and shoot the orderly. I then saw, as I was running toward the place, that the Russian dragged himself to the orderly and stabbed his eyes out with a dagger. When I arrived, the orderly was still alive, but he expired shortly afterward."[12]

Genital Mutilations

From the early days of the Polish campaign and throughout the war years, reports reached the War Crimes Bureau purporting to describe mutilations to the genitals. Investigation determined that in a number of cases soldiers had mistaken battle wounds for deliberate mutilations; therefore, the Bureau again sought primarily the sworn testimony of competent medical officers. The consulting legal medical officer at the Army Medical Office issued a memorandum of 8 November 1941 emphasizing the necessity of careful verification:

Experience in Poland and elsewhere shows that lay witnesses and even doctors . . . frequently err in this matter. Mere observation of a corpse is not sufficient to determine clearly whether the genitals are missing; frequently, witnesses jumped to this conclusion merely on the basis of the presence of blood or blood-colored putrid fluid in the genital area.

If indeed the genital organs are missing, then several possibilities must be checked, for instance, that the loss was not a result of destruction by worms . . . [or] a bullet injury. The same considerations apply to . . . alleged mutilations of the female breast, which in repeated instances in Poland turned out to be [the result of] the exit of bullets.[13]

A typical case of erroneous reporting was uncovered by Dr. Gerhard Panning in Yugoslavia, where he had been sent to investigate such allegations by the troops. On 16 October 1941 Dr. Panning submitted a medical opinion stating that the medical investigation carried out by a Dr. Grasser on 4 October 1941 had correctly concluded that the alleged mutilations corresponded to erroneous observations by laymen who had only seen that the genital area of Corporal Lötgers was very bloody. The blood had issued, however, from wounds on the upper thighs, and the presence of the undamaged genitals was established by photograph.[14]

In many other cases, however, medical investigation did confirm deliberate mutilation. On 20 August 1941 the medical officer of Infantry Regiment 239 stated under oath that "Private Bist did not die as a result of the bullet through the thigh but rather bled to death from the amputation of his testicles."[15]

In a medical report dated 4 July 1941 Dr. Hans Jacob Mattern described the corpse of Corporal Dohr, whose skull had been bashed in: "In the area of his genitals I discovered several 10-cm. incisions, which indicated that the enemy had attempted to cut off his genitals after having pulled down his pants. The left eye had been poked out of its socket. According to my medical findings the bullet wound in his chest was not the cause of death. Dohr had been incapacitated by this chest wound. It appears that the Russians took advantage of his defenseless state to beat him to death and sadistically abuse him."[16]

In yet another example Dr. K. G. testified on 13 March 1943: "The penis . . . appeared to have been removed by a clean cut. The medical officer of this fighting unit, Major Count von der Schulenburg . . . remembered Schulz well, since he had dressed his thigh wound one day before. . . . At that time there was no injury of . . . the genital organs."[17]

Experts in Forensic Medicine

The War Crimes Bureau made it a practice to submit reports dealing with mutilations, together with photographs and other documents, to the consulting medical officer at the Army Medical Office for routine verification. The following examples illustrate the cooperation between the two agencies.

Dr. Artur Jogerst was attached to Field Hospital 125 during the battle of Uman near Tscherkassy in the summer of 1942. On a path in the forest he found seven dead German soldiers lying in a row. In a sworn deposition taken before the court of Division 405, Dr. Jogerst declared: "Each soldier had his own knife sticking out of his skull. The skull caps showed fist-sized holes out of which blood and brain parts had spilled. . . . Under the head of each soldier a helmet had been shoved. This must have been done after the soldiers were already dead (since there was blood under the helmets). In my opinion the soldiers were still alive when the knives were driven through their skulls. . . . a corpse could not have bled in this fashion unless the wounds were inflicted immediately after death." [18]

As consulting medical officer, Dr. Panning commented: "The interpretation of the witness is erroneous . . . the correct explanation of the event must be sought rather on the assumption that the seven soldiers were killed by shots from behind at the nape of the neck thus causing large exits in the skull cap, and that then their own knives were stuck in the gaping holes. Judging by the witness's own description of the circumstances that a helmet had been subsequently placed under the neck of each corpse and that the corpses had been laid in rank and file, this case appears to be an example of sadism upon corpses. Such ignominious treatment of corpses, evidently executed with a view toward the impression that would be made on the discoverer, is not infrequent in our experience." [19]

A second example may be found in the investigations of the discovery of two mass graves in the village of Bessabetowka in July 1942. Lieutenant Lennartz, the company commander, explained that in the second grave, unlike the first,

we discovered that bestial tortures had been inflicted on the 56 comrades we found. . . . Most of the corpses were in uniform or at least half dressed. Only a single corpse was naked, that of Major Schönberg. There is no doubt that Major Schönberg was beaten up terribly, since his whole body was streaked with blood. . . . the medical orderly [Ernst] Rostin examined the body very carefully in the presence of numerous witnesses. He did not ascertain any wounds or entry or exit of bullets, so it may be concluded that Major Schönberg was beaten to death. Both feet of another corpse had been separated at the ankle joint, apparently cut by a scalpel or similar instrument. This can never have occurred as the result of an injury, since both feet exhibited the same kind of incision. . . . three corpses still had the hands shackled behind their backs.[20]

Dr. Panning's comments on the description of Major Schönberg's body began with its blood-streaked appearance: "Decomposition causes among other things deep red to reddish-black coloring of the skin and of adjoining tissues, which . . . can be distinguished from bleeding as a result of outside influences only by the expert. . . . Yet considering the special circumstances of this case, the evidentiary value of the observations does increase. The grave provided conditions similar to those in a refrigerator, as evidenced by the presence of snow and ice remnants in the excavation in mid-summer. We know from experience that corpses buried in very cold weather are better preserved than corpses buried in warmer weather." He went on to address other details:

A medical investigation and especially one for the purposes of medical jurisprudence should also have determined whether the injuries of the individual persons could have been fatal. . . . a medical orderly did examine the naked corpse for wounds. A deadly bullet or stab wound, which certainly would have been recognizable in view of the good state of preservation already described, could not be found. . . . The assumption that Major Schönberg was beaten to death is not vulnerable to criticism by enemy propaganda. It is well known that a beating, even without injuring internal organs, may well prove fatal by causing an embolism. In the case of Major Schönberg it appears that his torso was subjected to blows of sufficient force to injure visceral organs. . . . The assumption of the witnesses . . . that Major Schönberg's facial expression and mouth position indicated that he had screamed from pain is not persuasive. The corpse's mimicry is worthless—even shortly after death—as evidence of the final sensations, since it depends on coincidental internal and external factors such as rigor mortis, subsequent dislocation as a result of external pressure or tugging in the grave, loss of fluids, or accumulation of gases. Nevertheless this error of interpretation does not detract from the importance of the case.[21]

Guidelines of the Army Medical Inspector

In an effort to eliminate as many errors as possible, the Department of Science and Promotion of Health in the Army Medical Office issued on 12 June 1942 special guidelines for making medical findings.[22] The following excerpts indicate some of the problems:

> In the course of examining materials on enemy atrocities and violations of international law, which were submitted by the legal department of the Wehrmacht for review by experts in forensic medicine, many erroneous findings on the part of lay observers were found as well as erroneous interpretations on the part of medical doctors, as could be seen on photographs supplied. . . . It is sufficiently well known that in murder investigations one must expect a certain percentage of erroneous statements by witnesses; there are many different causes of these errors. Erroneous statements occur frequently in cases involving mass murder, such as in cases here dealt with. . . . In particular, we must point to the following typical changes that medical officers have frequently failed to take into account. In judging these cases we will refer to the extensive empirical evidence collected by this bureau in the course of investigating the murders that occurred in Poland, where similar assumptions by lay persons and doctors could be verified by autopsy in a number of cases. . . .
>
> In the frequently reported cases of extensive destruction of the skull, both lay witnesses and medical officers have almost without exception supposed that the destruction had been caused by blows with rifle butts, shovels, or hatchets. . . . Practically at no time have the medical officers stopped to consider the hydrodynamic effect of a rifle bullet fired at the skull. This is perhaps understandable, because this type of immediately fatal wound never arises in the daily work of the therapeutic doctor. In any event, it may be generally said that the reported findings on completely destroyed skulls with brains splattered out cannot be explained as having been brought about by the application of blunt force by hand; certainly such destruction was caused by a bullet or bullets. According to general empirical evidence collected by practitioners of forensic medicine, blunt force can cause this type of destruction only when it reaches the magnitude of machine injury (e.g., in an automobile accident) or of a fall from a great height. The kind of complete destruction involved in

these findings cannot be brought about by blows with belts, rifle butts, or axes, which according to experience cannot alter the structure of the human skull so completely.[23]

The guidelines go on to insist that in examining eye injuries and suspected mutilations of the tongue or of the genital organs, the doctor should always take into account other possible explanations for the destruction or removal of tissue or body organs: genuine military injuries, decomposition of the body, or damage caused by animals. The conclusion emphasized the importance of careful medical investigation and reporting:

> In view of the extreme cruelty practiced by the Soviets on wounded as well as unwounded prisoners and also on ethnic minorities in their own territory, some persons may at first think it is unimportant to correctly reconstruct the procedure employed in the individual case or that it is immaterial whether the destruction of the skull was caused by a bullet or by blows with a rifle butt. The reaction of the foreign press to our publications on the atrocity murders in Poland showed, however, that foreign public opinion understandably relies on examination of our allegations by their experts, who would of course not fail to detect gross errors such as those described above. Just to take one case as example, it would be easy for an enemy expert to poke fun at the allegation that a Soviet star had been branded on a body. The substance of the matter—namely, the fact that the person killed had been shackled, that is, that he was a prisoner and that he had been murdered with a shot at close range—would appear in the light of the other allegation equally incredible. . . .
>
> Therefore it appears necessary to remind all medical officers responsible for writing such reports . . . of a fundamental rule of forensic medicine: to lay down a clear statement of the findings to which any reasoning about the use of a particular instrument shall be added, if at all, together with essential critical reservations. Only then will the medical report achieve its rightful place in the vital investigation of violations of international law.[24]

Since the files of the Army Medical Inspector are very incomplete, it is no longer possible to determine to what extent these guidelines were in fact observed in subsequent years. The records of the War Crimes Bureau do show that witness depositions dealing with mutilations were regularly submitted to the Army Medical Inspector for routine review and that the Bureau relied on the judgment of forensic medicine experts to separate erroneous allegations from those that correctly described mutilation, in violation of international law.

Official German publications during the two world wars were issued as "white books" or "white papers" intended to present the German side of a given question. This chapter is concerned only with white books dealing with violations of the laws of war (not with those on historical or diplomatic topics) and the role of the War Crimes Bureau in their formulation.

The German Foreign Office had the exclusive authority to issue official white books, but no clear decision had been made at the beginning of the war regarding the right of other government agencies to issue similar publications. When the War Crimes Bureau compiled five volumes of witness depositions on atrocities allegedly committed by Polish soldiers and civilians before and during hostilities in September 1939, no clash with the Foreign Office took place, because the Bureau did not publish the volumes but only forwarded copies to various government agencies, including the Foreign Office. One year later, after the French campaign, the Bureau did print a "black book" on violations of the laws of war by French soldiers and civilians; this very much resembled the official publications of the Foreign Office, which, jealous of its prerogatives, reacted promptly. In a note dated 14 December 1940, Councilor Stalberg informed the deputy chief of the legal department of the Foreign Office: "I must point out that publication of white books is exclusively within the competence of the Foreign Office. The proposed distribution outside of Germany of a white book issued by the High Command of the Wehrmacht is likely to arouse much opposition by the Foreign Minister. Thus I consider it necessary to inform the High Command not to do anything with this exposé except in close cooperation and with the approval of the Foreign Office."[1] In order to avoid an altercation, the Bureau limited the circulation of its "black book," advising all recipients that its use was restricted and that its contents were not to be published or passed on to persons outside the Wehrmacht.[2]

Not satisfied with its victory, the Foreign Office again objected to the second volume of the Bureau's compilation of French war crimes. On 10 May 1941, Conrad Roediger expressly warned the legal department of the Wehrmacht: "The Foreign Office requests that . . . the printed report 'French illegal warfare 1939/40' and any other reports with similar content . . . shall be made public only with the approval of the Foreign Office. At present the publication of this printed report is politically undesirable."[3]

Two days before, the legal department of the Foreign Office had gone even further in dictating to the Wehrmacht: "The present printed report because of its form and cover gives the impression that it is an official German white book. The Foreign Minister reserves for himself the use of this form for publications on foreign policy matters; the OKW shall therefore choose a different shape and a different color for all future publications."[4] Thereafter, the War Crimes Bureau employed smaller-sized paper when, for example, it published, in April 1943, a 24-page booklet on the Grischino massacre.[5]

In spite of this apparent rivalry, the Bureau did work closely with the Foreign Office in the preparation of white books. Johannes Goldsche himself did most of the talking with the Foreign Office, mainly with Kurt Jagow, head of the Archive Commission. Sometimes Rudolf Lehmann, intervened in order to add weight to Goldsche's arguments. It was Lehmann who forwarded to the Foreign Office the Bureau's report "War Crimes in Crete"; in a letter dated 16 September 1941 he turned the tables by advising that the material could not be published by the Foreign Office without prior permission: "Any use of the material dealt with in this exposé as well as of the material on Russian war crimes requires observance of the censorship guidelines issued by the propaganda department of the Wehrmacht High Command. Publication in Germany of the material on war crimes in Crete requires . . . also the approval of the Air Minister and Commander in Chief of the Luftwaffe."[6]

Evaluation of German White Books

The evidentiary value of German white books during World War II varies greatly. Some consist almost exclusively of sworn witness testimony as compiled by the War Crimes Bureau; these can be said to be fairly reliable, whereas those white books including everything from newspaper articles to Gestapo reports must be taken *cum grano salis.*

The first two German white books dealing with the war in Poland represent a nadir of bad taste and cheap propaganda. On page 187 of "The Polish Atrocities against the Ethnic Germans in Poland" and on page 283 of the enlarged "Documents of Polish Cruelty" appears a "document" numbered 109 under the loud heading "In the Hell of Bereza-Kartuska." The editors simply reprinted a newspaper article from the *Posener Tageblatt* of 27 October 1939 —taking it at face value as the credible report of a Mr. Kopiera, the former director of the Schicht plant in Warsaw—purporting to establish the murder of 158 Germans at the Bereza-Kartuska internment camp.

This "document" was included even though a thorough investigation on the spot had disproved the allegations. In November 1939 a special commission—two military judges, a medical doctor, members of a propaganda company, and two foreign journalists—had been sent to investigate whether twelve to fifteen German pilots had in fact been killed at Bereza-Kartuska. Although the commission's report appears to have been lost, the files of the Foreign Office show that Gunther Altenburg had sent a representative to join the commission and report back to the Foreign Office.[7] According to his account, the pilots were not executed at all but were sent on a transport to Pinsk. The commission further established that though many ethnic Germans at Bereza-Kartuska had been beaten and otherwise mistreated, only three had been killed. In his report of 6 January 1940, Altenburg summed up: "The conclusions of this official commission do not substantiate the allegation in Document 109 that 158 Germans were murdered at Bereza-Kartuska. I do not think it is possible in view of the commission's thoroughness and its method of interrogating witnesses that such an event as the murder of so many Germans could have escaped its attention."[8]

In light of this finding several members in the Foreign Office pleaded for the removal of the document. On 10 January 1940 Ambassador Hans Dieckhoff wrote directly on the report: "Now as ever I believe that an official publication should contain only such documents as are absolutely correct. . . . If the atrocities are true, they should be published; if they are not entirely true, then they should not be published."[9] But a day later, Councilor Günter Lohse of the Press Department contended that it would be too expensive to take the document out of the white book, and anyway, the Foreign Office had already pointed out in a footnote that an official investigation of the case was still in progress.[10] Thus it was decided to keep the objectionable "document" 109 so as not to delay publication of the German-language version of the white book. Lohse did propose taking it out of all foreign-language editions, and in fact it is missing in the English version, titled "Polish Acts of Atrocity against the German Minority in Poland," which was published in New York in the spring of 1940.[11]

Besides this kind of false information there were more serious manipulations and exaggerations. For instance, the original manuscript version of the white book spoke of 5,437 murdered Germans; the published edition claims 58,000 dead and missing—the "official" figure fabricated by Goebbels for his propaganda machine. In implementing this political falsification, the German Foreign Office had to telegraph its embassies in Washington, Buenos Aires, Rio de Janeiro, and elsewhere: "On page 17, line 10 from the top, insert the figure 58,000 instead of 5,000."[12] This internal message did not become known until after the war, but in other countries there was so much skepticism about German allegations that the white book on Poland had little propagandistic success. Moreover, the Polish government-in-exile had been faster in publishing its own "black book"[13] denouncing the widespread and indiscriminate killings perpetrated by German ss and sd soldiers in occupied Poland.[14]

Other reasons why the German white books met with hostility in neutral countries include their racist tone: the clumsy attempt to make all Polish people and soldiers appear to be *Untermenschen* ("lower humans") or common criminals exposed the white books as reckless compilations of hate propaganda, not worth attention or discussion. Instead of letting documents speak for themselves, the editors added shrill absurdities: "After all this we should not be surprised that Poland in waging war failed to observe the simplest rules of international law and of humanity, for which the Poles substituted bestial terror and animal subhumanity."[15]

Although not quite so extreme, the white book "Documents of British and French Atrocities" also contained a number of improbable allegations. Again, there was the problem of timing: alleged British and French "atrocities" had to be collected as soon as possible, even if more speed meant less accuracy. On 4 June 1940 Altenburg telegraphed the German consul in Holland: "The Foreign Minister has directed that a white book on cases of pillage, arson, evacuations, and other atrocities committed by British and French soldiers be immediately compiled. Testimony should be in the form of protocols and should be sent together with pictures to the Foreign Office immediately."[16] The white book contains a number of sworn depositions, but the bulk of the published material consists of unconfirmed reports and allegations.

In the years 1941 and 1942 the Foreign Office published a white book on the war in Crete and three on the war in Russia. These consisted primarily of sworn witness testimony compiled and verified by the War Crimes Bureau and therefore may be taken more seriously as historical sources. On 24 November 1942 the Foreign Office asked the government of Switzerland as Protecting Power to deliver to the British government the official German white book titled "Violations of International Law by British Forces and by the Civilian Population of Crete" as a form of official German protest.[17] Because a year and a half had elapsed since the fighting in Crete, investigations by the British government were hardly to be expected; moreover, the British Foreign Office had already responded to the general accusations in the German press in the summer of 1941 after making a number of inquiries among the British senior officers involved. An internal evaluation dated 5 November 1941 had summed up: "At the time of the fighting in Crete, and shortly thereafter, the Germans accused British troops, as well as the Cretans, of numerous atrocities. . . . On the authority of General Freyberg and other senior officers, it was stated that, after full investigation, German claims were proved to be without foundation."[18]

Two more years would elapse before the British Foreign Office again had occasion to go back to the German white book on Crete, after the Germans repeated their accusation in a diplomatic note dated 5 September 1944. This time, however, the legal adviser at the British Foreign Office, Patrick Dean, made an interesting admission in an internal memorandum dated 10 November 1944: "The breaches of the rules of war alleged against British troops have been made the subject of a German white book and, as far as I remember, a number of instances appeared to be fairly well established."[19] This comment remained internal, of course, but it shows that the British were taking seriously the witness testimony compiled by the Wehrmacht War Crimes Bureau, even if they had not believed the wilder accusations in the German press three years earlier.

Photographic Evidence

Whenever possible, the Bureau tried to obtain photographic evidence to accompany witness testimony. Most of the pictures, often of poor quality, were taken by individual soldiers with their own cameras; sometimes a member of a propaganda company could be called to the scene in order to produce more professional photographs illustrating the case investigated. The Bureau made these pictures available to the Foreign Office, which used them extensively in the two white books on Poland. They were so shocking, however, that they detracted from the propagandistic effect. As the German Embassy at Bern reported on 3 May 1940 to the Foreign Office: "We have frequently observed that the recipients of the white book [in Switzerland] get upset not about the atrocities committed by the Poles but about our publishing such horror pictures."[20]

In the course of the war in Russia the Bureau received photographs of thousands of killings and mutilations, which Goldsche, as usual, made available to the Archive Commission at the Foreign Office. On 8 September 1941, however, Jagow responded on behalf of the Archive Commission that Foreign Minister Joachim von Ribbentrop had decided against their publication.[21] Thus the three Russian white books consist preponderantly of witness testimony, though pictures were again used to illustrate those on Katyn and Vinnitsa.[22]

When nations at war sever direct relations, any further diplomatic contact between them is usually achieved through a neutral state chosen as the Protecting Power. At the beginning of World War II, Great Britain chose the United States as Protecting Power, while Germany asked the government of Switzerland to represent German interests in Great Britain. When Germany declared war on the United States in December of 1941, Switzerland became Protecting Power for all three belligerents.[1] Diplomatic exchange between Germany and the Soviet Union was far less conventional.

The Third Reich and the Anglo-Americans
One of the tasks of a Protecting Power is to communicate one government's accusation of another's violation of international law. The German Foreign Office, for instance, would send a note to the German Embassy in Bern, Switzerland; the embassy would transmit that note to the Swiss Foreign Office (called the Federal Political Department), which would telegraph the note to the Swiss Embassy in London or Washington, which would bring it to the attention of the British or American government. After due investigation an official answer would be drafted by the British Foreign Office or the U.S. Department of State and telegraphed to its embassy in Bern for delivery to the Swiss Federal Political Department, which would complete the circle by informing the German Foreign Office through the Swiss Embassy in Berlin.

Although the Undersecretary of State Ernst von Weizsäcker in the German Foreign Office once told Swiss Minister Hans Fröhlicher during a meeting in Berlin that the Reich did not consider it worthwhile for a belligerent state to make official protests to another belligerent state, the Reich did in fact make frequent use of this old custom of international relations. However, as Weizsäcker put it, "the Reich . . . limits itself to making a statement of the facts for the protection of its legal position."[2] Thus the Germans avoided the use of the word "protest" by renaming their diplomatic notes "Communication of the Government of the Reich" to the Protecting Power. These communications were, of course, traditional protest notes, which the Reich asked the Protecting Power to transmit to the British or American Government.[3]

The German Foreign Office obtained its information about violations of the laws of war from many sources—first of all through the War Crimes Bureau but also through its own liaison officers at the High Command of the Army, Navy, and Air Force, in the Wehrmacht propaganda department, and with the armies in the field. The Bureau however, besides making its documents available to the Foreign Office, often itself recommended lodging a protest with the Protecting Power and sometimes prepared the draft of the note.

Perhaps the most frequent cause of protest was the treatment of German prisoners of war, one of the most celebrated cases being the shackling of German soldiers taken prisoner by British commandos at Dieppe in August 1942.[4] Another case involved the misuse of German POWs on dangerous assignments close to the front line. On 20 December 1944 the Bureau sent to the Wehrmacht operations staff a copy of the sworn deposition of Private Hans Greiss, who alleged that he and other German POWs had been forced to dig trenches at the American battle front close to Kirchberg, Jülich, in November 1944. Greiss stated that he and his comrades had been compelled to work under German artillery fire and that the resulting casualties included two dead and twenty wounded. Goldsche recommended lodging a diplomatic protest against the British and American governments, "since this case entails a very serious violation of the Convention on the Treatment of Prisoners of War (Articles 7 and 9)."[5] The operations staff passed the recommendation to the German Foreign Office, which agreed and transmitted an official protest on 26 January 1945.[6]

As in previous cases, the U.S. State Department took the matter seriously and had an on-the-spot investigation carried out; however, the report of the Office of the Inspector General of the U.S. 9th Army, dated 25 April 1945, concluded that "the purported facts given in the protest are too indefinite, contradictory and lacking in plausibility to warrant further investigation." Evidently, because several towns have the name Kirchberg and because of the time that had elapsed there was great difficulty in finding anyone who knew anything at all about Greiss or about the practices he described.[7]

Other German protests dealt with Anglo-American air warfare, especially with the alleged bombing and machine-gunning of ambulances, hospital trains, and field hospitals; the Bureau files report a great many such attacks in Italy. On 30 November 1944 the Bureau forwarded three sworn depositions: "In view of the increased frequency of Anglo-American attacks on medical units, we advocate lodging protest against both the United States and Great Britain. The nationality of the planes involved can be determined with certainty only in a few instances."[8]

On 6 December 1944 the German Embassy in Bern delivered a long note protesting twelve air attacks on German medical units in Italy during the six weeks from 1 September to 16 October 1944 by British and/or American fighter-bombers. The note emphasized that the German armed forces had taken every precaution to make army medical establishments clearly recognizable even to high-speed aircraft; moreover, all the attacks listed had taken place in good weather and far from any legitimate military targets. Identical notes were transmitted by the Protecting Power to London and Washington: "The government of the Reich expects that the British [American] government will not only make a thorough investigation and call the guilty parties to account but also prevent the recurrence of such infractions of international law by the immediate issue of more stringent orders to strictly observe the Geneva Convention."[9]

Upon receipt of this note, the British and American governments ordered the investigation of all twelve cases.[10] On 11 February 1945 British Air Vice-Marshal R. M. Foster reported that British planes had definitely not been involved in nine of the attacks complained of. In two others, British planes had in fact been on strafing missions, but in one case the pilots had not seen any red cross markings on the buildings and, in the other, did not see them until after the attack had been completed.[11] On 13 February 1945 the U.S. Adjutant General's office reported that a full investigation revealed responsibility in only two cases: "At 0810 hours the flight began a strafing run on 5 or 6 vehicles . . . not until the leader's machine-gun fire had driven one of the vehicles off the road was he close enough to discern red crosses marked on the vehicles; he immediately ceased firing and ordered the rest of the flight mission to hold their fire. . . . At 1545 hours a vehicle was fired on by this flight. . . . It was only after the vehicle had been strafed that it was recognized as an ambulance. No further attacks were made after the red crosses were distinguished."[12]

On the basis of these reports the U.S. War Department explained the attacks to the State Department, which in turn transmitted a statement to the Swiss Minister in charge of German interests in the United States: "Because of the nature of these attacks it was virtually impossible to see the red cross markings until after the attacks had begun. Had the pilots taken more time to examine each target at close range prior to attack, they would have been subjected to prolonged enemy fire. Whenever the markings were seen, the attacks were immediately broken off."[13]

The complaint-and-investigation procedure functioned in similar manner with respect to the bombardment of a hospital at Dunkirk in October of 1944. The German legation in Bern transmitted the following note to the Protecting Power on 1 November 1944:

> The commander of the German base at Dunkirk, currently under British siege, reports that when negotiating with the commanders of the British troops for a short armistice to permit the evacuation of the civilian population from the city he also asked them to spare the hospitals in Dunkirk, to which the British agreed. When shortly thereafter, on 14 October, a hospital was subjected to artillery fire and damaged, the German commander of Dunkirk officially protested to the British commander. In spite of this another hospital was again bombarded at night, although there were no military objectives in the vicinity. There were also wounded British soldiers in the hospital. Since the German commander had informed the British troops about the exact location of the hospitals in Dunkirk, it is presumed that the bombardment was deliberate and not mere stray shots.[14]

One month later, on 2 December 1944, the British government informed the Protecting Power:

> His Majesty's Government have made the fullest enquiry into the incident referred to by the German Government. As a result it has been established that no shell fire was aimed at the hospitals or hospital areas

notified by the German Commander to the British Commander at Dunkirk. Far from there having been no military target in the vicinity, there were in fact legitimate targets within 300 yards and 500 yards from the hospital concerned and the attention of the German Commander was drawn to the fact that these and other targets were very close to the hospital line. . . . His Majesty's Government declare therefore that British artillery fire has not been directed at the hospital areas indicated by the German Commander in Dunkirk and reiterate that it is their invariable practice to respect the immunity of hospitals under international law.[15]

At this point it would be well to mention that on numerous occasions the British and American governments on their own initiative communicated to the Swiss government such occurrences as they thought involved a violation of international law by their own troops. For example, on 19 November 1944 the British legation in Bern conveyed to the Swiss government a communication regarding the sinking of the German hospital ship *Tübingen* in the Adriatic south of Pola; the German government did not submit its official protest until 24 November 1944.[16]

And again, when some 140 German prisoners of war died of suffocation on 15 March 1945, while being transported from one POW camp to another in France, the United States government decided to inform the Protecting Power immediately. On 18 March 1945 General Dwight D. Eisenhower telegraphed to General George C. Marshall: "I have not yet found out the cause of the death of the German prisoners, recently reported to me, nor do I know who is responsible. It is irritating to have such things occur, because I certainly loathe having to apologize to the Germans. It looks as if this time I have no other recourse."[17] After consultations with the British government, the American legation in Bern conveyed a communication to the Swiss government: with the approval of the State Department, Eisenhower addressed a statement to the German High Command expressing regret over the deaths of the POWs and promising a full inquiry into the case and punishment of those responsible.[18]

The German Foreign Office continued processing documents from the War Crimes Bureau and churning out protest notes until the very last weeks of the war. One of the latest bears the date 25 March 1945, barely six weeks before the final collapse of the Reich. To the post-war historian it may seem remarkable indeed that while most of the Reich was occupied by Allied troops and the Russians were preparing for the final assault on Berlin, the Foreign Office could serenely issue a diplomatic note protesting eleven attacks on medical facilities in Italy:

> The German government has repeatedly had occasion to protest to the British and United States governments concerning violations of the Geneva Convention for the Protection of the Wounded and Sick of Armies in the Field. The latest reports listed below . . . substantiated by witness testimony under oath and by trustworthy accounts of witnesses, have strengthened the conviction of the German government that these continued attacks . . . constitute intentional systematic violations of the abovementioned Convention. . . . The German government . . . requests that the incidents be investigated, that appropriate action be taken against the guilty, and that all measures be taken to ensure that such totally inexcusable incidents will not recur.[19]

The Third Reich and the Soviets

Diplomatic protection as it functioned between Germany and the United States and between Germany and Great Britain never materialized between the two great European totalitarian powers; neither Hitler nor Stalin wanted it. Early in the hostilities between them, however, the Soviet Union did approach Sweden, and Germany approached Bulgaria, for very limited Protecting Power services.

On 19 July 1941 the Swedish legation in Berlin conveyed a Soviet note of 17 July offering to observe the rules of war set out in the Hague Convention IV of 18 October 1907, if the German government would do likewise. Because the Soviet government had abrogated all treaties signed by the Tsarist regime, the Convention would not apply to its soldiers without some such gesture. (The Soviet government, did not, however, offer to subscribe to the Geneva Convention of 27 July 1929, which it had never signed.) Of course, it is an open question whether the Soviet Union made the offer in good faith or whether this was no more than one of its frequent propaganda ploys. Whatever the case, the German government did not take the offer seriously. Whereas in other theaters of war the killing of prisoners had been a rare exception, thousands of German POWs had already been liquidated by Soviet forces during the first weeks of fighting. In the light of this experience, which was extensively documented by the War Crimes Bureau, Germany considered the Soviet suggestion a kind of bad joke, as the official answer of the Foreign Office indicates:

> The German government can only express its utter astonishment at the fact that the Soviet government considers itself justified in referring to the observance of international law rules with respect to the treatment of prisoners of war and thereby to bring up the question of reciprocity in spite of the conduct thus far shown by Soviet soldiers toward German prisoners of war. . . . the state of the corpses of German soldiers found by advancing German troops and the testimony of German soldiers who have fallen in Russian hands and then been liberated establish that Soviet soldiers have murdered and tortured German prisoners in bestial and indescribable fashion.[20]

At approximately the same time the International Committee of the Red Cross transmitted to the German Foreign Office a statement by the Soviet Red Cross protesting German air attacks on Soviet field hospitals. As a matter of course, the German Foreign Office passed the complaint on to the legal department of the German Air Ministry: "In order to respond to the Soviet allegations with greater propagandistic impact, it is necessary to determine which cities mentioned in the telegram are now in German hands and whether investigations on the spot can yield evidence to show the untruth of the allegations. Such evidence can be submitted eventually to representatives of the International Committee of the Red Cross for rechecking and may be used for other purposes."[21] On 23 July 1941 the High Command of the Air Force responded with a tone of indignation:

> It is wholly out of the question that the Luftwaffe may have deliberately attacked hospitals or medical transports. . . . in view of the well-known Soviet practice of destroying everything behind them, it is more likely that the Soviets have themselves destroyed their own hospitals. Moreover, the Luftwaffe refuses to devote any attention to Soviet protests with respect to the observance of the Geneva Convention or of the Prisoner of War Convention, since the Soviets have thus far conducted themselves in a manner totally outside international law. As proof we enclose, for your information but not for publication, a number of photographs and the transcript of a report dealing with the torture of German pilots and the murder of members of the Luftwaffe in Lvov.[22]

This internal communication reflects the subjective conviction on the part of German officers that the Red Army did not observe the laws of war, notwithstanding the representations made by the Soviet government to the Swedish Protecting Power. It was therefore with little expectation of success that the German Foreign Office, from the beginning of the campaign in Russia, took repeated steps to inquire into the fate of German soldiers missing in action and believed to be in Russian captivity. On 20 August 1941 it informed the legal department of the Wehrmacht and the special bureau for foreign intelligence that the Bulgarian Foreign Office had been approached as intermediary and that the Bulgarian legation in Moscow was attempting to establish whether there existed a prisoner-of-war camp some ten kilometers south of Moscow's Tushino Airport. The Bulgarian legation was further asked to try to arrange a visit to this and other camps by the International Committee of the Red Cross, which had already inspected prisoner-of-war camps for Russian soldiers in Germany.[23] As expected, however, the Soviet government informed the Bulgarian legation that it declined to answer such inquiries.[24] The ICRC, which had offered all belligerents its services in exchanging lists of prisoners of war and communicating messages, was similarly refused permission to visit POW camps in the Soviet Union. Nor did it receive any lists of prisoners, even though the governments of Finland, Italy, Hungary, Rumania, and the Reich had transmitted the names of Soviet prisoners of war. This lack of reciprocity led to the Reich's decision to discontinue the practice of communicating names to the ICRC.[25]

In the incomplete records of the War Crimes Bureau and the German Foreign Office, no other instances of quasi-Protecting Power activities with respect to the Soviet Union are to be found. Given the character of the confrontation between Hitler and Stalin, any attempt at diplomatic intervention was almost a priori condemned to failure: since each totalitarian belligerent was committed to annihilating the other at whatever cost, restrictions on the way to total victory were considered a waste of time.

Besides supporting diplomatic notes and filling the pages of official white papers, the documentation collected by the War Crimes Bureau was used in preparing war crimes trials against Polish, French, Russian, Yugoslavian, and other Allied prisoners of war.

The first step toward a trial on such charges was to determine whether a suspect mentioned in a deposition was being held as a prisoner of war under German jurisdiction. In cooperation with the Armed Forces Central Bureau for Casualties and Prisoners of War,[1] the War Crimes Bureau located many suspects and frequently also further witnesses.[2] It then forwarded the pertinent documents to the appropriate military court with a recommendation for court-martial.[3] At the commencement of a judicial hearing against a prisoner of war, it was the obligation of the detaining power's Foreign Office, pursuant to Article 60 of the Geneva Convention of 1929, to notify the Protecting Power. Upon the completion of judicial proceedings, a transcript of the judgment was forwarded as a matter of course to the Bureau as central documentation center.[4]

The Question of Jurisdiction

There is no doubt whatever that a detaining power may try a prisoner of war for offenses committed during internment. At the outbreak of World War II it was not entirely clear, however, whether a prisoner of war was subject to the military courts of the detaining power for offenses committed *before* his capture. Many World War I POWs had been punished for such post-capture offenses as breach of discipline, attempted escape, striking a guard, and the like, but there was little experience in the field of prosecuting "war crimes." The prevalent view held that there was no personal liability of the soldier; indeed, Article 3 of the IVth Hague Convention of 1907 made a belligerent party "responsible for all acts committed by persons forming part of its armed forces." According to this provision the injured state could claim reparation or compensation from the home state of the person committing the violation of international law, but was the injured state precluded from prosecuting the offender if he became a prisoner of war?

Neither the 1907 Hague regulations on land warfare nor the 1929 Geneva Convention relative to the treatment of prisoners of war answered this question. The penal sanctions set forth in Articles 45–67 of the Geneva Convention appear to apply primarily to offenses committed during internment: "Prisoners of war shall be subject to the laws, regulations, and orders in force in the armed forces of the detaining power." What this article failed to specify was whether submission to those laws applied retroactively.[5] National manuals on military law were more specific. For example, Article 59 of (Lieber Code, 1863) the American "Instructions" provide that "a prisoner of war remains answerable for his crimes committed against the captor's army or people before he was captured and for which he has not been punished by his own authorities"; the British "Manual" provides that "a prisoner of war who committed an offence against the customs of war—such for example as stabbing or robbing wounded men—may be considered to have forfeited the character of a prisoner of war, and be punished with death for his crime."[6] The German *Kriegsgebrauch im Landkriege* lists specific rules of international law and then adds that "whoever breaks these rules shall be prosecuted by his State. If he is taken prisoner, he is subject to punishment by [foreign] court-martial."[7]

The legal experts in the *Ausland-Abwehr* bureau of the Wehrmacht High Command challenged the view set forth in the American and British manuals and stated in a memorandum dated 30 December 1940 respecting a previously concluded trial:

A sentence has been passed on a prisoner of war because of an offense that he may have committed before he became a prisoner. This is fundamentally wrong. The sole purpose of imprisonment is to prevent an enemy soldier from further actions. . . . It is not admissible in international law to equate imprisonment as a prisoner of war with other cases in which a person falls within the jurisdiction of another state, whether by entering the territory of the other state or by extradition from another state. In the first case, existing criminal charges may be pressed without limitation; in the second case, only to the extent agreed to by the extraditing state. The prosecution of a prisoner of war because of offenses which he committed against the detaining power before his imprisonment would equate imprisonment with an extradition without conditions. . . . This violates both general principles of international law and also the soldier's code of honor. Since the function of military courts with respect to foreigners consists solely in carrying out with due process such necessary military measures as further the war effort, the execution of the death sentence against a prisoner of war for . . . offenses committed before imprisonment must be considered as killing a defenseless enemy and therefore violates . . . the Hague Regulations on Land Warfare. . . . For the violation of [those] regulations . . . only the state is liable in international law, and there is no individual criminal responsibility. Pursuant to this view the individual can be criminally punished by an enemy state only when his home state refuses to assume the responsibility, does not cover the soldier's act, and consents to his punishment by the enemy state. Obviously, this can occur only in cases of gross violations of the laws of war which display a dishonorable attitude that damages the reputation of his army. Only in such cases can war crimes trials be conducted without disadvantageous political and propagandistic consequences.[8]

This position did not prevail—partly because it was not shared by the Allies[9]—yet interestingly enough, it seems that during the war, Germans refrained from trying British and American prisoners on war crimes charges (though Hitler planned to do so; see below), and neither Great Britain nor the United States tried any German prisoners for war crimes prior to the German unconditional surrender. Evidently, neither side wanted to give the other a reason to retaliate.[10] Germany did not hesitate to try prisoners of war of other nationalities, however.

Trials of Polish Prisoners of War

During and after the German invasion of Poland the Bureau carried out extensive investigations of war crimes allegedly committed by Polish soldiers and civilians against German soldiers and the German ethnic minority in Poland, and numerous trials followed.

No Protecting Power was ever notified of these proceedings. According to Judge Walter Lichtenheldt, who was responsible for the prisoner-of-war department in the Wehrmacht's legal division, the Geneva Convention of 1929 "had no application with regard to Polish prisoners of war because Poland had ceased to exist."[11]

A major problem for the investigators was that witness testimony rarely named the perpetrators; it dealt chiefly with events, victims, and survivors. Only after a great many Polish civilians and prisoners of war had been questioned could the Bureau arrive at the names of some of the suspects. Even then, the majority of criminal proceedings had to be discontinued either because the suspect was not a prisoner of war or was "clearly not the culprit" (some discontinued proceedings were later reopened in the light of new evidence, however).

When investigations did lead to trials, they were held before special courts in Polish cities. One such case involved Sergeant Luciusz Kurczynski, who according to witness testimony killed two German prisoners of war shortly before German troops marched into the town of Grodzisk in September 1939. The Special Court in Lodz sentenced him to death on 28 November 1939 because he had known "that according to the laws of war he had only the choice to evacuate both prisoners or to let them go free. He also knew that even his superior could not order him to kill the two prisoners, since prisoners of war and military internees, as the accused knew, could not be killed even pursuant to Polish law except if sentenced by a court, and no sentence had been passed against the two prisoners."[13]

Similar trials were still taking place several years later. Captain Sigmund Rakocy was sentenced on 6 March 1942 and executed in April for having ordered the killing of German prisoners in September 1939. Another suspect, Private Jan Lysiak, could not be found; Private Andreas Felerski was acquitted (Felerski had allegedly held up a prisoner who did not want to stand up, so that he could be shot). Another midwar trial ended on 15 January 1943 when a Captain Lesik, accused of having ordered the execution of seven German prisoners of war, committed suicide.[14]

The following case illustrates the bureaucratic and unspectacular methods used in these criminal investigations. A Polish lieutenant had testified against his comrade Zmudzinski, claiming that he had killed a German prisoner of war named Rhode, who had resided in Düsseldorf, worked as a locksmith, and been married to a woman called Martha. An investigation carried out by the Düsseldorf police department failed to confirm the residence of the locksmith Rhode. Since no other evidence existed against Zmudzinski, the Special Court in Warsaw dismissed the proceedings on 10 November 1941.[15]

The trial with the largest number of accused was that of Captain Jan Drzewiecki and thirty-seven others. Drzewiecki had led a special troop of Polish reserves assigned to evacuate a number of ethnic Germans from the western zones of Poland. The forced march began in Torun on 3 September 1939 and lasted for eleven days, at the end of which some 230 Germans had lost their lives.[16] The trial before a Special Court in Bromberg ended on 1 April 1942: twenty-one of the Polish prisoners of war were condemned to death; one was sentenced to five years' imprisonment; sixteen were acquitted. The rationale of the court was laid down in a judgment of 177 pages.[17]

In view of the fact that no suspects could be found for most of the specified crimes, some fanatical Nazi Party members—particularly functionaries of the occupation government—started thinking in terms of reprisals. When the criminal investigation of the murder of a married couple by the name of Nickel had dragged on for four years but yielded no suspects, the frustrated prosecutor proposed to the High Command of the Wehrmacht that collective penalties be imposed on all Polish soldiers who had been in the area of the crime. The legal department rejected the proposal on 19 February 1944, referring to the express prohibition of collective penalties in the Geneva Convention of 1929. The prisoner-of-war department also disapproved: "A reprisal might have been appropriate if carried out by the fighting troop immediately after discovery of the crime, but a collective penalty is out of the question after more than four years have elapsed."[18]

According to an incomplete list of judicial proceedings against Polish prisoners of war, it appears that at least 252 cases were investigated, of which some two-thirds ended in dismissal. Death sentences were passed on at least twenty-eight persons; at least twenty-one were acquitted.[19]

Trials of French Prisoners of War

In the months of May and June 1940, during the fighting between Germany and France, German military courts initiated proceedings against French soldiers for alleged violations of the laws of war and against French civilians for fighting as irregular combatants, or *franc-tireurs*. One well-known case involved the killing of the crew of a Heinkel 111 that crash-landed near Vimy in northern France. The court-martial met in Doullens under Judge Albert

Lochner. The trial of three French civilians on 6 June 1940 ended with the death sentence against all three; the sentence was carried out on 29 June 1940 in Doullens.[20] In another case, four German airmen were severely manhandled by forty to fifty armed farmers and *gendarmes* after they crash-landed in a field. The court of the German 5th Armored Division passed the death sentence on two of the farmers in Brest on 23 June 1940; three others were acquitted because of insufficient evidence.[21]

After the armistice with France on 22 June 1940 the prosecution of other suspected war criminals was the subject of some controversy. On 25 August 1940 the High Command of the Luftwaffe proposed that French courts try their own soldiers. The German Armistice Commission, however, responded on 29 August that it would be inopportune to burden the French Delegation with such matters; better to postpone the question until the war was over and a peace treaty could be drawn up. The legal department of the Wehrmacht pleaded for the prompt commencement of criminal proceedings, but the armistice agreement made no provision for such proceedings. A proposal that French authorities deliver French suspects for trial by German courts not only promised an undue burden on the German side but recalled uneasy memories of the Reich's post–World War I resistance to the demand of the victors that Germans be delivered for trial before French courts. Finally, the German Armistice Commission proposed that only the gravest cases be investigated and then, given sufficient evidence, prosecution be demanded of the French government.[22]

Rudolf Lehmann commented on this proposal extensively in a memorandum to *Ausland-Abwehr* on 2 September 1940:

French soldiers and civilians frequently offended, robbed, and mistreated German prisoners of war. Thus far they have hardly been called to answer for their conduct. . . . Pursuant to the Reich Criminal Code [23] . . . these offenses may be prosecuted according to German law. . . . Although the victims generally cannot identify the perpetrators, we know from the experience of the courts with the Polish murders that a number of the perpetrators will be convicted. We should consider whether extradition should be demanded. The decision is solely political, but the legal department of the Wehrmacht would submit the following points of view for deliberation:

An objection to the demand for extradition is that it would be a repeat performance of the demand that France made of Germany in 1919. We succeeded then in persuading France that it would be advisable to refrain from actually extraditing the accused. Now we would have to face the same arguments on the French side which we ourselves pressed against extradition.

Thus we should leave the trial of the perpetrators . . . in the hands of *French justice*. By doing this we would avoid the accusations which foreign countries would certainly raise with respect to unfair and harsh justice, and at the same time France would have to try her own citizens for war crimes and thereby admit that Frenchmen have gravely violated the laws of war. . . . we have an opportunity to discuss these matters with the French within the Armistice Commission. . . . The legal department of the Wehrmacht requests to be kept informed of the outcome of discussions at the Foreign Office so as to continue taking its part in further preparatory work.[24]

At a meeting of the Armistice Commission in Wiesbaden on 25 September 1940, Maximilian Wagner and Alfons Waltzog elaborated further: "There is an enormous body of incriminatory evidence. . . . It is essential to bring these offenders to justice in all serious cases. . . . The question of jurisdiction may be answered as follows: Perpetrators in German prisoner-of-war camps or in occupied French territory can be brought before German military courts; perpetrators in the unoccupied part of France shall be dealt with by the French courts. . . . The main difficulty . . . consists in finding the perpetrators. . . . even when it is known who committed the crime, a time-consuming investigation must be carried out to discover his whereabouts, so as to determine whether jurisdiction lies with a German court."[25]

On 26 November 1940 Lehmann proposed that the Foreign Office approach the Armistice Commission to expedite the process of commencing war crimes trials before French courts and under German supervision. Out of political considerations, however, the Foreign Office declined to pursue the matter.[26]

In the meantime the Bureau had produced its first massive documentation on alleged French violations of international law. Upon receipt of the second volume the Foreign Office reacted on 8 May 1941 with a clear indication that no demand would be made of the French government to prosecute its own citizens until the Foreign Office saw fit. A similar communication was sent on 10 May 1941 to the Wehrmacht High Command. After numerous consultations between Lehmann and Foreign Office Councilor Roediger, the legal department of the Wehrmacht agreed to observe the wishes of the Foreign Office in order to help improve relations with the French government. Lehmann even ordered a stay of execution of all death sentences in occupied France.[27]

Nevertheless, the Bureau had continued to collect and prepare the evidence for war crimes trials. Wagner informed the Foreign Office on 23 May 1941 that a number of significant cases were ready for submission to French authorities, but on 8 June the Foreign Office again expressed its reservations: "For the time being it does not seem advisable to approach the French government with respect to the prosecution of French war criminals in unoccupied territory by French courts. The Foreign Office may review this matter at the appropriate time and rely on the above-mentioned note."[28]

In fact, the Foreign Office routinely reconsidered the matter every three months. Not until the Germans and Italians invaded the rest of France in December 1942, however, did the Foreign Office again turn to the legal department of the Wehrmacht. On 23 January 1943 Roediger wrote to ask Lehmann "whether the Wehrmacht had taken or was planning to take measures with respect to a criminal prosecution of French war criminals in the previously unoccupied part of France,"[29] and apparently the question was again discussed in February 1943, but no criminal proceedings seem to have been undertaken at this time.

Still, in the northern part of France that had been occupied since June 1940, German military courts did routinely prosecute the cases that came to their attention, although with the passing of time they tended to render milder judgments than those passed in Vimy and Brest. On 29 April 1941 the military court in Paris tried ten French civilians who on 10 May 1940 had mistreated and robbed the crew of a Heinkel 111 that had crash-landed nearby. Two of the accused were acquitted; eight were convicted of assault rather than treated as *franc-tireurs*. The highest sentence was three years' imprisonment, and three of the convicted were released immediately, their imprisonment awaiting trial being counted against the sentence.

The trial of Lieutenant Jules Levresse had greater political impact than routine trials against alleged *franc-tireurs,* since the accused was a French officer from a prominent family.[31] He was charged with violating Article 7 of the 1929 Geneva Convention, which provides that as soon as possible after their capture, prisoners of war shall be evacuated to depots sufficiently removed from the fighting zone to put them out of danger. Apparently, Levresse had failed to evacuate a number of German prisoners and had thereby exposed them to the danger of German artillery fire; according to the testimony of the survivors, a number of them were wounded and two died.

In this case the Foreign Office sent proper notification of the trial to the United States as Protecting Power, as provided in Article 60 of the 1929 Geneva Convention.[32] On 27 October 1940 the German military court of the 269th Division convicted Levresse of multiple murder, under Article 211 of the German penal code, and condemned him to death; in November the sentence was confirmed by the Army High Command and—pursuant to the German ordinance on criminal procedure—had next to be submitted to Hitler as commander-in-chief of the Wehrmacht. In a memorandum dated 30 December 1940 the *Ausland-Abwehr* objected to the death sentence, and on 30 January 1941 it appealed to the legal department of the Wehrmacht to support a petition for clemency.[33]

Meanwhile, the French government had taken up the matter, and on 28 January 1941 Marshal Philippe Pétain directed his defense minister, General Charles Huntzinger, to appeal to the German military authorities: "As father of my people and of my soldiers I cannot be indifferent to the fate of an officer whose record of service and excellent leadership prove his high moral character and when his soldierly honor cannot be questioned. I am also concerned about the grief of a young wife, who as a model of brave womanhood awaits in anguish the execution of the sentence against her husband." In conveying this appeal to Field Marshal Wilhelm Keitel as head of the Wehrmacht High Command on 30 January 1941, Huntzinger asserted that it was far from his intention "to question the high sense of duty of the members of the competent military court," yet in view of the respect that Levresse enjoyed among both his superiors and his comrades, and because the combat situation was so confused, the sentence should be reduced.[34]

Keitel then submitted the case to Hitler, who took his time in making a decision; not until 24 May 1941 did he order the sentence changed from death to imprisonment. On 29 May 1941 Rudolph Lehmann noted that political considerations had determined the outcome.[35]

Levresse was taken to Bockenheim Prison in Frankfurt am Main; on 23 February 1943 he was transferred to the hard-labor prison at Bruchsal and on 3 August 1944 to the Wehrmacht prison in Munich.[36] He was repatriated to France on 16 May 1945.[37]

Criminal Investigations of British and American Prisoners of War

In June of 1941, upon the conclusion of the campaign in Crete, the German press announced that special courts had been set up in Crete to try British and Cretan prisoners of war for atrocities committed on German parachutists.

Since the United States was then acting as Protecting Power for Great Britain, the American Embassy in Berlin reported this development to the State Department in Washington, which in turn informed the British Foreign Office on 10 June 1941, adding that "certain punitive measures, at least with respect to the Cretans, appear to be necessary for the morale of the parachute troops."[38] On 5 August 1941 a German military tribunal in Crete convicted John Zazaronakis of *franc-tireur* activities and of plundering the bodies of dead soldiers. The court sentenced Zazaronakis to death because "the situation in Crete and the security of German soldiers on the island require drastic measures for the sake of deterrence and by the same token it is imperative to carry out the sentence as soon as possible." The execution took place the same day.[39] The government of the United States as Protecting Power did not learn officially or unofficially of any trials actually carried out against British prisoners of war, however. It may be assumed that none took place, since on 2 October 1941 the American Embassy in Berlin reported that the press campaign against British prisoners of war had subsided and that war crimes trials were unlikely.[40]

During 1942–43 (when Germany had declared war on the United States and the Swiss government had assumed the role of Protecting Power for both Great Britain and the United States), the German government gave no indication that it planned war crimes trials against British or American prisoners of war. This situation changed following 16 December 1943, when the Soviet Union inaugurated the first war crimes trial against members of the German armed forces at Kharkov: three German prisoners of war who had been captured at Stalingrad were accused of having murdered Soviet citizens in specially constructed gas vans. Captain Wilhelm Langheld, Corporal Reinhard Retzlaw, and Lieutenant Hans Ritz were convicted of atrocities upon the Soviet people and hanged on 19 December 1943. Numerous British and American journalists attended the proceedings and the execution.[41]

It is interesting to note that Hitler reacted the same day. During a military conference at the "Wolf's Lair" in East Prussia, he "expressed his intention to respond to the sham trial at Kharkov by instituting similar proceedings against British or American officers who have committed violations against international law, and ordered the compilation of relevant materials."[42]

The Navy High Command, following Hitler's directive, asked *Ausland-Abwehr* and the War Crimes Bureau to furnish the necessary documents, and the Bureau promptly forwarded two memoranda—"Violations of the Laws of War by the British Army"[43] and "Violations of International Law by the British Armed Forces and by Civilians on Crete"[44]—and documents relating to low-level air attacks on German civilians. The German Foreign Office issued the official pronouncement at a press conference on 22 December 1943: "The German military courts will shortly deal with American and British prisoners of war against whom serious war crimes are charged and who have not yet been tried"; German newspapers and radio elaborated further, announcing that British and American pilots who had bombarded nonmilitary objectives and who had machine-gunned civilians in low-level flights would be put in the dock.[45]

Reacting to German reports, the Swiss *Neue Zürcher Zeitung* commented on 24 December 1943: "The German threat of taking a reprisal for the trial at Kharkov by punishing British and American fliers who are prisoners of war in Germany has given rise to much concern in American official circles, although some observers believe that the primary purpose of the German announcement was to split the Allied camp." The British Foreign Office took the matter with equanimity, manifesting a "wait and see" attitude. On 11 January 1944 it telegraphed the British Embassy in Washington: "We have been considering whether any public statement could usefully be issued, but have reached the conclusion that, short of expressly abandoning our right to try German war criminals, there is nothing we could say that would not involve the danger of driving the Germans, who appear to be still hesitating, into a position from which they might find it difficult to withdraw. In reaching this conclusion, we have been influenced by the fact that under the Geneva Convention we cannot object to trials in Germany provided they are properly conducted."[46]

Two and a half months later the press secretary of the German Foreign Office repeated that preparations for the trials were in progress.[47] Yet no such trials were ever held. Apparently the evidence collected by the Bureau did not suffice to establish the guilt of individual prisoners of war. There were enough witnesses who could testify to the shooting of shipwrecked German sailors or the machine-gunning of farmers in the field by low-flying Allied planes, but the crimes were anonymous. None of the members of the Royal Navy and Air Force or the American pilots in German prisoner-of-war camps could be identified as having been personally involved. Other considerations may also explain the failure of German courts to prosecute American and British prisoners of war. Joachim Rudolphi, head of the legal department of the German Navy, surmises that Admiral Karl Dönitz did not like the idea of prosecuting members of the Allied navies and put a damper on Hitler's proposed retaliation; moreover, Hitler's own interest appears to have subsided: "Although I was never called in to confer with Hitler, I know from others that in the first burst of anger he often had the idea of taking immediate reprisals. But frequently nothing happened at all, because he never came back to it again."[48]

In the course of the war a number of British and American prisoners were in fact put on trial, and death sentences were carried out in a handful of cases. But these trials involved not war crimes but rather offenses committed in prisoner-of-war camps such as insurrection or attacks on camp personnel. During the last months of the war a number of British and American pilots who had been shot down over Germany were lynched by civilian mobs; most, however, were taken prisoner by local police and treated as prisoners of war.[49]

Trials of Russian Prisoners of War

The first part of the Barbarossa Jurisdiction Order issued by Field Marshal Keitel on 13 May 1941—the "Decree on Exercising Military Jurisdiction in the Area of Barbarossa and Special Measures by the Troops"—provided that the military courts and the courts-martial were not competent for crimes committed by enemy civilians.[50] *Franc-tireurs* were to be liquidated ruthlessly by the troops in combat or while fleeing, though commanders-in-chief of the army groups could, by agreement with the competent commanders of the air force and the navy, reinstate jurisdiction of the Wehrmacht courts for civilians in areas sufficiently pacified. Pursuant to this order, countless Russian civilians and persons only suspected of *franc-tireur* activities were summarily shot by the troops or passed on to the SD for execution.[51]

Yet it appears that military courts did function in a number of cases and actually afforded the accused a fair trial; many were acquitted. Where the military courts functioned, a modicum of due process was observed, and the War Crimes Bureau received reports of the judicial investigations. For instance, on 23 September 1942 the witness Martin Niesse testified: "In the course of the search for the two missing soldiers we discovered that they had been murdered by Russians. We identified two Russian civilians as the perpetrators . . . they were tried by a German court-martial and were executed by five men in our battalion. Before the two Russians were executed, our battalion commander had them point out the graves of the murdered Germans. The bodies were exhumed and we could see that they had been mutilated: the eyes had been put out, the tongues had been cut off, and one of them was missing a finger. . . . I myself saw the mutilations."[52]

As in the other theaters of war, war crimes committed by regular troops were within the jurisdiction of the German military courts. Trials took place as a matter of course without press coverage or the propagandistic trimmings of the Kharkov trial. A German court-martial met, for instance, on 4 December 1943 in Saborownja and tried four Russian soldiers on charges of having killed a German prisoner of war and of mutilating the body. They were sentenced and executed on 6 December 1943.[53] In another case the German court in Orscha passed the death sentence on a Russian Army surgeon, Nikolai Amirow, who had shot his German patient after receiving an order from his commissar Tumanewitsch, as testified by two Russian witnesses, prisoners of war Klutschanski and Sagalajew.[54]

But relatively few trials could be held in the field shortly after the crime. Though many killings of German prisoners by their Russian captors were discovered, the witnesses could very seldom give the names of the perpetrators, most of whom in any case were not in German captivity.[55] Sometimes, however, the Bureau did succeed in locating the suspects with the assistance of the Wehrmacht's personnel department. Usually a fairly long time elapsed between the beginning of the investigation and conviction of the culprit. For instance, two Russian prisoners of war, Lieutenants Pawel Jegorenko and Andrej Meljnikow, testified on 5 December 1941 at the officers' POW camp in Pogegen that they had seen Captain Iwan Ogorodnikow shoot seven defenseless German prisoners of war on the Island Oesel. Not until 12 September 1942 could the Bureau discover that Captain Ogorodnikow was in POW Camp 350 in Riga. On 17 September the Bureau recommended a court-martial. Before it was called, the witnesses Jegorenko and Meljnikow again gave sworn testimony, on 1 October 1942 and 10 February 1943, respectively. At a trial held before the court of Division 401 at Insterburg, East Prussia, Ogorodnikow was convicted of murder on 23 March 1943; the death sentence was confirmed on 10 June and carried out on 5 July 1943.[56]

In the majority of cases, however, the investigations were discontinued or the accused acquitted for lack of evidence. On 27 December 1941 the Luftwaffe court in Münster discontinued the investigation against the Russian prisoner of war Jakow Ratin; not only did he deny having murdered a Lieutenant Peters, but "Sergeant Kownatzki . . . who belonged to the same unit as Lieutenant Peters and who had been seriously wounded with him . . . has declared that he could positively identify the murderer but that the accused is totally unknown to him."[57] And on 10 May 1943 the court of Division 173 in Würzburg dismissed criminal proceedings against Colonel Alexander Tawanzew. In a deposition of 23 June 1942, "Russian prisoner of war Vitale Tschegaew inculpated Russian prisoner of war Colonel Tawanzew of shooting a German prisoner of war after interrogation near Djakowo in November 1941." Colonel Tawanzew, however, "vigorously contested" the charge, and no confrontation was possible because the whereabouts of the accuser were unknown: "Under these circumstances the charge of having murdered a German prisoner of war cannot be proved."[58]

Lists of War Criminals

The compilation of names of purported war criminals plays an important role in preparing for war crimes trials. During World War I the Prussian Bureau of Investigation prepared two lists of alleged British and French war criminals. During World War II the War Crimes Bureau similarly tried to discover the names of Allied war criminals and succeeded to a certain extent by taking extensive depositions of Allied prisoners of war. While American and British prisoners seldom cooperated, Polish and Russian prisoners did provide the names of many comrades who were later found to be in German prisoner-of-war camps.

Lists of Allied war crimes and criminals were expected to prove valuable not only for judicial purposes but also in the propaganda war. As late as 21 January 1945 Field Marshal Keitel decreed:

All enemy war crimes against members of the armed forces of Germany and of countries allied with Germany shall be collected retroactively since the outbreak of the war and continuing through the future, as well as war crimes against members of the armed forces of Germany and of countries allied with Germany who are in enemy captivity and against German and other civilians. This list should include the names of enemy commanders who according to captured documents or witness testimony have given orders to their subordinates to commit war crimes. . . .

The armed forces shall make sure that all units down to companies and batteries are immediately informed about the importance of compiling enemy war crimes and that they be instructed to do so every eight weeks, and henceforth in the course of interrogating enemy prisoners of war that the names of perpetrators and their superior officers be discovered.[59]

The collected data were to be forwarded immediately to the department of propaganda. It is almost certain that the Bureau, too, prepared a list for the propaganda unit, but none has been found in the existing files.[60]

Among the more notorious crimes of the German armed forces in World War II was the taking of hostages from among the civilian population of occupied countries. Throughout Europe innocent civilians were executed in reprisal for the actions of local partisans or as a means of striking terror in the population; Lidice,[1] Oradour-sur-Glane,[2] Putten,[3] Skela,[4] Borisovka,[5] Shitomir[6] are only a few of the names we remember from the International Military Tribunal at Nuremberg. It is true that reprisals were also taken by other belligerents,[7] but the German practice of executing ten or more civilians for each German soldier killed was a clear offense against the principle of proportionality and accordingly constituted a grave violation of international law.[8]

Although the War Crimes Bureau received detailed reports of partisan attacks and especially of mutilations committed by Soviet partisans on German soldiers, it was not sent reports of the German reprisals that often followed. Only occasionally, when a specific reprisal plan was submitted to the Army High Command for approval, was the information supplied to the Bureau for its records.

Reprisals in Russia

In August 1941 a partisan group ambushed a German bus properly marked with a red cross and carrying nineteen German wounded. Driver, staff, and all wounded were killed, a number of them even mutilated. The High Command of the German 17th Army considered possible reprisals, including the execution of two Russian generals and all officers captured after the battle of Podwisskoje, and proposed informing the Russians of the reprisals taken by dropping leaflets over their lines. On 12 August 1941 General K. H. von

Stülpnagel rejected the plan: "The opposite of the desired result would take place. (1) According to the concurring testimony of prisoners of war in all ranks, Soviet resistance is partly the result of [the soldiers'] fear of being shot after capture. Announcing such a reprisal would thus confirm Russian atrocity propaganda to Russian soldiers and provide proof of those allegations. The consequence would be a hardening of their stance. (2) Moreover, the efforts of German propaganda aimed at breaking their morale and at encouraging desertion by entire troop contingents under their officers would be thwarted."[9] Hence, the projected reprisal was never carried out.

Several months later a similar case gave rise to renewed discussion. The intelligence section of the High Command of the 17th Army reported to Army Group South on 16 January 1942: "We may not expect results from reprisals. Since the beginning of the war the Russians have been telling their soldiers that we kill Russian prisoners of war. Moreover, our taking reprisals would probably have no effect . . . on Russian political leaders. Reprisals have a purpose only when they are openly announced. They would then provide proof of the defamatory allegations of Russian political leaders and harden the Russian will to fight. Essentially, we would ruin through such reprisals very important propaganda possibilities and badly blunder by not taking advantage of the disintegration of the Russian Army."[10]

In spite of these sober tactical considerations, very often reprisals were taken by the troops without checking back with higher authorities. Any discovery of mutilated corpses particularly increased the danger of indiscriminate revenge on enemy prisoners of war, though whether reprisals were indeed taken largely depended on the German officers involved: some permitted their troops to take revenge; others protected defenseless prisoners from being massacred. When 596 German prisoners, wounded men and female radio personnel were killed and many of them mutilated in Grischino in February 1943, remembers one of the German judges who interrogated witnesses and survivors, "you have no idea how much trouble the commanders and company chiefs had . . . to restrain the German soldiers from killing every Russian prisoner of war of the Popov Army. The troop was very bitter and angry. You cannot imagine the vehemence of the soldiers after they had seen what had happened."[11]

The escalation of bitterness sometimes took other forms of expression. For example, there was growing hostility toward the enemy among medical orderlies and doctors who were sickened by the repeated occurrence of deliberate mutilations inflicted on wounded German soldiers. One of several such documents in the records of the War Crimes Bureau is the report of a battalion doctor to his division doctor asking for instructions: "Please advise me how I should conduct myself in the future toward wounded Russians. After witnessing the criminal way in which the enemy has treated our wounded, I find it difficult to behave as I had hitherto considered to be my duty."[12]

Reprisals in Maritime Warfare

The High Command of the German Army, Navy, or Air Force, debating the pros and cons of reprisals against the enemy, frequently turned to the War Crimes Bureau for documentation. The decisive criterion, of course, remained the expedience of the reprisal in the particular case.

In view of numerous reports of attacks by the British Royal Navy and Royal Air Force against defenseless German shipwrecked sailors, the German Navy seriously debated taking reprisals in September 1942 and asked the Bureau to compile a list of the twelve most significant cases: three instances in Narvik on 10 and 13 April 1940 and nine during the Cretan campaign in May 1941.[13] But because these cases were too old to justify a reprisal in late 1942, another instance was sought which could be used as a more immediate justification. As it happened, the German minelayer *Ulm* had been sunk by a British destroyer on 5 September 1942, and some of the survivors claimed to have been shot at in the water.

When the *Ulm* incident came to the attention of Hitler, he wanted to take reprisals immediately, but the naval war staff objected because the general practice on the part of the Royal Navy had been to rescue German shipwrecked crews; reported cases of shooting at men in the water represented exceptions. Moreover, further investigation of the *Ulm* incident failed to establish a deliberate attack:

"The casualties, in particular the two reported woundings, occurred while the crew members were abandoning the ship that was still afloat. The enemy bombardment evidently was directed at the ship itself and not at the crew. Since the *Ulm* gave no indication of surrender, the enemy was entitled to continue the bombardment . . . in similar cases we ourselves would act in the same fashion. . . . it must be considered whether [reprisals] would not result in greater disadvantage for us if the enemy should adopt similar measures. . . . In this respect it is important to note that thus far it has not been proved that the known cases of enemy attacks on German shipwrecked have been motivated or covered by order of a British authority. Thus we must reckon that the promulgation of a German order would be used by enemy propaganda in a way whose consequences are still very difficult to calculate."[14]

When the Italian hospital ship *Arno* was sunk by British planes on 10 September 1942,[15] the German naval war staff and the Italian command discussed the possibility of a coordinated policy of reprisal in the Mediterranean but, all pros and cons considered, finally decided against any retaliation: "It does not seem to us expedient to take reprisals against British hospital ships, since the enemy use of hospital ships in the Mediterranean is of minor importance, while for Italy and Germany it is imperative to transport our own wounded and sick from North Africa for reasons of both morale and supply." Moreover, "it has not yet been determined whether on the part of the British a deliberate attack on the hospital ship took place or whether the attack occurred by mistake, as was the case with the attack on the British hospital ship *Somersetshire* by a German submarine. If as a result of reprisals hospital ships on both sides lose their immunity, this is likely to be more damaging for us than for the enemy."[16]

The Shackling of Prisoners
Perhaps the most notorious example of an official German reprisal concerned the shackling of prisoners of war following the British commando landing in Dieppe, France, in August 1942. As witness depositions show, numerous Germans who had been surprised by the British and who could not be immediately treated as prisoners of war were tied up for the duration of the commando action. In retaliation, Hitler ordered that all British prisoners of war in Germany should be similarly tied up. As counterreprisal the British government ordered German prisoners of war to be shackled.[17] Only through the constant efforts of the International Committee of the Red Cross was this vicious circle of reprisals and counterreprisals broken.[18]

The decree of 4 September 1939 gave the War Crimes Bureau authority to investigate not only enemy violations of international law but also "such accusations as are raised by foreign countries against the Wehrmacht." The surviving 226 volumes of Bureau records, however, include only a single volume on German war crimes. It is not known whether relevant records were lost or deliberately destroyed, or whether the Bureau—for whatever reason—failed to investigate other German war crimes. More important, the available records give no indication whether the members of the Bureau received any official or unofficial communications regarding the mass murders of Jews at German concentration camps or about the criminal activities of the ss in Russia.

It is true that the Bureau was granted no authority to investigate the activities of the ss, and even with respect to alleged crimes committed by the Wehrmacht its competence extended only to those that were made the subject of official protests from foreign powers. For knowledge of these the Bureau depended on communications from the German Foreign Office, which alone was authorized to respond to foreign protests submitted through the Protecting Power. Yet it should also be noted that the German Foreign Office and the Wehrmacht operations staff frequently dealt with foreign accusations directly, without ever referring the cases to the Bureau for more thorough inquiry or even for its information and files. Alfons Waltzog remembers seeing a number of relevant documents that had been submitted to the High Command of the Wehrmacht and on which Field Marshal Keitel had written in his customary lilac-colored ink: "Do not involve WR": that is, keep the legal department and the War Crimes Bureau out of the matter.[1] In fact, however, it may well be that no official diplomatic protests were ever lodged with the Protecting Powers Switzerland and Sweden on behalf of the Jewish population of occupied Europe.[2]

Still, the postwar historian cannot help asking whether the members of the Bureau knew what was happening in the Nazi concentration camps. It is hard to imagine that those whose daily work entailed investigation of crimes and atrocities did not at least hear rumors about the most unspeakable atrocity of the century, but there are no documents, personal notes, or diaries indicating any such knowledge, official or otherwise.[3] Had they known, the question immediately arises, what would they—or what could they—have done to expose it?

Order No. 1
Other Germans at the Nuremberg trials tried to excuse themselves by claiming ignorance and explaining this ignorance on the grounds of Hitler's fundamental "Order No. 1" with respect to the keeping of official secrets—including, of course, the *Sonderbehandlung* (special treatment) of the Jews and the *Endlösung* (Final Solution) of the Jewish question, which was classified *geheime Reichssache* (literally, Reich secret matter, the highest level of state secret). The so-called *Führerbefehl Nummer 1*, dated 11 January 1940, specified that (1) no one shall know about secret matters that do not belong to his own range of assignments; (2) no one shall learn more than he needs to fulfill the tasks assigned to him; (3) no one shall receive information earlier than is necessary for the performance of the duties assigned to him; (4) no one shall transmit to subordinate officers, to any greater extent or any earlier than is unavoidable for the achievement of the purpose, orders that are to be kept secret.[4]

One of the most amazing single documents in support of the thesis that knowledge of the exterminations was limited to a relatively small percentage of Germans is Heinrich Himmler's Posen speech of 4 October 1943 to top ss leaders: "Most of you know what it means when 100 corpses lie there, or when 500 corpses lie there, or when 1,000 corpses lie there. To have gone through this and—apart from a few exceptions caused by human weakness—to have remained decent, that has made us hard. This is a page of glory in our history *which has never been written and which is never to be written*."[5]

There were, of course, visible signs of abuses against Jews, but deportation to the east was not perceived even by the victims as a step toward extermination. Even persons high in the Nazi hierarchy appear to have been kept ignorant of the truth. In the spring of 1943 Henriette von Schirach, the wife of Baldur von Schirach,[6] witnessed the deportation of Jews from Amsterdam and went to Hitler to protest. Hitler was at first silent and then told her it was none of her business.[7] Also in the spring of 1943 Himmler was questioned by Hans Lammers, the chief of the German chancellery, about rumors of exterminations in the East. Himmler replied that only deportations were taking place, by order of the Führer.[8]

The Nuremberg proceedings and serious postwar testimonies provide further indication that senior officials in the German government may have remained unaware of the worst abuses. Nazi press secretary Hans Fritzsche, one of the three principal accused to be acquitted at Nuremberg, denied on the stand having had any knowledge of the exterminations. Of course, he had heard Allied radio broadcasts that were not accessible to the German population, but when he inquired about these reports at the competent offices, he was assured that it was all enemy atrocity propaganda. During his interrogation on 27 June 1946 he stated that in February or March 1942 a middle-ranking ss leader of the Ukraine had written to him to report the killings of Jews by an ss unit. Fritzsche called on Gestapo Chief Reinhard Heydrich, who explained that "special details of ss men had been misused on various occasions. . . . He told me that he would have an investigation started immediately." Shortly thereafter, Fritzsche was called to military service and sent to the 6th Army in the Ukraine. There he attempted to conduct some investigations himself, but he was always told that "Yes, there were some court-martial sentences. The reason for these sentences was sabotage."[9] On 28 June 1946 Fritzsche stated:

The German people were unaware of the mass murders of the Jews and assertions of them were considered rumors; reports that reached the German people from outside were officially denied again and again. . . . The Russians, after they recaptured Kharkov, started legal proceedings during which killing by gas was mentioned for the first time. I ran to Dr. Goebbels with this report and asked him about the facts. He stated that he would have the matter investigated and would discuss it with Himmler and with Hitler. The next day he sent me a notice of denial. . . . Dr. Goebbels explicitly informed me that the gas vans mentioned in the Russian legal proceedings were pure invention and that there was no actual proof to support it. It was not without reason that the people who operated these vans were put under the ban of strictest secrecy. If the German people had learned of these mass murders, they would certainly no longer have supported Hitler.[10]

ss Judge Georg Morgen testified at Nuremberg that three persons were charged with the extermination of the Jews: the former commissioner of the Criminal Police in Stuttgart, Christian Wirth; the chief of the Jewish section of the Gestapo, Adolf Eichmann; and the Auschwitz commandant, Rudolf Hoess. The detachment organized by Wirth himself for the purpose of exterminating Jews was known as *Aktion Reinhard* and was purposely kept small; Himmler personally took the oath from its members and declared explicitly that anyone who said anything about the action would be put to death. Selected Jewish prisoners with connections abroad were made to write letters telling how well they were treated at Auschwitz, so as to convey the impression that these well-known people were alive and well.[11] It appears that even much of the Gestapo did not know what was going on; for instance, the Security Police of Lublin reported Wirth's killings to the Reich Criminal Police office, apparently unaware that the orders came from the very top.[12]

When it became apparent that Germany would lose the war, Himmler ordered the exterminations halted in October 1944; the camps were to be destroyed before they could be liberated by the Allied forces. It is reported that in April of 1945 Hitler ordered the evacuation of the remaining concentration camps so that the atrocities would not be discovered, and that he was "raging for days" because Buchenwald and Bergen-Belsen fell nearly intact into the hands of the horrified Allies.[13]

Yet, having recognized all this, the historian still finds it unsatisfactory to explain the general inaction of the German population—and, more particularly, the apparent inaction of members of the War Crimes Bureau—by the *diabolus ex machina* of Order No. 1. It cannot be disputed that this order made it very difficult and risky to disseminate any information about the official murder of Jews, gypsies, and other victims; moreover, it is probable that the original competence of the Bureau was curtailed by other government agencies. But given the magnitude of the crimes, it is not acceptable to claim that investigation of them would have fallen outside the scope of the Bureau's authority. Thus the moral question remains unanswered. Only the discovery of additional files could shed light on the uncertainties about this aspect of the Bureau's work.

German War Crimes in North Africa

The one volume of the Bureau's records dealing with the investigation of Wehrmacht war crimes concerns the North African campaign. On 15 September 1943 the Swiss legation in Berlin transmitted to the German Foreign Office an official protest of the British government, alleging that on the night of 20–21 April 1943 three British prisoners of war had been killed by German soldiers near the Djebel-Djaffa Pass, and that on 30 April 1943 a German soldier had faked his willingness to surrender near Medjezlelbab.[14]

The British note was forwarded by the German Foreign Office to the *Ausland-Abwehr,* which in turn wrote on 1 October 1943 asking the War Crimes Bureau "to investigate the allegations and to propose an answer. . . . Since the investigation of the facts is expected to take some time, we consider it appropriate to submit a provisional reply." Accordingly, on 8 October the Bureau approved the following interim response: "The allegations made in the note of 15 September 1943 are being examined. The investigations will take considerable time, and therefore a final response must remain open. The High Command of the Wehrmacht is, however, in a position to state that German soldiers in the field have been unequivocally ordered to observe the rules of land warfare and in particular Article 23 of the Hague Regulations, and that there is no doubt that German soldiers have acted accordingly."[15] On the same day the Bureau wrote to the operations staff requesting that the commander-in-chief for the North African region investigate the allegations. The request was denied on the grounds that "the events described in the note . . . cannot be verified because of the changed conditions."[16]

The British allegations were not investigated at all, but the German Foreign Office did not want to remain silent. The Bureau was therefore asked to draft an answer rejecting the allegations as "highly improbable" and accusing the British in turn of war crimes in North Africa as well as those in Dieppe, Sark, and Crete that were documented in the Bureau's files. A senior officer of the legal department of the Wehrmacht, Werner Hülle, suggested listing only such British violations as had occurred in North Africa and none from other theaters of war. Goldsche rejected this suggestion on 13 January 1944; however, he considered the violations in Crete to be materially relevant, especially because the "illegal ruses of war" employed by the British there were similar to those that the British were accusing the Germans of practicing in North Africa.[17]

On 9 February 1944, therefore, Goldsche submitted to the German Foreign Office the draft of a note replying to the British protest. It described nine instances of apparent British violations and also focused on British commando practices. Because of delays occasioned by the air bombardment of Berlin, the German Foreign Office did not evaluate Goldsche's draft until 10 August 1944. Conrad Roediger, the expert for international law, endorsed Hülle's objections and disagreed with the Bureau's recommendation: "We consider it more appropriate to keep our response with respect to violations of international law by British soldiers as short and precise as possible and to limit it to cases that occurred in North Africa and the eastern Mediterranean theater."[18] Thereupon, Erich Albrecht, deputy chief of the legal department of the German Foreign Office, had a new draft prepared.

But considering that nearly a year had elapsed since the first British protest and that the Swiss legation in Berlin had communicated British reminders on 28 October 1943 and 16 March 1944,[19] it is not surprising that London found the German note of 5 September 1944 (transmitted by the Swiss Federal Political Department on 3 October 1944) both inadequate and arrogant. D.L.S. of the British Foreign Office commented: "This is curious. It is clear that the Germans have not made any investigations and I cannot imagine why after waiting a year they should now have decided to send this very weak reply. I do not see much point in answering it." British legal adviser Patrick Dean added: "I doubt really whether at this stage of the war it is necessary on legal grounds to dispute the allegations made on page 2 of the German note, particularly as they have first been made in a reply to us by the German Government."[20]

Repatriated Medical Personnel

Sometimes the War Crimes Bureau was asked by other government agencies to render a legal opinion on a given question of international law. On 29 March 1944 the High Command of the German Navy requested an opinion on British accusations against alleged German violations of the 1929 Geneva Prisoner of War Convention. The question at issue was the employment by Germany of repatriated German medical personnel. On 27 April 1944 Hermann Huvendick answered on behalf of the Bureau:

> If the British Foreign Minister [Anthony Eden] asserts that reemployment of repatriated medical personnel against Russia constitutes a seri-

ous violation of both Conventions of 1929,[21] he is no doubt in error in this generality. Indeed, according to the relevant regulations . . . exchanged medical personnel may be reemployed as such, that is, as noncombatants. But a broader interpretation of these regulations allowing a change of status of medical personnel . . . in order to employ them as combatants is not permissible in the opinion of the War Crimes Bureau. It is true that the Convention for the Amelioration of the Conditions of the Wounded and Sick does not contain any provision prohibiting the employment of repatriated medical personnel as combatants. But in the opinion of the Bureau the Convention undoubtedly rests on the premise that noncombatants remain noncombatants and that therefore repatriated medical personnel can be employed only in medical service. . . . It is feared that should Germany employ repatriated medical personnel as combatants, the British government would cease their repatriation.[22]

The jurists at the Navy High Command, however, were less restrictive in their interpretation and persevered in trying to find a way of construing the Convention that would allow the redeployment of auxiliary or part-time stretcher-bearers. On 5 May 1944 they submitted an argument that seems hair-splitting but gains in persuasiveness upon rereading:

Foreign Minister Eden dealt in his declaration only with the reemployment of auxiliary stretcher-bearers. With respect to this category of medical personnel, Article 9 of the Geneva Convention of 1929 provides that they "shall enjoy the same treatment as the permanent medical personnel if they are taken prisoner while carrying out their functions." In our opinion the "if" clause implies that both belligerents have freedom of choice as to how they should employ such military personnel; thus they can turn them into combatants at any time by removing their insignia. . . . Pursuant to the equally clear text of Article 12, auxiliary stretcher-bearers captured while carrying out their functions may not be retained by the enemy. If we should follow the view of the Bureau, then the belligerents would lose their freedom in the use of those auxiliary stretcher-bearers who without justification are captured by the enemy and provisionally retained and who according to Article 12 should be returned without conditions and as soon as the war situation allows. This change in favor of one belligerent and to the detriment of the other cannot in our opinion be deduced from the general meaning of the Convention in the absence of a specific provision such as in Article 18, Paragraph 6 of the Convention.[23]

It would have been interesting to learn what the Bureau had to say about this line of reasoning. Unfortunately, because he was overburdened with other tasks and because other governmental agencies were capable and competent to issue such legal opinions, Huvendick declined to go into the matter again: "The War Crimes Bureau asks that future matters dealing with purely legal questions be submitted directly to the head of the legal department of the Wehrmacht and not to the Bureau."[24]

Apparently, the question was then submitted to the legal department of the Wehrmacht, which resulted in a general order from the High Command restricting the employment of repatriated auxiliary stretcher-bearers to medical service. In a note dated 31 December 1944 the German Foreign Office so informed the Swiss Federal Political Department: "The German Government accordingly gives assurance that no member of the German medical service now to be repatriated . . . will be employed in military capacity other than that which his protection under the Geneva Convention justifies."[25]

Victims of German War Crimes during the Allied Invasion

Following the Allied landing in Normandy on 4 June 1944,[26] when numerous British, Canadian, and American units reported that the Germans were taking no prisoners,[27] it did not take long for the governments of Great Britain and the United States to appeal to the Protecting Power. The Swiss legation in Berlin delivered to the German Foreign Office a British note dated 1 August 1944, describing some of the incidents: "Supreme Commander of Allied Expeditionary Force received reports . . . that after capture by German armed forces certain Canadian officers and men had been shot. . . . On or about June 8th one Canadian officer and 18 other ranks met their death in the vicinity of Pavie in the Department of Calvados, Normandy, at or near Chateau Audrieux. . . . His Majesty's Government are left in no doubt that they were wilfully murdered by members of the 12th ss Panzer Division (Hitler Jugend), 12th ss Reconnaissance Battalion by order of certain of their officers."[28]

The governments of Great Britain, South Africa, Australia, New Zealand, and India demanded that "an immediate searching investigation" be made and that those German officers and men who were "responsible for this flagrant violation of laws and customs of war respecting prisoners of war" be punished and that the German government "promulgate strict orders which will prevent the repetition in future of such an occurrence."[29] Another protest note dated 7 September 1944 described an incident involving the killing of seven Canadian soldiers at or near Mouen, Normandy on or about 17 June 1944.[30]

Long before the official diplomatic protests reached the Germans, the allegations had been extensively publicized by the press, particularly in Switzerland. For this reason the German Foreign Office asked the Wehrmacht operations staff in July 1944 to investigate. This time the War Crimes Bureau was informed but not directly involved in the investigation process. Instead, the operations staff went directly to the commander-in-chief for the Western Theater, Field Marshal Günther von Kluge, who answered on 17 July 1944: "Commander-in-Chief West does not know of any such incident as notified from Bern. Since any such incident would surely have been reported, Commander-in-Chief West considers this message to be one only intended to harass."[31]

Yet the case was not dropped; instead, the intelligence department was given the task of pursuing the investigation.[32] The official German answer to the protests of 1 August and 7 September 1944 was not forthcoming until 31 December. It challenged the conclusions of the British commission that investigated the killings because neither the content of the witness testimony nor the names of the witnesses were given; therefore, it rejected the British accusations as "defamation of the Wehrmacht," asserting that the High Command of the Wehrmacht had carried out "thorough investigations" and failed to discover wrongdoing on the German side. But the note went on to admit that "the investigations of the alleged killings near Chateau Audrieux could not be completed because the majority of the members of the 12th ss Panzer Division had been either killed or captured in the first days of the invasion. With respect to the alleged killings near Mouen, the investigations were similarly negative, since those units of the 12th ss Reconnaissance Battalion had been wiped out in the fighting on 26 July 1944."[33]

This German note was transmitted by the Swiss legation on 11 January 1945. In the meantime, however, still another British protest—dated 6 December 1944—had reached the German Foreign Office. It contained a catalogue of further killings of prisoners of war involving members of the

11th ss Division, one Gestapo official, and a patrol of the 752nd Infantry Regiment.[34]

This new British note was followed by another German investigation. In February 1945 the new Commander-in-Chief West, Field Marshal Gerd von Rundstedt, reported that all ss units that had been in the area at the time had been questioned without any results; further questioning was still being carried out among survivors of the 752nd Infantry Regiment. As to the accusation that a second lieutenant of the 272nd Battalion and an officer of the 997th Infantry Regiment had ordered their men to shoot all Allied soldiers taken prisoner, von Rundstedt reported: "The vagueness of the accusations renders investigations very difficult. Although the numbers of the regiments are given, we have no clue by which to identify the officers responsible among the company leaders and to establish whether the alleged order to kill prisoners of war was in fact given."[35] On 28 February 1945 the German Foreign Office again consulted the Wehrmacht operations staff, but the results are unknown. In view of the impending collapse of the Reich, it is doubtful that the inquiry was actually pursued any further.

Malmédy

On 30 December 1944 the State Department in Washington requested the Swiss legation to transmit the following protest to the German government: "A group of 15 survivors have reported that on 17th December in the fighting south of Malmédy [in Belgium] about 190 members of an American field artillery observation battalion were taken prisoner by German forces. The prisoners were stripped of their valuables and equipment, herded into a field, and submitted to machine-gun fire from tanks at a range of approximately 100 feet."[36]

The note demanded that the German government investigate the killings and punish the guilty. This incident, too, had already been widely publicized in the Swiss press and promptly denied by the German government. Yet while the German Foreign Office issued an official démenti, it also ordered an immediate investigation. On 1 January 1945 the Ic officer at von Rundstedt's headquarters reported: "Thus far the investigations have been negative. Therefore we believe that the accusations constitute nothing but foul enemy agitation."[37]

Interestingly enough, the inquiry was pursued even after this negative report, although the war was quickly drawing to a close. After the 1st and

2d ss Corps and a special unit called Solar[38] reported in the negative, a large number of American prisoners were questioned about Malmédy by a special detail for prisoner-of-war interrogations. Apparently, nothing came of these investigations, yet on 29 January 1945 the operations staff wrote to *Ausland-Abwehr* that the Malmédy investigations should by all means be continued: "Commander-in-Chief West should be advised of the new order . . . of 26 January 1945, in which the Führer expressly commands the observance of the principles of the Geneva Red Cross Convention."[39]

Although the imminent German collapse was clear to all, the German Foreign Office pursued its work routinely and submitted its official answer to the Swiss legation on 8 March 1945: "The German military authorities ordered that an immediate inquiry be made as soon as they heard in enemy radio reports about the alleged shooting of 150 American prisoners of war in the Malmédy area; the inquiry has established that the report is not true. Pursuant to the memorandum of the Swiss legation, new investigations were carried out by the German troops that had been engaged in the Malmédy areas during the period in question. These investigations have similarly established that American prisoners of war have not been shot. The report that 15 so-called survivors allegedly made to the State Department is therefore false."[40]

Yet American investigations during and after the war established that 142 American soldiers had in fact been machine-gunned in a field near Malmédy. The German units involved were easily identified after the war, and a trial against seventy-three former ss soldiers began on 16 May 1946 at Dachau, the former Nazi concentration camp near Munich. The accused, presenting their version of the events, claimed that the American soldiers—caught by surprise by the German armored attack—did surrender and were in the process of being sent to the rear of the German lines, but that in the confusion of the second day of the Battle of the Bulge, a new wave of German tanks apparently mistook the Americans in uniform for regular combatants. Counsel for the defense also noted that according to the testimony of some American witnesses—that no shots fell until the American soldiers started to flee—the killings were so closely related to the fighting that the case for deliberate murder was rendered somewhat tenuous. Nevertheless, on 16 July 1946, forty-three of the accused received the death sentence; thirty were condemned to long prison terms.[41]

Five years after the Nuremberg and the Dachau trials the American

Military Government in Germany implemented a policy of reconciliation and amnesty in the course of which the commander-in-chief of the U.S. armed forces in Germany, General Thomas T. Handy, reduced the sentences of many of the Malmédy convicts and changed all death sentences to life imprisonment. Without expressing a doubt about their actual guilt, General Handy explained his decision of 31 January 1951 by conceding mitigating circumstances, since the killings had "occurred in connection with confused, volatile and desperate fighting."[42]

To the American reader of the late 1980s it may appear outlandish that in the early 1940s German lawyers were planning a new codification of international law that would better correspond to German interests. To the German experts in international law in 1940–41, however, it appeared entirely likely that Germany would win the war; accordingly, it was logical to prepare for the teutonic *Endsieg* and the Pax Germanica.

The lawyers in the legal department of the Wehrmacht were particularly involved in drafting new norms for the postwar period. This chapter outlines the Wehrmacht conception of a new international order under German leadership, as reflected in hitherto unpublished memoranda.

Uses of the Investigations of the Prussian Bureau

After World War I the vanquished Germans could hardly expect the victorious Allies to prosecute their own soldiers for such violations of the laws of war as those in the Baralong case;[1] the Treaty of Versailles demanded only the punishment of German war criminals. Hence, the files of the Prussian Bureau of Investigation were never used as evidence against British or French soldiers. But the files did not entirely lose their value; they were studied by a special Parliamentary Committee in 1919–27, and parts were published in the five-volume *Völkerrecht im Weltkrieg* (International Law during the World War), which caused much discussion in Germany, where memories were still relatively fresh.

More important, perhaps, the files of the Prussian bureau were used in the training of military judges. A number of particularly complex cases were adapted to teach young judges how to evaluate difficult situations on the basis of previous experience. Shortly before the outbreak of World War II, as the imminence of actual conflict grew apparent, the legal department of the Wehrmacht had a list of cases elaborated for submission to military judges and legal advisers of military commanders: "We have purposely chosen a number of cases the solution of which is not entirely without problems."[2] The teaching materials included alternative solutions to nine *franc-tireur* cases, five cases involving wounded and medical personnel, three on the determination of prisoner-of-war status and its cessation, two on espionage, one on the taking of hostages, and three on military necessity or emergency.

The materials were discussed at a conference on 26 June 1939 which was chaired by Rudolf Lehmann and attended by numerous army, navy, and air force judges as well as members of the foreign affairs bureau and the Wehrmacht propaganda department. Also examined were cases involving reprisals and the use of dumdum munitions. One of these concerned an order given by French General Vuillemot on 8 February 1918: "The division commander has been informed that a kind of tacit agreement between our front troops and the enemy appears to be practiced with respect to the transportation of the wounded after battle. The 69th Infantry Regiment reported on 5 February that a troop of seven Germans moved under the protection of the red cross flag from the woods of Le Pasy to Beau Mont. Nothing was reported about an attack upon this important objective. This practice must cease. The Division Commander orders expressly that every German, regardless where and when, even those engaged in transporting wounded, must be immediately taken under fire."[3] The participants at the conference agreed with Lehmann that the lower ranks should not be punished for obeying such an order, because "the violations cannot be seen as the individual acts of enemy soldiers but as acts of the enemy state. . . . Settlement of the injustice is conceivable only by way of reprisal."[4]

Within a few months after this conference Hitler unleashed World War II, and the War Crimes Bureau, as the Prussian bureau's successor, assumed the task of studying the application of international law to concrete situations in armed conflict.

The Gladisch Committee

What would the laws of war have looked like if Hitler had won? In the summer of 1940, when Germany expected to win, Field Marshal Wilhelm Keitel as head of the Wehrmacht ordered the establishment of a special committee to formulate the laws of war in a way more in keeping with the long-term interests of "Greater Germany." Keitel appointed this committee on 14 August 1940 under Admiral Walter Gladisch[5] and laid down its tasks as follows: "The moment of the restoration of the peace will give us an opportunity to attain the recognition through all states and thereby the binding force of those norms of the laws of war that have been particularly advantageous for us in this war. . . . This moment appears to be the most propitious for perfecting the laws of war, since Germany's might will then be greatest and thus will prevail in having such norms adopted as further its interests. Moreover, the war experiences of the immediate past can be best evaluated now."[6]

Although not directly involved in the committee's drafting assignment, the War Crimes Bureau as collecting center for matters of violations of the laws of war received a copy of the Gladisch Report of 3 December 1940. Its introduction presents a dry, positivistic view:

> Conventions in international law are the reflection of the political power constellation. . . . The interests of those states strongest on land and sea and in the air determined the structure of hitherto applicable principles for the waging of land, naval, and air warfare. In substantial fields they fail to correspond with German interests; especially in those where Germany could not throw enough weight on the scales at the time of codification. This is most obvious in the law of naval warfare, which represents primarily British interests.
>
> The current war gives reason to expect revolutionary changes in the strategic state of affairs and a shift of power in all fields of warfare. These changes must be reflected in the future laws of war. Germany will be able to demand at the end of the war a new law that takes into account its own and the continent's interests, and as speaker for a united Europe it shall prevail. A convention that sets up rules of warfare with binding force for all states, including for the first time binding rules for air warfare, is a political goal that promises to be of service to German military interests. Such a convention must take into account the newest experiences, especially in this war, and those provisions which through military and economic development have been rendered obsolete or . . . impractical must be eliminated.
>
> The demands to be made by Germany at the end of the war must in the meantime be delimited. The laws of war may not be so extreme as to make the waging of war by a state impossible. Nor may neutrality legis-

lation be so restrictive that a state would prefer to enter a war rather than preserve its neutrality. Every provision in international law which does not observe these limits will find no voluntary recognition among the majority of states and thus will not serve German interests . . . being applicable only in such places and at such times as Germany could enforce [it]; practically it would be no better than the absence of all law. Germany, even at its greatest deployment of power, is interested neither in a dictated international law nor in a state of anarchy in international law.

The next section deals with the political state of affairs expected to prevail at the conclusion of hostilities: "We assume a peace following victory by Germany. . . . The hypothetical situation can be characterized as follows: Germany stands at the head of a European bloc of states of which England is not a part. Germany has colonies in Africa and naval bases in the Atlantic and a sufficiently powerful war fleet as well as a commercial fleet. As possible enemies we must consider England and the United States, and secondarily Russia. Pursuant to this hypothesis, Germany could be confronted by a constellation of powers over which it is not so overwhelmingly superior as to be able to afford a complete absence of commitments with respect to the laws of war. Moreover, it is probable that there will be strong neutral states that would have to be taken into account in drafting the new law of war."[7]

The Gladisch committee went on to formulate a long list of topics to be evaluated by a larger commission. Among other points its members considered whether Article 2 of the Hague Regulations of 1907 with respect to the *levée en masse*[8] should not be changed. They proposed to forbid the use of colonial troops in Europe, to clearly define the criminal jurisdiction of the occupying power over the population of occupied territory, to declare the arming of commercial ships illegal, to place rescue aircraft under the protection of the Red Cross, and to define the military character of paratroops and infantry transported by air.

Other Memoranda

Rudolf Lehmann issued a memorandum on 2 September 1940 in which he discussed the legal lessons to be learned from the Wehrmacht's war experiences to that point:

> Investigations . . . have shown that French authorities have violated the provisions of the Geneva Conventions . . . in ways that make prosecution

difficult or impossible. In countless cases they failed to provide medical attention to the wounded or to take adequate measures to assure the feeding and decent quartering of prisoners of war. These acts of omission can be traced to a deliberate disregard of obligations that had been assumed. . . . it is clear that these French omissions cannot be punished under German law; similarly, it is doubtful whether they can be brought within the scope of French criminal provisions. Thus it should be considered whether it would be advisable to introduce special penal norms to enable punishing serious violations of international law in Germany and also by the French government.

He concluded, however, that for the time being no such special legislation should be drafted for fear that England would do likewise: "Since we do not expect objective application of such penal provisions on the part of the enemy, this may . . . endanger our submarine and air crews. Thus it would not be advisable to create a new penal sanction for violations of international law."[9]

The extant Bureau files reveal no subsequent memoranda on the further development of international law. On 28 April 1942, however, *Ausland-Abwehr* made its proposal for the systematic study of war diaries, stressing the compilation of material relevant to international law:

After the future conclusion of the peace, when relations between nations become more normal, international law will also experience new impulses. It is to be expected that Germany will play a leading role. Would it not be appropriate to start compiling wartime events in which international law is affected in some way and to evaluate this material with a view toward formulating a future international legal order? . . . we should consider, for instance, the war methods employed by the Russians that were and are very far from an open and honorable way of fighting. Surely all three sections of the Wehrmacht have already begun collecting the most important events as material for a future international law. It is doubtful whether the war diaries are also being consulted. It would appear worthwhile to consider doing so.[10]

The War Crimes Bureau took up this recommendation and wrote the army, navy, and air force legal departments to send in all reports that could be considered valuable additions to the other materials already at the center; the events described in war diaries "could be of great value at the end of the war ... in formulating new principles of international law."[11]

Germany's reversals from 1942 on, however, rendered this projected use of both war diaries and the Bureau's investigations irrelevant if not illusory. Still, the existence of such memoranda reveals much about the mentality of those lawyers in the legal department of the Wehrmacht who were responsible for the evaluation of reported cases of Allied war crimes. The chapters in Part II of this book illustrate how they investigated and analyzed specific cases or complexes.

PART II / SPECIFIC CASES

The War Crimes Bureau was set up on 4 September 1939 in response to the proliferation of reports of grave violations of the laws of war allegedly committed by members of the Polish armed forces. The Bureau's first assignment—and the first specific cases described here—consisted in verifying these allegations of abuses against both German soldiers and German civilian minorities throughout Poland—primarily in former German provinces (Posen and West Prussia) ceded to Poland in the Treaty of Versailles. Readers should bear in mind throughout the following chapters that these investigations reflect the German viewpoint and that the Allied position must still be considered in the light of whatever new evidence may become available.

Early Investigations

Since the German Army judges had to continue advancing with their respective divisions, the Bureau did not at first turn to them for assistance but instead sent several resident members on special assignment to various regions in Poland. Navy Judge Ulrich Schattenberg left Berlin on 7 September 1939, together with Inspector Dirks, and from 9 to 13 September they took numerous depositions at Bromberg and the nearby village of Hohensalza. Upon returning to Berlin, Schattenberg turned over the depositions and other collected evidence in a file entitled "Bromberg I," which also included numerous protocols, photographs, and press reports.[1] He summed up as follows:

> I took sworn depositions of over forty ethnic Germans. . . . Each witness gave testimony about the murder of at least two or three relatives; in a number of cases entire families were liquidated. . . . During house raids the soldiers and the mob first stole all money and valuables and

then plundered and devastated the homes. The men, regardless of age —from thirteen- or even ten-year-old boys to old men of seventy and eighty—were in nearly all cases brutally killed. Only in a few cases did the murderers merely shoot their victims. Most were beaten with crowbars, rifle butts, clubs, or stabbed so that their faces were deformed beyond recognition. . . . I even saw the partially burned corpses of murdered ethnic Germans. Many Germans had to watch the murder of their fathers, brothers, or children without being allowed to relieve their pain if they did not die immediately. While this was going on, they were even insulted and jeered at by the soldiers and the mob. In other cases they were forced to witness the murder of their relatives before becoming themselves victims and beaten or shot to death.[2]

The testimony of 12 September 1939 of the widow Johanna Giese is representative of the hundreds of protocols in the Bureau's files:

On Sunday 3 September 1939 between eleven and twelve in the morning we were in the cellar of our house. Polish soldiers and civilians entered our lot. They ordered us to come out of the cellar. After we came out, one of the soldiers claimed that someone had been shooting out of our house. . . . But we didn't have any weapons at all in the house. My son-in-law was the first to leave the cellar. At that moment a Polish civilian shouted that all Germans had to be shot. My son-in-law was immediately shot by one of the soldiers. The bullet severed the jugular; he received three more bullet wounds in the chest and throat. . . . My son Reinhard Giese had also been with us in the cellar. He was nineteen years old. When he saw that my son-in-law had been shot, he tried to flee. He succeeded in jumping over the fence into our neighbor's lot. But they pursued him and shot him. In the evening I was able to recover the corpse . . . he had been shot in the chest.[3]

Air Force Judge Alfons Waltzog, another resident member of the Wehrmacht legal department, interrogated other witnesses in Bromberg between 8 and 16 September and also visited some of the sites involved. For instance, after a witness named Kurt Kaliske described the deliberate burning of the Lutheran Church at Bromberg-Schwedenhoehe on 4 September 1939, Waltzog and his clerk Hanschke went to see for themselves. "The church, a red brick building, and the vicarage were totally destroyed by fire," he reported.

"Only the ruins of the outside walls have remained. The church was entirely plundered. . . . One steps over debris and bent rods. Altar and baptismal fountain have been demolished. Under the belfry on top of the debris are also the broken bell and the clockwork. Still on the tower is the clock dial, the hands marking 1745 hours."[4]

Vera Gannot testified on 14 September 1939 about her family's experiences:

On Sunday afternoon (3 September) around two, Polish soldiers and civilians approached our house. . . . The Polish civilians said: "Germans live here." Then the soldiers started shooting. . . . My father was the first to be forced out. The Poles asked him where he had his machine gun. My father did not understand the question, since he could not speak Polish. I went out . . . to help my father, since I speak Polish. I asked the Poles what we had done to them and pleaded for my father. But the Poles yelled back: "Down with the German swine." My father received several rifle butt blows to his face and on his body; he was then stabbed with a knife. He fell to the floor and was shot six times. The soldiers moved on after telling the civilians they could plunder the house or set it on fire. . . . After a while another horde of soldiers and civilians arrived. . . . The Poles tore my clothes off and forced me naked onto the floor. Some ten men held me down. . . . one of the Poles . . . consummated the rape.[5]

Another military judge, Joachim Schölz, was sent to Upper Silesia and Krakow to investigate reports of the murder of German prisoners of war by Polish soldiers. On 17 September he took the deposition of former POW Kurt Lemser at the Krakow military hospital:

On 9 September 1939 our music corps [of 31 men] marched from the front toward Sagan, since the bus in which we had been traveling could not keep up with the fast advance of the troops. . . . at the entrance to a town, which I believe is called Stopnica, we suddenly saw Polish soldiers. . . . The Poles were at first surprised and then fired at us with rifles and a kind of antitank gun. . . . later we were joined to a group of 16 German prisoners and taken to a churchyard. Seven or eight men had to step out and stand with their faces to the church wall. . . . Suddenly German artillery hit the town. Thus we had to turn around and march next to the Poles. . . . after we had marched for about an hour an escort of 50 to 60 men directed us down the roadside ditch to a hay-covered barn. There we had to stand in two rows. The Poles, who had been ahead of us, moved behind us, and we heard them load their rifles. We knew that our last moment had arrived, and shortly thereafter they started firing at us. I and other comrades managed to run away in the twilight. The Poles fired madly with rifles and machine guns after us, who were fleeing, and at our comrades standing by the barn . . . only 12 of the 45 or 46 prisoners survived.[6]

In order to confirm Lemser's allegations, Judge Schölz also took the depositions of four other survivors at the Krakow hospital for the Bureau's files in Berlin.

As the news of such abuses were published and magnified by the German press, Marcel Junod of the International Committee of the Red Cross asked for a conference with Rudolf Lehmann, requesting documentary evidence from Bromberg, Upper Silesia, and Galicia. On 27 September 1939 Lehmann made an extensive report to the German Foreign Office on his conversation with Junod and asked that copies of the files "Bromberg I" (including the Schattenberg report) and "Pless and Stopnica" be forwarded to Junod.

Lehmann summed up these investigations as follows: "The climax of the Polish murders was reached on 3 September 1939 between ten or eleven in the morning and three in the afternoon. . . . Official excuse for the slaughter of the German population was the accusation—mentioned by almost all witnesses—made by the Polish soldiers and civilians that shots had been fired out of the houses of the ethnic Germans or that guns and munitions were hidden there, making a search of the houses imperative. Under this pretext the Polish soldiers and their helpers entered the homes of the Germans, where they could best liquidate their victims. In every case without exception where this pretext was used, the witnesses swore that it was completely unfounded and that it was raised by the Poles only to give their brutal actions against the Germans a certain appearance of legality."[7]

Further Investigations: September–October 1939
In view of the great number of reports reaching Berlin every day, Judges Schattenberg, Waltzog, and Schölz were soon sent back to Poland. Maximilian Wagner, head of the international law branch of the Wehrmacht legal

department, also empowered them to call upon the local military courts for assistance. On 20 September 1939 he issued the following document to Waltzog: "With reference to the Army Decree of 4 September 1939 . . . you are entrusted with the most thorough investigation possible of the crimes committed by Polish irregulars in and around Bromberg. You are empowered to call upon the military courts there for assistance in taking sworn depositions of witnesses and experts and for the evaluation of other documentary evidence." And on 21 September: "The responsibility for the judicial investigation remains in your hands . . . the local military courts may carry out investigations only in exceptional cases and upon your petition and to the extent you consider appropriate, so as to avoid duplication of witness and expert depositions."[8]

In the following weeks the War Crimes Bureau called upon many military judges stationed in Berlin and recruited judges from other commands as well. As early as 15 September 1939 the Bureau had turned for assistance to the military court at Prague, which sent to Berlin three judges, Hans Boetticher, Georg Hurtig, and Horst Reger, who were immediately sent off on assignment.[9] Their first report, dated 29 September 1939, describes their work in the province of Posen between 18 and 28 September:

> Witness depositions were not limited to ethnic Germans but also extended to Polish persons. . . . Polish soldiers, especially the infantry, were much involved in the murders. . . . In the majority of cases the victims were first arrested under some pretext . . . most often following German air attacks. The following are the most common grounds for the arrests, when grounds were at all given: alleged possession of weapons, ammunition, and secret transmitters; giving light signals to German planes; espionage; and giving shelter to spies. But in many cases it sufficed for the arrest if the victim affirmatively answered the question whether he was German and of the Lutheran faith. . . . From the entire province of Posen the ethnic Germans, who had evidently been arrested according to a special list, were driven toward Kutno. . . . During the march continuous abuses were committed by the military escort . . . primarily against those who because of weakness or advanced age or disease could not walk fast enough.[10]

In addition to the victims of these deportations there were killings of ethnic Germans in other parts of the province, especially in the eastern and southern districts, where some extraordinarily brutal murders were committed. Entire families were liquidated. The men were not always merely shot but frequently slaughtered with all sorts of tools before the eyes of their relatives, who had also been advised of their impending death. Many of the corpses were discovered with severe mutilations. . . . At Tarlova near Kolo, Polish soldiers hunted down with machine guns a large number of Germans. Witnesses reported finding some 130 corpses strewn about on the field like hares after the hunt. . . .[11]

In three cases it could be established that the Polish Army did not treat members of the Luftwaffe who had jumped out of their stricken planes as prisoners of war but shot them instead. Only some of the witnesses have been interrogated thus far, because many who had particularly gruesome experiences are still physically and psychically so shaken that taking depositions did not appear advisable.[12]

The report of the three judges was supported by the sworn testimony of many witnesses, such as that of Olga Teske from Gross-Neudorf before Judge Boetticher:

On Wednesday, 6 September 1939, I was on the property of my uncle Karl Hackbarth in Gross-Neudorf. My brother Albert Teske was there too. Around 1:30 P.M. five Polish soldiers arrived and started searching for weapons and ammunition, alleging that someone had fired from the house. There were, of course, none there. Lying in bed they found the farmer Erich Busse from Gross-Neudorf, who had already been shot in the lung by Polish railroad workers and who had sought refuge at the Hackbarth house. . . . they ordered him to dress and come out. While he was dressing, the soldiers went into the room of the widow Luedke, who lived in the same house together with her daughter. They demanded to see Miss Luedke's husband and did not accept the fact that she was unmarried. Since they did not find her husband, they asked my brother, Albert Teske, to come out. They then left with Busse and my brother Albert and stated they were taking them for interrogation. Both were later found dead some 12 kilometers away.[13]

After the occupation of the town of Hohensalza by German troops, businessman Otto Hoffmann was commissioned by the magistrate to look for the places where ethnic Germans had been murdered and buried. By the time of his deposition before Judge Hurtig on 22 September, he had found three mass graves containing a total of thirty-five corpses.[14]

Since new witnesses were constantly being located, the War Crimes Bureau commissioned Boetticher, Hurtig, and Reger to undertake further investigations in Poland. This time they traveled separately and from 2 to 17 October took witness depositions at Thorn, Straczewo, Alt-Bogen, and Chiechocinek. On his way to Poland, at the university clinic in Breslau, Judge Reger interrogated a wounded German civilian, Karl Schmidt, who testified as follows:

> On Tuesday, 5 September 1939, Polish troops [infantrymen] retreating from the west came through our village of Neutecklenburg . . . [and] took me and 14 other ethnic Germans out of our houses and led us away. . . . We were six men and nine women. Among them were my wife Hertha Schmidt, née Grawunder, my mother-in-law Wilhelmine Grawunder, née Becke, my brother-in-law Paul Grawunder, and my sister-in-law Else Grawunder. On our way we were threatened with rifle butts if we did not walk fast enough. . . . Some two kilometers away from the village we had to stand facing a water ditch. After they had taken our money and watches, they started firing at us from behind at a distance of 20 to 30 meters. I stood at the furthermost left and was therefore the last one to be shot. The bullet struck me on the right side of my chest. I did not lose consciousness but let myself fall into the ditch. All those who were not already in the water were thrown in. Most were crying out terribly. Once again the Poles shot at them. My brother-in-law was thrown on top of me, but I managed to keep my head above water. The Poles then left. About half an hour later I risked crawling out of the ditch. All was quiet, and no one gave a sign of life; only two dogs howled that had also been shot.[15]

It is important to repeat that the military judges made a point of hearing not only Germans but as many Poles as possible. On 14 October 1939 Judge Boetticher took the sworn testimony of Boleslaw Kasprzyszak: "On Monday, 4 September 1939, I was with the 63-year-old Richard Gerth. . . . around nine in the morning a Polish soldier came on the lot. His bicycle was broken, and I had to help him repair it. . . . When he was finished, he demanded that the old man Gerth give him food, drink, and tobacco. I told him that everything was already gone. Then he yelled: 'Enough! Put your hands up.' . . . I could get away and run for the door. At this time I heard the first shot and then the second. Then I saw that the soldier sat on his bicycle and rode away. . . . I saw Gerth lying dead on the floor."[16]

Judge Zornig, assigned to the area of Langenau and Alt-Flotenau, interrogated Arnold Schallhorn on 1 November: "The village of Langenau had some 135 ethnic Germans. . . . from 3 to 6 September 1939, 23 of them were murdered, primarily by Polish soldiers [there follows a list of names of men, women, and children aged 6 to 75]. Most of the barns were destroyed by arson. Furthermore, the Poles plundered all valuables and destroyed what they could not carry with them."[17]

Investigations in the Lodz district were assigned to Judges Schattenberg, Wolfgang Zirner, and Wilken von Ramdohr.[18] Their interrogations covered not only wartime abuses but also a series of events in the summer of 1939.[19] Among the cases of arrest and maltreatment of Germans investigated by Judge von Ramdohr from 7 to 27 October 1939 was the testimony of Erna Brodöhl from the village of Pabianice:

> On 5 August 1939 my brother Hugo drove to Sieratz to pick up two friends who were staying at the home of a common acquaintance. . . . On the way back, on 7 August 1939, they were stopped and searched by a Polish major. They were sent to the jail at Widawa. . . . I drove to Widawa with the mother of one of the two friends who had been arrested, and we learned there that the three had been transferred to the jail at Sieratz. This was on 11 August 1939. On 26 August we received a letter from the Sieratz jail informing us that my brother had hanged himself. When we arrived at Sieratz in order to be present at the funeral, we were told that my brother had already been buried on 25 August. It wasn't until 6 October 1939 that I could have the body of my brother transferred here. The condition in which my brother's body was found in the jail's coffin clearly showed that he had not hanged himself but rather that he had been beaten to death by the Poles.[20]

Julius Brodöhl, the victim's father, described the condition of the body: "The feet were tied with a thin cord. The body lay on wood shavings. . . . The shavings under the head and under the back were impregnated with blood. . . . It is out of the question that my son would have taken his own life; the lawyer who visited him two days before his death has told us that my son was in good spirits because he expected to be released soon."[21]

Judge Zirner also investigated another apparent murder that occurred shortly before the outbreak of the war. On 12 October 1939 Wanda Quast stated under oath: "In the night of 30–31 August 1939 around ten-thirty our windows were smashed by Poles . . . the fragments of the glass panes flew in the room and hit us in the back. My mother jumped out the side window; Erwin Jüngling ran out the door and into the fields. We all hid ourselves . . . at 6 A.M. Mrs. Steinberg from the neighboring house . . . came and informed us that the brother-in-law lay murdered in the field. We then went to the place. He was lying on the side, his head on one arm." Corroborating testimony came from a second witness, Wenzel Brutke: "In the night of 30–31 August 1939 my windows, like the windows of all the Germans in the area, were smashed; the perpetrators were members of the Polish reserve, who had to go into active duty. I am a neighbor of the Quasts, with whom Erwin Jüngling was staying. . . . Jüngling fled in the night and was killed by the Poles. I saw the corpse the next morning."[22]

On 21 October 1939 Alex Busse testified before Judge Zirner: "In the last months before the war . . . the western association of the Poles incited them against us ethnic Germans. The consequences of this agitation were burnings and many killings in this district. Even before the war German farmsteads were set afire by the Poles at night."[23]

Such examples establish that there had been persecution of the ethnic Germans before the war, but the War Crimes Bureau files do not establish large-scale killings before September of 1939; thus, they contradict Nazi propaganda of the "great terror," which was used by Goebbels and the *Völkischer Beobachter* to justify Germany's invasion of Poland. Still, Polish propaganda tried to justify Polish actions against the ethnic Germans as punishment for the traitorous activities of a "Fifth Column." Hence, part of the task of the Bureau was to ascertain to what extent Germans in Poland had engaged in espionage or other activities detrimental to the security of the Polish state.

Among the witnesses questioned in this regard by Air Force Judge Wilhelm Bockisch was the Polish Sergeant Palicki from Bromberg, who described how a shooting incident that began on 3 September 1939 in the northern part of Bromberg aroused nervousness in the Polish barracks because rumors went around that German parachutists had landed; the soldiers then went to town and arrested a number of ethnic Germans. Palicki asked the guards whether anybody had actually seen any Germans shooting, but no one had.

In the evening around 1730 the battalion commander Major Slawinski called the other officers to a meeting, which I also attended. Major
Slawinski made the following statement: "Gentlemen, there is no evidence at all to establish *franc-tireur* activities on the part of the Germans;
get this idea out of your heads." He explained . . . that not a single German use of arms could be established and that the shootings had been
started by the retreating soldiers of the 9th and 27th Infantry Divisions.
. . . Lieutenant Kopczynski . . . indicated that he and "a number of
other persons had searched the Lutheran cemetery . . . because it was ru-
mored that the Germans had set up a machine gun there. But nothing
at all could be found." Sergeant Tyrakowski . . . also declared that all
reports of shootings on the part of the German population had proved
to be unfounded. Whenever the relevant persons were questioned about
the precise course of events, they could not give any such information.[24]

The testimony of many German witnesses similarly rejects the *franc-tireur*
theory. In this connection it is significant to note that after the collapse of the
Polish government and the German military occupation of the western half
of the country, no resident German was honored for anti-Polish *franc-tireur*
activity.

Evaluation of the Testimony
The dossiers prepared by individual judges and special commissions were
systematically collected, evaluated, and compared by the staff of the War
Crimes Bureau in Berlin. Because of the gravity and number of the crimes
investigated, Rudolf Lehmann conferred with the members of the Bureau on
30 September, 18 October, and again at the end of October 1939.[25] But because reports of abuses continued to arrive in Berlin, depositions of witnesses
were taken through the summer of 1940. Bureau members Martin Heinemann and Lothar Schöne were sent on special mission in November 1939 and
January 1940 to military hospitals throughout the Reich, where ethnic Germans and Wehrmacht soldiers were still convalescing; Bureau chief Johannes
Goldsche personally questioned those at military hospitals in the Berlin area;
and since witnesses were spread throughout Germany and the occupied areas
of Poland, the Bureau requested the assistance of more than fifty military
courts as well. On 30 November 1939, for instance, Lieutenant Udo Ritgen
gave a sworn statement before Judge Otto Mackel of the 21st Infantry Divi-

sion. Ritgen, who had been wounded and taken prisoner during the Polish campaign, reported that he and other German POWs had been subjected to serious ill-treatment by Polish soldiers, officers, and civilians.[26]

Some twenty local civilian courts were also requested by the Bureau to obtain the sworn deposition of witnesses residing within their jurisdictions. Thus on 29 January 1940 the county court in Hirschberg took the deposition of Lieutenant Ernst Freiherr John von Freyend concerning his experience as a POW in Poland. He stated that although he was seriously wounded, he was first robbed by Polish soldiers, then forced to march; when he could no longer walk, he was stabbed twice with a bayonet in the area of his kidneys, and his nose was broken.[27]

On the basis of the material collected and evaluated by the War Crimes Bureau, six volumes of documents and commentary were assembled, each containing approximately 500 pages: (1) Polish atrocities in Bromberg, Pless, and Stopnica; (2) Polish atrocities committed against ethnic Germans and prisoners of war in the province of Poznan; (3–4) violations of the laws of war by the Polish Army; (5) the massacre of ethnic Germans in Lodz; (6) Polish murders of ethnic Germans (an addendum). In the available records of the Bureau there is no statistical study establishing the number of victims among members of German communities or German armed forces in Poland (although it is probable that such a computation was at least attempted); hence, there are widely diverging estimates. The most heated debate concerns the number of ethnic Germans killed or missing. For instance, the Polish West Institute (*Institut Zachodni*) in Posen published in 1959 a study by Karol Pospieszalski titled *The Case of the 58,000 Volksdeutsche*, which estimates some 2,000 ethnic German victims of excesses by Polish civilians and soldiers. Pospieszalski explains that the rapid advances of the German army in Poland were perceived by the Polish population as the result of Fifth Column activities on the part of the resident German minority, and the prevailing atmosphere of surprise, nervousness, fear, and bitterness "undoubtedly led to heedless excesses against the local Germans."[28] The noted Dutch historian Louis de Jong suggests that of "the 750,000 to 1,000,000 ethnic Germans in Poland, several thousand lost their lives in the wake of the panic over Fifth Column activities."[29]

Lacking definitive figures, the Federal German Archives in Koblenz commissioned in the 1960s a major project that involved the questioning of 6,106 persons and the collection and evaluation of 400 reports of eyewitnesses.

This material establishes the murder of at least 3,841 named ethnic Germans. When it is considered that this result was obtained more than twenty years after the events and that only witnesses residing in the Federal Republic of Germany could be located and questioned, it would appear that the actual number is probably well in excess of that figure.[30]

The records of the War Crimes Bureau dealing with this question comprise the depositions of 593 witnesses before 44 military and civilian judges;[31] these refer to approximately 1,000 named victims and 3,500 to 5,000 additional unnamed victims among the ethnic Germans. Of course, it is no longer possible to determine to what extent the reports of killings overlapped; nevertheless, since the records *are* incomplete and since it is hardly possible that the German judges were able to locate and interrogate *all* surviving witnesses, the figure of 6,000 murdered ethnic Germans would appear a reasonable estimate.

German Crimes in Poland

The German invasion of Poland with all its attending horrors and aberrations also provided ample evidence of the criminal plans of the Nazi regime in putting the racist *Herrenvolk* (Master Race) theories into practice. A grave dilemma emerged for many Germans, particularly for military judges who were expected to investigate enemy war crimes while their own government was itself engaged in official criminality against Jews and non-Jews in Poland, both of whom were seen by the fanatical Nazis as *Untermenschen* (subhumans).[32]

Many German judges were spared an early confrontation with the excesses of the Nazi state, but others did learn of some activities of the ss and sd. Alfons Waltzog, in the course of his investigations of Polish atrocities, also witnessed German crimes about which he felt compelled to report to his superior, Maximilian Wagner: "International law appears different in practice than in theory. At the High Command of the Wehrmacht we discussed the question of who had the authority to order the execution of hostages. Here the ss special security units [*Sicherheitsdienst*] have executed hostages arbitrarily, *franc-tireurs* without court-martial. It required considerable effort on the part of the judge competent for the occupied zone behind the lines to stop these killings. . . . Today I learned from the current head of the local Gestapo that last night 20 Poles, so-called criminals, had been shot without trial. There are also 50 Poles in an internment camp here; they have been held for eight days in a cellar, which I myself have visited. They too were supposed to be shot."[33]

At about the same time an ss storm trooper and a police sergeant killed some 50 Polish Jews in the zone occupied by the German 3rd Army. The military court of the Kempf armored division initially charged the two with murder, and the prosecutor asked for the death penalty. The court, however, held on 13 September 1939 that the accused were guilty only of manslaughter; it sentenced the storm trooper to three years' imprisonment and the police sergeant to nine years' hard labor, recognizing as mitigating circumstances that "because of the numerous atrocities committed by the Poles against the ethnic Germans, they were in a state of high irritability."[34] Perhaps an explanation for this scandalously lenient sentencing may be found in the fact that the three-man court-martial was composed of a Wehrmacht judge and two ss jurors (*Beisitzer*).

A different case occurred in October 1939 in Polish Upper Silesia. There General Otto von Knobelsdorff ordered an SD functionary arrested who claimed to have authority to execute fifty to sixty persons. The SD man alleged that according to intelligence information, the persons in question intended to carry out acts of sabotage against the German troops; therefore, he claimed the authority to have them executed without legal proceedings. Knobelsdorff informed the man's SD superiors of his arrest and categorically rejected as a matter of principle any requests to have him released.[35]

A sad example of unsuccessful opposition to Nazi abuses involves the fate of the Wehrmacht commander-in-chief at the Eastern Front, General Johannes Blaskowitz, who demanded in October 1939 that two ss colonels (*Standartenführer*) be court-martialed on charges of murder and plundering.[36] When they were not, Blaskowitz sent two explicit protests to Hitler.[37] In the second, dated 6 February 1940, he observed: "The attitude of the Wehrmacht troops to the ss and to the police alternates between disgust and hatred. Every soldier feels offended and repulsed by the crimes being committed in Poland by citizens of the Reich and representatives of the executive power. A soldier cannot understand how such crimes can remain unpunished, crimes that occur in a sense under the army's protection."[38] General Blaskowitz was replaced on 5 May 1940, and Nazi crimes in Poland did not abate; Auschwitz-Birkenau, Lublin-Maidanek, and other abominations were yet to follow. The full horror of Nazi exterminations in Poland would not be disclosed until the Nuremberg trials.

In the course of the German invasion and occupation of Belgium, Holland, and northern France, the High Command of the Wehrmacht received allegations of the abuse of civilians by British and French troops and of crimes against members of the German armed forces committed by Allied soldiers and civilians. As it had done in the Polish campaign, the War Crimes Bureau sent a number of military judges to investigate and document events in the Western theater of war. The liaison officers between the German Foreign Office and German forces in the West similarly collected material, which the Foreign Office then used to compile a white book on violations of international law by the Western Allies. Moreover, a special propaganda company was assigned to carry out *in loco* investigations in the province of Zeeland.[1]

Allied Crimes against Civilians

The internal correspondence of the offices involved and the investigatory procedures themselves show that there was no fabrication of atrocity stories but rather the methodical collection and evaluation of evidence. Nor was there any attempt to blame the Allies for destruction that may have been caused by the Germans themselves. For example, one investigation of what the Germans had suspected was wanton arson by retreating Allied troops concluded: "The causes of the destruction of the town of Middelburg are not altogether clear. The mayor of the town insists that the destruction of the town, including the city hall and the church, was caused by German bombs and artillery. The allegations of the mayor are difficult to refute."[2]

Other investigations in the Netherlands also failed to produce evidence of Allied impropriety: "Consultations in The Hague, Rotterdam, and Breda rendered an entirely negative result. Plundering or other violations of international law cannot be clearly established. In the course of three visits in Breda and numerous conversations with mayors, police commissioners, etc., it became apparent that the French evacuation was carried out in a fashion that hardly gives rise to objection. The greater number of those persons evacuated from their homes could return after a few days. Notwithstanding a few marginal cases, stores and private homes were not plundered.[3] The evacuation and return of the civilian population was carried out in an orderly fashion, in keeping with the prevailing circumstances."[4]

Dutch Flanders was occupied by Belgian and French troops until 28 May 1940. No major battles took place in this area, and the Bureau investigations uncovered only minor theft: 1,212 florins were stolen in the village of Hulst on the night of 19–20 May 1940; the mayor of the town of Axel reported citizen claims of 4,352, 93.72, and 143.54 florins and a list of items "pilfered by unknown persons: a jar containing 8 pounds of butter, 6 pounds of butter wrapped in paper, a vessel containing 4 pounds of pork lard."[5]

Official inquiries in Belgium and northern France rendered more substantial results. In June 1940 the War Crimes Bureau commissioned one of its members, Martin Heinemann, to carry out special investigations in Louvain, Brussels, and Aix la Chapelle. At the same time the Bureau sent Alfons Waltzog to Louvain and then to France, where he focused primarily on the use of explosive (dumdum) ammunition by the Allies.[6] In addition, the military commanders-in-chief in Belgium and northern France were requested to obtain the sworn deposition of witnesses through the military judges attached to their divisions.[7] Judge Jansen, for instance, investigated reported instances of plundering in the Belgian town of Geeraardsbergen, and on 20 August 1940 he took the deposition of the Belgian witness René De Clercq: "On Sunday morning, 19 May 1940, around five o'clock I saw English soldiers enter my house at 39 Meersch Street. . . . [where] I own a store and a tobacco shop. The English soldiers took merchandise, shirts, razor blades, rings, watches, and canned goods. . . . I was too afraid to go there to stop the plundering, since the English soldiers had set up a machine gun there and were threatening with it. . . . I also observed that English soldiers plundered the house of my neighbor, the school director Arthur Van den Berghe. . . . I later confirmed that the soldiers had opened trunks and boxes in both houses and stolen the contents."[8]

On 5 December 1940 Judge Wehner took the deposition of Belgian butcher Alphons de Smedt concerning a death in the town of Okegem near

Ghent: "On Saturday, 18 May 1940, the English were in Okegem and interned some 100 to 120 persons, including women and children, in my house. Guards with bayonets were posted at both doors. I did not see Theofiel de Beenhouwer among the interned persons. When the English retreated, my daughter noticed that practically all the beer bottles at her restaurant had disappeared. I proceeded to look for the bottles and found a mound of freshly dug earth in a ditch on the other side of the street. . . . Since I suspected the beer bottles were there, I cleared away the earth and found underneath the corpse of Theofiel de Beenhouwer."[9]

Judge Wehner also investigated the death of the farmer Benoit Vernaillen. On 6 December 1940 Wehner took the depositions of three witnesses. On 3 February 1941 the fifteen-year-old son of the victim, Franz Vernaillen, testified: "On 18 May 1940 I was with my father cutting hay in the field. At around 3:00 P.M. I was with the horse a few meters away from my father, who was swinging the scythe, when suddenly three shots were fired. Immediately thereafter I saw two English soldiers come from the area of the shots. I cannot say whether they were carrying guns with them, since I did not pay attention to that. When I saw them, they were at a distance of about 200 meters. And while they approached me, I saw that my father was lying on the ground and that he had been hit by a bullet. The English soldiers ordered me to go home . . . besides the two Englishmen I did not see anyone else at the scene of the crime."[10]

It was also reported that at Fournes (Veurne) eight civilians had been shot. Town secretary Joris de Burchgraeve gave a sworn deposition on 15 April 1941 before Judge Last:

Whereas the conduct of the English troops during the first days after their arrival did not give rise to any complaints, the situation changed in the evening of 29 May 1940.[11] That night many English soldiers entered the empty homes and shops in order to steal all sorts of beverages, particularly wine, liqueurs, cognac, whiskey, etc. The English soldiers were not hindered because most of the local population had fled, and the remaining civilians, including the mayor of the town, were not allowed on the streets. As soon as a civilian went out on the street on 29 May, he was ordered back into his home. On 30 and 31 May the soldiers shot at civilians who went out on the street. I personally saw that in the evening hours of 29 May 1940 English soldiers threw furniture and other private property out of the windows of evacuated houses into the streets. Then they noisily piled up this furniture in order to build barricades. Doors and windows of many homes were broken, since the owners had locked them before leaving. Around ten-thirty in the evening soldiers knocked at my door. . . . they ordered me with their revolvers to leave the house within five minutes. I can speak some English, so I asked them where I should go, since there were also members of my family and other persons in my house. When the soldiers could not answer my question, I demanded that an officer should come. The officer similarly insisted that we abandon the house, but he could not tell me where we should go. Thus, together with all the persons in my house, I went to the farm of a friend some two kilometers away from Veurne. We stayed there until the first German troops arrived on 1 June 1940.

About seven or eight in the morning of 1 June I returned together with a friend to my home in Veurne. Although the house door and the windows had been broken by the explosions, the interior of my house was intact. Not a single item was missing. The German troops were already in the town. On my way there I saw the corpse of the seventy-year-old retired civil servant Demeulenaere, who had been shot on Oost Street. The next day I also saw the corpse of the laborer Florizoone, who had been shot on Statie Street. I learned from friends that both persons were shot by the English soldiers on 31 May 1940 because they were seen on the streets. Friends also told me that six more persons, including two women, were killed when they went out on the street.[12]

In the town of Meenen the popular Belgian cyclist Julien Vervaecke was killed. The report of the investigation into his death, dated 22 August 1941, describes the events as follows:

In connection with their retreat the British in Meenen wanted to blow up the Leie bridge, which connects Meenen with the road to Halluin and Roncq. Before that they set up a barricade . . . and took out the furniture from the neighboring houses, including the hotel of the Vervaecke family. . . . Vervaecke left the air raid shelter on 24 May 1940 and went to his home to get food for his family. In so doing he came across the English troops who were taking furniture out of his house. Knowing Vervaecke's impulsive character, it is probable that he protested. . . .

The situation may have been aggravated by the fact that Vervaecke could not speak any English and did not speak French very well. Vervaecke was arrested by the English soldiers and taken to the Park Torris in Roncq, where he was shot. These events are confirmed by witness testimony. . . . In view of the war operations, it is at first understandable that British troops arrested Vervaecke when he opposed their use of his furniture for building barricades . . . [but] further measures taken by the British soldiers against Vervaecke were brutal and a gross violation of international law.[13]

The Bureau also investigated cases in which French troops were involved. The most important appears to have been the shooting of some twenty-one prisoners in Abbeville on 20 May 1940; some of them were Belgian nationalists and fascists, but others were Jewish refugees from Germany —who, ironically, had been arrested upon the outbreak of the war.[14] (The War Crimes Bureau itself was apparently not involved in the Abbeville investigations but only received copies of the inquiry from the liaison officer of the German Foreign Office at the High Command of the Fourth Army, Consul-General Schattenfroh.)[15] The most significant testimony is that of Paul Winter, a Danish engineer who had also been detained by the French and who managed to escape during a German air attack. Twenty-one corpses were found at the place where Winter claimed that the executions had taken place, and his testimony was used in a German Foreign Office propaganda brochure, "The Crimes of Lille and Abbeville." Testimony was also obtained from the Belgian journalist Achiel Mareel, who together with fifty-one other prisoners had been transferred from Abbeville to Rouen. He was separated from the others, however, so that he was not a direct witness of the killings.

Long before the Bureau completed its own investigations with regard to the Western theater, the German Foreign Office published "Documents of British-French Cruelty: The War Conduct of Britain and France in the Netherlands, Belgium, and Northern France in May 1940." This 1940 white book contains primarily reports of war crimes allegedly committed by the Allies against civilians in the areas under military occupation. The statements are not supported by judicial investigations, however, and the accuracy of some is clearly open to question, yet it is fairly certain that a number of the violations described did take place. Internal documents not intended for publication attest to the German conviction that the Allied troops did, in fact, commit a variety of crimes. For instance, the report of the commander-in-chief for Belgium and northern France, dated 5 December 1940, reads in part: "It has been established that violations of international law . . . were committed both by French and by British soldiers and officers. These violations include the killing of civilian persons, deliberate shooting at and threatening of civilians, destruction of buildings through arson and bombardment, devastation of the interior of private homes, and plundering."[16]

Crimes against German Soldiers in France

From the available Bureau records it appears that investigations of crimes committed by Allied soldiers and civilians against members of the German armed forces were far more extensive in France than in Holland and Belgium. A typical report is that of noncommissioned officer Karl Michaelis, who on 9 June 1940 was wounded in a village near Le Havre. On 6 September 1940 Bureau member Karl Hofmann took his deposition at the military hospital in Neubrandenburg, where Michaelis was convalescing:

> In the course of the battle I received two superficial wounds in my left lower and upper arm, and then a bullet through my right upper arm . . . gradually our ammunition ran out, so that we had no choice but to surrender to the British. . . . Because of my wounds I was unable to continue fighting and lay on the ground. Together with me were Corporal Magdanz and a reserve soldier, who was superficially wounded. . . . Since we had become defenseless, my [five] men put away their rifles and stood next to the barn. At that moment the British came from behind the barn, some 15 to 20 men. . . . I know for a fact that my men had their arms up and that none of them had any weapon when the British soldiers arrived. Without speaking a word, the British aimed at my comrades and shot them, although none of my comrades had made any aggressive move. On the contrary, and I must repeat this, my comrades were standing with their arms raised. . . . In the shooting I myself received another superficial wound, in the neck. The three reserve soldiers and Corporal Leibner were dead on the spot. Corporal Magdanz passed away some ten minutes later. After the shooting the English came up to us and turned the bodies around, including me, and even kicked the corpses, apparently to see whether we were still alive. I myself cried out because I experienced great pain in my arm when they grabbed me.

. . . one of the English soldiers who, like the others, was very close to me, aimed his rifle at me. At this moment an English sergeant suddenly came from behind the barn and vigorously shouted at the other soldiers. Through his intervention I was spared. . . . This British sergeant, who was himself wounded, stayed with me for the duration of the battle and also dressed my wounds.[17]

Although there are relatively few reports of British war crimes in the field, the Bureau incorporated a selection of them into an unpublished document, "Violations of the Laws of War by the British Armed Forces."[18] Many of the depositions obtained concern the ill-treatment or lynching of German air crews following an emergency landing or parachuting in France. On 11 October 1940 Lieutenant Rudolf Gaudé testified before Judge Ufer that on 16 June as he and Sergeant Herrig "were still in the air—we jumped out at an altitude of about 1,500 meters—two French Moranes repeatedly circled around us and shot at us. I was not hit, but Sergeant Herrig was probably killed in the air during the second attack. I found him the next morning some 1,000 meters away from the place where I had landed. He was dead and one leg had been completely shot off. I had seen when he was still in the air that he threw back his arms and his head. There is no doubt that his wound was brought about by a direct hit from the airplane's cannon."[19]

Another case concerned noncommissioned officer Karl Fritz Wöllner, who on 14 May 1940 had to jump out of his airplane over Sedan at an altitude of 3,500 meters. On 23 September 1940 he was summoned to testify before Judge Schmidtel in Saxony. He stated under oath that at an altitude of about 500 meters he was hit in the upper thigh by machine-gun fire from French ground troops.[20]

French civilians too participated in the machine-gunning of disabled airmen parachuting to the ground. Because this widespread practice frequently led to the accidental killing of British and French as well as German airmen, it became necessary to issue orders against such indiscriminate attacks. For instance, Abbeville headquarters were instructed on 15 May 1940 to shoot only at groups of at least three parachutists.[21]

German airmen making emergency landings on French ground had considerable difficulty in surrendering and were frequently subjected to continued fire.[22] Sergeant Josef Schweiger stated under oath before Judge Kommert in Esslingen am Neckar:

After we landed we immediately abandoned the plane, first the radioman, noncommissioned officer Anschau; then the mechanic, Sergeant Zimmer; then the observer, Corporal Hopf; and finally I as pilot. All this time we were the targets of some 150 to 200 French soldiers at a distance of 40 to 50 meters. Corporal Hopf was shot through the left thigh while lying next to the plane on the ground. I was hit in the right thigh. . . . we were promptly encircled by the French soldiers. . . . we raised our arms to show that we wanted to surrender. In spite of this they continued shooting at us . . . shouting and yelling madly. Each of us was beaten with rifle butts. I also saw when they hit Hopf, who was lying next to me. While I was prostrate on the ground I received a blow on my head and momentarily lost consciousness. Later on I developed a big lump on the right side of my head. I also received rifle blows and kicks from all sides all over my body.[23]

On 5 June 1940 Sergeant Hans Belles landed near Corbigny, Auxerre. His deposition was taken on 4 September 1940 by Judge Gerhard Schuldt of the Giessen court:

I myself had been hit by a ricochet in one of my upper ribs. Two other members of the crew were also wounded. Since I speak French, I went up to the farmers working in the fields in order to ask them to . . . obtain medical assistance for my comrades. Although I had thrown away my gun and the farmers who were coming toward me saw this—they were about 25 civilians with hunting and infantry rifles—they took aim at me, whereupon I stood still and told them what I wanted. After they promised to help, I went back to my comrades, who were hiding in bushes close to the burning aircraft. As I started to walk back, one of the civilians shot at me . . . at a distance of about 10 meters. The huntsman fired twice with his shotgun. At least 28 pellets had to be removed from my entire body. French police eventually arrived and took us into custody.[24]

German infantry soldiers also found it difficult to surrender, and some were killed in the attempt. Corporal Kurt Wiegand stated under oath on 15 October 1940:

Our cannon was out of operation, and we had to surrender because we ran out of ammunition. Upon Lieutenant Frank's order we put down our rifles and took off our belts, stood up, and raised our arms to show that we were surrendering. . . . Behind us there were already a number of French infantry soldiers . . . [who] discussed among themselves for a moment and then opened fire on us. Lieutenant Frank and Corporal Palland were killed. There were also several dead and wounded among our infantrymen. The French soldiers then ordered us with sign language to move back. . . . We still had our arms raised. A French soldier (it may have been a sergeant) stood in the tower of an armored vehicle and shot at us with a pistol. Trute was first hit in the stomach, and he fell to the ground. Since he was not dead, the Frenchman emptied his magazine at him. He was hit by almost every bullet and died immediately. The French soldier then ordered me to lie down, but when I saw that he started loading his weapon again, I stood up and retreated with my hands up. The Frenchman shot at me several times but did not hit me.[25]

On 25 September 1940 Corporal Wilhelm Ermlich told his story under oath before Judge Schorn:

The French soldiers . . . started searching the fields right and left of the road. . . . Noncommissioned officer Hartmann ordered us to stand up without our weapons. We did this and raised our arms to indicate that we were surrendering. Some seven Frenchmen came up to us. The rest of them, about 70 men, stayed on the road about 20 meters away. By comparison we were only one noncommissioned officer and four men. . . . Suddenly another Frenchman from the road came down to us, pushed his comrades away, and closely observed us. . . . He then yelled "Captain" four times in the belief that Hartmann was an officer. At this point the Frenchmen who had first come up to us opened fire at very short distance, although we still had our hands up and did not make any move that could have been interpreted as resistance or an attempt to escape. When I saw that Corporal Pfeifer, who stood at our extreme left, got a bullet in his forehead, I let myself drop to the ground. . . . The next moment . . . Hartmann and Corporal Tittmann, both of them wounded, fell over me. Private Stahn, who was standing a bit farther away, was probably hit at about the same moment. I then heard the Frenchmen reload their guns and fire five shots at us on the ground. This time I was hit in the thigh, but I did not move, so as not to show that I was still alive. The Frenchmen then left. I cannot say what regiment they belonged to.[26]

The German campaign in the West had started on 10 May and ended on 22 June 1940 with the signing of the French armistice. For this period of six weeks the War Crimes Bureau obtained the depositions of several hundred witnesses, many of them German soldiers who were liberated from French captivity after the armistice. Some 400 of these sworn statements were printed in two special reports prepared for internal use by the Bureau, one in September 1940 and another in April 1941. The first dealt with French breaches of the Geneva Convention on the Treatment of Prisoners of War, classified as extortion of information on military secrets; killing of defenseless wounded soldiers; attacks on airmen after forced landings; ill-treatment, shackling, bad conditions of detention, inadequate rations, compulsion to perform military assignments; and confiscation of private property. The second divided violations of the Geneva Convention for the Amelioration of the Condition of the Wounded and Sick into breaches against the red cross; misuse of the red cross; and inadequate medical attention.

For political reasons, in order not to counter the official policy of reaching an entente with France, these two reports were distributed only to a very limited circle, with specific instructions that their content was not to be published, copied, or given to persons or agencies outside the Wehrmacht —except those copies made available to the German Foreign Office (which, however, never published any part of them).[27]

The French Resistance

The War Crimes Bureau files are very incomplete with regard to possible violations of the laws of war by members of the French resistance (*Forces Françaises de l'Intérieur,* or FFI) in the years 1941–44—or, for that matter, concerning violations committed by regular French forces following the Allied Normandy invasion and subsequent liberation of French territory from German occupation—but a few documents remain.

One of the most important cases concerned the fate of German POWs who had been taken prisoner in the Haute-Savoie in August 1944 and whom the FFI threatened to execute if the German government refused to grant the FFI combatant status and POW rights in captivity. When Berlin declined to answer the ultimatum, eighty German prisoners were "executed" by the FFI near Annecy on 2 September 1944.[28] The Bureau obtained confirmation of the killings by questioning some returning prisoners who were exchanged for wounded and sick French prisoners. Depositions were obtained, for instance, from Private Rudolf Diepold and Sergeant Georg Fackler.[29]

Following the German television broadcast of the War Crimes Bureau (see Note on the Sources) documentary in 1983, several additional witnesses identified themselves and forwarded their testimony. One such witness was Anton Gottschaller, who had been taken prisoner by the FFI in Annecy on 19 August 1944 and who had described the events in an affidavit dated 4 February 1954.[30] Concerning the victims from the Annecy POW camp, Gottschaller stated:

> In the early hours of this Saturday 34 persons were called out alphabetically by name. . . . One of those called was Fritz Lössl, a medical orderly for many years, who was wearing his red cross armband. This fact caused a certain hesitation on the part of the Frenchmen, who consulted among themselves for a while, but finally Lössl remained in the list. The 34 men were then led away.
>
> Some time later nine other prisoners and I were assigned to a work detail. We were led in a rush toward Sacconges. At this place we received five picks and five shovels. About one kilometer beyond Sacconges . . . we saw a truck out of which our comrades who had been led away earlier in the morning were descending. There was an exchange of words between two clergymen who apparently had also come in the truck— Lutheran Pastor Höchstetter and Catholic priest Fritz Völker—and the French commander, Major Barrelet. From their agitated tone, I assumed that our comrades were to be shot. Barrelet stated that it was irrelevant whether the persons had themselves committed any offense: "You all cried out 'Heil Hitler' and now you will pay for it." Preparations for the executions were made, and the first group was taken away. Thereupon I heard wild shooting in all directions. Some men of this first group attempted to escape, without success. Together with the work group, I had to collect the bodies. There were ten bodies. We were then ordered to dig a mass grave in the fallow land nearby. We . . . were not allowed to look up, but from a distance of some 20 meters I saw that three further groups of ten men each were executed: that is, 40 men in all. Six officers

had been added to the 34 men who had been picked up in the morning.
. . . The dead were then buried in the grave.

Forty other German POWs from the camp at St. Pierre de Rumilly were
executed the same day at Habère-Lullin. Although Gottschaller was not a
direct witness, he personally knew some of the victims, and his 1954 affidavit
includes what he was able to find out, both during his captivity and in a more
thorough investigation after his release in 1947:

> The execution detachment from Annecy also went on 2 September 1944
> to the camp of St. Pierre de Rumilly, some 30 kilometers northwest of
> Annecy. In the afternoon of that day 40 prisoners of war were called by
> name. Some of them were not there, because they had been assigned to
> a work company outside. The missing places were filled arbitrarily; some
> persons volunteered (Dietzsch and Hoffmann), thinking that they were
> being assigned to another work company. This also explains why two
> Austrians are on the list of dead, who from the French side would cer-
> tainly not have been selected for execution. These 40 men were executed
> on the same afternoon at Habère-Lullin. Five wooden posts were set up,
> and the men were shot five at a time. The next group of five was required
> to carry the bodies of their dead comrades. A Catholic priest (French-
> man) was present. A woman had intended to beat the men with a bat,
> but she was prevented from doing so. In the same evening the 40 bodies
> were returned in coffins. On Monday (two days later) they were buried.
> . . . On Sunday a representative of the International Committee of the
> Red Cross had come by auto and made photographs of the coffins. We
> were informed of this execution by the French. The details of the killings
> were given to me on 23 July 1947 by a camp comrade, the Lutheran Pas-
> tor Hermann Blanke. . . . On this day he also spoke with two witnesses
> of the execution, a teacher from Habère-Lullin, M. Duret, and an old
> farmer, whose farm is across from the field where the executions took
> place. Both described the events in concurring fashion.

It is a sad arabesque to these killings that the Reich government subsequently did agree to provide nominal rolls of FFI members held prisoner
in Germany and gave verbal assurance to the International Committee of
the Red Cross "that members of the FFI taken by the Germans would be
treated as prisoners of war."[31]

CHAPTER FIFTEEN / CRETE

The German invasion of the island of Crete in the Mediterranean commenced in the morning of 20 May 1941. After heavy fighting the British, Australian, and New Zealand troops were evacuated on 31 May. In those four days great losses were suffered on both sides: some 4,000 British soldiers and sailors were killed, 12,000 taken prisoner, and 18,000 evacuated; it is estimated that 4,000 German soldiers and sailors perished.[1] The involvement of the Cretan population as irregular soldiers contributed to the substantial battle losses and later gave the Germans an excuse to carry out draconian reprisals.

During the first days of the fighting an unusually high number of violations of the laws of war were reported. The first sworn depositions were taken on the island on 26 May. In all, some 150 witnesses were questioned by twelve German Army, Navy, and Air Force judges. Although the depositions continued all through the summer, at least until 25 August 1941, the War Crimes Bureau completed in July a long study titled "Enemy Violations of International Law during the German Engagement in Crete," which evaluated the extensive documentation already collected.[2] The study comprises chapters dealing with killings and mutilations, misuse of the German flag and German uniforms, *franc-tireur* activity, and attacks on German transport by sea and the killing of German shipwrecked survivors.[3]

The Bureau forwarded this study to the German Foreign Office, which used substantial parts of it in an official white book titled "Violations of International Law by British Armed Forces and by Civilians in Crete," which was published and distributed in 1942.[4]

Official Reports

Quite valuable to the Bureau in preparing the study were not only the depositions themselves but the reports submitted by Army Judge Joachim Schölz, Air Force Judge Roland Rüdel, and medical officer Dr. Hellmuth Unger.

Judge Schölz had had considerable experience in questioning witnesses and victims in Poland, following which he had continued working in the legal department of the Wehrmacht in Berlin. Called upon again to carry out investigations on the spot, he flew to Athens and then to Crete, where he interrogated 32 witnesses between 26 May and 4 June 1941. His report of 4 June summed up his impressions:

> The content of the sworn depositions is complemented and confirmed by the statements that officers and men have given on the basis of their own experience and on reports of third parties. Through the sworn depositions the following violations of international law are established without doubt:
>
> 1. Many parachutists were subjected to inhuman treatment or mutilated.
>
> 2. During the battle around Suda Bay on 27 May 1941 the first Mountain Infantry Regiment No. 141 had to retreat temporarily to a better position because of enemy superiority and on account of the difficult terrain. (a) All wounded who could not be transported were murdered. (b) Many of the corpses found the next day had been mutilated.
>
> 3. Warships of the Royal Navy attacked German shipwrecked soldiers, whose [transport] ships had been sunk some 100 kilometers from Crete and who were drifting helplessly in the water.
>
> 4. British soldiers misused the German swastika flag, parts of German uniforms, and the white flag.
>
> 5. Greek civilians participated in the fighting as *franc-tireurs*. . . .

According to the sworn testimony of witnesses, who confirmed and complemented one another, there is the following evidence that the wounded left behind were murdered: Scouting patrols that returned to the battlefield one or two hours after the fight and burial details sent the following day found 124 dead and not a single man wounded. . . . A corporal who had a shot only in the shoulder lay there with his own knife through his throat. . . . Many of the dead had in addition to other injuries stab wounds or shots through the head or through the heart.

The number of shots through the head and heart was remarkably high, although the battalion had been attacked primarily with machine guns. Two of the dead had serious stab wounds that had not issued any blood. Before withdrawing, the enemy must have dealt each German soldier, whether dead or alive, a lethal stab or bullet wound to make sure that no living remained behind. . . .

I believe that the British and the Greek soldiers as well as the civilian population may all be guilty. The British took prisoners at first and probably treated them well. After the fall of Chania the Germans pursued them, and this made it difficult for them to transport or feed the prisoners. It is possible that they then tended not to take prisoners and thus did not spare the wounded men. In my opinion Greek soldiers and civilians are also suspect. . . . It is necessary to investigate the events thoroughly before we can determine the extent to which Greek soldiers were guilty of maltreating and mutilating members of the German armed forces, such as the parachutists.[5]

Judge Rüdel, in charge of investigating allegations about crimes committed against parachutists, first questioned numerous wounded soldiers who had been flown to hospitals in Athens. Their testimony convinced the chief of staff of the 11th Air Corps, Major General Alfred Schlemm, that a special commission under intelligence officer Major Johannes Bock should be sent forthwith to Crete to continue on-site investigations. Rüdel, as a member of the commission, flew to Crete on 28 May 1941. On 14 July he submitted a long report more favorable to the British military than to the Cretan civilian population. He summed up:

On the basis of sworn testimony of German soldiers who participated in the fighting on Crete, [plus] interrogation of Greek and British soldiers, and aided by photographic evidence, we could establish the following:

1. Participation of civilians and policemen in open battle on all battlefields, especially in the western parts of the island; in some areas civilians offered organized resistance according to military principles. The civilian population, including youngsters about ten years old, fired with all sorts of weapons, also with dumdum and hunting ammunition. Bush and tree snipers were repeatedly observed. . . .

2. Dead and wounded soldiers were robbed and deprived of parts of their clothing, primarily by the civilian population.

3. On corpses of German soldiers countless mutilations have been established; some had their genitals amputated, eyes put out, ears and noses cut off; others had knife wounds in the face, chest, stomach, and back; throats were slit, and hands chopped off. The majority of these mutilations were probably defilement of the dead bodies; only in a few cases does the evidence indicate that the victim was maltreated and tortured to death. A number of corpses were found with hands, arms, or legs tied up; in one case the corpse had a cord around his neck. . . .

4. On the enemy side the use of German uniforms, especially parachutist combinations and steel helmets, was observed. Similarly, in order to deceive the other side, they signaled with swastika flags.

5. Shipwrecked soldiers of the light squadron "West" . . . which had been attacked and partly destroyed by British warships in the night of the 21–22 May, were shot at by the British. Soldiers swimming in the water with life vests or paddling their lifeboats were fired upon and many killed or wounded. . . .

From these investigations it appears that the mutilation of corpses and the maltreatment of soldiers were committed almost exclusively by Cretan civilians. In some cases survivors observed that civilians fell upon dead soldiers, robbed them, and cut them up with knives. In only one case were enemy soldiers involved in such acts; on the contrary, the British attached great importance to the proper treatment of prisoners of war, prevented abuses by Greek soldiers and civilians, and did all that was necessary in the medical field. On the other hand, the shooting of shipwrecked was carried out exclusively by British warships. It is difficult to determine how it was that the civilian population of Crete participated in the fighting and committed atrocities; the statements made by the Cretans and by the British prisoners must be taken *cum grano salis,* because they each tend to put the blame on the other.[6]

On the question of mutilations, Dr. Hellmuth Unger was called upon to evaluate the evidence. In a memorandum dated 19 June 1941 to Air Force Medical Inspector Hippke, Unger reported:

1. The head medical officer at the air force hospital in Saloniki knows of only one case of stab wounds, and this was a soldier who had numerous stab wounds in the throat, chest, and stomach. A woman is said to have inflicted the wounds. . . .

2. In the hospital at Athens there was supposed to be a large number of mutilated soldiers, yet upon questioning the doctors there we could not find a single case; the doctors knew in general that mutilations had taken place in Crete, but the mutilated had already died on the island.

3. On Crete itself: at Chania I received the first authentic statement through medical officer Dr. W. Roddewig . . . [who] himself had seen the mutilations and immediately photographed them. There were mutilated corpses from the battle of Castelli Kisano. It is reported that of the 57 parachutists who had landed there, 40 had been mutilated by stab wounds in the throat, chest, stomach; by amputation of the testicles; or by putting out the eyes. The entire material on these cases was given to intelligence officer Captain Mors. The remaining 17 men were spared such treatment because they were able to entrench themselves in a prison. . . . As reprisal for these atrocities Dr. Roddewig stated that 200 male residents of Castelli Kisano had been shot.

Judge Rüdel later commented on the statements of Dr. Roddewig that the numbers given were too high. He was not able to give me more precise information at the time, because the entire documentation had already been sent to Reichsmarshal Göring. Judge Rüdel summed up that according to his depositions six to eight cases had been established by the salvage corps in Castelli Kisano;[7] in other towns, fifteen other cases; near Rethymnon, three or four cases together. It could not be determined whether the mutilations were inflicted on the still living or only on the dead. None of those mutilated still lives. All explanations given on questioning indicate that no enemy soldiers were involved in the mutilations or defilement of corpses; bestialities are attributable exclusively to fanatical civilians. The fair fighting methods of the British and the New Zealanders were also duly noted by Judge Rüdel. . . .

4. On my flight back from Athens to Berlin I had the opportunity of speaking with two gravely wounded soldiers who had participated in the battles near Rethymnon. They were Corporal Harry Kurtz . . . and Sergeant Rudolf Greve. . . . Both soldiers stated that they were eyewitnesses of cases of torture and mutilation committed against German parachutists near Rethymnon and that they were prepared to give further information thereon.[8]

Eyewitness Reports

Concurrent with these sober investigations of what had actually happened in Crete, the German press launched a virulent campaign against the fighting methods of the British army and of the Cretan population, exaggerating both the number of the victims and the nature of the mutilations. Probably a considerable percentage of alleged cases of mutilation did not entail deliberate torture but resulted from hand-to-hand combat; the unusually high number of reports concerning the loss of eyes could similarly be explained in many cases by the mere fact that the corpses were found after decomposition had begun in the Mediterranean heat of late May.[9]

Still, some reports came from soldiers who were aware of this possibility. In a statement to Judge Oskar von Jagwitz on 29 July 1941, Corporal Friedrich Meyer asserted that "in the case of the body of the German parachutist lying on his back, I could clearly establish that his nose and both ears had been cut off and the eyes poked out. I observed this quite carefully. Such changes on the face could not be the result of decomposition, since the corpse was at most one day old."[10]

Moreover, a number of German soldiers stated under oath that they saw mutilations being carried out. On 11 June 1941 Judge Schölz obtained the following deposition from Corporal Erich Fiedler: "On 20 May 1941, shortly after we landed with our parachutes, we were taken prisoner by British soldiers, Greek soldiers, and civilians in the vicinity of Castelli. . . . I myself was wounded and lay under the body of a dead German sergeant. A civilian rolled over the body of the sergeant, took a knife out and stabbed him repeatedly. I saw with my own eyes how he cut the sergeant's eyes out. Once he missed, but then he struck in the middle of the eye, turned his knife two or three times inside the socket, and pulled it out. Then he did the same with the other eye."[11]

Only a limited number of mutilations could be subjected to forensic medical examination. One doctor called upon to examine suspicious injuries was Helmut Zänker, who stated in his deposition of 11 June 1941 before Judge Schölz: "In a number of cases the ears had been cut off. I also established cuts and gashes in the area of the nose. Both eyes of a soldier, I believe a lieutenant, had been put out. The eye sockets were completely empty and the edges had crusts of clotted blood. I have no doubt whatever that the stab wounds were inflicted after the men had fallen into enemy hands. The wounds were all in the same area of the chest or of the throat so that it is impossible that they would have been inflicted in exactly this fashion during combat."[12]

Since the German press was accusing British troops of committing atrocities, British General Bernard Freyberg ordered an investigation; the results, published in July of 1941, rejected all German accusations as unfounded.[13] Nevertheless, the records of the War Crimes Bureau do contain a number of sworn statements by German soldiers who claimed to have witnessed violations of the laws of war by British soldiers. Corporal Martin Premm testified before Judge Rüdel:

> Shortly after jumping over Crete on 20 May 1941 I came upon four wounded comrades who were attempting to bandage each other. In order to have better cover, I moved down to a ditch near the four men. From there I observed that three Cretan civilians with bayonets and a British soldier, also with a bayonet . . . stabbed the wounded soldiers repeatedly with the bayonets . . . for about five to ten minutes. The comrades cried out in pain. The British soldier, who had been observing the Cretans, took out a grenade and placed it in the middle of the German wounded and rushed away with the Cretans. After the grenade exploded, the four men continued moaning . . . until dark. . . . I could not assist them while they were being attacked, because I myself was out of ammunition. Of the four dead I knew Corporal Freitag and Private Martin, both of the 10th Storm Regiment. The crying and moaning ceased after I heard some shots in the area; I assume that the four were finished off by a British patrol.[14]

On 27 May 1941 Corporal Rudolf Dollenberg gave the following deposition to Judge von Jagwitz: "A comrade of another company, whom I did not know by name, was wounded in the chest. He lay some 70 meters away from me. I could clearly observe that he was alive. . . . Suddenly a New Zealand soldier rose and went up to the comrade, who remained lying on the ground and moaning. The New Zealander took the German's rifle away and smashed his head with the butt."[15]

On 31 May 1941 a soldier named Rudolf Bachmann stated before Judge Steiner: "I lay in a vineyard and was taken prisoner by the British. From a distance of 60 to 70 meters I saw that eight or ten British soldiers were occupied with a wounded German parachutist in a ditch. They removed his uniform. While the wounded soldier lay on the ground, a British soldier shot him with his pistol at short distance."[16]

On 28 May 1941 Judge Reinecke took the deposition of Corporal Hans Brück: "The British soldiers followed us and took Corporal H. prisoner. I succeeded in hiding so that they did not find me. At a distance of three to four meters I saw them press him to the ground and then shoot him in the mouth with a pistol."[17]

On the same day Judge Reinecke also obtained a deposition from Corporal Wilhelm Noh: "I observed from a distance of some 30 meters that a wounded parachutist cried out for help. Thereupon a British soldier wearing a British helmet came up to the wounded soldier, shot and killed him."[18]

From this brief selection of sworn eyewitness accounts, it is apparent that at least some British soldiers did commit war crimes on Crete. Still, it is not necessarily surprising that the British investigation in July did not confirm the German allegations, since many of the perpetrators themselves probably fell in battle or were taken prisoner by the Germans; nor is it probable that the British, Australian, and New Zealand soldiers who did manage to escape from Crete would have accused themselves of war crimes. Moreover, at the time of General Freyberg's inquiry the German depositions had not yet been communicated to the British government; precise information as to time, location, or the regiment involved in specific cases was not made available until the publication of the German white book in 1942.

The white book is silent, however, on the draconian measures of reprisal taken by the Germans on Crete. As early as 31 May 1941 the German commander-in-chief ordered reprisals—without, of course, any prior judicial determination of guilt of the persons executed. Göring, upon receiving copies of depositions concerning the killing and mutilation of parachutists, ordered that these crimes should be punished;[19] as a result, the villages of Skines, Prasses, and Kandamos were destroyed and the male population executed.[20]

Germany's surprise attack on the Soviet Union on 22 June 1941 opened a new and far more brutal phase of the war. Hitler had already given the so-called "Commissar Order," intended to deny prisoner-of-war status to commissars (special political officers integrated into the armed forces), and he had set the tone for the treatment of Russian soldiers by stating categorically to his generals that "the Russian soldier is no comrade."[1] He knew, of course, that the Soviet Union had not signed the Geneva Prisoner of War Convention of 1929, but, more importantly, he saw his Eastern neighbors as sub-humans and Stalin as a ruthless and determined adversary. Certainly, both sides anticipated a more barbarous struggle than that being waged in the West.

Atrocity reports were not long in coming: the Soviet Union accused the German Air Force of attacking Russian hospitals;[2] the War Crimes Bureau received a flood of reports, dating from 22 June on, describing the killing of German prisoners of war. Scouting patrols were especially hard hit, and many mutilated corpses were found by the troops that followed close behind. A number of mass shootings were reported in areas where the Russian troops had been flanked on both sides and had to retreat very fast in one direction, so that they chose not to take any prisoners and to shoot any that they already had.

The Massacre at Broniki

On the road from Klewan to Broniki in the Ukraine on 1 July 1941, some 180 German soldiers of the 2d Infantry Regiment 35 (motorized), 6th Infantry Regiment 119 (motorized), and 5th Artillery Regiment 60—mostly wounded men—were taken prisoner by the Russians. According to the report of Judge

Wilhelm Heinrich of the 25th Infantry Division, dated 2 July 1941, the bodies of 153 of them were found.[3] Beyond interrogating witnesses, Heinrich went to the field where the massacre had taken place and directed the investigations himself. Lieutenant Franz Kröning identified the bodies and in the course of a second search discovered twelve more corpses some 200 yards away from where the others had been found.[4]

But not all German soldiers who had been taken prisoner were killed; some had succeeded in fleeing to the woods when the massacre started. Judge Heinrich took the depositions of six survivors—one of them, Private Michael Beer, barely four hours after the shooting on 1 July: "Together with some 150 to 200 comrades who were not wounded or very lightly wounded I was taken to a clover field some 20 yards left of the road. Suddenly the Russians started shooting at us . . . after the first shots we dispersed. In spite of continuous fire from machine guns and automatic rifles I was able to escape down the ditch to the left of the road." Private Beer was also called upon to identify some of his dead comrades on 2 July, "since there was practically no one who knew them all. . . . We then buried them outside the church in Broniki."[5]

Another survivor, Corporal Karl Jäger testified before Judge Heinrich on 12 July 1941:

After being taken prisoner . . . other comrades and I were forced to undress. . . . We had to surrender all valuable objects including everything we had in our pockets. I saw other comrades stabbed with a bayonet because they were not fast enough. Corporal Kurz had a wounded hand and . . . could not remove his belt as quickly as desired. He was stabbed from behind at the neck so that the bayonet came out through the throat. A soldier who was severely wounded gave slight signs of life with his hands; he was kicked about and his head was battered with rifle butts. . . . Together with a group of 12 to 15 men I was taken to a spot north of the road. Several of them were completely naked. We were about the third group counting from the road. Behind us the Russians commenced the executions . . . panic broke out after the first shots, and I was able to flee.

Survivor Wilhelm Metzger, interrogated several months later by Judge Siebert, corroborated the description: "The Russians . . . grabbed everything we had, rings, watches, moneybag, uniform insignia, and then they took our coats, shirts, shoes, and socks . . . they started liquidating the various groups with machine-gun fire and hand grenades. I cannot describe what happened in detail, since I took advantage of the confusion to run away."[6]

One victim who could not flee was Private Hermann Heiss, who lay severely wounded in the field. He was almost dead when German soldiers found him on 2 July 1941 and took him to a field hospital. It was not until 26 November 1941 that a member of the War Crimes Bureau, Judge Lothar Schöne, could take his statement at a hospital in Beelitz-Heilstätten near Berlin: "My hands were tied up at my back . . . and we were forced to lie down. . . . a Russian soldier stabbed me in the chest with his bayonet. Thereupon I turned over. I was then stabbed seven times in the back and I did not move any more. The Russians evidently assumed that I was dead. . . . I heard my comrades cry out in pain. Then I passed out. The following morning I was found by German soldiers. I saw that the head of my comrade was split open. Most of the others were dead . . . [or] died later as a result of their wounds."[7]

In all, twelve survivors and witnesses of the Broniki massacre testified under oath before four different military judges,[8] enabling the Bureau to obtain an almost complete picture of what had happened. Similar reports coming in from other divisions gave rise to the suspicion that the Russians were not taking any prisoners of war, and the Bureau set itself the task of determining whether this practice responded to an order from the higher echelons of the Soviet Army.

Sources of Information

For the entire duration of the Russian campaign, reports of torture and execution of German prisoners did not cease. The War Crimes Bureau had five major sources of information: (1) captured enemy papers, especially orders, reports of operations, and propaganda leaflets; (2) intercepted radio and wireless messages; (3) testimony of Soviet prisoners of war;[9] (4) testimony of captured Germans who had escaped; and (5) testimony of Germans who saw the corpses or mutilated bodies of executed prisoners of war.

From 1941 to 1945 the Bureau compiled several thousand depositions, reports, and captured papers which, if nothing else, indicate that the killing of German prisoners of war upon capture or shortly after their interrogation was not an isolated occurrence.[10] Documents relating to the war in France, Italy, and North Africa contain some reports on the deliberate killing of German prisoners of war, but there can be no comparison with the events on the Eastern Front. On the other hand, it must be emphasized that the Russians did take prisoners: according to official reports, 175,000 Germans in 1941–42; 220,000 in 1943; 560,000 in 1944; and 2,200,000 in 1945 (these figures refer to Germans who were not immediately killed upon capture but sent on to POW camps; even so, their chances of survival were slim—as were those of Soviet prisoners of war in German camps).[11] Thus, one cannot speak of a uniform Soviet practice with respect to the German prisoners of war; some were luckier than others. It is with these reservations that one should approach the following selection from the documents of the War Crimes Bureau.

Among captured Soviet documents, was a report of Operations No. 11 of the staff of the Soviet 26th Division, one kilometer west of Slastjena, dated 13 July 1941, 10:00 A.M.: "The enemy left approximately 400 dead on the battlefield. Some 80 Germans had surrendered and were executed."[12]

A captured report of the commander of a Soviet company, Captain Gediejew, dated 30 August 1941: "Three minethrowers, one officer killed, three P.T. guns, four machine guns, 15 wounded men shot."[13]

In the notes of a Soviet medical officer, B.J., who was taken prisoner: "All prisoners of war who had belonged to the German Army were executed during the operations near Odessa. . . . In the course of the fierce resistance of the Red Army . . . from 4 to 6 November 1941 a small group of Germans was taken prisoner. They were all shot. . . . Near Sevastopol no prisoners were taken. More precisely: prisoners were executed."[14]

The diary entry of a fallen officer of the 61st Cavalry Regiment for 24 December 1941: "The second squadron took three Fritzes—probably incendiaries. Two of them were killed without interrogation; one was sent under guard of two men to the Division staff. His fate was, however, the same."[15]

From the diary of an engineer named Andrejev, who fell near Sevastopol in June 1942: "In a village near Bija Sala the German prisoners were shot. A young fellow was in charge of the executions, and he went about asking who should do the shootings. An older soldier . . . asked for a machine gun, shouted: 'For my family, for my son, for my mother,' and mowed all of them down."[16]

In a battle report of the 109th Armored Brigade, dated 2 July 1942: "From the crews of two German tanks we took two prisoners. We liquidated the other Hitlerites."[17]

Excerpts from reports of the Partisan Group Polk 13, which were seized by the Germans in October 1943: "Losses among enemy prisoners: 13 policemen and two Germans who were burned in a stable" (5 August 1943); "During our raid on the police at Rjassny we killed six Germans and took one prisoner, who was shot after interrogation" (7 August 1943); "On 7 October a German supply column was ambushed. A cavalryman who accompanied the supply column was captured and later shot" (8 October 1943).[18]

From the Bureau's extensive documentation on intercepted Soviet radio and wireless messages, the following illustrations are representative. On 6 September 1942: "The three men will now be shot. . . . I still need the Fritz F. He should now show me the ditch and the positions. That means we have to wait with this one."[19]

On 7 July 1943: "The enemy suffered great losses. We captured 13 enemy machine guns and turned them on the enemy. . . . We did not take any prisoners. . . . They were all liquidated."[20]

On 17 March 1944: "Do you have any prisoners there?—Yes, two men. I shall interrogate them. . . . I forbid you to shoot them, because I want to see them first. The rest we can take care of here just as well." "We took prisoners belonging to the 4th Mountain Infantry Division, Regiment 13, Company 9. . . . You know what we did with them. They will never come to you." "Yesterday you sent me twelve men. The guards had to go back, so I had the prisoners shot."[21]

Soviet Justification for the Killings

Captured Soviet documents and the testimony of many witnesses provide a wide spectrum of explanations for the frequent liquidation of German prisoners of war.

1. German soldiers who did not surrender: "A sharp distinction is made between soldiers who surrender and those who fall in Soviet hands after battle. The former are treated well; the latter may be immediately shot without an order."[22] "Lieutenant Karpenko officially ordered that every German soldier taken prisoner while still carrying a weapon should be immediately shot. Only such German soldiers will be sent to the rear who voluntarily desert to our side."[23]

2. Wounded soldiers: "A gravely wounded soldier was captured, but on the way the older Sergeant Kabulow killed him with his bayonet because he

was seriously wounded."[24] "Why should we bother to carry him—his hands and feet are frozen."[25]

3. Neither means nor time to transport the prisoners: "Twenty kilometers west of Storozyninc in the Bukovina . . . some 300 to 400 Romanian prisoners of war, including a number of German officers and noncommissioned officers, were shot on orders of the Regiment Commander, Major Ssawelin, primarily because . . . we had no way of transporting them, and he did not want to be burdened with them."[26] "As soon as the enemy opens fire, shock troops must immediately withdraw and take the prisoners along. If it is not possible to take the prisoners, they must be liquidated."[27] "I had the German prisoners of war shot because I did not have the time to interrogate them."[28]

4. Prisoners who refused to give military information: "We did not succeed in making the third soldier talk. We had to shoot him."[29] "Those soldiers who talked were sent to the rear; those who didn't were shot near the place where they were captured."[30]

5. Insufficient food: "When I spoke to Gribow about it, he admitted the killing and commented: 'Do you want us to feed the prisoners with bread while the Germans kill our prisoners?' The same day and place, two more German prisoners of war were shot under orders of the same *Politruk*."[31]

6. Nazis and officers: "Party members were executed whether officers or soldiers."[32] "While I was in the Soviet Army I heard from the commissars that we should not capture fascists but liquidate them on the spot."[33] "The commissar mentioned that every German officer was shot after interrogation."[34] "In the 29th Armored Division . . . we had an order from the Army High Command that senior German officers captured at the front should be sent back for interrogation, while junior officers should be shot because they are supposed to be more loyal to Hitler."[35]

7. Rewards for high casualty figures: "We have a division order according to which every Red Army soldier who shoots twenty German soldiers gets a three-day vacation at home . . . the order of the day is: kill more German soldiers; that is the basis for our victory."[36] "Red Army soldiers must enter a written commitment to kill several Germans in battle. The commissars keep records in small books . . . those who can claim many killings are raised in rank or decorated."[37]

Clearly, the German aggression against the Soviet Union was met with vehement cruelty; captured Soviet documents and intercepted radio messages largely confirm and strengthen the testimony of German and Soviet witnesses. The foregoing statements, only a few of the thousands compiled by the War Crimes Bureau, justify the conclusion that they cannot all be dismissed as exaggeration. Nor can they be simply explained as reprisals for German atrocities (although the latter undoubtedly account for many instances): similar incidents occurred throughout the entire Eastern Theater of war and commenced immediately upon the outbreak of hostilities.

Soviet War Propaganda versus Official Guidelines
In order to understand the atmosphere in which such treatment of German prisoners of war was possible, it is necessary to keep in mind the crimes committed by the SS *Einsatzgruppen* (task force) and the great hardships imposed on the Soviet population by the German occupation. In addition, Soviet war propaganda was designed to instill fanaticism in the Red Army troops and incite them to annihilate the German enemy without mercy. A leaflet that circulated in areas already occupied by the Germans admonished the Soviet civilian population to "obtain weapons and rise against the Germans, destroy them to the very last man. Wreak vengeance upon the German-fascist scoundrels. Take revenge for the raping of your wives. Avenge the torture committed on the people. Avenge the destruction of your cities and villages. Take revenge for everything. Blood for blood. Death for death."[38] Another, intended for the Soviet population of the Leningrad and Talin districts, was found on 25 March 1942: "The officers and soldiers in the green coats are not human but wild animals. . . . destroy German officers and soldiers as you kill mad dogs."[39]

Many Soviet authors'turned from literary production to violent propaganda. Among these, Ilya Ehrenburg was one of the most prolific; he wrote for the front newspaper "Red Star" and produced many political leaflets. In one of these, captured in large numbers on 9 September 1942 by the 4th German Armored Army, the last paragraph reads as follows:

> The Germans are not human beings. Henceforth the word German means to us the most terrible curse. From now on the word German will trigger your rifle. We shall not speak any more. We shall not get excited. We shall kill. If you have not killed at least one German a day, you have wasted that day. . . . If you cannot kill your German with a bullet, kill

him with your bayonet. If there is calm on your part of the front, or if you are waiting for the fighting, kill a German before combat.[40] If you leave a German alive, the German will hang a Russian and rape a Russian woman. If you kill one German, kill another—there is nothing more amusing for us than a heap of German corpses. Do not count days; do not count miles. Count only the number of Germans you have killed. Kill the German—this is your old mother's prayer. Kill the German— this is what your children beseech you to do. Kill the German—this is the cry of your Russian earth. Do not waver. Do not let up. Kill.[41]

In sharp contrast to Ehrenburg's propaganda, the Resolution of the Commissars of the U.S.S.R. of 1 July 1941—a copy of which was captured by the German Army in August of 1941—prohibits (a) insulting or maltreating prisoners of war; (b) employing force or threats to obtain information; (c) robbing prisoners of parts of their uniforms, clothing, shoes, personal items, documents, or medals and decorations. Special regulations pertaining to this decree were to be explained to the prisoners of war in a language they could understand; all rules and orders applying to them were to be posted on bulletin boards where prisoners could read them.[42]

As illustrated above, however, Soviet military records, intercepted radio messages, and the testimony of countless Soviet prisoners of war indicate that Soviet commissars and soldiers largely ignored this resolution. Moreover, certain captured documents show that higher Soviet authorities knew the resolution was not being followed. One finds, for instance, many orders prohibiting the practice of killing prisoners before they could be sent to the rear for interrogation. In September of 1941 two such documents were taken in the area occupied by the German 2d Army.

The first is a communication of the central office for political propaganda of the Soviet 5th Army, dated 30 June 1941, addressed to commanders and chiefs of political propaganda and signed by Major General M. I. Potapov, commander-in-chief of the 5th Army:

It has frequently occurred that Red Army soldiers and commanders, embittered by the cruelties of the fascist thieves . . . do not take any German soldiers and officers prisoner but shoot them on the spot. As a consequence of this practice it is difficult for the leadership to determine enemy formations, the political and moral state of the German Army. . . . At the same time this practice is bad from the political point of view, since our task consists in inducing the German soldier to desert to the Red Army. If they find out that prisoners are shot, the influx of deserters stops. I therefore order: (1) It must be made plausible to all fighters and commanders that killing captured soldiers and officers is detrimental to our interests; prisoners must be sent to the rear without delay so that they may be processed. (2) I categorically forbid shootings on individual initiative.[43]

The second document, dated 14 July 1941, originates from the Soviet 31st Corps and is directed to all chiefs of counterintelligence and all deputy commanders responsible for political matters. It bears the signature of the chief of the propaganda department of the 31st Corps, Commissar Ivantschenko:

At this time of struggle one recognizes in the party political work . . . politically damaging and even criminal deficiencies. . . . Red Army soldiers and commanders do not capture enemy soldiers and officers. . . . prisoners have been strangled or stabbed to death. Such behavior toward prisoners of war is politically damaging to the Red Army; it embitters the soldiers of the fascist army; it hinders the process of disintegration; it gives the officers of the fascist army evidence with which they can lie to their soldiers about the "horror" of imprisonment by the Red Army and thus strengthens their will to fight. . . . every means of political persuasion [must] be used to explain to all units that such behavior toward the prisoners of war is unworthy of the Red Army and very damaging. To make clear that the German soldier—worker and farmer—does not fight voluntarily; that the German soldier, when he is captured, ceases to be an enemy. To take every measure necessary to capture soldiers and especially officers.[44]

Similar orders were issued on 28 December 1941 by the commander of the 168th Cavalry Regiment, Colonel Pankratow: "There have been a number of cases lately in which officers have failed to deliver to the regiment's staff German fascist prisoners of war, who have been liquidated on the spot, so that we have lost the opportunity of learning about the condition of the enemy. I order: All prisoners of war shall be delivered to the regiment's staff under the personal responsibility of the chiefs of departments and of the political officers."[45]

Significantly, most orders prohibiting the execution of prisoners of war prior to interrogation say nothing about what to do with the prisoners after interrogation. One decree, however, having specified that "captured enemy soldiers and officers must be sent to the higher staffs for interrogation," went on to say: "The fighting men and officers must know that the enemy will not be spared anywhere . . . but for the sake of the war effort we need prisoners of war, and therefore we must take them. We will have plenty of time to deal with them. None of the intruders will leave our country alive."[46]

As the war continued, there were other good reasons not to kill prisoners besides the hope of extracting military information. As one Soviet prisoner stated in December 1942, "Our officers forbade our killing of German prisoners of war as was frequently done last winter. We urgently need their labor."[47] Apparently about this time the leadership of the Soviet Army decided to clamp down on unauthorized lynchings. On 8 March 1943 a captured Soviet lieutenant stated: "Lieutenant General Below, commander-in-chief of the 61st Army, following an order of Army General Zhukov, ordered that German prisoners of war should no longer be shot."[48]

A number of captured documents indicate that an effort was made at various levels of the Soviet Army to stop the widespread killing of prisoners by threatening disciplinary action against the responsible officers. On 27 March 1942 all commanders and commissars of the 17th Division were informed of a decision of the Army War Council following an incident in which, "in spite of the fact that the military situation did not hinder the delivery of the soldier to the regiment staff [for interrogation], platoon commander Kudriavzeff took this soldier some 300 to 400 meters away from the place where he had been captured and shot him. By this act he violated the order of the People's Commissars for Defense of the U.S.S.R. and of the Army War Council. The Army War Council has instituted court-martial proceedings against platoon commander Lieutenant Kudriavzeff and emphasizes that similar cases will be prosecuted in the future. This order shall be communicated to all platoon commanders."[49]

The files of the German War Crimes Bureau cannot, of course, provide a full picture of the practice of Soviet courts-martial, but it appears that such efforts did not have much success: Bureau documents indicate that the killing of captured Germans continued unabated through the years 1943–45, however much Soviet policy on the highest level may have disapproved.

Responsibility for the Killings

While it is not easy to establish the degree of knowledge and of responsibility of the higher echelons of the Soviet Army, it was the testimony of countless Soviet prisoners of war that most of the shootings of German POWs were ordered by commissars and lower-rank officers. On 27 November 1941 several Soviet prisoners declared: "The *Politruk* of the ninth company ordered that all Germans were to be killed and no prisoners taken. He repeated this order in front of the assembled company."[50] On 19 January 1942 Lieutenant Vassili Kisilov wrote a statement in his native Ukrainian: "The regiment's commissar ordered that no prisoners be made; all Germans must be killed. None may stay alive."[51]

On 23 August 1942 a Sergeant A.K. accused his commissar of killing German prisoners of war after interrogating them: he "ordered some 150 Russian soldiers present to fall in and then delivered a speech . . . 'You must remember that you will be executed if you fall into German hands. The Germans are men of the lowest class. They fight against Stalin.' At this point the commissar drew his pistol and shot the German corporal and the older soldier."[52] On 17 July 1942, when Sergeant P.S. similarly accused his commissar, Nikolai Nedostupov, also a prisoner of war, Nedostupov was confronted with the allegations. He admitted that he gave the order to take no prisoners when they were attacking and that he condoned the maltreatment of German wounded and prisoners: "I know that I went beyond the order of our army leadership, which only requires us to kill prisoners if we cannot transport them."[53] On 9 December 1942 another prisoner, Lieutenant A.O., stated that "Germans [who] were captured while no officers were around . . . were immediately shot. Officers, however, took care that they were sent to the rear. Most commissars order in all cases that they be shot."[54]

Lieutenant M.S. reported the shooting of forty-six German prisoners of war, including four officers, without prior interrogation: "The Regiment Commander of the 123rd Infantry Regiment of the 22nd Infantry Division, Major Ivan Alexandovitch Kulikov, and the regiment's commissar August Otmichalski both gave the execution order. Other Russian officers in the area who expressed their indignation . . . were depicted as traitors by Otmichalski and threatened with being shot themselves."[55] The statement of another Soviet officer, Major K., appears to reinforce the case against the commissars: "The regiment commanders must deliver prisoners of war to the division, the division to the corps, the corps to the OGPU. . . . But in practice . . . when prisoners are on their way to the battalion or to the regiment, most commissars order that they be shot . . . politically ambitious company leaders also have them shot on their own initiative. The OGPU interrogates the prisoners about their political views. Those who are sympathetic to Communism are treated well. Whoever expresses 'fascist' or 'capitalist' ideas is immediately shot. . . . An order to kill German prisoners of war has never been given by higher military authority. But no officer is in a position to prohibit a commissar from giving [such] instructions."[56]

All these and other statements seem to establish the responsibility of the commissars. But many Soviet officers on various levels similarly ordered or at least condoned the killings. For example, Captain W.P. testified on 21 October 1941 that "every Russian officer on the front knew that parachutists were liquidated by a special unit of the NKVD."[57] And a Soviet colonel, on 21 February 1942, related that "five soldiers of the NKVD carried out the execution [of a German pilot] in the presence of the commander-in-chief of the 3rd Army. . . . The general was the senior officer among [those] who were there at the time."[58]

The Alleged "Stalin Order"

The question arises whether Soviet commissars were acting exclusively on their own initiative or with Stalin's tacit or express approval. Witness testimony collected by the War Crimes Bureau indicates that commissars frequently quoted Stalin to justify the killings—although this does not necessarily mean that Stalin in fact knew how he was being quoted.[59] On 22 December 1941 a Soviet prisoner of war stated: "Sometime between 4 and 8 December 1941 . . . our platoon commander read us an order from Stalin according to which . . . all German prisoners of war and all captured German wounded should be shot immediately."[60] A Soviet propaganda leaflet found by the German 16th Army in December 1941 ends with a quotation from Stalin printed in big letters: "The Germans must be killed to the last man; they have fallen into our homeland as occupiers. No mercy to the German occupiers. Death to the German occupiers."[61] Alfred Frauenfeld, representative of the Foreign Office (VAA) at the High Command of the 16th Army sent these and various intelligence reports to Berlin on 11 January 1942, confirming the general impression that German prisoners of war were being liquidated on Stalin's orders.

On 18 January 1942 four Soviet prisoners of war gave a sworn statement to the interrogating German judge: "From 6 November 1941 our *Politruk* repeated every day at roll call that Stalin had ordered in his radio speech of 6 November 1941 that all Germans found on Russian soil, regardless whether they are *Volksdeutsche* or captured German soldiers, were to be liquidated to the last man. We were instructed to act accordingly."[62] Another Soviet prisoner asserted on 25 January 1942 that "every Russian soldier received a mimeographed Stalin Order in which harshest treatment of the Germans was specifically demanded. According to this order every German soldier was to be liquidated."[63] On 26 November 1942 Sergeant P., a captured member of a Soviet penal unit, also maintained that "the guiding principle was Stalin's word from November 1941: 'Extermination of the Hitler generation.'"[64]

Contrary to the impression given by the foregoing statements, other witnesses testified that the process was more selective. On 16 April 1942 Commissar A.L. declared under oath: "The standard for dealing with German prisoners of war in the Red Army is Stalin's order of November 1941, according to which all prisoners of war who fight to the end or who are captured with the weapon in their hands are to be shot. Only deserters are sent to the rear as prisoners."[65] On 12 January 1943 the intelligence department of the Center Army Group reported: "Soviet deserters have stated . . . [that] there is a Stalin order according to which every German soldier who is captured while fighting is to be shot. Only deserters are excluded from this rule. German soldiers with decorations are seen as great criminals, since they could only have received their decorations by killing very many Russians."[66] And on 2 January 1943 the Soviet prisoner of war Captain K.K., interrogated by Judge Schlitt, cited "a Stalin order, I believe from January or February 1942, according to which prisoners who put up resistance upon capture are to be shot. I do not know of any other Stalin order."[67] A German intelligence report of 10 August 1943, however, stated that under "a new secret order of Stalin," prisoners "waste too much time when they turn up individually. Only groups of more than ten prisoners should be sent to the interrogating organs. This instruction should be given from man to man and not to the assembled troop."[68]

Despite all this testimony, the Bureau's files contain still other depositions of Soviet prisoners of war who had never heard of any such Stalin order and who attributed the killings to independent action by the commissars: "Officers and commissars accuse each other of giving such orders."[69] According to the results of intensive questioning of numerous Soviet prisoners of war at Krzemieniec in July 1941:

> No general order has been given to kill all German officers, noncommissioned officers, and men upon capture. The shooting and torturing to death of German soldiers are explained by captured Soviet soldiers, commissars, officers, and doctors as stemming from individual or special orders given to the troops by commissars or officers or both. A junior commissar stated that such orders are given primarily by battalion and regimental commanders to whom the commissars are accountable. . . . Officers and two doctors allege that the orders discussed are given exclusively by the political commissar. These contradictions cannot be resolved, although the junior commissar was threatened with execution should it be established that he lied. In support of his allegation he referred to secret orders given to the commanders which he as junior commissar was not allowed to see.[70]

Even on 19 December 1941—*after* the alleged Stalin order of November 1941—the intelligence department of the 54th Army Corps communicated to Berlin the testimony of a Soviet lieutenant that "German prisoners are liquidated by commissars and members of the NKVD. He does not know of any order not to take any more prisoners."[71] Then, on 20 May 1942, the intelligence department of prisoner-of-war camp No. 240 transmitted to the Bureau the testimony of a Soviet captain who claimed that "according to a Stalin order of February 1942 no more prisoners should be killed, and they ought to be treated well."[72] And on 13 December 1942 a Soviet sergeant testified: "There is indeed an order of Stalin according to which prisoners of war may not be shot. But this order is secret and has not been circulated. There are certain exceptions, for instance, that fliers should all be killed as well as those who resist. By resistance is meant resistance during actual battle and not resistance after imprisonment. National Socialists are also liquidated."[73]

On 7 April 1943 the intelligence department of the 57th Infantry Division reported a Soviet deserter's statement that in mid-May of 1942 "a new Stalin order was read according to which the killing of prisoners of war was strictly forbidden. The main reason for this measure was lack of labor. At present rewards are being given for bringing in prisoners."[74]

Many Soviet prisoners of war, of course, were never asked whether they knew of any general order with regard to the treatment of captured Germans; the bulk of the Soviet depositions simply describe the killing of German POWs, and in those cases in which responsibility was clearly established, it appears that the orders came from Soviet officers or commissars. The documents contained in the War Crimes Bureau's files do not definitively answer the question of whether these Soviet officers were acting on their own account or pursuant to a general order from Stalin.

Perhaps the following explanation given by a Soviet prisoner of war comes closest to the truth: on 22 December 1941 the intelligence department of the 54th Army Corps reported that a Russian lieutenant "knows of a Stalin order issued about two months ago, according to which all occupiers are to be destroyed. This order has been interpreted in various ways. He himself understands it to mean that as many Germans as possible must be killed in battle but that the order has no application to prisoners, whether wounded or not. There are, however, other soldiers . . . of the opinion that precisely on the basis of this order it is imperative to liquidate the wounded, since these cannot work and have no utility whatever."[75]

If there were an absolutely authentic text of Stalin's speeches of 6 and 7 November 1941, there might be a clear answer to the question of whether Stalin did in fact issue a special order to liquidate German prisoners of war. The official Soviet text available today may not be complete[76]—or, of course, such an order could have been given orally and passed down through the network of political commissars. No contemporary captured Russian text of the speeches, no orders or propaganda leaflets citing excerpts of the speeches are to be found in the existing records of the War Crimes Bureau. The similarly incomplete files of the German Foreign Office indicate that in March 1942 the German 11th Army found a Russian brochure that was transmitted to the Foreign Office by its liaison officer, Werner Otto von Hentig. According to Hentig's transmittal note, the brochure contained the text of Stalin's report at the solemn meeting to celebrate the Russian Revolution, held in Moscow on 6 November 1941, and also the text of Stalin's speech of 7 November 1941 at Red Square after the Red Army parade.[77] Unfortunately, the brochure itself is missing from the files.

A passage from the speech of 6 November is quoted in a Foreign Office white book, "Bolshevist Crimes against the Laws of War and against Humanity": "Henceforth our task and the task of the People of the Soviet Union, the troops, the commanders, the political commissars of the Red

Army and the Red Navy, is to kill every German to the very last man. No mercy for the German intruders. Death to the German Occupiers."[78] But this particular passage is not included in the edition of Stalin's speeches published in the Soviet Union in 1967. The volume does include the following slightly less virulent appeals: "Now, we must achieve these goals, we must destroy the German war machine, we must annihilate the German occupiers to the last man" (6 November), and "To the total destruction of the German invaders. Death to the German occupiers" (closing words, 7 November).[79]

Obviously, such general appeals are subject to different interpretations; it cannot be said that they are equivalent to an order to kill German prisoners of war, even if broad interpretations led in practice to the slaughter of many thousands. It has been suggested that Stalin may have issued such an order on some other occasion, since various Soviet prisoners testified to the existence of secret orders to the commissars. But no such order or secret instruction can be established on the basis of the records of the War Crimes Bureau.

German Interpretations

Even in the absence of absolute proof of the existence of a Stalin order to that effect, the unpublished, internal remarks of the staff of the German Foreign Office show their genuine conviction that the Red Army was pursuing a policy of exterminating German POWs. This belief was based on the mosaic of captured Soviet documents, intercepted radio messages, and, principally, the statements made by Soviet prisoners of war. For example, the liaison officer of the German Foreign Office at the High Command of the Army observed in a transmittal note to the Foreign Office: "Enclosed please find several captured Russian papers which illustrate the methods of the Russian military in dealing with German prisoners of war. They prove once again that it is customary for the Soviets to liquidate German prisoners of war immediately after interrogation."[80]

On 28 August 1941 the liaison officer at the operational command of the German Air Force reported to the Foreign Office: "Soviet prisoners of war of the 40th Army Corps stated that all German officers taken prisoner were executed, since on the German side the Soviet political commissars were also shot."[81] Referring to the same report on 15 September 1941, the Wehrmacht operations staff replied to an inquiry from the German Foreign Office: "It is evident that the Soviets from the very first day of the war and throughout the front have been murdering the Germans in brutal fashion. The allegation that on the German side Soviet commissars who have been taken prisoner have been executed can only be understood as a belated pretext or excuse. Accordingly, there are no conclusions to be drawn."[82]

The same general opinion can be read again and again in the internal notes and observations of the War Crimes Bureau. In November of 1941 the Bureau's report "War Crimes of the Russian Army" contained a selection of the cases collected and evaluated. In the preface Johannes Goldsche wrote:

> The Soviet Union has . . . from the first day of the war employed a ter-
> ror policy, already characteristic of its brutal domestic practices, against
> defenseless German soldiers that have fallen into its hands and against
> members of the German medical corps. At the same time—apparently
> with the intention of masking its real conduct—it has made use of the
> following means of camouflage: in a Red Army order that bears the ap-
> proval of the Council of the People's Commissars, dated 1 July 1941, the
> norms of international law are made public, which the Red Army in the
> spirit of the Hague Regulations on Land Warfare are supposed to fol-
> low. . . . This . . . Russian order probably had very little distribution, and
> surely it has not been followed at all. Otherwise the unspeakable crimes
> would not have occurred.[83]

The Bureau's second report on Soviet crimes, dated March 1942, evaluated several hundred additional depositions of Soviet prisoners of war and numerous captured Soviet papers.

Bureau members, who of course knew of Hitler's criminal and controversial Commissar Order, debated whether the widespread Soviet liquidation of German prisoners could be seen as a kind of reprisal for Hitler's order to deny prisoner-of-war status to Soviet political officers.[84] Yet in an internal paper they expressed the view that the Soviet policy could not be interpreted as retaliation, "because the evidence presented unequivocally establishes that Soviet atrocities occurred in the same manner and at the same time in all the sections of the front and from the first day of combat." Further, in evaluating captured Soviet papers stipulating that German prisoners of war should not be executed, or should no longer be executed, the Bureau noted that these documents "do not manifest the least concern for treatment of German prisoners of war in a manner compatible with international law, but rather and exclusively they manifest the interest of staff headquarters to obtain intelligence information and their need to interrogate prisoners of war about enemy formation and other important military questions."[85] These and other memoranda and correspondence with the operations staff and the Foreign Office clearly show the conviction of Bureau members that Stalin was personally responsible for the killing of German prisoners of war, through either a general order or secret instructions to the political commissars.

Whether their belief was correct cannot be conclusively determined even today, but in any consideration of the question, certain remarks made by Stalin himself should not be dismissed out of hand. At the Teheran Conference in December 1943, according to Winston Churchill, "he said there were many toilers in the German divisions who fought under orders. When he asked German prisoners who came from the laboring classes . . . why they fought for Hitler, they replied that they were carrying out orders. He shot such prisoners."[86] Such a comment is no proof of a general policy, of course, but it does suggest a certain mentality, a certain atmosphere in which subordinate commissars and officers could assume their leader's tacit approval of the widespread killing of prisoners of war.

Stalin made a similar remark to Milovan Djilas in April 1945 when Djilas protested the behavior of Red Army soldiers in occupied ("liberated") Yugoslavia. "You have imagined the Red Army to be ideal," Stalin replied, "and it is not ideal, nor can it be, even if it did not contain a certain percentage of criminals—we opened up our penitentiaries and stuck everybody into the army. The Red Army is not ideal. The important thing is that it fights Germans—and it is fighting them well, while the rest does not matter."[87]

Thus, when the Red Army entered the Reich in October 1944, it was the civilian population of East Prussia that had to endure the lack of discipline and lust for revenge of Soviet soldiers. When the German Army temporarily took back the towns of Goldap, Gumbinnen and Nummersdorf, they discovered that hundreds of German civilians had been slaughtered and most of the women raped.[88] As Alexander Solzhenitsyn, then a young captain in the Red Army, recalls: "All of us knew very well that if the girls were German they could be raped and then shot. This was almost a combat distinction."[89]

Investigations of the killing of German prisoners of war in the Soviet Union became a matter of macabre routine for the War Crimes Bureau, but a few cases stood out because of the number of victims involved or the needless cruelty demonstrated. One such case was the December 1941 killing of some 160 German wounded who had been convalescing at a hospital in the city of Feodosia on the shore of the Black Sea.

Part of the documentation compiled by the Bureau is found in "Violations of the Laws of War by the Red Army," a report prepared in March 1942.[1] A year later, in February 1943, according to numerous notes and references in the Bureau's files, a special dossier on Feodosia was completed.[2] Unfortunately, this dossier appears to have been lost, but because transcripts of the depositions and copies of the reports do survive in other record groups, it is possible to reconstruct the events and compare numerous corroborating accounts from both German and Soviet witnesses.[3]

Feodosia, a port town on the Crimean peninsula, was captured by the German 46th and 170th Infantry Divisions on 3 November 1941. A few weeks later, however, Field Marshal Erich von Manstein, commander-in-chief of the 11th Army, withdrew most of the German forces in order to concentrate on the attack on Sevastopol, leaving behind only a minimum of troops and, of course, the wounded and incapacitated. On 29 December 1941, following maritime bombardment by the Soviet Black Sea Fleet, the town was overrun by Soviet forces, and the remainder of the German 46th Infantry Division was hurriedly evacuated. The fate of the 160 wounded Germans in Feodosia hospitals was learned only gradually.

On 3 January 1942 two German soldiers were interrogated about their knowledge of the Feodosia events. Corporal Heinz Splettströsser could give only hearsay information from "a comrade from coast artillery": "On the afternoon of 29 December 1941 he had observed that a Soviet truck full of wounded Soviet soldiers stopped outside the field hospital. Shortly thereafter he saw that wounded German soldiers were thrown out of the windows of the hospital by the Russian soldiers." Radio operator Georg Radke, who like Splettströsser was not an eyewitness, reported that a German soldier who had succeeded in escaping from Feodosia had allegedly seen the corpses of many German soldiers outside the Feodosia field hospital.[4]

The order of the day issued by the High Command of the German 11th Army on 14 January 1942 based itself on these and other reports: "The wounded and sick were evacuated from Feodosia with the exception of those who were not in a condition to be transported. With them remained a medical doctor and six medical assistants of the 715th Medical Corps. We must be prepared to learn of their heroic death."[5]

Although the 11th Army failed to take Sevastopol in December 1941 or even January 1942 (Sevastopol did not surrender until 1 July 1942), German forces were able to push back into the Kerch peninsula and to recapture Feodosia on 18 January 1942. There, soldiers of the 105th Infantry Regiment found the corpses of the wounded soldiers who had been left behind: most of them lay at the bottom of an embankment, having apparently been thrown down from a wall several meters high; others were buried or lay scattered on the frozen Black Sea beach, where evidently some of the wounded had been carried and left to freeze to death. The scene of these bodies covered with a sheet of ice was photographed by German Army cameramen and sent to the War Crimes Bureau as documentation.[6]

The German army judges in the area were so shocked that they proceeded to take the sworn testimony of witnesses without waiting for a specific request from the Bureau. On 25 January 1942 Judge Heinrich Fuchs obtained the deposition of a civilian Russian doctor, Jiri Dimitrijew. Soviet marines, he said, were the first to arrive, "later followed by infantrymen. The marines moved about the town in a state of complete drunkenness; already on the first day they came to the hospital across from the Palace and shot the German wounded convalescing there, some 30 to 35 German soldiers. . . . On the third day, that is, on 1 January 1942, a general order was issued that all Germans found in the liberated areas were to be liquidated. The commisars and NKVD officials entrusted this task to special details, who then went to the other hospitals. . . . There were about 60 wounded Germans in the city hospital, 25 in the palace hospital, and 30 to 40 in the technical building. In all, I estimate that about 160 Germans were executed during the period when Feodosia was reoccupied by the Russians."[7]

On 30 January 1942 Judge Fuchs took the deposition of a Crimean laborer, Konstantin Bursud, who had been employed as a male nurse: "I first hid in a cellar . . . since I feared that [the Russians] would shoot me as they shot all other Crimeans who had cooperated with the Germans. I could observe very little from my hiding place. On the first day of the Russian landing I saw primarily a special group of Red Navy marines who were finishing off about a dozen German wounded with axes and bayonets; this was at the square behind the hospital. . . . I can further report that the [marines] went about congratulating themselves on having thrown German wounded out of the windows of the hospital and then pouring water on them so that they would freeze."[8]

Another German judge, Walther Wilhelm, took the deposition of a German lieutenant, Hans Friedrich Döring, on 31 January 1942: "The corpses of some 50 German soldiers lie in two large rooms of the former German hospital. . . . Some of them still have their red hospital tags; on some . . . you can see that a leg was amputated. All the bodies are horribly mutilated. . . . immediately outside the hospital, to the right of the main entrance, there is a niche in the wall . . . and there lie the corpses of a number of German soldiers, some of them naked, others wearing only a shirt. The corpses are precisely next to each other in rows . . . covered by a sheet of ice. Evidently, the wounded soldiers were first carried there and then drenched with water so that they froze to death. On this group of corpses there were no mutilations like those mentioned above."[9]

Judge Günther Jahn took the deposition of a German doctor who had been evacuated from the Feodosia hospital and had returned three weeks later. On 2 February 1942 Dr. Rudolf Burkhardt testified:

I had heard that there was a big mound on the beach. I went there and saw a hand in a splint sticking out. Accordingly, I ordered that the mound be opened. After removing a few inches of sand, we discovered layers of corpses piled up underneath. According to what we had heard from the Crimean population, there should have been about 55 bodies, and this turned out to be the case. The next day I had the bodies taken out of the mound, and I was able to establish that these were the bodies of the seriously wounded from my hospital. I was able to identify a number of the bodies by their combat injuries. Most of the corpses still had splints or plaster dressings. . . . I was not able to establish whether the wounded soldiers had been exposed to water while they were still alive, since the condition of "wash skin" may also occur if a fresh corpse is drenched in water. . . . I did conclude that the wounded soldiers had been brought out on the beach while they were still alive, since upon examination I could determine first-, second-, and third-degree frost injuries on the uncovered parts of the body, which were most exposed to the cold. Frost injuries of this type do not occur on corpses. . . . The plaster dressings were broken in some cases, and blood and pus had issued from the cracks . . . again, my conclusion is that the wounded were still alive when their splints were broken. . . . About 50 meters from the mound I saw a corpse partly covered with sand that had blown over it; 10 meters farther I saw another corpse, this one enveloped in a sheet of ice because the surf had broken over it. . . . In a Russian cemetery the bodies of more than 100 German soldiers were found, which were taken to a house where I examined them. Among them were about 60 who had been treated for combat injuries, as evidenced by the splints and dressings. Clear signs on these 100 corpses justify the conclusion that the men were killed by blows with blunt instruments.[10]

Still a fourth German judge, Friedrich Lungwitz, took the deposition of a Russian male nurse, Assan Kalafatov, who had worked in the German hospital in Feodosia. On 14 February 1942 he testified: "Right after the sailors and officers arrived, two of the Russian members of the hospital personnel were shot because they had treated the German wounded. I myself and two other nurses fled immediately. . . . On 7 January 1942 the three of us walked back to the Villa Stamboli. . . . None of the wounded were still in the cellar where they had been accommodated . . . because of the bombardment of the town. We found them in another empty room in the cellar. They had been shot."[11]

The testimony of several witnesses make it apparent that an order was issued to kill every single German in Feodosia, whether wounded or not. On 24 January 1942 Gottfried Hagemann, a fifth German judge on special assignment with the High Command of the 11th Army, took the deposition of Corporal Anton Niedermair, the cook of an ambulance section, who had been captured by the Soviets on 29 December 1941 and scheduled for execution on 16 January 1942: "A Russian wearing a blue uniform, evidently a commissar, came up to me, put his pistol on my neck. . . . I felt a heavy blow and lost consciousness but only for a brief while. Upon regaining consciousness I heard several shots fired in the cell above. . . . On 18 January in the early morning civilians came and brought us water to drink. . . . Shortly thereafter German troops came to our rescue." [12]

Corporal Wilhelm Törber testified similarly before a sixth German judge, A. Diderichs, on 24 January 1942: "During 16 January 1942 we noticed while looking out the window of our prison cell that there was a certain anxiety among the Russians in the street. . . . About an hour later the prisoners were taken out of the cells one by one. I was one of the last, and they made me descend to the cellar. . . . I was shot from behind with a pistol, and the bullet entered in the right side of the nape of the neck and came out through my right cheek. At first I was unconscious, but I came back after a few seconds. After me another soldier was brought down to the cellar, and they did the same to him. . . . of the 40 to 50 German prisoners who had been there, only eight men remained alive." [13]

The Bureau's files contain further depositions taken at later dates, when witnesses who were advancing or retreating with the troops could be located. On 24 May 1942 Lieutenant Bernhard Balletshofer reported on the execution of 15 German prisoners of war. [14] Much later still, on 8 November 1943, Corporal Karl Ewen described the corpses of five German soldiers whose "faces could no longer be identified, since they were swollen. . . . I suspect that some of them were mutilated on the face." [15] Noncommissioned officer Heinz Wippich, who spoke Russian, was told by civilians that "the German wounded were thrown out of the windows of . . . the second floor of the building and that cold water was poured on them so that . . . they froze to death." [16]

Altogether, depositions of at least twelve witnesses were taken by seven judges. Many persons mentioned in the documents shortly thereafter fell in combat or died after the war, but nearly four decades later three of the examining judges, two important witnesses, and the photographer who took most of the pictures all remembered the events and confirmed the contents of the Bureau's protocols. On 12 March 1976 Walter Hackl provided copies of a dozen Feodosia photographs and the following statement:

I was the photographer assigned to Infantry Regiment 105 under Colonel Müller. Four or five days after the beginning of the German counter-offensive we arrived in the center of the town of Feodosia. . . . Somehow, perhaps from the Russian civilian population, we learned that horrendous things had happened in the German hospital. . . . The first thing we saw [there] was the senseless devastation, the totally ravaged rooms and equipment. Bottles and glasses with medicines were thrown about, trampled on the floor between overturned cupboards, chairs, beds, medical instruments, and bloody dressings. But where were the wounded? After a futile search we met on the street a civilian who . . . took us to the edge of the shore highway and pointed down to a long mound of sand. On our way down to the shore, an older couple approached us. . . . they both spoke German, and they told us with tears in their eyes all that had occurred in that place. The seriously wounded and the amputees had been carried down to the edge of the street and then thrown down six or eight meters to the shore, where two Russians beat their heads with iron clubs and finished them off. . . . German soldiers and POWs with shovels arrived and proceeded to lay out the bodies. . . . some of the wounded had not been killed immediately but instead carried to the beach and left in the surf so that the waves broke over them and they gradually froze to death. . . . the senior doctor from the German hospital . . . [who] had treated the wounded before the evacuation was able to identify them by name, one by one.[17]

During the Nuremberg trials, serious accusations lodged against the High Command of the Wehrmacht included the ill-treatment of the Russian civilian population in the Crimea. In this connection the defense collected numerous affidavits from German officers concerning not only the treatment of civilians by the Germans but also the treatment of German prisoners of war by the Red Army. On 2 July 1946 Lieutenant-Colonel Herbert Geitner stated: "After recapturing the town of Feodosia in mid-January 1942, the commander-in-chief of the 30th Army Corps, General Fretter-Pico, gave the order to distribute bread to the famished civilian population (mostly old men, women, and children). He did this although he knew that his own troops were suffering from chronic lack of food and that he would have to order the killing of a number of horses for food. He did this also in spite of the fact that the Soviet Army . . . had killed the German wounded who had been left behind in the hospital . . . by pouring water over them and leaving them to freeze to death." [15]

Three years later, in the Hamburg trial against Field Marshal Erich von Manstein, the defense made specific use of the Feodosia events, since the victims had belonged to Manstein's troops. Among other things, the defense introduced as evidence the German Foreign Office white book "Bolshevik War Crimes and Crimes against Humanity" (1942), which includes several of the witness depositions cited above.[19]

The Feodosia killings were not unique in a war that piled horror upon horror; many field hospitals were overrun and countless wounded soldiers murdered. Grischino offers yet another example of how the war Crimes Bureau investigated a major complex step by step and how it used the documentation.

In the night of 10–11 February 1943 a Soviet armored division succeeded in breaking through the German lines and occupying the Grischino area to the northwest of Stalino.[1] A German counteroffensive recaptured the area on 18 February 1943. What they found was a massacre. A judicial commission set up to investigate the murders determined that Soviet soldiers had killed 596 prisoners of war, wounded soldiers, nurses, and female communications personnel: 406 German soldiers, 58 members of the Todt Organization (including a Danish citizen),[2] 89 Italian soldiers, 9 Romanian soldiers, 4 Hungarian soldiers, 15 railroad and other officials, 7 German civilian workers, and 8 Ukrainian volunteers.

The first intelligence reports of 18 February 1943, immediately after the recapture of Grischino, contain the unsworn statements of three German soldiers, a member of the Todt Organization, and an Italian soldier. The Italian, Anesi Damaso, told the German intelligence officer: "On 18 February 1943 in the early morning hours I noticed that small groups of prisoners were taken from the room next to mine and that they were taken down to the cellar and then shot. They forced us into another room and then started shooting wildly into the room with machine guns and pistols. They also threw hand grenades at us. From the start I had thrown myself to the floor and kept low throughout, and thus I was not wounded."[3]

Franz Grabietz, a technician, had been captured on 11 February 1943 and avoided being immediately shot by claiming to be an ethnic Pole. But as the German counteroffensive became stronger, the Soviets decided to liquidate all prisoners of war: "When our group of seven came down to the cellar, we saw there the bodies of the 20 men who had been picked up before us. Since I was the first one of our group to enter the cellar, I saw what was awaiting us and hid myself as well as I could in a corner behind the corpses. Then they started shooting with machine guns and threw hand grenades into the cellar."[4]

The first judicial investigations did not take place until several weeks later. On 18 March 1943 Judge Berthold Goebel took the deposition of Corporal Rudolf Pecher, whose supply column, unaware of the enemy in Grischino, stopped there on 10 February 1943 on its way from Stalino to Dnjepropetrovsk.

The crew of the tank came out and took us prisoner, since we had no way to defend ourselves against the tank's machine guns. . . . two guards took us out on the road, where, upon orders of the tank commander who came toward us, we had to stand in a semicircle. He asked whether anyone could speak Russian. When I answered that I knew Russian, I was ordered aside. Besides that he asked the prisoners whether they were German. After I had been segregated, I heard him give the order in Russian: shoot them. Thereupon several Russians raised their machine guns and shot into the group of prisoners. Actually, they did not particularly take aim at my comrades. After that the commander came to me and asked whether I had seen what had been done with the prisoners and whether I was sorry for them. I said that I had seen it. He then wanted to know where I had learned Russian. I told him that I could speak Czech, which is related to Russian, and that in this way I was able to learn Russian. He then replied: "So you are really a Czechoslovak," which I confirmed, since I had seen what had happened to my comrades. . . . While the tank commander was speaking with me, I saw that another group of comrades was shot, and a little while later another group of 8 to 10 men . . . were similarly executed. . . . On the same day toward evening I was to go with an Italian and bring over the German vehicles. While I was doing this, I saw that still more Germans had been assembled, apparently denounced by the civilian population and taken out of their hiding places in the houses and cellars. After that I only heard the sounds of shots being fired, and when I returned to the scene I saw 12 to 14 corpses.[5]

Willi Knobloch, judge of the 333d Infantry Division, took the depositions of six further witnesses. Sergeant Bruno Bonkowski testified: "On 24 and 25 February 1943 Lieutenant Wusterack and I . . . saw a courtyard in which 10 to 15 men of the Todt Organization had been laid out in rank and file and executed. . . . in the vicinity of the military cemetery I saw in a house corpses piled up 1.5 meters high . . . they had been horribly mutilated. . . . outside a field hospital I saw a great many bodies, wounded soldiers who evidently had been carried out of the hospital and left outside to freeze. . . . in a house close by I saw seven or eight dead women, Red Cross nurses, communications assistants, and girls dressed in brown and gold uniforms . . . probably they were all raped by the Bolsheviks, since they were lying on their backs with their legs spread wide."[6]

Judge Knobloch, who had entered Grischino immediately after the town's recapture, inspected the bodies himself: "In a house I saw women with their legs spread apart. Judging by the uniforms they had been Red Cross nurses. Some of the bodies manifested mutilations: the attackers apparently tried to cut off their breasts."[7]

A more senior judge, Adolf Block remembers that after the 7th Armored Division recaptured the town, it was discovered that "the Russians had killed every single German they had found there. In the hospital the nurses had been first raped and then murdered. I was immediately sent there and was able to see with my own eyes what had happened. A nurse had a broomstick rammed between her legs. Some 120 Germans had been crowded into a storage room in the cellar of the train station and then mowed down with a machine gun. Two men survived the massacre, and their depositions were obtained. Both of them belonged to a construction company of the Todt Organization. One was a Frenchman and was spared because of that. The other, a German, also claimed to be a Frenchman, and that is why he survived. . . . As far as I can remember, the judge of the 7th Armored Division investigated this case and added photographic evidence."[8]

Judge Gerhard Wulle, who was attached to the commander-in-chief of the 1st Armored Army, carried out investigations in the area of Jekaterinovka, near Grischino.[9] Among witnesses from the local Ukrainian population were two women whose depositions were taken by an ad hoc judicial officer, a Major Wilhelm.[10] On 6 April 1943 Maria Martimjanova testified: "I clearly saw the events from a distance of about 100 meters: out of the open truck some 25 persons came down. . . . Some children . . . told me that they were

German soldiers; meanwhile, they had sat down and were in the process of taking off their shoes and their uniforms, which took about 20 minutes. I did not hear any orders. The naked soldiers then stood in a line, and suddenly many shots were fired at the soldiers, I think from behind. All Red Army soldiers present participated in the shooting."[11] Henja Sakurakina, a neighbor of Mrs. Martimjanova, stated that she was a Baptist, that she too had seen the truck arrive and the soldiers take off their clothes, but when she realized that they were going to be executed, she ran into the house because she did not want to see the killings.[12]

The War Crimes Bureau's efforts to find additional witnesses of the Grischino events were pursued over many months. Judge Knobloch recalls that "there was a specific request addressed to the court at Army Headquarters, which passed it down to the division courts: that is, not only to me but also to other division judges. The request named the witnesses from whom we were to obtain depositions."[13] Among them was Corporal Karl Thomas, who had been wounded and sent to a Berlin hospital, where he gave a sworn statement to Bureau member Martin Heinemann. He remembered seeing the corpses of three Red Cross nurses; one had the skull split open, and another had knife cuts in the upper part of the body.[14]

On the basis of the evidence it was able to compile, in July 1943 the Bureau prepared a 24-page report with photographs, "The Grischino Case," but the available records do not indicate how widely it was distributed. In any event, the Bureau continued to collect material about the case. More than a year later, on 18 June 1944, Friedrich Schümann took the sworn deposition of Sergeant Wilhelm Asche: "When I arrived at the northern exit of the town of Grischino, I saw there, lying on the road, the corpses of 10 German soldiers. They wore only pants, and their identification tags were still around their necks. The skulls of the corpses had been flattened, apparently by blows with heavy instruments. The skulls had been reduced to about ⅓ of their usual breadth. . . . Later, on the way from Grischino to Anenskaja, I saw hundreds of corpses of German soldiers . . . piled up on the street. All corpses were naked. . . . Almost all the bodies manifested mutilations . . . the nose and the ears had been cut off many of them. Other bodies had their genital organs amputated and stuck in their mouths."[15]

It is impossible to know how many more depositions the original files contained. As it did for Feodosia, the Bureau removed the originals from the general files and opened a special dossier on Grischino, and all the special dossiers—*Sondermappen* or *Sonderhefte*—have been lost.

Like Feodosia, too, the Grischino massacre was mentioned by the defense in the war crimes trial against Field Marshal von Manstein, though it apparently did not have access to the Bureau's documentation; instead, it introduced into evidence a long affidavit by one Karl Bender, dated 7 October 1949, which complements and confirms the Bureau's findings.[16]

Non-German Axis Soldiers

Although the War Crimes Bureau was primarily concerned with cases in which the victims were German soldiers, it did expand its field of activity in the course of the war to investigate several major crime complexes involving other members of the Axis armed forces.

A typical example is the deposition of the Spanish soldier Amadeo Casanova, taken on 19 March 1942 by Bureau member Lothar Schöne in a military hospital in Frankfurt an der Oder. Casanova, a member of the so-called Blue Division, which was composed of Spanish volunteers, stated under oath: "In December 1941 my company manned a defense post together with German troops north of Novgorod. . . . In the early morning hours of 27 December 1941 the Russians attacked us and encircled the Spanish company. Around 6:00 A.M. we undertook a counteroffensive in order to break the ring and succeeded in taking a village in the vicinity. A Spanish lieutenant and four Spanish soldiers who had gone ahead of us were wounded and fell into the hands of the Russians. Shortly thereafter we found [them] dead. In all five cases the Russians had nailed their heads to the ground with pickaxes."[1]

Another Spanish soldier, Manuel Ruiz, told his story before Judge Schöne the same day:

> After Christmas 1941 the first company of the Spanish Division was attacked by the Russians at its middle section, just north of Novgorod. Many wounded Spanish soldiers were captured. Some hours later another Spanish company was able to reoccupy the area, and I personally saw the bodies of Spanish comrades who had been murdered by the Russians. Three of them had been pierced with a pickaxe through the chest, another had had the ears cut off, another was missing an arm,

and still another had the genital organ amputated. Toward the end of December 1941—after the events described above—I saw a Red Cross ambulance standing on a road. . . . five wounded German soldiers who had been in the ambulance were lying on the ground. . . . All five had been killed with bayonets or knives, and two of them had had their genitals cut off.[2]

Italian soldiers who fell into the hands of the Red Army also fared as badly as the Germans. The Bureau's files contain a considerable number of depositions in which Italian soldiers describe the killing and torturing especially of wounded soldiers left on the field and later found murdered. Italians who were captured without being wounded were frequently interrogated (when Italian interpreters were available) and routinely shot afterward. Of the 596 Axis prisoners of war and hospital staff summarily liquidated by the Soviet Army in Grischino, 89 were Italians.[3]

At the end of World War II the new Italian government established that 84,000 Italian soldiers—presumed prisoners of war—were still unaccounted for. Their fate has remained unclear, and Italian requests to the Soviet Union for their return or for clarification as to where and when they died have been unsuccessful. Official Soviet history has claimed that many of the missing died in battle and that others who, after the fall of Mussolini in 1943, refused to continue fighting on the side of the Germans were actually executed by the Germans.[4] This allegation has been periodically repeated by the Soviet press, most recently by TASS in January 1987, which claimed that 2,000 Italian POWs were massacred by the Germans in August and September 1943 in Lvov.[5] They were purportedly members of the Italian *Retrovo* Division, including Generals Enrico Mangianini, Alfredo Fornaroli, and Giuseppe Giannotti. Investigations carried out by the Italian Ministry of Defense, however, indicate that there has never been a *Retrovo* Division, that in August and September 1943 there were only a few dozen Italian soldiers in the Lvov area, that they all returned to Italy, and that the generals named by TASS cannot be found on the lists of Italian officers.[6]

It is noteworthy that the Soviet prosecution at Nuremberg did not include among its accusations the massacre of Italian prisoners of war at Lvov; moreover, the relevant German war diaries and records of the High Command of the Wehrmacht do not indicate that such a massacre could have been perpetrated by the Germans.[7]

194

15

17

16

18

15. Judge Ulrich Schattenberg, first Bureau investigator in Poland, September 1939 (Zayas Archive)
16. Judges Ulrich Schattenberg, Wilken von Ramdohr, and Wolfgang Zirner (first three from left) on their mission to Posen (Zayas Archive)
17. Judge Alfons Waltzog, who carried out extensive investigations in Poland, Belgium, and France (Zayas Archive)
18. Judge Schattenberg taking the deposition of a witness in Bromberg (Zayas Archive)

19 **20**

21

19. Judge Horst Reger, who carried out investigations in Poland, September–October 1939 (Zayas Archive)
20. The Lutheran church in Bromberg-Schwedenhöhe (Bundesarchiv)
21. Foreign journalists at Bromberg in September 1939 (Bundesarchiv)
22. Member of German minority murdered near Bromberg in September 1939 (Bundesarchiv)

22

23

23. Murdered ethnic Germans near
Bromberg (Bundesarchiv)
24. *Volksdeutsche* widow at the grave of
her murdered husband (Bundesarchiv)

24

25. Heinkel 111 that landed in June 1940
near Vimy, France (Bundesarchiv)
26. Crew of Heinkel 111 lynched by French
civilians (Bundesarchiv)
27–28. Red Cross ambulances attacked by
low-flying Allied fighter planes in France
1944 (Bundesarchiv)

25

26

27

28

29. Soldiers' cemetery at Broniki (Zayas Archive)
30–31. Massacre at Broniki on 1 July 1941 (Zayas Archive)

30

31

44

45

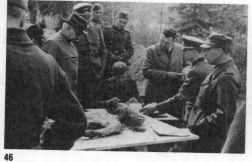

46

50

48

49

51

52

53

48. Objects found on the bodies of Katyn
victims (Bundesarchiv)
49. Memorial erected by Polish exiles in
London at Gunnersbury Cemetery
(Bednarski)
50. Members of the Polish Red Cross at
Katyn (Bundesarchiv)
51-52. Vinnitsa, 1944 (Bundesarchiv)
53. Mass grave at Witebsk (Bundesarchiv)
54. Autopsy at Witebsk (Bundesarchiv)

54

55

56

55. Commander Karl Smidt
of the destroyer *Erich Giese*
(Zayas Archive)
56. Judge Helmut Sieber,
who took the deposition of
Commander Smidt (Zayas
Archive)
57. Destroyer *Erich Giese* in
Narvik, 11 April 1940 (Zayas
Archive)
58. Hospital ship *Erlangen*
after attack on 15 June 1944
(Kludas)

57

58

59

60

61

59. Hospital Ship *Freiburg* after attack on 14 August 1944
(Kludas)
60. Captain Dietrich Hermichen on the *Tübingen* (Zayas Archive)
61. Hospital ship *Tübingen* sinking, 18 November 1944 (Zayas
Archive)

208

62. Goldap, East Prussia,
October 1944. The sign in
Russian reads: "Soldiers!
Maidaneck does not forgive.
Take revenge without
mercy!" (Bundesarchiv)
63–65. Civilians liquidated
in Nemmersdorf, sparing
neither old men nor children
(Bundesarchiv)

63

62

209

64

65

Most Russian and Ukrainian volunteers who fought in German uniform and fell into the hands of the Red Army were summarily shot, as abundantly documented in the Bureau's files. For instance, on 28 November 1943 the counterintelligence section of the High Command of Army Group A reported the statement of a Soviet prisoner of war:

> On 8 August 1943 the 42d Gwardejskaja Baklanow of the 13th Gwardejskaja Armored Division of the Fifth Army executed 165 German prisoners of war and 125 Russian volunteers. . . . The place of the shooting and of the mass grave may be seen on the attached map. . . . The Germans after their interrogation came out of the shack in groups of up to eight men and were immediately shot. The commander was Lieutenant-Colonel Kotelnik. The executioners were all drunk and shot wildly with machine guns, so that not all of the Germans were killed immediately. Two hours later a lieutenant and five of his men . . . laughed when they saw that several of the soldiers were still alive. These seriously wounded men were then brutally finished off.[8]

On 28 November 1943 Sergeant Kurt Kretschmer gave a deposition to Judge Wolfgang Schürmann in which he described another massacre: "When we came to the bodies of the executed soldiers, we discovered that a number of them were Germans and the rest volunteers. The German soldiers had been shot with machine guns; the volunteers had been beaten to death."[9] In April 1944 Corporal Josef Kuhn, who had escaped from Russian captivity and was convalescing at the military hospital in Troppau reported that the Russian volunteers captured with him were first interrogated, then beaten and executed.[10]

Ukrainian and Baltic Civilians

German military judges investigated reports of violations of the laws of war committed against civilians as well as soldiers: German civilians in Poland in 1939;[11] Belgian and Dutch civilians in 1940;[12] Baltic, Polish, and Ukrainian civilians from 1941 on. The introduction to the first of the Bureau's three volumes of selected cases on Soviet war crimes and crimes against humanity reads in part:

> Documents on Russian atrocities against Ukrainian, Polish, Latvian, and other minorities within the population of the Soviet Republic in the first

months of the war have been included together with the evidence of war crimes committed against members of the German armed forces. These documents, particularly those concerning the brutal murder of countless women and children, also illustrate the intentional and systematic character of the war conduct of the Soviet Army and thus provide an important addition and confirmation of other evidence contained in this volume concerning war crimes against German soldiers.[13]

The Bureau's files document by abundant examples the existence of a general Soviet policy to liquidate all political prisoners in the Ukraine and in the Baltic states rather than allow them to be liberated by the German Army. In the first days following Hitler's attack on the Soviet Union, large-scale liquidations took place in all NKVD prisons close to the front; not only political prisoners but priests and other religious leaders and a few German prisoners of war—mostly air crews captured after emergency landings—were killed. On 24 June 1941 some 500 political detainees were executed in Dubno. On 26 June, shortly before German troops occupied the town, the Ukrainian population had stormed the NKVD prison, but most of the detainees had already been executed; only a few wounded prisoners could be freed.[14] Not far away from Dubno, in a town called Luck, some 1,500 Ukrainian political detainees were liquidated in late June 1941.[15] In the northern district of the town, four mutilated bodies of German pilots were discovered in the courtyard of the NKVD administration building.[16] In another town called Sarni several hundred Ukrainian men and women were executed prior to the German arrival.[17]

On 17 July 1941, Ukrainian witnesses Gregor Turko and Roman Kurschmir testified about the killing of several hundred Ukrainians in the Dobromil district; the bodies were subsequently found in the NKVD prison and in several mass graves.[18] In Bobrka the mutilated corpses of 16 Ukrainians were found; in Zolkiew the murders of 50 to 60 Ukrainians were reported.[19] In Brzeznay 150 to 180 bodies were found in the NKVD prison, and in the cellar of a house nearby the mutilated corpses of 12 more Ukrainian victims.[20] In a smaller town located between Lvov and Tarnopol the bodies of 80 Ukrainians —men, women, and children—and several mutilated corpses of German soldiers were found.[21] In Rudki and Komarno approximately 200 Ukrainian men, women, and children were murdered, and there were mass murders of Ukrainians in Sambor.[22]

Military judges tried to investigate as many cases as possible, but there were numerous difficulties. Ukrainian witnesses, of course, had to be interrogated in Ukrainian. Moreover, because the German judges had to move on with the advancing German troops, they did not always have time to question all available witnesses. Still, an effort was made; the Bureau's files include, for instance, depositions taken in Tarnopol concerning the killing of some two hundred Ukrainian civilians and ten German prisoners of war.[23]

Mass liquidations took place throughout the Baltic states as well. On 25 June 1941 a Soviet armored vehicle arrived at an NKVD concentration camp near Kovno, in which some 450 Lithuanians were being detained. All civilian internees were forced to come out into the courtyard, including the Lithuanian guards, where they were mowed down by machine-gun fire. The Bureau obtained depositions from the survivors—in particular from a Doctor Garmus from Kovno—and numerous photographs of the massacred corpses are preserved in its files.[24]

A similar event was described by the liaison officer of the German Foreign Office at the High Command of the 16th Army: "I have just visited the former concentration camp near Pravieniski, where the Soviets murdered some 200 Lithuanians on 25 June 1941. . . . When the German formations advanced into Kovno on 24 June, the commissar and five other Soviets fled. On 25 June, however, the commissar returned in the company of Soviet troops. Around three in the afternoon the internees were forced out of their barracks to a place by the wire entanglement and there shot down with machine guns. . . . Only a few of the internees survived and could report on the killings."[25]

On 29 June 1941 in the town of Schaulen, Lithuania, seventy-two male corpses were counted. Dr. Bruss carried out autopsies and identified a number of deliberate mutilations.[26]

Among the German officers who wrote about these massacres after the war is General Walther von Seydlitz. He was with the invasion of Lithuania in the summer of 1941 and was captured at Stalingrad in January 1943. After being held prisoner in the Soviet Union for more than seven years, in July 1950 he was charged before a special Soviet court-martial in Moscow with war crimes during the first few days of the 1941 Lithuanian campaign. Seydlitz rejected the accusations and took advantage of the situation to tell the court what he had seen there: "Soviet authorities . . . massacred the civilian internees of the concentration camp at Alexandrovo, where they had rounded up opponents after their occupation of Lithuania in 1940. After this experience at Alexandrovo . . . you should understand . . . that some [German] soldiers . . . did not always conduct themselves in a restrained fashion." [27]

Seydlitz had previously asked his Russian interpreter whether he knew of the Alexandrovo killings, and the Russian had replied, "Yes, we had serious problems with the Lithuanian intelligentsia. This concentration camp was set up for them." [28] Seydlitz requested the Moscow tribunal to call his former military judge Alfred Holzki, who was also a prisoner of war in the Soviet Union, but the court neither summoned Holzki nor obtained his written testimony nor called any other witness for the defense. [29]

Still another Soviet concentration camp, near the town of Glebokie, was taken by the advancing Germans in July of 1941. Although the records of the War Crimes Bureau contain no depositions regarding the massacres there, Judge Hans Georg Jeremias—who took many depositions in other cases which are still preserved in the files—described the Glebokie events on 19 August 1975. As division judge of the 14th Infantry Division, which in July 1941 was advancing northeast of Vilnius in the part of eastern Poland that had been occupied by the Russians in September of 1939, Jeremias had kept a personal diary; one entry reads: "Two kilometers from the town of Glebokie there is a baroque monastery. It had been used by the Russians as a concentration camp for politically troublesome Poles. Annexed to the church were monastery cells which the Russians used as prison cells for the detainees. The church had also been emptied and used for purposes of internment. . . . In the courtyard of the church a mass grave was found into which the murdered Polish detainees had been thrown; they were piled up in several layers."

Jeremias adds: "I still remember that on the upper layer of bodies I saw some who appeared to have been strangled and still had a cord around the neck. The Polish population was inspecting the piles of corpses, looking for family members. I cannot say exactly how many bodies were in the mass grave. I had the impression that the Russians had liquidated all the detainees so that they would not be liberated by the Germans. It was the pattern, the same liquidations as were carried out in Lvov and many other places." [30]

Every scholarly analysis of the events that occurred in Lvov in the summer of 1941 is fraught with nonscholarly dangers: the dangers of emotional reactions, polemical disputes, quotations out of context, deliberate distortion and misuse for political purposes. Indeed, because this complex of murders has remained a politically sensitive issue for over four decades, it is prudent at the outset to distinguish three murder phases: (1) the measures taken by the NKVD against Ukrainian and Polish political prisoners in June of 1941; (2) the pogroms carried out by Ukrainian and Polish civilians against local Jews; and (3) the murders of 38 Polish professors and at least 7,000 Jews by the SD and SS.

In keeping with its limited authority, the War Crimes Bureau focused only on the crimes committed by the NKVD. Its files show that Bureau members knew about the local pogroms against the Jews (though no specific investigations of these were conducted) but provide no indication that they were aware of the SD and SS murders. This chapter is limited in scope by the available Bureau records and therefore concentrates on the first of the three murder phases.

In the early hours of 30 June 1941 the Polish-Ukrainian city of Lvov was occupied by the 1st Mountain Division of the German 49th Army Corps. There was little resistance, since Soviet troops had already abandoned the area. The intelligence section of the 49th Army Corps observed in its first report, dated that same day: "According to the account of Major Heinz, commander of a battalion of Regiment 800, thousands of brutally murdered persons were found in the Lvov prisons. The 1st and 4th Mountain Divisions are hereby ordered to assign journalists and photographers to cover these atrocities. The chief military judge of the Corps and the liaison officer of the

Foreign Office with the High Command of the 17th Army have been sent to Lvov to carry out in-depth investigations."[1]

The German investigations, then, did not originate with the Bureau; the number of victims was so great that three army judges immediately commenced inquiries on their own, without awaiting specific instructions from Berlin: Judge Hans Tomforde, with the 603d Garrison headquarters; Judge Erich Wilke, of the 49th Army Corps; and Judge Wilhelm Möller, with the High Command of the 17th Army.

The Testimony of German Witnesses

Barely a few hours after the German troops occupied Lvov the 603d Garrison headquarters moved in and began to investigate the extraordinary events that had preceded the German arrival. Upon learning of the mass killings, Judge Tomforde asked his medical officer Dr. Georg Saeltzer to accompany him to the former OGPU prison, to the Brygidky prison, and to the former military prison, known as Samarstinov. He interrogated a number of witnesses and prepared a preliminary report the same day.[2]

Wilke, chief judge of the 49th Army Corps, issued a report dated 1 July 1941: "The examination of the bodies found at the OGPU prison indicated that the killings had been preceded by torture. . . . The majority of the victims are Ukrainians; the rest are Polish. Witnesses also reported that in this prison two German wounded pilots had been interned. A Luftwaffe belt and a pilot's cap were found in the prison. In . . . one of the mass graves a Luftwaffe helmet was also found. Thus it must be assumed that these German airmen are among the bodies that could not be identified."[3] Judge Wilke remained in Lvov until 6 July and took the sworn depositions of numerous witnesses, including those of senior medical officer Dr. Richard Eckl, veterinarian Dr. Joseph Brachetka, and noncommissioned officer Kurt Dittrich.[4]

Further witness depositions, including those of Polish and Ukrainian detainees who had survived the liquidations at the prisons, were obtained by Judge Möller, on special assignment to the High Command of the 17th Army. On 6 July 1941 Möller took the deposition of Dr. Saeltzer, who had accompanied Tomforde to the prisons on 30 June 1941:

> The Brygidky prison . . . was still burning. There I met a young Ukrainian, aged about 24 years. . . . He claimed that 24 hours before, shortly before he was to be executed, he had succeeded in escaping from cell 3

of the left wing; he guided me through the cellars, the ground floor, and the first floor of the prison. The people who rushed in through the main entrance wailed and lamented while asking to see their relatives, with whom they had been in contact two days before by shouting from outside the prison. We discovered . . . in the first four cellars a considerable number of bodies, the upper layer being relatively fresh and the lower layers in the pile already in advanced decomposition. In the fourth cellar the bodies were covered by a thin layer of sand. In the first courtyard we found several stretchers stained with blood. On one of the stretchers I saw the body of a male who had been killed by a bullet through the back of the head. . . . I ordered that the cellars should be immediately cleared, and in the course of the next three days 423 corpses were brought out to the courtyard for identification. Among the bodies there were young boys aged 10, 12, and 14 and young women aged 18, 20, and 22, besides old men and women. . . .

From there I continued to the former OGPU prison. . . . We broke the door leading to the lower prison rooms and saw there 4 corpses at the foot of the stairway, among them a young woman aged about 20 years, who apparently was shot at the very last minute; in the first large room the corpses were piled up to about half the height of the room. . . . In the courtyard were two mounds of earth from which parts of corpses stuck out. There too the recovery of the corpses was immediately begun, and they were carried to the main courtyard. . . . In the second courtyard of the OGPU prison I found at one of the gates a Luftwaffe cap and a parachute belt. . . .

[At] the military prison in the northern part of the town . . . the stench of decomposition was so strong and there was so much blood under the mountains of corpses that we had to wear a Polish gas mask in order to enter the cellar and carry out the necessary investigations. Young women, men, and older women were piled up layer upon layer all the way to the ceiling. . . . The third and fourth cellars were only about three-fourths full. Over 460 corpses were taken out of these cellars. Many of the bodies showed evidence of serious torture, mutilations of arms and legs, and shackling. The recovery of the remaining bodies was stopped upon orders of the commander because as a consequence of the heat the decomposition of the bodies was already advanced, and there was no possibility of identifying the scantily dressed corpses.[5]

At the military hospital the bodies of three members of the Luftwaffe were found. Judge Möller ordered a medico-legal autopsy to determine the cause of death, and the pathologist of the 17th Army, Dr. Herbert Siegmund, was entrusted with the task. The corpses of four other German airmen found at the OGPU prison were also subjected to forensic investigation. On 3 July 1941 Judge Möller took a deposition from Dr. Siegmund, who explained that the first three soldiers had been shot dead in their hospital beds:

> The body lying on the left bed next to the window had a superficial skin wound on the right chest, the size of the palm of my hand. The wound was several days old and had been freshly dressed. Moreover, there was a more recent bullet wound inflicted by a 6.5-mm bullet through the skull slightly over the left ear; the exit wound was about one centimeter in diameter through the right temple, which was considerably destroyed. . . . The body on the middle bed had a broken jaw that had been professionally bandaged . . . the examination also established a fresh bullet wound on the left chest, four centimeters down from the nipple, in the area of the heart. The body on the third bed next to the wall had a large wound in the under side of the lower leg . . . a fresh bullet wound of the same caliber as that seen in the other corpses had been inflicted on the right side of the victim's stomach, some six centimeters under the costal arch.[6]

Examination of the four other fliers' bodies indicated that they had not been previously wounded. Three had been killed by a shot through the head; the fourth had no head injuries, but the rest of the body was in such an advanced state of decomposition that an autopsy was not deemed feasible.[7]

The officer responsible for removing thousands of corpses from the prisons and arranging for their proper burial was Lieutenant Walter Lemmer. In his deposition before Judge Möller, dated 7 July 1941, he stated:

> On the evening of [1 July 1941] I went to the Brygidky prison and observed that already a substantial number of corpses had been taken out of the cells and brought out into the courtyard. I estimated the number of corpses at about 200. . . . On the same night I arranged for the burial of 50 more bodies. They were carried to the Ukrainian cemetery and interred in a mass grave. . . . In the course of the next day some 300 bodies were buried. . . . But there were still countless bodies in the

cellar. They had been piled up layer upon layer all the way to the ceiling. The floor of the cellar was flooded with blood. It was not possible to carry out an orderly removal . . . because of the advanced decomposition of the corpses. It was not possible to enter the cellar without an oxygen apparatus. Upon orders of the city commander lime chloride was poured over the bodies, and the openings of the cellars were bricked up. I estimate the number of bodies still remaining in the cellar at about 1,000. It is possible that there were further cellars into which we were not able to go. . . .

Late in the afternoon of 2 July 1941 I began the task of clearing up the NKVD prison. . . . I estimate that there were some 150 corpses in the courtyard. . . . There were also corpses in the cellars which had been covered with sand. I cannot estimate how many. . . . the entrances were bricked up by order of the city commander of Lvov. The bodies . . . in the courtyard were taken to the Ukrainian cemetery for burial.

I had nothing to do with the clearing up of the Samarstinov prison. But I heard that the cellars . . . were similarly full of corpses. . . . On Friday, 4 July 1941, I went to the prison of the local courthouse. . . . According to the prison administrator there was a mass grave in the courtyard. I myself saw a grave mound of about 4 by 6 meters. The administrator further informed me that a large number of corpses remained in the cellars.[8]

The Testimony of Ukrainian and Polish Witnesses

Besides recording the confirming testimony of many more German officers and medical doctors, the German judges also took the depositions of numerous Ukrainian and Polish witnesses. On 4 July 1941 Josef Pilichiewicz, an employee of the surgery division in the Lvov hospital, testified before Judge Möller that on 22 June two wounded German soldiers had been brought to the hospital; on 29 June both were shot by the Soviet Commissars Loginov and Maslov. The responsible chief of section, Dr. Czeslav Sadlinski, stated on 4 July 1941 that he had treated three wounded German soldiers for broken bones; subsequently, he learned that all three had been killed by commissars. The nurse Sofia Gryglovna remembered that she had brought tea to these soldiers and that the two commissars chased her out of the room and told her that the wounded Germans would be shot. All three witnesses gave their testimony under oath.[9]

On 5 July 1941 Judge Möller interrogated a survivor of the massacre, the Ukrainian teacher Leo Fedoruk, who spoke with the aid of an interpreter: "On 17 March 1941 I was arrested at the school by members of the NKVD. . . . The shootings at the prison began two days after the outbreak of war . . . the following night we were taken into the interrogation room around one or two in the morning. Three persons sat at a table with a red cloth on it. One of them was a first lieutenant, the other person in civilian dress was the prison prosecutor. I could not recognize the third person because the room was lighted only by candles. There was a list on the table, and each prisoner was supposed to give his name. The three persons then decided who should be shot. Since my name was not properly written on the list . . . I was taken away to a solitary cell. . . . Only twelve persons survived, eight men and four women."[10]

Another Ukrainian survivor, Omelian Matla, testified before Judge Möller on 6 July 1941:

On 7 August 1940 I was arrested in my home by members of the NKVD on account of my links with the OUN [Organization of Ukrainian Nationalists] . . . on the second day after the outbreak of the war I noticed a lot of movement in the prison. . . . around five or six in the morning the door of my cell was opened and seven NKVD men came in with the prison director. . . . Someone shouted: "Lie down, you whores!" And at that very moment the shooting began. Twelve of us were immediately killed, two were seriously wounded, three . . . were not hit. I survived the massacre because one of the victims fell on top of me. . . . The NKVD men then rushed from cell to cell and shot down the detainees. After the last shots had been fired, I stood up. . . . Suddenly I heard them coming back. I crept under a corpse and smeared blood on my face. . . . The men again entered our cell and fired three more times. They continued from cell to cell, and then I heard, "Come quickly to the courtyard, the cars are ready to go." I remained a while longer in my cell waiting to see whether the NKVD men would come again.[11]

On 8 July 1941 Judge Möller took the deposition of Ukrainian teacher Bohdan Kazaniwsky, who had also been arrested by the NKVD because of his membership in the OUN. With the help of an interpreter, Kazaniwsky described his experiences at Brygidky prison: "On Tuesday, 24 June 1941, the NKVD men temporarily left the prison. We broke out of our cells and attempted to escape. The courtyard was blocked, however, and we were unable to get out. While we were standing in the courtyard, machine guns started firing at us. Numerous persons were wounded and others killed. We therefore retreated into the prison. The NKVD men returned and forced some 90 of us into a large cell. . . . During the following days persons were called out, and we heard then the shooting and the cries. Of the 90 only 22 survived. My name had, in fact, been called out, but I did not answer. On 28 June we heard many shots . . . after a while we discovered that civilians had entered the prison to free us. The NKVD men had already abandoned the prison. I estimate that the number of detainees at Brygidky prison was around 10,000, of whom only 600 to 800 came out alive." [12]

On 7 July 1941 Josefa Soziada, a Polish widow, testified before Judge Möller: "On Monday, 30 June 1941 . . . I went to the NKVD prison, because I had heard that German troops were already in town. I first went to the courtyard, where I at once saw numerous corpses, including those of three men whose color had turned dark, and of a woman who was totally naked. . . . through a window . . . I saw many corpses butchered on a table. . . . through another window I saw the body of a girl hanging from a lamp; she was about eight years old. The corpse was naked and had been hanged with a towel." [13]

On the same day Polish architect Ludwig Pisarek related that on 29 June he had gone to the NKVD prison to look for his brother, arrested in December 1940. "The prison had already been abandoned by the Russians, although the city of Lvov had not yet been evacuated by the Russians. I entered the prison and looked into the individual cells. These were scenes of horror. The cells were completely full with corpses. In a large room of 10 by 5 meters I saw bodies piled up to a height of about a meter and a half." [14]

Also on 7 July 1941 Irene Loesch, a Ukrainian housewife, testified that she had gone to the same prison on 28 or 29 June to look for her mother, "who had been arrested some three months before because of her religious convictions: as wife of a pastor of the Greek Orthodox church, she had asked a member of her parish why he did not go to church. When I entered the prison I immediately saw dead people in the first cell. The bodies were mutilated. . . . I saw a woman with a breast cut off. . . . Another woman had had her abdomen slit open; she had been pregnant. . . . Before that I had already been to the Samarstinov prison to search for my mother. There I could only see from the outside into a room that was filled up with corpses all the way to the ceiling."[15]

After numerous other Poles and Ukrainians were interrogated by the German judges, Möller drafted a report on 16 July 1941 which he sent together with the originals of all depositions to the War Crimes Bureau.[16]

Knowledge of Lvov Murders in the Outside World

The Bureau collected and evaluated information from various sources, and used part of its documentation on Lvov to prepare its first study of the war in Russia, "War Crimes of the Soviet Armed Forces," dated November 1941.[17] Numerous depositions were also used in the white book of the German Foreign Office titled "Bolshevist War Crimes and Crimes against Humanity," of which the British Foreign Office obtained a copy through its legation in Switzerland.[18]

One important non-German organization that participated in the investigations was the Ukrainian Red Cross. On 7 July 1941 it addressed an appeal to the German city commander: "Over 4,000 corpses have been found in Lvov's prisons . . . it is hardly possible to describe the condition in which the bodies were found. . . . Full of anguish and consternation because of the fate of all Ukrainians who remain in prisons and concentration camps throughout the Soviet Union, the Ukrainian Red Cross requests that the entire civilized world be informed by radio of these atrocities. In particular we urge the Swiss, Swedish, and Dutch Red Cross societies to take measures to protect the lives of those who are endangered so that they may still be saved."[19]

Information also reached the outside world through Polish confidential agents and others, such as the Polish professor Olgierd Gorka, who reported from Sweden that the Russians had killed some 160 Poles at the Brygidky prison before evacuating the town.[20] All these and other reports led the British Foreign Office to address a note to Soviet Foreign Minister Vyacheslav Molotov, who, predictably, rejected the accusations on 12 July 1941.[21] But when Sir Frank Roberts, a British foreign service officer involved in Polish-Russian relations during the war, mentioned the Gorka report to the foreign minister of the Polish government-in-exile, Edward Raczynski, he replied that there was "little doubt that the Polish and Ukrainian political prisoners in Lvov had in fact been liquidated as alleged."[22]

It was not until the Nuremberg trials, however, that Lvov was discussed at length in the international community—and then attention focused not on the NKVD killings described above but rather on the extensive liquidations carried out by the SD and SS. The Nuremberg indictment charged that "in the Lvov region and in the city of Lvov the Germans exterminated about 700,000 Soviet people, including 70 persons in the field of the arts, science, and technology."[23] On 15 February 1946 Soviet prosecutor L. N. Smirnov referred to a report of the "Extraordinary State Commission on Crimes Committed by the Germans in the Territory of the Lvov Region." According to that report, even before the German seizure of Lvov the Gestapo detachments were preparing lists of the most prominent representatives of the intelligentsia who were to be annihilated. He charged that mass arrests and executions began immediately after the seizure of Lvov.[24]

German SD documents introduced by the prosecution at the principal trial and later at the American trial of SS General Otto Ohlendorf (Nuremberg Trial No. 9) show that the civilian population of the city as well as the SD participated in the abuses; for instance, an SD report dated 31 July 1941 asserts that "the population rounded up some 1,000 Jews and drove them to the prison that had been occupied by the Wehrmacht." The same report continues: "The Lvov prisons were full with the corpses of murdered Ukrainians. . . . between 3,000 and 4,000. Reliable information also indicates that some 20,000 Ukrainians, of whom at least 80 percent belong to the intelligentsia, were deported to inner Russia. Similar conditions were observed in the neighboring towns, e.g., Dobromil, Sambor, and vicinity. . . . As reprisal for these atrocities 7,000 Jews were picked up and shot."[25]

Erwin Schulz, chief of a division of SS *Einsatzgruppe C*, which arrived in Lvov early in July 1941, reported in an affidavit for the Ohlendorf trial, dated 26 May 1947: "I saw the thousands of murdered persons and horrendous mutilations in Lvov. I smelled the awful stench of decomposing corpses that prevailed in the city and saw many weeping women, men, and children who were looking for their relatives."[26] Otto Rasch, chief of the SS *Einsatzgruppe C*, claimed that it was Jewish officials and civilians who had been responsible for the killing of the political prisoners, and thus he gave his *Sonderkommandos* an order from Hitler that reprisals were to be taken against guilty persons and against major suspects.[27]

In affidavits given for the Nuremberg defense, however, senior German officers who had been in Lvov briefly after its capture confirmed the SD and SS reports of the bodies found in the prisons and the reaction of local civilians, but also testified that the German military authorities had issued orders to prevent violence against the Jewish population.

General Max Winkler: "I remember [hearing] the figure of some 4,000 corpses. . . . As a reaction to these murders the Ukrainian population immediately started to drag the Jews out of their homes and to abuse them in the streets. . . . The provisional commander of Lvov, Colonel Fingergerst of the 49th Army Corps . . . succeeded in stopping [these excesses] by giving orders to German troops and sending special patrols through the streets."[28]

General Egbert Picker: "In the courtyard of the state prison I saw many rows of corpses, laid next to each other, many of them with the most grotesque mutilations. . . . I also saw in a small courtyard . . . some 15 corpses, apparently Jews who had been killed as reprisal by the local population shortly after the Russians evacuated the town. . . . Jews were being taken to the prison by local civilians wearing armbands, and in one case they were being beaten with a bat. . . . General Kübler . . . told me . . . that he had ordered such acts of violence by the civilian population against Jewish persons to be immediately stopped."[29]

General Hans Kreppel: "In the first hours after the occupation of Lvov I personally saw hundreds of bodies of murdered Ukrainians . . . I also remember an order of the 49th Army Corps forbidding the Ukrainian population to persecute the Jews." Similar affidavits were introduced in evidence by the defense in the trial against Field Marshal von Manstein (1949) in Hamburg.[30]

Postwar Investigations

In 1954 the U.S. House of Representatives established a Select Committee on Communist Aggression under the chairmanship of Congressman Charles Kersten of Wisconsin. At hearings in Munich, New York, and Chicago, hundreds of witnesses testified on a variety of topics, including the systematic killing of political prisoners by the NKVD. The committee's report reads in part:

> In every city in western Ukraine in the first days of the war, the NKVD and its agents shot all of the political prisoners, except a mere handful who were miraculously saved. One of those, Valentyna Nahirnyak, who had been connected with the theater in Rivne, has given a graphic account of her escape. She had been in a cell with seven other women. . . . A band of the murderers came into the cell and shot with their automatics at the

group until they fell. All but three were dead. A little later a man entered the cell and bayoneted all three of these, but Miss Nahirnyak's wounds were still not mortal, although she had received six bullet wounds and two bayonet cuts. The same process continued as the German armies advanced into the Eastern Ukraine. Here the Communists had more time than in the extreme west, but even in Vinnitsa some 700 bodies were found near the railroad station. In Kharkiv, one of the main prisons was closed and set on fire, while the NKVD remained on guard to prevent any assistance until the interior was destroyed and the inmates were all dead.[31]

Similar statements were given by other Ukrainian witnesses who testified before the House committee, including Bohdan Kazaniwsky, whose deposition had already been taken by the Germans in July 1941.

The Lvov case gained renewed attention in the fall of 1959 when the Soviet press mounted a major disinformation campaign against a minister in the West German Adenauer cabinet, Theodor Oberländer, accusing him of participating in the ss murders there.[32] On 5 September 1959 the *Radianska Ukraina* wrote: "Eighteen years ago the fascists committed a horrendous crime in Lvov in the night of 29–30 June 1941. The Hitlerites arrested on the basis of prepared lists hundreds of Communists, Communist youth, and non–party members and murdered them in brutal fashion in the courtyard of the Samarstinov Prison." These accusations were picked up by the Western press and eventually led to Oberländer's resignation. The investigation by the district attorney's office in Bonn, however, completely cleared him.[33]

At about the same time an international commission was set up at The Hague in the Netherlands to carry out independent investigations. The members were four former anti-Hitler activists, Norwegian lawyer Hans Cappelen, former Danish foreign minister and president of the Danish parliament Ole Bjørn Kraft, Dutch socialist Karel van Staal, Belgian law professor Flor Peeters, and Swiss jurist and member of parliament Kurt Schoch. Following its interrogation of a number of Ukrainian witnesses between November 1959 and March 1960, the commission concluded: "After four months of inquiries and the evaluation of 232 statements by witnesses from all circles involved, it can be established that the accusations against the Battalion *Nachtigall* and against the then Lieutenant and currently Federal Minister Oberländer have no foundation in fact."[34]

The extensive journalistic and historical activity of Ukrainians in exile further confirm the results of the investigations carried out by the War Crimes Bureau in 1941. Roman Ilnytzkyi's study condemns both the murders perpetrated in the Ukraine by the SS and the NKVD murders in Lvov.[35] A collection of documents dealing with Russian colonialism in the Ukraine devotes an entire chapter to the liquidation of Ukrainian political prisoners by the NKVD, not only in Lvov but also in Vinnitsa, Solotschiv, and a dozen other localities.[36] It reproduces numerous reports of Ukrainian eyewitnesses living today in the United States, Canada, and the Federal Republic of Germany.

Ukrainian journalist and author Borys Lewytzkyi wrote in 1960: "The responsibility of the Soviet authorities for the murders perpetrated in the Lvov prisons, and also for the murders in other prisons in Galicia and in the Ukraine, is clear and overwhelming; there is justification to suppose that in Soviet circles there were agitators who wanted to put the blame for these atrocities on the German army of occupation and on the Gestapo. It is known that the shooting of prison hostages took place even in Kiev; the Polish Embassy in Moscow later received many reports of specific instances in which senior Polish civil servants had been killed in the Kiev prisons. As for the killings in the Lvov detention centers, the entire population of the town and its vicinity knew what had happened during those tragic days in June."[37]

Further Investigations
Periodically, reports appear in the press that new mass graves have been "discovered" in the Soviet Union; again and again reference to the Lvov murders resurfaces, and there is a tendency even in the Western press to give some credence to Soviet propaganda and to assume that the Germans may indeed have killed the Ukrainian political prisoners at the Brygidky, Samarstinov and OGPU prisons. Surely, the Germans would have been capable of committing such crimes, but in this case the evidence is overwhelming that they did not.

Because of the persistent political misuse of the Lvov murders, it was necessary to find as many surviving eyewitnesses as possible. Only one of the German judges, Wilhelm Möller, and four Ukrainian witnesses could be located and questioned. On 20 August 1976 Judge Möller stated: "The copies of the depositions of witnesses about the events in Lvov which are before me describe the facts as I still remember them. . . . The investigations were carried out without any influence or pressure from any side or from any other agency."[38]

In December 1976 and again in December 1977 the author visited the Ukrainian witness Bohdan Kazaniwsky at his home in Philadelphia. He confirmed and expanded on his version of the events as described in his 1941 deposition and at the 1954 congressional hearings. Leo Fedoruk, another Ukrainian witness who had testified before Judge Möller, also granted an interview in Philadelphia in December 1977—as did Maria Strutynska, who had not been questioned by the Germans in 1941 but had testified before the international commission at the Hague in 1960. Mrs. Strutynska, the widow of a Lvov victim, journalist Mychailow Strutynskyj, stated: "When the Wehrmacht entered Lvov, all prisons were already full of murdered prisoners . . . there were two huge mass graves that had been superficially covered with earth; here and there an elbow or a foot was visible . . . When the Bolshevists left, they set fire to the Brygidky prison, and the Germans had to organize a special work force, which spent an entire week removing charred bodies."[39]

Still another witness who had appeared before the international commission was Mrs. A.K., who on 1 April 1977 remembered her experience as follows:

In the fall of 1940 I was arrested by the NKVD in Lvov because of my membership in the Organization of Ukrainian Nationalists. I was detained in the Samarstinov prison . . . until the beginning of June 1941. I was then transferred to the Brygidky prison because I was sick and I was supposed to be hospitalized for treatment of jaundice and kidney problems. But instead . . . I was thrown into the cellar of the prison. When the German-Soviet war broke out on 22 June 1941 I was detained in a cell in the cellar. The cell was bursting with other women detainees. . . . At short intervals the guards . . . called out individual prisoners or small groups, who then had to go out in the hallway with all their possessions. They kept calling people from Tuesday until Friday. . . . In the early hours of Saturday the voices of other prisoners from the higher floors became audible. . . . Right then we realized that there were no more guards in the prison, and so the detainees broke the door open and rushed into the halls. . . . I then went toward the Samarstinov prison, and on my way I met another woman with whom I had been interned . . . she told me that according to another Samarstinov detainee my brother had been murdered there. . . . I went to look for his body. Upon arrival I saw that a great many people were already standing outside the gate. . . . The bodies were laid out in four rows. I counted 40 corpses, among them 13 women. I was able to identify three women with whom I had shared a cell. . . . I saw that the corpses had many broken bones. Among the male corpses I could not find my brother, perhaps because I did not know what clothing he had been wearing in prison. I asked whether there were more bodies at the prison and received a positive answer. I was told, however, that the rest of the corpses . . . were unrecognizable as a result of advanced decomposition.[40]

Certainly all these statements should be carefully compared with others so as to discover possible errors or exaggerations; this principle applies to the testimony of all witnesses who have been victims of crime. But if a historian wants to study the reality of murders and persecutions, it is imperative to identify and interrogate the victims. Surely the victims have a better recollection of events than the perpetrators, who prefer to keep their silence or, better, to forget.

The mass murders of political prisoners by the NKVD in Lvov are still frequently confused with the anti-Jewish pogroms of the local population and with the liquidations perpetrated by the SD. Clear separation lines must be drawn between the three murder phases. With regard to the first phase, the War Crimes Bureau's investigations are thoroughly confirmed by the affidavits presented by the defense at the Nuremberg trials and by the subsequent inquiries of the United States Congress and the international commission at The Hague. The other two phases, on which the available Bureau records provide no information whatever, have been well documented in the records of a number of war crimes trials.[41]

Perhaps the only non-German war crime of World War II that has received worldwide attention is the 1940 liquidation of some 14,700 Polish prisoners of war by Soviet authorities. Only the bodies of 4,143 Polish officers were ever counted,[1] and there has been considerable controversy over the authorship of the killings since the German discovery of the mass graves in the spring of 1943 at Katyn Forest near Smolensk in the Soviet Union. Important studies have been published on this subject since the war, many of them by Polish authors.[2] This chapter gives only a brief survey of the facts and the issues involved and shows that subsequent non-German inquiries have largely confirmed the results of the German investigations of 1943.[3]

The War Crimes Bureau received its first reports from Soviet prisoners of war who had been interrogated by German officers and judges shortly after the German invasion of the Soviet Union. A communication dated 2 August 1941 refers to the interrogation of a Soviet POW named Merkuloff, who "claims to know with absolute certainty that all Polish officers who were taken prisoner by the Soviet Army in the course of the Russian-Polish war of 1939 have been executed."[4] At first the Bureau was unable to follow up on this information, because no graves had been found. Nor was any systematic effort made to find them, even after the Katyn Forest was occupied by the Germans in September 1941. Not until February 1943, when persistent rumors among the Russian population finally alerted the German occupation authorities, did they undertake a search of the area.

The ground was still frozen in February, and concerted digging could not start until the beginning of April 1943. Summer heat, however, led to an interruption of the digging in June, barely two months later. It was in this relatively short period that the 4,143 bodies were exhumed.

Johannes Conrad, a senior judge with the military court of the Center Army Group, went to Katyn to interrogate witnesses. Among these, Russian civilian Parfeon Kisseljeff stated on 27 February 1943 (and confirmed on 18 April 1943) that "in the Spring of 1940 for a period of four to five weeks three to four trucks full of men arrived every day in that area of the forest. . . . From my home I could hear the shooting and the human cries; they were male voices. We supposed that men were being executed. In the whole area no one really doubted that here Poles had been shot by the NKVD."[5]

Another Russian, Matwei Sacharow, stated: "I worked on the railroad from 1937 to 1941. . . . In the month of March 1940 freight trains arrived from the Tambov District, each train pulling five or six big cars. . . . As I learned from members of the military escort, the prisoners came from Kozielsk. . . . In my capacity as switchman I had the opportunity to remain in the immediate area and to observe the people taken out of the cars . . . most of the prisoners wore Polish uniforms and were officers. Among the civilians I was able to distinguish several priests. . . . the unloading of prisoners continued for 28 days. I determined this on the basis of my official records."[6]

Aware of the considerable propaganda value of their discovery, the Germans called upon one of their foremost experts in forensic medicine, Gerhard Buhtz, director of the Department of Forensic Medicine at the University of Breslau, to supervise the exhumation and to examine the bodies.[7] A commission of German experts in forensic medicine was quickly dispatched to Katyn and carried out numerous autopsies. The Buhtz report notes: "The absence of insect damage on the corpses indicates that the killings and interment took place in a cold season devoid of insects. The date of the killings may be set in the period from March to May 1940, as indicated by the evidence recovered on or near the corpses such as documents, wallets, diaries, and newspapers."[8]

In order to strengthen the credibility of the investigations carried out by Dr. Buhtz, the Germans invited a number of foreign observers, notably representatives from the International Committee of the Red Cross and the Polish Red Cross, foreign journalists from Sweden and Switzerland and other countries, and numerous British and American prisoners of war. In addition to the German doctors, an international medical commission was also established with prominent experts in forensic medicine from neutral countries and from countries under German occupation. They too performed autopsies and conducted other investigations that were duly recorded and promptly publicized: "Thus far seven mass graves have been opened, from which 982 bodies have been taken, examined, and 70 percent identified; autopsies were performed on several of the bodies. The exclusive cause of death was invariably found to be a shot in the back of the head. The date of the executions was March and April 1940, as evidenced by the written and printed documents found on the bodies, such as diaries and newspapers, and as reported by witnesses of the events."[9]

The Nuremberg Proceedings

The reliability of the German investigations and in particular of the report of the international medical commission was put to question at the Nuremberg trials. In fact, the indictment itself accused the Germans of committing the crime.[10] In July of 1946 the Soviet prosecution called Dr. Marko Antonov Markov, lecturer in forensic medicine at the University of Sofia, Bulgaria, as key witness to impeach the results of the international commission. Dr. Markov, who had been one of the twelve commission members, testified on 1 July 1946:

> At the end of April 1943 . . . I was told that I was to take part, as representative of the Bulgarian government, in the work of an international medical commission which had to examine the corpses of Polish officers discovered in the Katyn wood. . . . on Monday morning, 26 April, I flew to Berlin . . . and the other members of the commission arrived there too. They were the following besides myself: Dr. Birkle, chief doctor of the Ministry of Justice and assistant of the Institute of Forensic Medicine and Criminology at Bucharest; Dr. Miloslavich, professor of forensic medicine and criminology at Zagreb University, who was representative for Croatia; Professor Palmieri, who was professor for forensic medicine and criminology at Naples; Dr. Orsos, professor of forensic medicine and criminology at Budapest; Dr. Subik, professor of pathological anatomy at the University of Bratislava and chief of the State Department for Health of Slovakia; Dr. Hajek, professor of forensic medicine and criminology at Prague, who represented the so-called Protectorate of Bohemia and Moravia; Professor Naville, professor of forensic medicine at the University of Geneva, representative for Switzerland; Dr. Speleers, professor for ophthalmology at Ghent University, who represented Belgium; Dr. De Burlett, professor of anatomy at the University of Groningen, representing Holland; Dr. Tramsen, vice chancellor of the

Institute for forensic medicine at Copenhagen University, representing Denmark; Dr. Saxen, who was professor of pathological anatomy at Helsinki University, Finland. . . .

The commission arrived in Smolensk on 28 April, in the evening. . . . We stayed in Smolensk two days only, 29 and 30 April 1943. . . . No new graves were opened in our presence. We were shown only several graves which had already been opened before we arrived. . . . Near these opened graves were exhumed corpses already laid out. The only part of our activity that could be characterized as a scientific, medico-legal examination were the autopsies carried out by certain members of the commission who were themselves medico-legal experts, but only seven or eight of us could lay claim to that qualification, and as far as I recall, only eight corpses were opened. Each of us operated on one corpse except Professor Hajek, who dissected two. Our further activity during these two days consisted of a hasty inspection under the guidance of Germans. . . . As to the condition of the corpses in the Katyn graves, I can only judge according to the state of the corpse that I myself dissected. The condition of this corpse was, as far as I could ascertain, the same as that of all the other corpses. . . . In the head of the corpse I dissected there was a small hole, a bullet wound in the back of the head. . . . I dictated a report, on the spot, on the result of my investigation. A similar report was dictated by the other members of the commission who examined corpses. This report was published by the Germans, under Number 827, in their book.[11]

Soviet prosecutor L. N. Smirnov then asked Dr. Markov whether in his opinion the corpses could have been buried three years earlier (in 1940, before the German attack on the Soviet Union), or whether they must have been buried subsequent to that (after the Katyn area had been occupied by the German Army). Markov answered:

In my opinion these corpses were buried for a shorter period of time than three years. I considered that the corpse I dissected had been buried for not more than one year or 18 months. . . . The only [member of the delegation] who gave a definite statement in regard to the time the corpses had been buried was Professor Miloslavich from Zagreb, and he said it was three years. However, when the German book regarding Katyn was published, I read the result of his impartial statement regarding the corpse on which he had performed the autopsy. I had the impression that the corpse on which he had performed that autopsy did not differ in its stage of decomposition from the other corpses. This led me to think that his statement that the corpses had been in the ground for three years did not coincide with the facts of his description.[12]

Cross-examination by defense counsel Otto Stahmer, however, seriously impeached the credibility of Markov's testimony. The witness admitted that the commission had met with several Russians from the Katyn area, although he had first stated that its members had had no contact with the local inhabitants. In fact, the commission had interrogated several Russian witnesses, who had stated that the Polish officers had arrived almost daily at the railroad station near Katyn in the months of March and April 1940, that they had been taken in trucks to the wood of Katyn and never seen again. Dr. Markov also retracted his statement that he could not read German and admitted that letters and newspapers and identity papers had been found by members of the commission who were dissecting the bodies.[13] Stahmer introduced into evidence the German white book on Katyn and cross-examined Dr. Markov on many passages.[14]

An explanation for Markov's change of heart may be sought in his personal experience following the liberation of Bulgaria by Soviet troops in the fall of 1944. Markov had been promptly arrested as a German collaborator and brought before a People's Tribunal because of his participation in the international medical commission. In order to save his life, he revised his conclusions on Katyn, which he claimed to have signed under duress. After this confession and "correction" of the record, he was acquitted on 23 February 1945.[15]

By comparison it is illuminating to refer to the post–World War II testimony of François Naville of the University of Geneva, who in September 1946—when the Nuremberg trial was nearing its end—was attacked by a member of the Swiss Labor Party, Jean Vincent, because of his participation in the international medical commission. Albert Picot, vice-president and later president of the Conseil d'Etat (the Geneva cantonal government), asked Dr. Naville to explain his participation to the Geneva Grand Council, and Naville responded in a written report dated 24 September 1946:

It was on the night of April 22, 1943, that Dr. Steiner, medical adviser to the German Consulate General in Geneva, asked me whether I could and would leave on April 26 to join the committee of experts concerned. May I add in this connection that I have never concealed from anybody my outspoken . . . hostility toward Germany after 1914, caused by their foreign policy which I always considered dangerous for Switzerland. . . . Therefore I refused at first and suggested some other Swiss experts in forensic medicine. In the meantime, however, I contacted other persons. They told me that this was not a matter of rendering a service to the Germans, but of responding to the legitimate wish of the Poles, who demanded that an impartial investigation be made, and that it should be established whether anything had been done to produce a nominal roll of the dead officers, to proceed with the identifications as far as possible, and to inform the next of kin. Here I must remind you that, contrary to the practice followed by all the other belligerents, the Russians always refused to supply lists of prisoners of war . . . to the International Committee of the Red Cross[16] and that for a long time no news had been received of the 10,000 officers they had taken prisoner. When Dr. Steiner again invited me, therefore, I decided to accept.

Professor Naville's report further indicates that he was authorized to take part in the medical commission both by the Swiss military authorities and by the Federal Political Department. He also maintained that there was no pressure from the Gestapo:

I can definitely state that we were able to proceed undisturbed with our work as experts. . . . We were always able to discuss all matters freely among ourselves without the Germans being present. . . . As two of us could speak Russian, we were on several occasions able to talk to the peasants and Russian prisoners of war. We also contacted the medical personnel of the Polish Red Cross, who co-operated at the exhumation and were specially detailed to identify the bodies, make nominal rolls, and inform the next of kin. . . . We freely carried out about ten post-mortem examinations of bodies which had been taken, in our presence, from the lower layers of the unexplored common graves. Undisturbed, we dictated reports on the post-mortem examinations, without any intervention from the German medical personnel.

We examined, superficially but quite freely, about 100 corpses that had been exhumed in our presence. . . . we paid particular attention to the transformation of the fatty substances of the skin and internal organs, to changes in the bones, to the destruction of joint tendons, to changes and atrophies of various parts of the body, and also to all other signs which would testify to the time of death. Examination of the skull of a lieutenant, undertaken specifically by Professor Orsos from Budapest, at which I was present, brought to light a condition that virtually excluded the possibility of death having occurred less than three years previously. . . .

All the experts met on Friday afternoon to discuss and decide on the composition of the report. Only medical personnel took part in that discussion, but without any interference. Some of us made a draft of the final report, and it was submitted to me for signature on Saturday. . . . I offered several comments and asked for some changes and additions, which were immediately made. I do not know whether the same consideration was given to the observations and criticisms made by Dr. Markov of Bulgaria; I do not remember whether he intervened during our discussion at the meeting; but I was present when he signed the report on May 1 about noon, and I can state that he did not then make any objections or protests. . . . he was certainly not under any pressure or constraint while the commission of which he was a member was at work.[17]

It is perhaps regrettable that only Dr. Markov was asked to testify at the Nuremberg trial and that none of the other members of the commission had an opportunity to express their views there. Johannes Conrad, the German military judge in charge of the Katyn investigations and thus an important witness to the investigations, did give the following written affidavit on 25 June 1946: "I personally viewed the exhumation and observed that the corpses had a dried-up, mummified appearance; the uniforms were identifiable, all corpses had a shot in the head, some were gagged in the mouth, others had the arms shackled. On most of the bodies papers, jewelry, and money were found, thus facilitating the task of identification. All items found on the victims were classified and exhibited in a room. The diaries and letters found indicated that the execution of the Polish officers must have occurred in April 1940; as far as I remember, the last entries in the diaries found were dated 7 April."[18]

Conrad's affidavit, it seems, was not duly taken into account by the tribunal. Nevertheless, the Soviet prosecution failed to pin the blame on the Germans. The German officer named by the Russians as having been in charge of the massacre, Colonel Friedrich Ahrens, volunteered to testify; when it was proved beyond doubt that he was neither present at the alleged time of the massacre nor at that time commander of the unit accused, Signal Regiment 537, the Soviets claimed that his predecessor, Colonel Albert Bedenk, was responsible. Once Bedenk was produced by the German defense, the case was dropped. Significantly, the subject of Katyn did not appear in the final verdicts.[19]

The U.S. Congressional Investigation
Following the Soviet fiasco at Nuremberg further attempts were made to arrive at the truth, notably by a U.S. House of Representatives Select Committee, which was established in 1951 and issued its final report on 22 December 1952. The Select Committee interrogated, among others, Colonel Albert Bedenk, the German officer who preceded Colonel Ahrens as commanding officer of Signal Regiment 537,[20] and Dr. Helge Tramsen, the Danish member of the international medical commission, who refuted the "report" of a Russian medical commission that visited Katyn in January 1944, after the Germans retreated. He explained why the international commission made only "an extremely small number of post-mortem examinations," as charged by the Russian commission: the German experts in forensic medicine under Professor Buhtz had already carried out a considerable number of post-mortem examinations and about 900 identifications by the time the international commission arrived; under the circumstances it was sufficient to perform full autopsies on nine bodies selected at random.[21] The Select Committee tested Tramsen on his own credibility, his political persuasion, and his wartime activities during the German occupation of Denmark. As it happened, he had been a member of the Danish resistance for a year before he was called to serve on the Katyn commission (he had contacted the resistance movement to discuss whether he should participate at all) and was eventually arrested by the Gestapo and held for the last year of the war in a concentration camp.

The Select Committee also interrogated Dr. Ferenc Orsos, the Hungarian member of the international commission, who had been chosen by the other members to act as chairman. Dr. Orsos reaffirmed his conclusions that the bodies had been buried for about three years.[22] Other members who appeared before the Select Committee and confirmed their 1943 findings were François Naville of Switzerland, Vincenzo Mario Palmieri of Italy, and Edward Lucas Miloslavich of Croatia.[23]

Count Jozef Czapski, a Polish officer taken prisoner by the Russian Army in September 1939, also testified before the Select Committee. Approximately 15,000 Polish officers and men had been interned at the Soviet camps of Starobielsk, Kozielsk, and Otashkov; Czapski himself had been held at Starobielsk until 5 April 1940; when the evacuations began, he was segregated from the rest and sent with some others to the camp of Griazovec, presumably for further interrogation. At the time he assumed that the other officers had been scattered among various camps throughout Russia.

After Hitler's invasion of Russia in the summer of 1941 a Polish army in Russia was to be organized under the Polish General Wladislav Anders to fight the German Army. Czapski was deputized to organize a search for the needed officers. The list of names he prepared was presented to Stalin on 3 December 1941, but the men could not be found. On 2 February 1942 Czapski presented another memorandum to Soviet General Raichmann at the Lublianka (seat of the NKVD) in Moscow. At no time said Czapski, did the NKVD suggest that the missing officers could have fallen into the hands of the invading German army. In his capacity as Commissioner for the Affairs of Former Prisoners of War in the U.S.S.R., Czapski continued his research, although he had given up hope that the men would still be alive; none of the families of the missing officers had received letters from them after April of 1940. "We were fully aware," Czapski concluded, "that this could have been an act of the Germans, because we knew of the German atrocities, but we knew that in this case it was done by the Russians, because we were in Russia and we saw how the Russians had been evacuating these prisoners, and we knew that the Russians did not leave any prisoners to fall into the hands of the Germans. . . . Russia is the most centralized country in the world whenever it comes to issuing orders or directives or policy. Therefore, the full responsibility for this crime does not rest with some NKVD sadist; the full responsibility rests with Beria [chief of the NKVD] and Stalin."[24]

The congressional committee also heard the testimony of Wladyslaw Kawecki, a Polish lieutenant who had been taken prisoner by the Germans in 1939 and subsequently released, and who on behalf of the Polish Red Cross had participated in April 1943 with other Polish officials in an on-site inspection of the graves, where they examined some forty bodies. Kawecki also spoke with two Russians who worked on a farm near the forest and had seen the NKVD vans, known as the "black ravens," bringing soldiers into the Katyn woods in April 1940. In May 1943 Kawecki returned to Katyn with British, Australian, and American POWs to try to establish a list of the Polish officers found in the graves. His review of all the documents found on the bodies persuaded him that the massacre had been perpetrated by the Russians. Kawecki also reported to the congressional committee that in May 1947 in Italy he had been approached by an official of the Warsaw Government in Poland, Alex Dobrowolski, then adjutant to the Polish military attaché in Rome. Dobrowolski proposed to him that he recant his 1943 conclusions and presented him two copies of a statement already prepared for his signature; he even offered money—approximately $2,000—but Kawecki refused to recant.[25]

Among the American officers who visited Katyn in 1943, two testified before the congressional committee. Lieutenant Colonel Donald B. Stewart and Colonel John H. Van Vliet had been captured by the Germans in North Africa and had been taken to Germany as POWs. Although both were convinced of the Soviet authorship of the massacre, they refrained from making any statement about it during the war because they did not want to support the German propaganda effort. Only after their liberation did they report to American military intelligence and later to the congressional committee.[26]

Thus, after thoroughly reviewing the available documentation and questioning witnesses from many nations, the Select Committee concluded its nine-month assignment:

This committee unanimously finds . . . that the Soviet NKVD committed the mass murders of the Polish officers and intellectual leaders in the Katyn Forest. . . . there has not been . . . even any remote circumstantial evidence presented that could indict any other nation in this international crime. It is an established fact that approximately 15,000 Polish prisoners were interned in three Soviet camps: Kozielsk, Starobielsk, and Ostashkov in the winter of 1939–40. With the exception of 400 prisoners, these men have not been heard from . . . since the spring of 1940. . . . Evidence heard by this committee repeatedly points to the certainty that only those prisoners interned at Kozielsk were massacred in the Katyn Forest. . . . On the basis of further evidence, we are equally certain that the rest of the 15,000 Polish officers—those interned at Starobielsk and Ostashkov—were executed in a similar brutal manner. . . . Thus the committee believes that there are at least two other "Katyns" in Russia.[27]

Although the War Crimes Bureau investigated many mass graves discovered in the Soviet Union by the German Army, the Bureau's files shed no
light on the fate of the 6,000 Polish prisoners of war thought to have been
interned at Ostashkov or the 4,000 at Starobielsk. A newspaper of the Polish
government-in-exile in London, *Rzeczpospolita Polska* (Polish Republic) reported in June 1980 that pipeline construction workers had discovered a mass
grave containing the bodies of Polish officers in the vicinity of Orenburg in
the southern Urals, but that these are the Starobielsk POWs appears improbable in view of the distance; other indications place the site of the killings at
Dergachi, west of Kharkov and closer to the camp. It is also improbable that
the Russians, as some witnesses suggested, would have transported 6,000
POWs from Ostashkov to the White Sea, only to drown them there. If there
was an NKVD order to liquidate Polish POWs, it is more likely that the executions took place by simple shooting in the back of the head, in the Katyn
pattern, perhaps in the general area of Bologoye.[28]

Katyn and German Credibility
Since this book endeavors to test the credibility of the investigations of the
War Crimes Bureau and to look out for evidence of fabrication or "doctoring"
of documents, it appears legitimate to remark, as an ironic aside, that in
1969 the Soviet authorities unveiled a major war memorial at a place called
Khatyn, a Byelorussian village where the Germans are said to have killed all
the inhabitants. Khatyn, which is near Minsk, should not be confused with
Katyn, which lies some 160 miles farther east, near Smolensk, a provincial
city in Russia proper. It has been suggested that there was method in this
confusion of the issues. The indefatigable Katyn researcher Louis FitzGibbon
has found 1954 and 1956 Soviet maps that show Katyn but not Khatyn; a 1969
atlas of the U.S.S.R. that shows neither; and a 1974 map that shows Khatyn
but not Katyn.[29]

There are many ways of testing the truth of German allegations about
Soviet war crimes. External corroboration is an important method. In addition, a close analysis of the German sources—that is, an internal examination
into German investigative procedures and how the results of these investigations were internally evaluated—allows a certain judgment with respect to
the existence or nonexistence of a conspiracy to fabricate evidence.

Seldom have historians enjoyed the luxury of being able to study official government papers right across the board, as is the case with captured

German records from World War II. Although a number of documents were lost in air bombardments or deliberately destroyed in the last days of the war, the historian can nevertheless compare records from the German Foreign Office, Propaganda Ministry, Chancellery Office, Ministry of the Interior, High Command of the Wehrmacht, the legal offices of the armed forces, and so on. Had the Germans "fabricated" the Katyn case and, after murdering the Poles, attempted to pin the blame on the Russians, there would surely have been traces of the hoax. Yet a conscientious examination of many record groups in the German Federal Archives revealed again and again that all German officials in the various ministries and departments were convinced that the NKVD had perpetrated the massacres.[30]

Even the relatively obscure *Publikationsstelle Berlin Dahlem*, a research institution in Berlin specializing in questions concerning the German eastern provinces and central and eastern Europe, contains a report dated 29 May 1943 by a medical officer, one Dr. Lang, describing his personal observations at Katyn Forest in May 1943, including the discovery of other nearby graves containing the bodies of civilians. He concluded that the Katyn Forest had been a frequently used execution ground for the NKVD and estimated that there could be 50,000 bodies in the civilian graves just discovered.[31]

In another document the Russian engineer A. Danilowski, who was appointed by the Germans as mayor of a town in the vicinity of Smolensk, asserted that the Polish prisoners of war who had not been murdered at Katyn had been sent to hard labor on railroad construction in northern Russia, where they would all die of cold, hunger, and exhaustion; he spoke of a large contingent of Polish soldiers—not officers—assigned to the 160-mile railroad line between Tschibju and Koschwa.[32]

It should be further noted that the internal papers of all these ministries and research institutions were not intended for publication and thus reflect the subjective convictions of the officials involved. The very existence of these internal memoranda, reports, and file notes from a variety of offices and as many authors adds authenticity to the German allegations of Soviet responsibility for the Katyn massacre.

The first mass grave of Ukrainians in Vinnitsa was discovered by the Germans shortly after they occupied the town in 1941: 96 corpses, mostly of Ukrainian political prisoners and religious dissidents, were found in the courtyard of the civilian prison, victims of the general policy of liquidating prisoners when it became impossible to evacuate them prior to the arrival of German troops. The grave was about 20 meters long and 6 meters wide. The exhumations took place in the presence of a military judge named Schwarz, who collected the relevant evidence and had photographs taken for the documentation of the War Crimes Bureau.[1]

In another courtyard of the same prison a second mass grave was found, but those bodies were not exhumed.[2] It was not until two years later, on 25 May 1943, that as a result of the persistent rumors among the Ukrainian civilian population, digging was begun in other suspected areas of town and more graves discovered. In all, three major graveyards were found: the pear orchard with 38 mass graves, the old cemetery with 40 mass graves, and the People's Park with 35 mass graves.[3] Only some of the bodies were exhumed; weather conditions interrupted the digging, and it was never resumed because the Soviet Army reoccupied the area. By then, however, 9,439 corpses had already been counted.

Wartime Investigations
The Bureau did not get directly involved in on-the-spot investigations of the Vinnitsa murders but merely served as central documentation depot. In view of the political and propagandistic implications of the case, the judicial investigation was entrusted not to a military judge but to a senior civilian judge appointed by the Minister of Justice upon the request of the Minister

for the Occupied Territories. More than fifty witnesses were heard in Vinnitsa itself and in the neighboring towns by a team of judicial investigators under Judge Ziegler.

On 29 June 1943 a Ukrainian guard, Juri Klimenko, explained, "The area I was supposed to watch extended to the courtyard of the church. From there I observed in the fall of 1937 or 1938 that digging was going on in the cemetery every day and trucks arrived every night. Since that appeared suspicious, I went up to the fence and tried to peek through a crack. On several occasions I was able to observe . . . a number of holes in the ground of about two square meters, but I could not determine how deep they were. The trucks were transporting immobile objects under a tent cover which were then thrown into the holes. I could not see exactly what the rigid objects were, since I had to be very careful not to be discovered. . . . I did suspect at the time that the objects were corpses transported from the NKVD prisons. The trucks did not come from the hospital but rather from the town."[4]

On 3 July 1943 another Ukrainian guard, Atanasi Skrepka, testified: "I continued to be employed as a guard even after the area of the pear orchard was fenced off. . . . The trucks kept coming and going on a regular basis from 1938 until the arrival of the German troops. Usually two or three trucks came in a night, and then there was quiet for several nights, and then the trucks returned. Many times I observed traces of blood and . . . frequently smelled the stench of dead bodies. One day I climbed a tree, and from there I saw the open graves with the corpses in them. Apparently the graves were not yet full enough . . . to be closed up. Once I saw two persons who were walking toward the town and who stopped at the fence and tried to see through. Thereupon they were arrested by some guards and taken away; they have not been heard from since."[5]

Judge Ziegler summed up in his provisional report dated 18 July 1943: "From 1936 until the outbreak of war, especially in the period from late 1937 to early 1938, many ethnic Ukrainians from Vinnitsa and neighboring villages were arrested and have since disappeared. Thus far nearly 2,000 bodies have been exhumed. Judging by the number of graves already discovered but from which the bodies have not yet been exhumed, a conservative estimate would place the number of victims at 10,000. The persons arrested were mostly farmers and laborers and ranged between 40 and 50 years of age."[6]

Meanwhile, as in Katyn, the Germans had first sent in their own experts in forensic medicine, then invited foreign experts. The international medical commission that arrived in Vinnitsa in July of 1943 (some three months after the Katyn investigations) was composed of eleven doctors from Belgium, Bulgaria, Croatia, Finland, France, Hungary, Italy, the Netherlands, Rumania, Slovakia, and Sweden. From 13 to 15 July 1943 they carried out 11 full autopsies and 24 simple post-mortem examinations. The commission's expert opinion, signed on 15 July, reads in part: "All the corpses examined had bullet wounds in the back of the head or in the neck . . . with the exception of the lower neck shots, the cause of death was the head injury. From the information obtained from relatives and eyewitnesses, and from the documents found on the corpses as well as the medical examination of the decomposition of the bodies as described in the protocol . . . it may be concluded that the killings took place in the year 1938."[7]

The commission's conclusions confirmed the results of the medico-legal investigations already carried out by a team of German and Ukrainian doctors under a Dr. Schrader, director of the German Association for Forensic Medicine and Criminology. Schrader's provisional report of 16 June 1943 described the exhumation of 509 corpses, of which 171 had been subjected to post-mortem examination.[8]

The German Minister of Health, Dr. Leonardo Conti, thereupon appointed Dr. Schrader head of a German commission of thirteen professors of forensic medicine which from 27 to 29 July 1943 studied the work already done by Schrader and his assistants, visited the three grave sites, and carried out a number of autopsies. They arrived at the same conclusions as the international medical commission.[9]

Postwar Investigations

A decade later, as in the Katyn case, a special committee of the United States Congress turned its attention to war crimes reported from eastern Europe, including the Vinnitsa killings. The House Select Committee on Communist Agression, again chaired by Charles Kersten (Wisconsin), held hearings in Munich 30 June and 1 July, in New York 11–14 October, and in Chicago 18–19 October 1954. Among the sixty-eight witnesses heard by the committee, five testified on the events at Vinnitsa: Zenon Pelenskyj, Pavlo Pavlenko, Ihor Zhurlyvy, Ivan Rudenko, and Fedir Pihido.

Zenon Pelenskyj, a Ukrainian national and a journalist by profession, had been in Vinnitsa at the time of the discovery of the mass graves and the exhumation of the bodies. On 30 June 1954 he testified in Munich:

Some 1½ kilometers from the town on the north edge of a highway there was an orchard, and rumors claimed that in this orchard mass graves had been found. The NKVD had appropriated this orchard from somebody and fenced it . . . nearly 3 meters high . . . and there were rumors that behind this fence in the orchard some dreadful things had happened. Of course, you have to take into account, gentlemen, how it looked during the Bolshevik occupation. People talked about it only in a low whisper, and there was almost superstition about this place. . . .

Now in 1941 the German-Russian War broke out. The Germans occupied the district of Vinnitsa in July 1941. But no one bothered very much about this orchard. It was fenced in still. But in the [very cold] winter of 1941–42 . . . the population began to take this fence apart piece by piece and board by board. They used it for firewood. By the spring of 1942 there was no more fence. . . . I believe the first man who convinced the Germans in Vinnitsa [in 1943] that it might be of interest to investigate this orchard more closely, was Professor Dr. Doroshenko. He was a court physician and got permission from the German town commissar to make the first diggings. . . . At last, after some 2½ months, they dug up in this orchard 38 graves. . . . I saw them dig up hundreds of corpses from single pits and rebury them, and I saw that repeated for days and days, so the conclusion is reasonable that there must have been thousands of these corpses. . . . the population told the Germans that they suspected [also] . . . the old cemetery . . . and the so-called people's recreation park. . . .

Of course, after they had found these terrible places the Germans tried to make use of them, politically and propagandistically, so they invited committees to come and inspect the places. I remember at the beginning of July 1943 an official German committee came . . . consisting of three groups: specialists in forensic medicine . . . assisted by the local physicians; . . . the committee for the investigation of murder from the *Reichskriminalpolizeiamt*, Berlin; . . . [and] the delegation of the German Ministry of Justice. . . . The most important group . . . seemed to be the international committee of expert foreign forensic physicians which visited Vinnitsa in July 1943, and then on 15 July 1943 signed a protocol as a summary of their findings. . . . after the news about these terrible findings spread throughout the region . . . people started to come to Vinnitsa, for the most part women, mothers, sisters, sweethearts, and you could see in this orchard and the other two places lots of women coming and going. . . . There were not very many identification cards with the people in the graves, and most had to be identified by their garments. . . . A great many of these people were identified.[10]

Ihor Zhurlyvy testified on the same day that his own father had been arrested by the NKVD and was never heard from again. Zhurlyvy was in Vinnitsa when the international commission of forensic medicine experts was inspecting the graves: "The members of the commission themselves directed which bodies or corpses were to be taken out of the graves, and they personally conducted an inspection of the bodies. The examination was generally conducted in the following manner: The head was cut open—I am describing what I saw with my own eyes—and the bullets taken out. Then various other types of examinations were performed. Also the members of the commission interrogated Ukrainian wives who had recognized bodies of husbands."[11]

In its final report, the congressional committee concluded that the NKVD had carried out a policy of systematic terror in the Ukraine, claiming thousands upon thousands of lives, including the 9,439 counted Vinnitsa victims.[12]

Years later, in 1971, the U.S. Senate Judiciary Committee published yet another investigation of NKVD killings, including Katyn and Vinnitsa.[13] Other non-German sources of the postwar period have likewise confirmed the German allegations as documented by the War Crimes Bureau. The Ukrainian exile press has published many studies of NKVD massacres; the documentary collection "Russian Colonialism in the Ukraine" includes the Vinnitsa massacre and a statement by Ukrainian witness Ihor Zhurlyvy.[14]

One of the most difficult tasks of the War Crimes Bureau consisted in clarifying the fate of German shipwrecked sailors and air crews downed in the ocean. In the majority of such cases an investigation is impossible because there are no survivors and therefore no witnesses. The chances of surviving in a shark-infested sea are very limited and even smaller if enemy planes or ships attack the wounded and drowning men.

Nevertheless, the Bureau was able to collect at least one hundred depositions from survivors of such incidents. In view of their testimony, one might be tempted to draw the conclusion that Anglo-American planes and warships attacked German shipwrecked personnel as a matter of course. Yet the thousands of Germans saved by American and British ships are proof that it was Anglo-American policy to rescue shipwrecked survivors; sometimes Germans were taken on board even though the presence of other German vessels endangered the rescuing vessel.[1] As a rule, however, British and American cruisers and destroyers did not attempt rescues if there were German U-boats in the area, and rescues by submarines—given their limited space—were infrequent.

In the evaluation of witness testimony certain psychological considerations must be taken into account; the personal danger inherent in battle frequently distorts the perception of those who are fighting for their lives. Misinterpretation and exaggeration are by no means rare, and shipwrecked persons tend to assume that gunfire in their direction is aimed at them, disregarding the fact that there are frequently other legitimate military objectives in the immediate vicinity—perhaps including the ship they have abandoned. The situation is more serious, of course, if it is established beyond doubt that shooting has continued after the ship has gone down or if the shipwrecked are sufficiently far from other targets that any shooting in their vicinity can only be explained as being aimed at them.

Are there any conceivable circumstances under which an attack upon shipwrecked survivors may be termed legitimate? In the specific case of the sinking of the *Erich Giese* near Narvik, Norway, in April 1940, the German Naval War Staff concluded that British destroyers had deliberately attacked the German survivors and surmised that "the British will try to justify their actions by stating that the customs of war permit shooting at shipwrecked crews if it is certain that in the absence of this use of arms, and because of the nearness of enemy occupied land, the shipwrecked would be immediately reintegrated in the enemy armed forces."[2]

No official or unofficial British statement in support of this theory is known;[3] perhaps the German Naval War Staff assumed an unwritten order. (Interestingly enough, there are indications that some officers of the United States Navy thought it valid to shoot at survivors if they could easily swim to the shore of enemy-held territory, even though it would seem that the answer to the dilemma would lie in rescuing and thereby capturing them.)[4]

In the files of the War Crimes Bureau there are many borderline cases where it is difficult to judge whether or not a violation of international law took place, in some it appears that Allied forces actually did shoot at German shipwrecked survivors.

Narvik

During the German invasion of Norway in the spring of 1940 one of the important strategic moves consisted in occupying the port of Narvik in the north, close to the 69th parallel.[5] Hitler sent ten destroyers full of troops and carried out a successful landing. In the meantime, however, sixteen British destroyers and the battleship *Warspite* were on their way to Narvik and entered the fjords precisely as the empty German ships were setting out for their home port. In two major sea battles on 10 and 13 April 1940, all ten German destroyers were wiped out. Soon thereafter the German press accused the British of shooting at German survivors desperately trying to swim ashore in the icy Norwegian waters.

It was through these press reports that the War Crimes Bureau first heard the allegations. On 25 June 1940 Maximilian Wagner wrote on behalf of the Bureau to the High Command of the Navy requesting that depositions from witnesses be obtained. On 1 August the navy ordered a special court to examine the facts, putting Navy Judge Helmut Sieber in charge: "The investi-gations shall be carried out with the necessary thoroughness and expediency and shall be submitted directly to the High Command of the Navy."[6]

On 8 August 1940, prior to Sieber's arrival in Wilhelmshaven, where most of the Narvik crews were stationed, the depositions of a number of survivors from the destroyer *Anton Schmitt* were obtained by a naval officer. Sieber's investigations followed on 15 and 16 August, including the interro-gation of four crew members of the *Erich Giese*, which had been sunk on 13 April 1940. Since Captain Karl Smidt, former commander of the *Giese*, had been reassigned to navy headquarters in Paris, Judge Sieber was sent there to continue the investigations. On 27 August 1940 a preliminary report was transmitted to the Navy High Command in Berlin: "Prior to 6 August 1940 it was not possible to determine who had been shot at by the British in Narvik while swimming in the water, since the destroyer crews were either on leave or transferred. Before Judge Sieber was directed to investigate this matter, we had been able to determine that crew members of the destroyers *Erich Giese* and *Georg Thiele* were involved . . . also the shipwrecked crew of the destroyer *Anton Schmitt*."[7] In the meantime depositions from survivors of the other destroyers had been obtained on 22 August, and the protocols were sent to Sieber.

Pursuant to his orders, Sieber traveled to Swinemünde in Pomerania, where he obtained depositions from several officers and members of the crew of the *Georg Thiele*. On 10 September he was back in Kiel to take the deposi-tion of the *Thiele*'s commander, Max Eckart Wolff. On 16 September he for-warded the sworn protocols and a final report to the Navy High Command, which in turn forwarded the file to the War Crimes Bureau. Sieber's evalua-tion is characterized by a careful analysis of the legal situation. He concluded that a violation of international law had taken place only in the case of the *Erich Giese*. Interrogations in the other cases had established that the British artillery fire most probably was aimed at the destroyers. Even though many sailors had been killed or injured by pompom fire and shrapnel, the distance from the attacking ships was so great that the gunfire could not reasonably be assumed to have been aimed at men in the water. This was also the opinion of Captain Friedrich Böhme, commander of the *Anton Schmitt*, who had been rescued by a Swedish cutter. He explained to Judge Sieber on 16 August: "Several members of my crew alleged that they had been shot at from British merchant ships. Later we captured some 250 British sailors. There is no proof that they actually fired any shots. We did not find any weapons. It may be assumed that they threw them into the water as soon as they realized their hopeless situation. It is out of the question that the shooting observed by the crew could have come from the British warships, which lay at the entrance of the port. The distance was much too great; I estimate it at more than three kilometers."[8]

Similarly Captain Wolff of the *Georg Thiele* testified on 10 September: "The distance to the British destroyers exceeded four kilometers during the shooting. It is obvious that shells would not only hit the destroyer but also fall short or wide of the mark, and therefore it is understandable that the survivors swimming in the water were endangered."[9]

Wolff went on to explain that the situation was entirely different with respect to shooting that took place after the survivors had reached the shore. As they started to climb the rugged fjord cliffs, 4-cm. pompoms and 12-cm. shells exploded all around them; one shell burst in the middle of a group of survivors and killed six. Wolff concluded: "It is clearly established that the British did not aim their fire at the abandoned destroyer but at the crew members . . . it is important to note that the entire crew was unarmed and were only trying to save themselves and the wounded they were carrying."[10] Judge Sieber was of the opinion, however, that although shooting at defenseless survivors in the cliffs was certainly harsh, it did not entail a violation of international law: while it is prohibited to shoot at shipwrecked in the water, it is not expressly prohibited once they reach land, even if they are unarmed; this, he said, is analogous to land warfare, which permits shooting at the fleeing enemy whether or not he is armed.

The events surrounding the sinking of the *Erich Giese* on 13 April 1940 presented an entirely different situation, as Captain Karl Smidt explained during his Paris deposition on 23 August 1940:

> While the crew of some 200 men was swimming in the water, the British destroyers opened fire against us with machine guns and cannons. Several times from the pressure in the water, I felt the explosion of a shell. . . . However, I did not see anyone hit. The crew did suffer casualties through machine-gun fire, which was clearly identifiable by its whistling sound. . . . Reports made to me by members of the crew after reaching land . . . indicated that a number of soldiers had been hit. . . . the civilian steward Masula was wounded by a shot that grazed his head, but the

wound did not endanger his life. Several days after the battle the engine-man Ospelkaus was washed ashore, and we saw that he had been shot in the head, a wound which he could only have received in the water. Other reports submitted immediately after the battle clearly established that several soldiers were killed while swimming in the water. Those who had been swimming in their vicinity observed that their heads were suddenly all bloody and they ceased moving. According to undisputed testimony the British also directed heavy fire at the rafts, even one raft that had no oars and simply floated in the fjord. The British did take nine men prisoner from this raft.

Smidt emphasized that the continued shooting was aimed exclusively at the shipwrecked, since "after abandoning ship there was no belligerent activity on the German side, not even from the shore." He concluded, "It would have been easy for the British to rescue the survivors from the water and thereby prevent them from rejoining the German troops in Narvik."[11]

The sailor Josef Wilzius testified on 16 August 1940: "A British destroyer fired at us while we were swimming. . . . The shots could be seen and heard. They fell in the midst of us. About 500 meters from land I heard my comrade sailor Reddemann cry out. . . . I saw that he was bleeding in the head. I called him and he did not answer. He did not move any more."[12]

Engineman Heinz Backus stated on 17 August 1940: "I saw continuous foam spraying from the machine-gun bullets as they hit the water. . . . I am convinced that this fire was exclusively intended to hit the crew of the *Erich Giese*, since nowhere in the vicinity was there either a German or a neutral ship. We were the last destroyer.[13] And on land there were no German resistance nests. . . . I myself saw a comrade hit by a bullet in the water; his head sank and he did not swim any more. . . . We were very upset about the behavior of the British, since we had rescued twenty shipwrecked British sailors three days before, on 10 April."[14]

Among those German sailors who were hit in the water was Josef Linn. "After we had abandoned ship and were swimming toward land," he recalled on 4 May 1974, "I was hit by a bullet in the upper arm, but I did not ex-perience any pain, since the extremely cold water had a numbing effect. . . . When I reached the land I was unable to climb ashore and had to be pulled out of the water."[15]

Other members of the crew stated that they saw the British shoot at a raft carrying, among others, Captain Ernst Günther Kray and the ship's doctor. It was this raft without oars that the British intercepted some two hours later, thereby capturing the survivors. Captain Kray survived the war to become German naval attaché in London. On 9 April 1974 he recalled the rescue operations: "Our first artillery officer and the second watch-keeper in their life jackets were killed right next to me by machine gun fire. . . . I know with certainty that at the time of the shooting our ship was silent. The battle had already ended. . . . The British destroyer *Foxhound* later approached our raft and sent out a cutter to pick us up and bring us on board. That was the ship's doctor and two or three crew members."[16]

Two other rafts were also attacked by British destroyers before being intercepted by the *Foxhound*, which arrived later on the scene and had not been involved in the shooting.[17] The attackers were probably the *Bedouin* and the *Cossack*, although their logs do not provide any indication that they had shot at shipwrecked Germans.[18]

A report of 16 April 1940 from the British destroyer *Icarus* reacted to the German allegations that British destroyers had attacked shipwrecked German sailors. Although the *Icarus* had not been engaged in battle with the *Erich Giese*, it had heard a British radio message to the *Foxhound*: "If you are not otherwise engaged, pick up any Germans in the water."[19] The *Icarus* regarded this message as a confirmation of the traditional British policy of rescuing survivors and therefore a refutation of the German charges.

The fact that the *Foxhound* did in fact rescue survivors, however, does not exclude the possibility that other destroyers may have behaved differently. In view of the unanimous testimony of the surviving crew of the *Erich Giese* immediately after the events and their consistent assertions ever since, it appears certain that they were indeed attacked while they were swimming ashore. The reconstructed log of the *Erich Giese* also contains a succinct and matter-of-fact entry: "The enemy opened machine-gun fire upon the survivors swimming in the water. Several soldiers were hit. One of the survivors who was wounded superficially by a bullet that grazed his head reached the shore."[20] This was the steward Erich Masula, who told Judge Felix Reich on 5 November 1940: "I myself received two superficial wounds on the back of the head. The corpse of our civilian cook, Bernhard Machens, was later fished out of the water. He had received a shot through the head. . . . I cannot suppose that the British machine-gun fire could have been aimed at any other objective than us."[21]

It is interesting to compare these sober descriptions with the propagandistic tone of such contemporary publications as the navy newspaper *Die Kriegsmarine*, which attempted to recreate the atmosphere with a strong emotional appeal and much rhetorical embellishment:

> Last to abandon his ship was the commander. Three red rafts had been thrown overboard, and now the survivors of the brave crew drifted, some of them on the rafts, the others swimming . . . 1,000 meters from shore. The British destroyers turn around—surely they want to rescue the shipwrecked, take them on board, as one owes to a courageous enemy, as this very crew had done for the survivors of the *Hunter*. But no—the incredible comes to pass: the British approach the men drifting in the water in order to liquidate them with machine guns. Not only that; they even direct their machine-gun fire at those lucky ones who had reached shore, who thought themselves saved: these are fiends who want to appear as decent seamen, as civilized men. Shots through the head and on the back of the neck are proof of this new British atrocity.[22]

It is not known whether the German government submitted an official protest note to the British government. However, the voluminous records of the Sieber and Reich investigations were evaluated by the War Crimes Bureau, and on 28 January 1941 Johannes Goldsche delivered a speech to the German Association for Military Politics and Military Sciences, "Violations of International Law by the Enemy in the Present War," in which he dealt extensively with the *Erich Giese* case.[23] This material was also incorporated in a bulky study prepared by the Bureau, "Violations of the Laws of War by the British Armed Forces."[24]

The *Osia Paraskevi*

One of the gravest instances of shooting at German shipwrecked survivors took place in May 1941 in the Aegean, shortly before the commencement of the German assault on Crete. Judge Georg Prechtel obtained depositions on 18 May 1941 from six witnesses of the event, the Greek captain and the crew of the caïque *Osia Paraskevi*.[25] An interpreter named Felix Ruggiero assisted. According to the caïque's owner, Joanis Mamaloucas:

> On 12 May 1941 my ship *Osia Paraskevi*, a caïque weighing 35 tons, sailed to Kavalla under orders of the German port commander of Kastron [Chios] on the island of Lemnos. We sailed out at eight in the morn-

ing. On board were Captain Theodoros Mamaloucas (my uncle), myself, three sailors, Tsiwelekis, Keleris, and Daniel, the engineman Nasoa, two Greek civilians, and four German soldiers: to wit, an officer, a noncommissioned officer and two men. . . . Around 12 noon the ship was some 35 kilometers or 20 miles northwest of Kastron. . . . Suddenly at a distance of about 1,000 meters a submarine came up behind us and fired three shots over the ship. I ordered the ship to stop immediately. The German officer . . . gave the captain his shirt and told him to signal with it. . . . In the meantime the submarine had approached to about 20 meters. One of five or six men on the tower of the submarine shot with his pistol at the German officer, who then descended with the other three soldiers below deck. . . . A man on the tower with a full beard spoke to us in a foreign tongue and by gesticulating ordered us to go on the lifeboats and to move away from the ship. . . . we recognized it as English because of the way it sounded, since we as seamen had frequently been together with British sailors and had heard them speak. At first we had thought it was an Italian submarine . . . but it could not be, since we know the sound of Italian very well. . . .

While the crew and the Greek passengers were still on board, the German soldiers also came out from below deck. The officer and a soldier with eye-glasses were in uniform, the other two in swimming trunks. They were threatened from the submarine tower with a machine gun . . . and the bearded man . . . signaled them to go back below deck. . . . At this point my crew and I went on the lifeboat and paddled away from our ship; at about the same time the submarine started moving backward. When we were some 10 meters away from the *Osia Paraskevi*, the cannon on the tower started shooting . . . the first round must have hit the caïque below water, since it went up in flames, and the German soldiers, whose clothing was already burning, emerged from the inside of the boat . . . they did not get around to jumping overboard, since the boat suddenly sank under them. After the ship disappeared, the four Germans were swimming . . . then the machine gun on the tower opened fire on the shipwrecked and continued shooting until each German had been hit and sank beneath the water.[26]

Judge Prechtel obtained similar depositions from the other five Greek witnesses, who took the oath in the Greek Orthodox manner: "I swear by God to have spoken the whole truth."[27]

On 26 May 1941 the High Command of the German Navy sent the depositions to the War Crimes Bureau.[28] Meanwhile, the case had also come to the attention of the German press, which exploited it for propaganda purposes; it occasioned vigorous accusations against the British government at a press conference in the German Foreign Office in Berlin on 4 July 1941.[29]

It appears that the British submarine involved was the *Rorqual*. We read in its log for 12 May 1941:

> *Rorqual* went alongside and it was seen that there were Greeks in the caïque; after much shouting and gesticulating they were induced to abandon ship into the boat, and one round of H.E. was fired into the caïque at 50 yards range; there was a big explosion with great flames and most of the caïque disintegrated; the bow remained above surface for about 30 seconds and a dozen or so German soldiers in uniform rushed up the hatch amid the flames shrieking horribly and afraid to jump into the water. The explosion was a heavy one and there must have been explosives aboard the caïque and it seems likely that there were more German soldiers below who were killed by the explosion. There were no German survivors.[30]

Judging by the date, location, and description of the events, it is almost certain that the *Rorqual* report corresponds to the case investigated by Judge Prechtel, even though no mention is made in the British log of shooting at survivors.[31] The German version gains in credibility to the extent that the witnesses were all Greeks and not a priori anti-British. There are close parallels to the *Baralong* case in World War I, when American sailors were the witnesses.[32] It is regrettable that the Greek survivors of the *Osia Paraskevi* were never questioned after the war. On 26 July 1978, however, Judge Georg Prechtel recalled the depositions made thirty-seven years before, because "the case had caused a stir with much indignation. At the time I was the judge of the 164th Infantry Division, and in this capacity I was ordered by the High Command of the 12th Army by telegram dated 17 May 1941 to interrogate the Greek witnesses. After so many years I cannot make precise statements on the witnesses, but it is certain that according to established practice I would not have taken their depositions if they had not seemed credible to me. . . . The location of the deposition was according to my notes the town of Xanthy, northeast of Kavalla."[33]

Crete

The German invasion of Crete began just a week after the *Paraskevi* incident. The attack was primarily carried out by paratroopers, but 2,331 additional troops were to be brought to the island by sea. This endeavor proved to be a disaster for the Germans: the caïques were intercepted by the Royal Navy, and most were sunk or burned in the night of 21–22 May 1941. According to unpublished German figures, however, only 327 of the soldiers aboard them lost their lives; the majority of the shipwrecked were able to reach one of the Aegean islands.[34]

Nevertheless, many of the survivors reported having been attacked while they were swimming in the water. Others, whose caïques had not been destroyed, witnessed the machine-gunning of lifeboats by the British. Corporal Walter Segel stated before Judge Sauermann:

> Together with my troops I went on board a Greek caïque on 17 May 1941 and we sailed from Piraeus in order to land on the western shore of Crete on 20 May to give support to the parachute troops. We sailed in a convoy of 21 ships that was attacked by British warships near Crete in the night of 20–21 May from 2210 in the night until 0330 in the early morning. The British scanned the seas with searchlights, attacked individual ships with artillery fire, and after sinking them, switched on smaller searchlights to look for the shipwrecked, who were holding on to rubber boats or similar gear, and opened fire on them with machine guns and small-caliber cannons. I could observe the shooting clearly . . . individual men in such rubber boats suddenly sank. . . . The British did not even attempt to rescue any of them. I saw at least twenty groups of survivors who were illuminated by the British and then sprayed with bullets. My own ship that had the number 107 or 103 was only lightly damaged.[35]

On 26 May Judge Oskar von Jagwitz interrogated Willi Wall, a survivor of the caique S-3, which had been sunk on 21 May around 2330 hours:

> Since the searchlights had repeatedly illuminated our lifeboat, we tried to move far away . . . after about two hours a British warship found us with its searchlights and attacked us with machine guns and artillery fire. We threw ourselves down on the bottom of the rubber boat to give the impression that it was empty. We clearly heard the bullets whistle

past and the artillery shells hit the water close to us. Yet neither the boat nor those in it were hit. In the meantime, rough seas had come up so that we frequently disappeared in the waves. . . . During the night we rescued four comrades from another ship. . . . [who] told me that they had tried to swim to a warship in order to be rescued; they abandoned this intention after they saw that the ship they had supposed was Italian was in fact British and opened fire both on the rubber boats and on the swimmers.[36]

A survivor of the caique S-12, Sergeant Karl Riep, told Judge Roland Rüdel that "many soldiers in the water cried out for help. The British shot at them too, and the cries for help were silenced. I can state with certainty that this shelling could only hit the shipwrecked, since in the direction of the shooting there were no larger ships of the first marine squadron."[37] And a sailor from another caïque, Ernst Stribny, reported to Judge Joachim Schölz on 28 May 1941 that despite his ship's white flag, six British ships opened fire on it and continued to shoot at the men who jumped into the water and tried to swim away. Heavy machine-gun fire "sprayed all around us for several minutes. I was wounded in my right shoulder. . . . we suffered the most from the heavy cruiser, which moved criss-cross amid the shipwrecked and continuously shot at us. And in its wake many comrades were pulled into the depths by the suction of the propellers. The British did not rescue a single man."[38]

A similar case had already been reported to Judge Schölz by Lieutenant Walter Henglein on 23 May 1941. He had been on a two-masted Greek fishing boat with some 80 Mountain Infantry troops: "We unfurled a white towel at the stern and most of the crew signaled with white handkerchiefs. The English must have seen these signs of surrender, since they were at a distance of 150 to 200 meters, and we clearly saw that they were watching us with binoculars. Nevertheless, they shot . . . some ten to fifteen shells from a cannon with caliber 2.5 or 3.7 cm. The shells hit the deck and wounded some twenty men. We tried to bring the wounded below deck and were then hit by a 7.5-cm. shell that destroyed the infirmary room and everything in it. . . . I ordered "abandon ship" and was the last man to jump into the water . . . when I had swum some 50 meters from our boat, machine-gun bullets splashed in a semicircle around me."[39]

Corporal Karl Grimm, a survivor of the same boat, added: "They fired mainly with machine guns but also with artillery. My feet were repeatedly lifted by the water pressure caused by the shells that exploded around me. . . . A comrade swimming directly next to me was hit in the head by a machine-gun bullet and sank. I estimate that at least ten men were killed in the water. . . . It is almost incredible that anyone survived."[40]

A sailor named Valentin Zaremba completed the picture: "At first I saw some 50 men swimming about; a quarter of an hour later we were only 22. All missing comrades were victims of British bullets; the sea was completely calm, and everybody had a life vest, so that actually no one could have drowned. . . . we were especially upset that the British . . . stood along the entire railing and watched how we were individually liquidated. The shooting lasted something like a quarter of an hour."[41]

The caïque S-109 was attacked around 9:30 on the morning of 22 May. Judge Rüdel took the deposition of the ship's doctor, Ernst Thalheim, who described an attack on his lifeboat: "We were some 400 meters away from our ship. The British cruiser was at a distance of 700 to 1,000 meters. No one in our rubber boat was wounded or killed, but three air cells were hit by the shell, so that one side of the boat sank deeper in the water. Neither from our ship nor from the rubber boats did anyone shoot at the British, nor did we have any weapons at all in the lifeboat. One more thing: our ship was shelled after the white flag had been hoisted."[42]

The logs of the British Navy report the sinking of many German caïques in the Mediterranean in the month of May 1941 but contain no reference to the shooting of the shipwrecked Germans.[43] After the invasion of Crete the frequency of German reports of British attacks on shipwrecked soldiers decreased notably. One of these later reports was made on 15 September 1941 by gunner Rudolf Krobath to Judge Wilhelm Landwehr: "On 8 July 1941 I had been assigned to the machine-gun area of the caïque LV that was bringing vacationers from Chania to the Continent. . . . Around 3:00 A.M. a British submarine came up and fired a cannon shot at our caïque, hitting the engine. The caïque stopped but did not sink. The entire crew and passengers put on life vests and jumped overboard. The British submarine sent a detail to our caïque and blew it up with explosives. While we were swimming in the water, the British submarine shot at us with machine guns for about 15 minutes. The British used tracer bullets. Two men were killed and two seriously wounded. I myself was wounded superficially in the head."[44] Another survivor of the same ship, Corporal Alois Walder, reported to Judge Hochegg: "The submarine shot at the rubber boats, and at the crew swimming nearby, with tracer ammunition. Then the gunner changed his aim and shot directly at us. . . . We submerged our heads, and the bullets swept over us."[45]

Air Attacks

The files of the War Crimes Bureau disclose that shipwrecked German survivors were shelled not only by enemy warships but sometimes also by enemy airplanes; frequently, the victims were not only German sailors but also German air crews whose planes had been shot down over the sea.

A typical case was reported by Horst Buchholz, whose plane was shot down by British Spitfires on 19 August 1942 over Dieppe, France. In his deposition before Judge Piest, Buchholz stated: "Our wireless operator, petty officer Iger, and I came down some three kilometers from the shore, threw off our parachutes, and rendered our swimming vests serviceable. We tried to swim to shore but made very slow progress owing to the strong ebbtide and also because Iger was wounded. . . . several Spitfires flew at a height of about ten meters and fired constantly at us in the water. They must have hit Iger, who was swimming behind me, because I heard him call out my name . . . but I could not see him any more. I assume that his swimming vest was hit and that he immediately went down. . . . In my opinion the Spitfires attacked us deliberately and not by accident . . . there being no other military objectives around."[46]

Several other German planes were shot down over Dieppe on the same day, and Corporal Hugo Lemser reported a similar Spitfire attack: "I saw the bullets hit the water. I tried to dive but could hardly go down because of the life vest. . . . There is no doubt at all that the British fighter deliberately attacked me, since there were no other objectives in my direction. . . . There were no ships or boats in my vicinity."[47]

Numerous incidents of this kind were reported in the Mediterranean, especially after the Allied invasion of Italy. On 21 June 1944 a rescue launch was attacked and sunk by American fighter planes, which then continued to strafe the survivors, Corporal Fritz Schiedlauske and the Italian pilot Umberto Pagan. Corporal Schiedlauske reported:

At 9:00 A.M. I was ordered to rescue shipwrecked. My comrades and I sailed on an Italian fishing boat with red cross markings. Size of the boat: 10 meters long, 2 meters wide; size of the red cross: one square meter.

American fighter planes flew over us until about 11:00 A.M. We held up the red cross in the flight direction, and the planes turned around and flew toward the coast.

A second fighter squadron flew over us and took objectives on land under fire. But then they turned around and flew out to sea, went into position by looping over us, and opened fire even though we waved the red cross flag at them. The boat sank. We were four in the crew. Two were killed and two seriously wounded. Even while we were swimming in the water, gravely wounded, the planes attacked us again. . . . I cannot say with certainty how many approaches they flew over us.[48]

Umberto Pagan provided a more poignant description: "On 21 June 1944 . . . my brother and I rushed with two German soldiers to rescue German shipwrecked. The red cross that we flew was plainly visible to the American fighter planes, but . . . they strafed us with machine-gun fire . . . my brother and a German soldier died instantly. The other German and I were seriously wounded. In spite of our wounds we jumped in the water, since our boat was sinking. . . . the Americans continued their attack and wounded us again. The fighter pilots, who saw that German comrades were coming to rescue us, shot at them too."[49]

British Policy

There is no doubt that official British policy was in keeping with the laws of war. But this did not preclude discussion of the limits of the laws of war in the British ministries—particularly, discussion of the possible military advantages of a harsher policy toward shipwrecked enemy crews.

Early in 1943 the German submarine commander Hans Diedrich von Tiesenhausen, who had been rescued by a British destroyer after his submarine was sunk, submitted a protest to the British government and asked that it be forwarded to the Protecting Power. He alleged that after his submarine had shown the white flag, British planes continued the attack and machine-gunned the shipwrecked crew. Von Tiesenhausen's report was considered at a British Foreign Office meeting on 3 June 1943. Legal advisor Patrick Dean, who chaired the meeting, advised against forwarding the report to the Protecting Power. He had already argued at the Air Ministry on 14 May 1943 that an airplane cannot capture a submarine; it can only sink it. "The surrender of such vessels should not be accepted unless Allied surface craft in the immediate vicinity are in a position to ensure their capture. In all other circumstances the attack should be pressed home in spite of the flying of a white flag. It has been agreed that for operational reasons this policy should as far as possible be concealed from the German Government . . . if it became known to them, they might institute reprisals against captured British seamen."[50] Yet Dean did not succeed in having his point of view adopted; instead, the Air Ministry drafted very clear instructions for fighter pilots: "In no circumstances is the crew of a U-Boat in the water to be subjected to any form of attack."[51] On 28 May 1943, Dean objected that "circumstances can be imagined (e.g., when a U-Boat crew are swimming from their sunk or damaged U-Boat to an enemy war vessel) where one would have thought that attack upon them from the air was justifiable."[52]

Dean's point of view parallels the German hypothesis with respect to Narvik, that the crews of British destroyers considered it justifiable to shoot at the German shipwrecked because any German sailors who reached land would be incorporated into the German forces there. And it may be that the British destroyers in Narvik acted according to this unwritten policy—but other attacks on shipwrecked survivors were less easily rationalized. A case in point was the machine-gunning of the shipwrecked crew of the U-852 by four British fighter planes on 3 May 1944 near Bender-Beila, Somaliland, which was in British hands so that there was no danger whatsoever that the German crew would join other German forces on land. In fact, the survivors were all taken prisoner shortly after the landing.[53]

This incident is not devoid of historical irony: it was this very U-boat that two months earlier, on 13 March 1944, had sunk the steamer *Peleus* in the Atlantic and machine-gunned a number of Greek survivors.[54] After the war, in criminal proceedings before a British military court in Hamburg, the commander of the U-852, Heinz Eck, defended his actions on grounds of operational necessity, arguing that Allied air surveillance was very intensive in the Atlantic and that late in 1943 four German U-boats had been discovered in the same area and sunk by fighter planes.[55] He contended that he had never ordered the killing of survivors; rather, he gave an order to destroy all floating wreckage to prevent Allied planes from using it to find and destroy his ship—even though he knew that a number of shipwrecked would be hit by the shelling and that those not hit would have a much smaller chance of surviving without the larger floating objects to cling to.[56]

In fact, three Greek sailors did survive to testify against Eck. The British court rejected his defense of "operational necessity" and sentenced him and two of his officers, Lieutenant August Hoffmann and the ship's doctor Walter Weispfenning, to death.[57] The court also refused to consider the Bender-Beila incident, which the defense had not failed to mention.[58] Evidently a *tu quoque* defense was psychologically impossible at the time.

In comparison with air and land warfare there were relatively few atrocities in the war at sea. Nevertheless, besides the infrequent attacks upon shipwrecked crews (discussed in the preceding chapter), in a number of instances German and Italian hospital ships were bombarded and sunk.

The Soviet Union, for instance, refused to recognize any German hospital ships. Shortly after the onset of the German-Soviet war on 22 June 1941, the German government notified the Soviet government that the German hospital ships *Stuttgart*, *Berlin*, *Rügen*, and *Strassburg* would operate in the Baltic Sea. The Soviet Union responded with the following note: "Having established that the German government systematically and in a treacherous manner violates international treaties and conventions, German observance of the Hague Convention cannot be relied upon. Considering that the Soviet government has already protested the German Army's bombardment of Soviet hospitals in spite of elementary norms of international law, the Soviet government has every reason to believe that the German government will not abide by the Hague Convention and that its hospital ships will be misused for military purposes. Therefore the Soviet government cannot consent to granting immunity to the notified ships pursuant to the Hague Convention."[1]

It was no surprise, then, when the German hospital ship *Alexander von Humboldt* was bombarded on 22 August 1941 as it was entering the Gulf of Petsamo (Pechenga) in the Barents Sea, and the *Pitea* on 2 September 1941 as it was leaving Venta (Windau) in the Baltic.[2] But the Soviet Union's unilateral action in refusing to recognize German hospital ships could not be deemed to have rendered the attacks legal, because the immunity of hospital ships is part of customary international law.[3] Therefore, the War Crimes Bureau recorded the deposition of numerous witnesses in both cases.

German hospital ships were endangered not only by the categorical So-viet denial of immunity but also by the British policy of selecting which hospital ships they would recognize and which they would not. Although the Hague Convention does not set any size requirements, the British gov-ernment refused to recognize the smaller German hospital ships, such as the *Bonn, Erlangen, Freiburg, Hüxter, Innsbruck, Konstanz,* and *Saturnus.* The High Command of the German Navy commented on the British refusal to recognize the *Bonn* (478 tons) and the *Konstanz* (1,441 tons) in a note to the War Crimes Bureau: "This policy not only conflicts with the letter and the spirit of the Convention on Hospital Ships, which sets no limits whatever with respect to their tonnage, but contrasts with the practice of the United States government, which has recognized both vessels without any reserva-tions. The British government has repeated its 1940 objection to the smaller hospital ships, claiming that these vessels had the primary purpose of picking up unwounded air crews after they went down over the sea. The British took this position in 1940 probably in connection with the air offensive against En-gland and in order to hinder as much as possible the execution of Operation Sealion [the projected German invasion of the British Isles]. This objection does not have any justification whatever with respect to hospital ships in the Mediterranean."[4]

Pursuant to their declared policy, the British Navy and Royal Air Force regularly attacked the smaller German hospital ships—though finally, in 1944 they did recognize the *Erlangen* (3,509 tons) and early in 1945 the *Freiburg* (both of which they had earlier attacked).[5] British warships also disturbed the traffic of German hospital ships by forcing them to take a certain course or by detaining them for weeks and even months, as indicated in the records of the German Navy although not always the Bureau's files.[6] Moreover, though the British did attack primarily the smaller hospital ships, every now and then a larger ship was also hit; British pilots evidently had some difficulty in deciding which ships enjoyed immunity. In May 1943 the Bureau compiled a list of those that had been bombarded, comprising nine German hospital ships and ten Italian hospital ships (including the sinking of the *Po, Arno, California, Giuseppe Orlando,* and *San Giusta*).[7]

As the bombardment of hospital ships continued, the Bureau compiled a second list of twenty-four cases covering the period from May 1943 to December 1944,[8] including thoroughly documented attacks on the *Erlangen* on 13 and 15 June 1944[9] and on the *Freiburg* on 14 August 1944.[10] On the basis of these records the German government submitted protest notes to the British government: for instance, a note of 1 November 1944 described attacks on the *Hüxter*, *Innsbruck*, *Erlangen*, *Bonn*, and *Saturnus* as well as upon hospital trains bearing the red cross.[11]

The most significant case on the Bureau's list was the sinking of the *Tübingen* (3,509 tons) on 18 November 1944 at 0745 hours GMT (Central European Time) near Pola, south of Cape Promontore in the Adriatic. The case was all the more remarkable considering that Great Britain had recognized the *Tübingen* as a hospital ship and the British Mediterranean Command knew its exact course. Yet two British Beaufighter planes attacked and sank it.[12]

Apparently, the sinking came as a surprise to the British Foreign Office; in the afternoon of the same day it communicated the news to the Swiss government as Protecting Power.[13] The Swiss telephoned the German legation in Bern, which in turn cabled the German Foreign Office in Berlin: "Hospital ship *Tübingen* pursuant to assurances given sailed on 17 November . . . from Bari to Triest. British authorities have been informed that the hospital ship was attacked in the early hours of today by a British plane and severely damaged. The British have ordered an immediate investigation."[14]

The British government sent a second, more extensive note to the Protecting Power on 19 November 1944.[15] The official German protest followed on 24 November:

On 18 November 1944 at 0745 hours near Pola the German hospital ship *Tübingen* was attacked by two double-engine British bombers with machine guns and bombs so that it sank, although the course of the hospital ship had been communicated to the British government well in advance of its voyage to Saloniki and back for the purpose of transporting wounded German soldiers. Numerous members of the crew were thereby killed and wounded. The German government emphatically protests the serious violations of international law committed by the sinking of the hospital ship *Tübingen*. The German government demands that the British government take all necessary measures to prevent the recurrence of such—undoubtedly deliberate—violations of international law. It further reserves the right to draw the appropriate consequences of this and many other violations of international law, especially such as were communicated to the Swiss legation in Berlin by verbal note of 1 November 1944.

This note was forwarded to London by the Swiss on 27 November 1944.[16]

The British Air Ministry had already ordered an inquiry on 18 November 1944,[17] and on 29 November the British Foreign Office informed its legation in Bern that an investigation of the case was in progress.[18] On 19 November the Royal Air Force headquarters in the Mediterranean had telegraphed the Air Ministry: "The report is too long and intricate to lend itself to summarizing in a signal, but the incident was the result of a curious mixture of bad luck and stupidity."[19] It appears that through a chain of errors on the part of the British pilots and a misunderstanding in the wireless transmission, the order was in fact given to attack the ship. The official British answer, submitted to Germany on 4 December 1944, explained that

> four aircraft circled the ship, but as the leader was still unable to identify her he decided to signal sighting details to base and to request instructions. For technical reasons he was unable to transmit the signal himself and he therefore instructed the second aircraft in his section to do so.
>
> The captain of the second aircraft . . . had identified the ship as a hospital ship and incorrectly assumed that his leader had done so too. He supposed, however, that there must be some special circumstances justifying an exception from standing orders prohibiting attacks on hospital ships and transmitted a message to the following effect: "1 H.S. 350" (one hospital ship—course 350 degrees) and giving her position. Owing to atmospheric conditions, this message was received by base incorrectly and read to the following effect: "1 H.S.L. 350" (one high-speed launch —course 350 degrees) with a position in the middle of the Gulf of Venice. A second version of this message showing the position of the ship as overland in the Istrian Peninsula and requesting instructions was later retransmitted by another station, but it again incorrectly referred to a high-speed launch.
>
> These messages were then brought to the notice of the controlling officer, who ascertained that no Allied high-speed launch was in the position indicated in the first version of the message, which was in any case many miles from the *Tübingen*'s position, and gave orders to attack. On receipt of these orders the leader, who was still unaware that the ship

was a hospital ship, instructed his section to attack. It was not until he passed over the ship after completing his attack that he distinguished the name *Tübingen* on her side and realized her identity.

His Majesty's Government have given instructions that the circumstances attending this attack shall be fully investigated at a court of enquiry with a view to preventing any similar incident, and that if the facts disclosed justify such a course, appropriate disciplinary action shall be taken. . . .

Although as stated above, his Majesty's Government regret the sinking of the ship in the circumstances described, they cannot refrain from remarking that had the *Tübingen* been properly illuminated at the time of sighting in accordance with international practice, the leader of the section would have had no difficulty in identifying her as a hospital ship and the incident would thus have been avoided. They trust that care will be taken to ensure that in the future, all German hospital ships are illuminated in poor visibility in such a way as to leave no doubt as to their identity.[20]

As was to be expected, the German authorities too devoted considerable time to investigating the circumstances of the sinking. On 23 December 1944 ship's captain Wolfgang Dietrich Hermichen, first officer Günter Quidde, and the third officer Heinrich Bruns made sworn statements before German Navy Judge Franz Nadenau; on 29 December they were followed by chief engineer Ernst Frenz, second officer Martin Messeck, and third engineer August Glander.[21] The statement of Captain Hermichen casts doubt on part of the British version:

Both British planes flew 60 to 70 meters right over our ship. With the unaided eye I saw the British colors on the fuselage. Even if the planes had not recognized us before as a hospital ship—something which is, I think, out of the question because of the extraordinarily good visibility —at the very latest, at this moment they must have realized that we were a hospital ship. After both planes had flown over the ship, they turned around and flew one by one over the ship, one plane from starboard and the other from port, and attacked us again. The bombardment was repeated about six times from starboard and about three times from port.[22]

Obviously, a key question is whether the ship was immediately identifiable (as the Germans claimed) or whether the visibility was impaired (as the British contended). Second officer Martin Messeck, who was responsible for illumination, explained: "Shortly after 7:00 A.M. I ordered our electrician Kessenich to turn off the night illumination. The sun had risen already about 6:30 A.M. . . . During my watch the weather did not change. After sunrise we had perfectly calm weather. . . . Shortly after 7 A.M., after the night illumination had been turned off, four fighter bombers circled over us. Yet they turned around and flew southward. They were clearly British planes. I saw their colors."[23] According to the Germans the ship was attacked between 7:45 and 8:05 A.M. and sank at 8:20 A.M. There was enough time to put down lifeboats, and two members of the crew, sailors Töllner and Heuer, were able to take pictures of the sinking ship. The photographs, which survived the war, show good visibility and calm seas.[24]

On the basis of these depositions the High Command of the German Navy submitted a preliminary report to the German Foreign Office, rejecting the British allegations: "The note's contention that the incident would have been avoided if the Tübingen had been duly illuminated can only be termed an inadequate excuse, considering that a German court has now taken statements from the captain of the Tübingen as well as the first and third officers, according to whom a mistake about the identity of the ship as a hospital ship was completely out of the question because of the clear weather."[25] The German Foreign Office then transmitted a second protest note on 29 January 1945:

The investigation which the German government has carried out does not support the British hypothesis that the sinking of the hospital ship occurred because of a chain of errors, the first link of which was the incorrect behavior of the hospital ship. According to sworn testimony by German witnesses, the circumstances were as follows:

On 18 November the Tübingen was on its way from Bari to Triest in the north Adriatic Sea. During the entire voyage the ship made transmissions on radio and on the 600-meter wave, so that the enemy knew its general location. Shortly after 7 A.M. Central European Time, four single-engine fighter bombers, which were identified as British, flew over the hospital ship, which was duly painted as such.[26] The planes circled . . . and flew southward, without carrying out any attack. The weather was clear, there were no clouds, the sea was calm, there was practically no wind, the sun had just risen, when at around 7:45 A.M. Central European Time two double-engine British "Boston 3" bombers approached the *Tübingen* from the south. The planes circled over the ship and opened fire with rockets and machine guns. The attack lasted almost fifteen minutes, during which the planes flew over the ship at a height of 30 to 60 meters, bombarding it twelve times. The planes left the scene only after they saw that the ship was lost. In the light of these facts there is no doubt whatever that the crews of both attacking planes knew that the ship they were attacking was a hospital ship. There is no room here for the possibility that they might have been in error. The allegation is equally untrue that the *Tübingen* was not sufficiently illuminated when the first four fighter-bombers sighted it. Because of the very clear weather the *Tübingen* was at this time unmistakably recognizable as a hospital ship . . . even from a great distance.[27]

A communication of the High Command of the German Navy to the War Crimes Bureau indicated that the casualties were one dead, three missing and presumed dead (including the ship's chief medical officer, Dr. Neumann), and 16 wounded.[28]

Faced with the problem of whether to answer this second, more emphatic note,—with the war nearing its end and the German collapse only a matter of weeks away—the British Foreign Office decided to do nothing: "We feel here that little good will be done by continuing the controversy and that if any reply is considered necessary, it should be confined to a reassertion of the facts set out in our note to the Germans."[29]

There are still a number of open questions about the sinking of the *Tübingen*, and German and British opinions still differ. On 18 August 1976 Captain Hermichen reiterated his supposition that the British attack was deliberate and that it served a very good military purpose: the hospital ship service in the Adriatic was very necessary to take the pressure off the railway between Trieste and Montenegro; without hospital ships, the wounded would have had to be transported by rail or plane, thus using facilities that were sorely needed for the war effort.[30] This theory has some persuasive value, considering that the British apparently had a concerted policy of hindering

German hospital ship service as much as possible: for example, by repeatedly detaining them (as it did the *Gradisca*, *Freiburg*, *Bonn*, and *Konstanz*) in port for weeks at a time.[31]

On the other hand, the inquiry carried out by the British Air Ministry makes credible the possibility that a chain of errors did in fact take place, that unusual circumstances accounted for the regrettable sinking of the hospital ship. No official order to sink the *Tübingen* has ever been found, and British policy is quite unequivocally against the bombardment of red cross vehicles and vessels.[32] British documents not intended for publication or for use in war propaganda clearly show that both the Air Ministry and the Foreign Office were surprised and embarrassed by the event.

Ten years lie between the original publication of *Die Wehrmacht-Unter-suchungsstelle* and this somewhat abridged American edition. In those ten years the author has had the opportunity to consult further materials in American, British, and Swiss archives and to interview more judges and witnesses with regard to the specific investigations described here. This new material has been incorporated into the subsequent German editions and, of course, into this newest version.

Press reaction to earlier editions in German-speaking countries was very broad. Daily newspapers and scholarly journals alike described the publication of part of the War Crimes Bureau's files as something new and sensational, perhaps the most important discovery of World War II records in thirty years. The book attracted favorable reviews in newspapers and magazines, including the *Frankfurter Allgemeine Zeitung*, *Die Zeit*, and *Der Spiegel*, and such scholarly journals as *Die Historische Zeitschrift*; it has appeared in four hardbound and two paperback editions.

In the non-German-speaking world, however, the book has made rather less impact. In 1980 the *Manchester Guardian* commended it, noting that "no German historian had touched the documents out of concern that a study of Allied war crimes could be interpreted as an attempt to set off German against Allied injustices." In 1981 the *American Journal of International Law* reviewed the work at greater length and made a useful observation about the Malmédy trial, which has been duly taken into account in Chapter 11 of this edition.

When the two-part television special based on the book was broadcast on German prime-time television in 1983, NBC's *Today* show reported on it, and the *Los Angeles Times* gave it extensive coverage, noting that "the aim of the German series was to show that war itself is a crime, a point emphasized in commentaries in the series, including one by Benjamin Ferencz, one of the American prosecutors at the Nuremberg war crimes trials of Nazi leaders." (By contrast, predictably, the Soviet news agency TASS called the documentary a "terrible lie.")

Hundreds of German readers and television viewers sent letters, documents, and even pictures, for which the author is very grateful; their input is reflected in this edition. Yet in spite of the considerable success of the book and the broadcast, no American publisher showed immediate interest in bringing an English-language version to press, nor did comment, addition, or rebuttal come from American, British, French, Polish, or Soviet historians or ex-soldiers with specific knowledge of the events described. Perhaps the American edition will now enable some Allied veterans to contribute to confirming or disproving the German investigations.

Following World War II, historical research into war crimes understandably concentrated on the investigation of Nazi crimes against humanity. Besides the sheer number and enormity of those crimes, one of the reasons for giving so little attention to non-German abuses was the lack of concrete evidence of violations of the laws of war by the Allies during that conflict. This continued to be the case until the files of the Wehrmacht War Crimes Bureau were declassified and made available to scholarly research. No comparison is possible between Nazi and Allied crimes; nevertheless, the existence of 226 volumes of German records on alleged Allied war crimes requires examination.

Of course, publication of all 226 volumes of the Bureau's records would have been impracticable; nor does this book pretend to be a "documentation" of Allied war crimes. First and foremost it is a history of the German office that was responsible for investigating allegations of such crimes. Because it is based primarily on German testimony, the Allied position on each and every case should be made known. The principle of *audiatur et altera pars* applies here as elsewhere; hence, the appeal made in the German editions is hereby repeated, that all persons with knowledge about these events come forth to complete or correct the information presented in this book.

Meanwhile, what, if anything, can be learned from the existence of this German agency and from the investigations contained in its surviving records? As this book shows, the War Crimes Bureau was not established to fabricate documents on Allied war crimes: its records are genuine; its investigations were carried out methodically, in a judicial manner. The Bureau was not cut after Goebbels' Propaganda Ministry. Yet it is useful to stress what the book does *not* mean or imply: surely it does not compare Allied with Nazi war crimes, nor does it diminish the guilt of the Nazi war criminals condemned at Nuremberg and elsewhere. A so-called *tu quoque* argument is not possible here, either historically or morally. On a different plane, however, the book does encourage the reader to reflect on the individuality of suffering. One should try to put oneself in the situation of every soldier subjected to torture or abuse, of the prisoner of war who thinks that the madness of war is over, only to discover the cruelties of imprisonment or the barbarity of summary execution.

The reader should also consider that all soldiers—including enemy soldiers—have certain human rights, regardlesss of the criminality of their governments. The laws of war, which apply to all belligerents, were adopted to make war less savage and to limit suffering, not to grant special privileges to those who claim that they are the victims of aggression or who assert that they are fighting for the good cause, that theirs is a "holy war." Indeed, and perhaps surprising to many Anglo-American readers who may never have reflected beyond the German stereotype, the investigations described in this book manifest again and again the subjective conviction of the German military judges in the field and of the staff members of the Bureau that the German armed forces were fighting honorably, in compliance with the Hague and Geneva Conventions, while those on the other side—that is, we, the Allies—were violating those Conventions. The German judges were ordinary men, wrapped up in the routine of their work. They were not cynics; there is not one jaded remark among the thousands of observations and comments that accompany their investigations. As unbelievable as this may seem to the Anglo-American reader, the German military judge in 1939 to 1945 saw himself as a protector of generally accepted human values. It was not until after the German unconditional surrender, after the collapse of the Nazi hold over all German media, that many Germans—including military judges and Bureau members—were confronted with the full reality of Nazi crimes and the crushing responsibility for the Holocaust. The wrenching journey from the relative quiet of their bureaus to the unsettling realization of the Nazi nightmare had to be accomplished by these men in the postwar period. During the war years many were living in a moral and intellectual vacuum, professionally limited to the confines of their daily juridical tasks.

History is made up of more routine and banality than many historians would care to admit. Indeed, one of the most interesting revelations contained in the records of the Wehrmacht War Crimes Bureau is precisely that it existed as a well-functioning office that routinely compiled and investigated reports of alleged war crimes and even continued to prepare official protests against the Allies well into the spring of 1945, only a few weeks before the final collapse of the Third Reich. Even more significant is the fact that the United States and British governments took the German protests seriously and also continued investigating and answering them through April of 1945.

Most important, however, the study of these files shows that in wartime there is a constant danger of excesses, of violations of the provisions of the Hague and Geneva Conventions, and that this problem affected every party to the conflict to a greater or lesser degree. It is the responsibility of scholars and lawyers to focus attention on this difficult chapter of contemporary history in order to determine in *which* situations *which* war crimes were committed and thereby help prepare the ground for a better observance of the provisions of humanitarian law in armed conflict. Yet the ultimate concern must remain the eradication of the source of these violations—that is, the prevention of war itself. Certainly this is the important lesson to be learned from the present study into the crimes of the Allies in the Second World War.

This book, which does not claim to be more than an introduction to a painful subject matter, is essentially an antiwar book. *Dulce et decorum est pro patria mori* (Horace) was the Latin maxim that justified the death of Rome's soldiers. For thousands of years rulers have glorified war and sought to justify their power and the shedding of enemy blood by the claim that victory was in itself proof of virtue and honor. Heroic deeds became mythology and heroes were venerated as gods.

Thrust into a murderous war, men and women often do perform heroic deeds, take colossal risks in the name of some goal perceived as noble and good. Among the military rank and file there are extraordinary individuals capable of great sacrifice, prepared to endure profound suffering, and ready to die for a cause. But let us not elevate such heroism to the rank of mythology. Let us honor those individuals without making a religion out of war. For there are not only heroes in war but also criminals—and as Vietnam has shown us, war crimes have not been committed exclusively by one people in history, nor just by one or the other party to a struggle. In every armed conflict heinous war crimes have been committed; most of them have gone unpunished.

Today, after countless fratricidal wars, Western thinking recognizes that dying for one's country may be necessary but that death on the battlefield is not sweet, nor is it a positive value in itself. War is neither glory nor honor. It is horror upon horror, injustice, agony, and waste.

NOTES

The following abbreviations are used throughout the notes.

ADM	Admiralty
AJIL	*American Journal of International Law*
AOK	Armeeoberkommando (High Command of an Army)
BA	Bundesarchiv (federal archives of the Federal Republic of Germany), Koblenz
BA-MA	Bundesarchiv-Militärarchiv (military archives of the Federal Republic of Germany), Freiburg
BA-ZN	Bundesarchiv-Zentralnachweisstelle (personnel files), Kornelimünster
BB	Bundesarchiv-Bern (Swiss Federal Archives)
E.W.	European War
FO	Foreign Office, British
H	Heer (Army, German)
ICRC	International Committee of the Red Cross
IMT	International Military Tribunal, Nuremberg
IMT	42-volume published records of the Nuremberg trials
KTB	Kriegstagebuch (War Diary)
NA	National Archives, Washington, D.C.
NOKW	Nazi-Oberkommando der Wehrmacht (series of Nuremberg documents)
NSB	Niedersächsische Staatsbibliothek, Göttingen
OKW	Oberkommando der Wehrmacht (High Command of the Armed Forces)
PA	Politisches Archiv des Auswärtigen Amtes (Political Archives of the German Foreign Office), Bonn
PH	Preussen Heer (Prussian Army, record group from World War I in BA-MA)
PRO	Public Record Office

RG   Record Group in NA

RM   Reichs-Marine (Reich Navy, record group in BA-MA)

VAA   Vertreter des Auswärtigen Amtes (liaison officer of the German Foreign Office)

VfZ   *Vierteljahrshefte für Zeitgeschichte*

VR/KR Völkerrecht/Kriegsrecht (record group in PA)

WO   War Office, British

WR   Wehrmacht Rechtsabteilung (Legal department of the Wehrmacht)

INTRODUCTION

1 Information from Joachim Heinemann, son of former Bureau member Martin Heinemann, in a letter to the author, 14 July 1976.

2 See also Robert Wolfe, ed., *Captured German and Related Records* (Athens, Ohio, 1974).

3 Information from George Wagner, National Archives; Microfilm Publication T-77, Rolls R1458–98, Modern Military Branch, Military Archives Division, National Archives, Washington, D.C.

4 United States of America v. Josef Alstötter et al., in Herscht Lauterpacht, ed., *Annual Digest and Reports of Public International Law Cases* (London, 1947), case 126, pp. 278ff. Cf. Hermann Weinkauff, *Die deutsche Justiz und der Nationalsozialismus* (Stuttgart, 1968), esp. Hitler's Reichstag speech of 26 April 1942, attacking the independence of the judiciary (pp. 147ff.). See also Ingo Müller, *Furchtbare Juristen: Die unbewältigte Vergangenheit unserer Justiz* (Munich, 1987); Lothar Gruchmann, *Justiz in Dritten Reich, 1933–40* (Munich, 1987).

5 As recorded by Admiral-General Hermann Böhm, 22 August 1939, IMT, 41:25, Raeder doc. 27 (all translations from the German, French, and Russian are the author's unless otherwise specified).

6 IMT, 4:243–44. Cf. Jürgen Runzheimer, "Der Überfall auf den Sender Gleiwitz" (esp. the 1949 report of the station's director), VfZ, 1962, pp. 408ff.

7 Transcript of author's interview with Hans Boetticher, 20 April 1976, p. 13.

8 See Karol M. Pospieszalski, *The Case of 58,000 Volksdeutsche* (Poznan, 1959), pp. 70, 63, 120ff. The Central Bureau's list, of course, may well have been incomplete.

9 IMT, 1:54. In September 1976, when an obelisk commemorating the death of the Polish officers was erected in London, over vehement Soviet diplomatic protest, the official British statement was that "it has never been proved to Her Majesty's Government's satisfaction who was responsible." The London *Times*, however, observed: "Enough has been published to convince anyone who is not a dedicated defender of the Soviets that the massacre did take place in 1940, when Katyn was under Soviet and not German control." See also the editorial in the *Frankfurter Allgemeine Zeitung*, 18 September 1976, p. 1; and the Polish exile journal *Polish Affairs* 98 (December 1976): 6ff.

10 "Temoinage oculaire de notre correspondant particulier sur le front oriental," *Le Courrier*

de Genève 306 (7 November 1944): 1, quoted in Alfred de Zayas, *Die Anglo-Amerikaner und die Vertreibung der Deutschen*, 7th rev. ed. (Berlin, 1988), pp. 82–83. See also Alfred de Zayas, *Nemesis at Potsdam*, 3d ed., rev. (Lincoln, Neb., 1988), esp. pp. 60–69.

11 Geneva Conventions of 12 August 1949, Articles 49 (I), 50 (II), 129 (III), 146 (IV).

12 Geneva Conventions of 12 August 1949, Articles 47 (I), 48 (II), 127 (III), 144 (IV). For all citations of the Hague and Geneva Conventions, see Dietrich Schindler and Jiri Toman, *The Laws of Armed Conflict* (Leiden, 1973).

CHAPTER ONE

1 Schindler and Toman, *The Laws of Armed Conflict*; Rudolf Bernhardt, ed., *Encyclopedia of Public International Law* (Amsterdam, 1981–88), vols. 3–4.

2 Henri Dunant, *Un Souvenir de Solférino* (Geneva, 1862).

3 At the Hague Peace Conferences there was considerable disagreement between the Great Powers and smaller powers, esp. with regard to the legality of partisan (guerrilla) warfare and the participation of civilians in armed conflict. See "Combatants" in vol. 3 of Bernhardt's *Encyclopedia of Public International Law*.

4 A Protecting Power is a neutral nation asked by one belligerent nation to represent the rights of its citizens in the other belligerent nation(s). See s.v. "Protecting Power" in Bernhardt, *Encyclopedia of Public International Law*, vol. 9; A. Janner, *La puissance protectrice en droit international* (Basel, 1948); P. von Muralt, *Die Schweiz als Schutzmacht* (Basel, 1947); Dietrich Schindler, "Vertretung fremder Interessen durch die Schweiz," *Schweiz. Jahrbuch* 1 (1944): 130ff.

5 Art. 3 of Hague Convention IV (1907) provides: "A belligerent party which violates the provisions of the said regulations shall, if the case demands, be liable to pay compensation. It shall be responsible for all acts committed by persons forming part of its armed forces."

6 "Gray books," "white books," and the like (each European country having a designated color) are official compilations of a government's diplomatic documents and internal papers and reports. Their main purpose is to inform the country's legislature and the public about foreign policy; they also play an important role in war propaganda. See s.v. "Colour Books" in Bernhardt, *Encyclopedia of Public International Law*, vol. 9.

7 On the issue of mutilated hands, see L. L. Klotz, *De la guerre à la paix* (Paris, 1924), pp. 33ff.; Lord Arthur Ponsonby, *Falsehood in War-Time* (London, 1928), pp. 78ff.; Harold Lasswell, *Propaganda Technique in World War I* (London, 1927), p. 82; Horace C. Peterson, *Propaganda for War* (Oklahoma City, Okla., 1939), p. 37; James D. Squires, *British Propaganda at Home and in the United States* (Cambridge, Mass., 1935), pp. 66ff.

8 Lord James Bryce, *Report of the Committee on Alleged German Outrages* (London, 1915).

9 Leon Friedman, *The Laws of War* (New York, 1972), pp. 777, 868–82; Ingo von Munch, "Llandovery Castle," in Karl Strupp and Hans-Jürgen Schlochauer, *Wörterbuch des Völkerrechts* (Berlin, 1960–62), 2:420; F. von Zwehl, *Die Versenkung der Llandovery Castle*, 1921.

10 Lasswell, *Propaganda Technique*, p. 81; Peterson, *Propaganda for War*, pp. 60ff.; *Le régime des*

prisonniers de guerre en France et en Allemagne au regard des conventions internationales, 1914–1916 (Paris 1916).

11 Johannes Bell, ed., *Völkerrecht im Weltkrieg* (Berlin, 1927), 2:147, 145. Cf. *Documents on British Foreign Policy 1919–1939,* 1st ser., 9 (1960): 608 (British list, 97 cases; French list, 334 cases; Italian list, 29 cases; Belgian list, 334 cases; Polish list, 51 cases; Rumanian list, 41 cases; Serbian list, 4 cases).

12 Claude Mullins, *The Leipzig Trials* (London 1921); "Judicial Decisions Involving Questions of International Law," *AJIL* 16 (1922): 674ff.; Arnold Toynbee, *Survey of International Affairs, 1920–1923* (Oxford, 1925), pp. 96ff.; "Minutes of the Proceedings of the Seventh General Meeting," *Transactions of the Grotius Society* 8 (1923): xixff.

13 For the text of the judgment, see *AJIL* 16 (1922): 708ff.; also *Amtliches Weissbuch über die Kriegsverbrecherprozesse,* Reichstagsdrucksache. 1. Wahlperiode 1920–24, no. 2584, p. 254ff.

14 *AJIL* 16 (1922): 674ff., 696ff.; Mullins, *Leipzig Trials,* pp. 87ff., 67ff., 151ff.

15 Bell, *Völkerrecht,* 2:185–86.

16 Kriegsministerium, *Militäruntersuchungsstelle für Verletzungen des Kriegsrechts: Belgien, Löwen* (Berlin, 1915). Cf. Peter Schöller, *Der Fall Löwen und das Weissbuch* (Cologne, 1958). See also Franz Petri and Peter Schöller, "Zur Bereinigung des Franktireurproblems vom August 1914," *VfZ* 9 (1961): 234–48.

17 See pp. 7, 13, 14, 98 of the Kriegsministerium report (n. 16).

18 "Die Völkerrechtswidrige Führung des belgischen Volkskrieges."

19 Cf. Bernhard Duhr, *Der Lügengeist im Völkerkrieg* (Munich, 1915); Fernand van Langenhove, *Comment nait un cycle de légendes* (Paris, 1917); Jules Valery, *Les crimes de la population belge* (Paris, 1916).

20 Kriegsministerium, *Militäruntersuchungsstelle für Verletzungen des Kriegsrechts: Denkschrift über den belgischen Volkskrieg, Zusammenfassende Darstellung* (Berlin, 1917). Cf. the Belgian side, which claims that there never was civilian warfare in Belgium: Fernand Mayence, *La Légende des franctireurs de Louvain* (Louvain, 1928); R. P. Oszwald, *Der Streit um den belgischen Franktireurkrieg* (Cologne, 1931).

21 "Erwiderung auf die von der Französischen Regierung erhobenen Anschuldigungen," BA-MA, PH 2/35.

22 "Die Beschiessung der Kathedrale von Reims," BA-MA, PH 2/28.

23 Peterson, *Propaganda for War,* p. 61: "In many instances the soldiers of the Allied armies used church towers and private houses as cover for their operations."

24 "Frankreich und das Kriegsrecht: Schandtaten an der Front," BA-MA, PH 2/27.

25 Bell, *Völkerrecht,* 2:338ff.

26 BA-MA, PH 2/26, p. 1.

27 Lothar Kotzsch, "Baralong Fall," in Strupp and Schlochauer, *Wörterbuch des Völkerrechts,* 1:157.

28 Excerpts of the testimony of American witnesses before the American consul in Liverpool are contained in the exchange of telegrams between the American Embassy in London and the State Department in Washington, published after the end of the war: *Foreign Relations of the United States*, 1915, supp., pp. 527ff., 577, 604ff.; *Foreign Relations of the United States*, 1916, supp. 1, pp. 79ff.

29 "Denkschrift der Deutschen Regierung über die Ermordnung der Besatzung eines deutschen Unterseeboots durch den Kommandanten des britischen Hilfskreuzers 'Baralong,'" BA-MA, PH 2/25; English text in *AJIL* 10, supp. 1 (1916): pp. 8off.

30 *Foreign Relations of the United States*, 1915, supp., p. 605.

31 *AJIL* 10, supp. 1 (1916): 86. See also Bell, *Völkerrecht*, 2:493.

32 "Schwarze Liste derjenigen Engländer, die sich während des Krieges gegenüber deutschen Heeresangehörigen völkerrechtswidrigen Verhaltens schuldig gemacht haben," BA-MA, PH 2/25, pp. 13ff.

33 According to the official record, Deputy Chief Johannes Goldsche continued in this capacity until his separation from military service on 31 December 1919. Thus it would appear that the bureau was not dissolved until that date at the earliest.

34 Geheimes Staatsarchiv Preussischer Kulturbesitz (Berlin), I. HA Rep. 84a, no. 11763, pp. 18–23.

35 Bell, *Völkerrecht*, 2:270.

36 Art. 34 provides in part: "The German Parliament has the right, and, upon motion of one-fifth of its members, the obligation, to establish investigatory committees. Such committees shall establish the facts in public proceedings. . . . The courts and administrative offices are required to comply with the committee's requests for production of evidence; the files of government offices shall be opened to the committee, if so requested."

37 Bell, *Völkerrecht*, 1:4, 19ff.

38 "Verletzungen der Genfer Konvention durch Deutschland-feindliche Staaten während des letzten Krieges."

39 Bell, *Völkerrecht*, 2:273ff., 3:31ff.

40 Ibid., 3 (pt. 1): 23ff.

41 Ibid. (pt. 2): 715ff. At the time of the completion of Meurer's report, the fate of 15,747 (9.38 percent) German prisoners of war in Russia had been determined: they had perished. The fate of 51,213 (30.45 percent) still remained unknown. K. W. Böhme of the German Red Cross writes on this point that "158,104 German soldiers who were prisoners of war in Russia 1914–1918 perished, that is, 39.4 percent" ("Absicht oder Notstand?" 1963, p. 9). Cf. Nicholas N. Golovine, *The Russian Army in the World War* (New Haven, Conn., 1931), p. 103, according to which 70,000 Russians perished as prisoners of war during World War I. Golovine estimates the number of Russian POWs at 2,415,000 (p. 93), for a death toll of 2.8 percent.

42 *Völkerrecht im Weltkrieg*.

43 PRO, FO 371/24423, Doc. C 6639ff.

44 PRO, ADM 199, vol. 140:17.

45 Captured Soviet papers, in PA, Kult. Pol. Geheim, vol. 112, "Berichte des Legationsrates Graf Bossi-Fedrigotti"; cf. BA-MA, RW 2/v. 158, pp. 178, 180.

46 Captured Soviet papers, PA, Kult. Pol. Geheim, vol. 167.

47 Telegram to the British Foreign Office, signed Kuibyshev, PRO, FO 371/30921, Doc. C 10825.

48 "Punishment for War Crimes—the Inter-Allied Declaration," signed at St. James's Palace, London, 13 January 1942 (H.M. Stationery Office).

49 U.N. War Crimes Commission, *History of the United Nations War Crimes Commission* (London, 1948), p. 118.

50 NA, R659, Doc. 740.00116 E.W. 1939/566.

51 "A History of the War Crimes Office, 25 September 1944–30 June 1945," p. 1 (4-2 DA A, Office of the Judge Advocate General, NA).

52 Captured U.S. papers, BA-MA, RW 2/v. 87, p. 14.

CHAPTER TWO

1 Lehmann (1890–1955), Senatspräsident of the Reichskriegsgericht in 1937, Ministerialdirektor and Chief of the Wehrmacht-Rechtsabteilung 1938, was tried at Nuremberg (OKW Trial, Case 12) and sentenced in 1948 to seven years' imprisonment.

2 Trial of Wilhelm von Leeb (OKW Trial, Case 12), NSB, Proceedings of 16 July 1948, p. 7726.

3 *Heeresverordnungsblatt* 1939, Teil C, Blatt 26, 15 September 1939, p. 310. The same text was published in the *Luftwaffenverordnungsblatt* 1939, Part A, 18 September 1939, p. 230; and in the *Marineverordnungsblatt*, vol. 70, 1939, p. 633.

4 *Deutsche Justiz*, 1939, p. 1611.

5 Deutsche Gesellschaft für Wehrpolitik und Wehrwissenschaften.

6 BA-MA, RW 2/v. 30, pp. 2ff.

7 Ibid., 61, pp. 13ff.

8 Ibid., 24, p. 6a.

9 See Chapter 11.

10 BA-MA, RW 2/v. 164, p. 22.

11 Ibid., 34, p. 2.

12 Information from Günther Arnolds and his wife, whom the author visited on various occasions, 1978–82.

13 On 18 November 1946 Rudolf Lehmann prepared from memory an organizational chart of the legal department of the Wehrmacht, including the War Crimes Bureau; see Nuremberg Doc. NOKW-397.

14 The author has on repeated occasions visited Karl Hofmann in Giessen. Hofmann was taken

prisoner by the Soviets toward the end of the war and was not released until 1955. After his return to the Federal Republic of Germany, he continued his career as a public prosecutor. He has never written about his personal experiences as a Bureau member or a prisoner of war.

15 The originals of the Yugoslavian depositions are lost; only transcripts may still be found in BA-MA, RW 4, and in PA, Kult. Pol. Geheim. The author received further information from Eugen Dorfmüller in letters dated 3 July and 11 September 1976.

16 The building at Blumeshof was completely destroyed in a major bombardment, November 1943, as were whatever Bureau records had remained there.

17 Sentence of the Feldkommandantur 580 St. L. no. 7/39, BA-ZN.

18 Information from BA-ZN, 13 September 1977; information from the Deutsche Dienststelle, Berlin, 14 April 1978.

19 Transcript of author's interview with Willi Knobloch, 1 July 1976, p. 12.

20 Allgemeine Heeresmitteilungen, issued by the High Command of the Wehrmacht, 7 August 1940, p. 377. See also Section 9, "Behavior in Occupied Territory," pp. 47ff., BA-MA, record group B II 2 d/g2.

21 IMT, 40:74–79, Dönitz Doc. 49, Affidavit of Navy Judge Fritz Jaekel. The author has photocopies of some 150 such judgments.

22 Gericht des Admirals der Westküste Norwegens St. L. J. no. 18-40, BA-ZN, RM 45, Norwegen-G St. 536.

23 Gericht des Admirals Skagerrak St. L. J. III no. 3213/44, BA-ZN, RM 45, Nord-G Fr. 7012.

24 IMT, 40: pp. 78–79, Dönitz Doc. 49.

25 IMT, 34:249ff., doc. C-50.

26 Just Block, Die Ausschaltung und Beschrankung der deutschen ordentlichen Militärgerichtsbarkeit während des 2. Weltkrieges (Diss. jur. Würzburg, 1967), p. 68. See also Helmut Krausnick, "Kommissarbefehl und 'Gerichtsbarkeitserlass Barbarossa' in neuer Sicht," VfZ 25 (1955): 682ff.

27 IMT NOKW-3357; Lehmann Doc. 212.

28 Block, Die Ausschaltung und Beschrankung, p. 70; Lehmann Docs. 222–37.

29 Affidavit of Gotthard Heinrici for the Nuremberg Trials, 12 July 1946, Peace Palace, IMT Doc. 1619 (Laternser Papers).

30 Affidavit of George Lindemann in Neu Ulm, 21 June 1946, Peace Palace, IMT Doc. 1601b.

31 Affidavit of Eberhard von Mackensen, 8 July 1946, IMT Doc. 3066; affidavit of Adolf Block, Neu Ulm, 23 June 1946, Peace Palace, IMT Doc. 1601. Also letter from Block to author, 27 April 1976.

32 Affidavit of Otto Dessloch, 18 June 1946, Peace Palace, IMT Doc. 501.

33 Affidavit of Georg von Küchler, Neu Ulm, 5 July 1946, Peace Palace, IMT Doc. 507.

34 Transcript of author's interview with Erich Kuhr, 7 February 1976, p. 13.

35 Transcript of author's interview with Horst Reger, 19 February 1976, p. 2.

36 Gericht der Feldkommandantur 454, Rechtshilfeliste 3/43. The Judge Viktor Wimmer, presiding, also carried out many investigations for the Bureau and took the depositions of witnesses in crimes committed against German POWs. See the Sieber Papers in the Archives of the Navy Officers Association in Bad Godesberg, West Germany.

37 There are many more examples in the records of the defense of Field Marshal Erich von Manstein, PRO, WO 235/590, and in the records of the defense of the Wehrmacht at Nuremberg. Since none of the defense affidavits for the Wehrmacht were published in the 42-volume *IMT* series, the originals should be consulted at the Peace Palace in The Hague.

38 Letter of Walter Hoffmann to the author, 23 November 1975.

39 Transcript of author's interview with Wilhelm Weber, 1 July 1976, p. 1.

40 See Christian F. von Hammerstein, *Mein Leben* (Munich, n.d.), esp. pp. 56ff. Hammerstein was initially with the Lutheran Church but in 1935 joined the legal department of the navy and later the legal department of the air force.

41 Personnel file in BA-ZN, H 2-8242. Research in the Nazi Party archives and complete party membership files at the Berlin Document Center shows that none of the foregoing persons was ever in the party or in any of its associations.

42 Hubert Schorn, *Der Richter im Dritten Reich* (Frankfurt am Main, 1959), p. 170. Regarding party membership, former Army Judge Willi Knobloch explained on 1 July 1976: "Very many of us who were not in accord with the things that were going on in the political arena decided to turn our backs on the county and district courts and chose to transfer to military justice" (transcript of interview, p. 18).

43 Weber interview, p. 1.

44 Transcript of author's interview with Grünewald on 13 November 1975, p. 3. Grünewald's predecessor as chief of military justice in the field, Erich Lattmann, was similarly opposed to the Nazi Party and resisted the various endemic pressures to join it (transcript of author's interview with Lattmann, 12 March 1976, p. 3).

45 Block letter, 27 April 1976.

46 *Deutsche Justiz*, 1934, p. 632.

47 Article 26 of the Wehrgesetz of 21 May 1935, *Reichsgesetzblatt* I, p. 609. See also decrees of 21 June 1935 and 6 December 1939, *Politisches Handbuch 1938*, pt. 1, vol. 1; Manfred Messerschmidt, *Die Wehrmacht im NS-Staat* (Hamburg, 1969), p. 94; Manfred Messerschmidt and Fritz Wüllner, *Die Wehrmachtsjustiz im Dienste des Nationalsozialismus* (Baden-Baden, 1987).

48 Otto Schweling, *Die deutsche Militärjustiz in der Zeit des Nationalsozialismus* (Marburg, 1978), pp. 130ff. Cf. *Wir klagen an!* issued by the Ausschuss für Deutsche Einheit in East Berlin, 1959, pp. 149ff.

49 Ger van Roon, "Graf Moltke als Völkerrechtler im OKW," *VfZ* 18 (1970): 12–61; van Roon, *Neuordnung im Widerstand: Der Kreisauerkreis innerhalb der deutschen Widerstandsbewegung* (Munich, 1967); Helmuth James Graf von Moltke, *Dokumente* (Berlin, 1986).

50 Hermann Bösch, *Heeresrichter Karl Sack im Widerstand* (Munich, 1967).

CHAPTER THREE

1 Moltke, *Dokumente*, pp. 21, 175–76; Freya von Moltke, Michael Balfour, and Julian Frisby, *Helmuth James von Moltke 1907–1945: Anwalt der Zukunft* (Stuttgart, 1975); van Roon, *Neuordnung im Widerstand*, with a list of Moltke's articles and memoranda in the field of international law. Unfortunately, the records of *Ausland-Abwehr* were largely destroyed by air bombardment.

2 Van Roon, "Graf Moltke," pp. 12ff.

3 BA-MA, RW 2/v. 79, p. 147.

4 Ibid., p. 280; 80, p. 257.

5 Ibid., 87, p. 13.

6 Ibid., 158, pp. 218, 221.

7 Ibid., 79, pp. 161, 163ff.

8 Ibid., 80, pp. 144, 256.

9 PA, VR/KR, vol. 82/3.

10 For the structure, competence, and staff of the propaganda department, see W. Keiling, *Das deutsche Heer 1939–1945: Gliederung, Einsatz, Stellenbesetzung*, 3 vols. (Bad Nauheim, 1956–70), esp. 42/ii, 1–19. See also Ortwin Buchbender, *Das tönende Erz* (Stuttgart, 1978), p. 22ff.

11 See Chapters 17, 18, 20.

12 Certified copy of the order in the private papers of former Army Judge Alfons Waltzog. The author has interviewed Waltzog on three occasions.

13 The author interviewed Lattmann on 12 March 1976 and Grünewald on 13 November 1975.

14 BA-MA, RW 2/v. 168, p. 226; ibid., 149, p. 248.

15 Sonderkommando des OKW zur Aufdeckung bolschewistischer Greueltaten und Völkerrechtswidriger Handlungen.

16 BA-MA, H 20/290, pp. 272ff.

17 Ibid., p. 260.

18 See Chapter 21. The records of the *Sonderkommando Buhtz* have probably been destroyed or lost, since they were kept at the Institute for Forensic Medicine of the University of Breslau, which was occupied by Soviet forces in the spring of 1945. Buhtz died as the result of an accident on 26 June 1944.

19 The text of this directive has not been found in Western archives; it may be that the Germans themselves destroyed all the official papers when the Army Medical Office abandoned its headquarters in April 1945, shortly before the Russian Army closed its ring around Berlin. See Hans Hartleben, "Die organisierte Entwicklung des Heeres-Sanitätswesen von 1930–43," *Wehrmedizin* 1 (1977): 62.

20 BA-MA, RW 2/v. 184, p. 131.

21 Ibid., pp. 136, 137ff.

22 Beratender Gerichtsmediziner beim Heeres-Sanitätsinspekteur.

23 BA-MA, H 20/293, pp. 158ff.

24 BA-MA, RW 2/v. 196, p. 284.

25 BA-MA, H 20/293, pp. 150–51.

26 BA-MA, RW 2/v. 158, p. 290.

27 Ibid., 204, pp. 116ff.

28 Ibid., 202, p. 227.

29 Ibid., 167, pp. 93, 96.

30 Ibid., 139, pp. 57, 103.

31 Ibid., 158, p. 254.

32 Ibid., 61, pp. 70, 103.

33 PA, Kult. Pol. Geheim, vol. 174.

34 BA-MA, RW 2/v. 162, pp. 252, 254, 256.

35 Von Hentig Papers, PA; author's interview with Werner von Hentig, 31 August 1976.

36 PA, Kult. Pol. Geheim, Akten des VAA beim AOK 11, von Hentig.

37 PA, Kult. Pol. Geheim, Akten des VAA Schutt, AOK 9, vol. 168.

38 BA-MA, OKW 962, p. 23, and OKW 12, pt. 1, p. 105. The head of the international law department in the Demobilization Office was Walter Cartellieri, and his deputy was Bureau member Lothar Schöne, but the latter was still in Freising, Bavaria, when the Dönitz government ceased to exist: letter of Schöne's widow, Gertrud Schöne, to the author, 1 March 1979. See also Institute für Zeitgeschichte, Munich, Microfilm MA-208, p. 71 (OKW 962).

39 See Marlies Steinert, *Die 23 Tage der Regierung Dönitz* (Düsseldorf, 1967); and Walter Lüdde-Neurath, *Regierung Dönitz*, 3d ed. (Göttingen, 1964).

CHAPTER FOUR

1 See Chapter 13.

2 *Ausweis*, issued 8 September 1939; original in possession of Alfons Waltzog.

3 Transcript of author's interview with Karl Hofmann, 5 May 1976, p. 13.

4 BA-MA, RW 2/v. 190, p. 283.

5 Schweling, *Die deutsche Militärjustiz*, p. 130.

6 See Chapter 2.

7 Transcript of author's interview with Judge Arndt (formerly of the Supreme Court of the Federal Republic) 1 July 1976, p. 21.

8 The record group *Fremde Heere Ost* contains very extensive documentation of Soviet war crimes against German soldiers, but also against non-Germans: Poles, Lithuanians, Estonians, Latvians, Ukrainians, Crimean Tatars, and others; BA-MA, RH 2/579.1, RH 2/657, RH 2/663, RH 2/665, RH 2/682, RH 2/690, RH 2/1177, RH 2/1231 are some of the more important files.

9 *Feindnachrichtenblatt*, no. 10, 9 July 1941: BA-MA, RH 20-6/489.

10 General *zur besonderen Verwendung* (for special duty). This post was created in the High Command of the Army on 1 October 1939. Eugen Müller was the first General z.b.V.

11 BA-MA, RH 20-6/489, p. 82 (AOK 6 KTB Ic/AO of 21 June to 15 July 1941).

12 PA, Kult. Pol. Geheim, VAA Frauenfeld, vol. 120, 12 November 1941.

13 BA-MA, RH 20-6/515, 516, p. 589 (KTB Ic/AO).

14 BA-MA, RW 2/v. 168, pp. 120ff.; author's interview with Stankeit, 31 August 1976.

15 BA-MA, RW 2/v. 168, p. 119. In Hellenthal's files there is a copy of his transmittal letter of 4 July 1941 to the German Foreign Office and also of Dr. Stankeit's report: PA, Kult. Pol. Geheim, Akten des VAA beim RH 20-6, Hellenthal.

16 BA-MA, RW 2/v. 168, p. 124.

17 Letter of Rudolf von Schönfeld to the author, 8 May 1978.

18 BA-MA, RW 2/v. 168, pp. 128ff.; author's interview with Erich Kuhr, 7 February 1976.

19 BA-MA, RW 2/v. 168, p. 130. The author was also able to locate the witness Georg Wendler and the court clerk Willi Schumacher, and send them photocopies of the 1941 depositions. Schumacher answered on 25 February and Wendler on 5 April 1976. Both confirmed the accuracy of the depositions and the authenticity of their respective signatures.

20 BA-MA, RW 2/v. 175, p. 197.

21 See Chapter 23.

22 BA-MA, RM 54/40.

23 BA-MA, RW 2/v. 234, p. 52. The files in this part of the Bureau records are particularly incomplete; nevertheless, the newspaper report may have been inaccurate, since the Bureau did not include the case in its 1943 special list, "Enemy Attacks on Hospital Ships": BA-MA, RW 2/v. 40, pp. 22ff.

24 See Chapter 24.

25 BA-MA, RW 2/v. 79, pp. 17, 18.

26 ICRC, *Report of Activities during the Second World War*, vols. 1–3 (Geneva, 1948).

27 BA-MA, RW 2/v. 129, passim.

28 Deposition of Luftwaffe Sergeant Manger, ibid., 92, pp. 5, 27.

29 Deposition of medical orderly Wenzel, ibid., pp. 5, 24ff.

30 Deposition of Major Noster, ibid., pp. 6, 32ff.

31 Deposition of noncommissioned officer Gugel, ibid., pp. 5a, 28ff. See also ICRC, *Report of Activities*, 1:333ff. In the Soviet Union, however, German prisoners of war were frequently employed in cleaning up minefields. See the documents of the defense in the Manstein Trial (1949), PRO, WO 235/594.

32 BA-MA, RW 2/v. 92.

33 Ibid.

34 Ibid., 72, pp. 12ff.

35 Traditionally, combatants have been members of the armed forces of a party to a war or members of militias or volunteer corps fulfilling the following conditions set forth in Art. 1 of the 1907 Hague Regulations on Land Warfare: "(1) to be commanded by a person responsible for his subordinates; (2) to have a fixed distinctive emblem recognizable at a distance; (3) to carry arms openly; and (4) to conduct their operations in accordance with the laws and customs of war." See s.v. "Combatants" in Bernhardt, *Encyclopedia of Public International Law*, vol. 3.

36 ICRC, *Report of Activities*, 1:522–23; Kurt Böhme, *Die deutschen Kriegsgefangenen in französischer Hand*, (Munich, 1971), in Maschke, *Zur Geschichte*, 13:155 n. 292. Cf. Frits Kalshoven, *Belligerent Reprisals* (Leiden, 1971), pp. 193ff.; Hans Luther, *Der französische Widerstand gegen die deutsche Besatzungsmacht und seine Bekämpfung* (Tübingen, 1957), p. 79.

37 BA-MA, RW 2/v. 72, pp. 12ff. Following the television documentary of 18–21 March 1983 (see Note on the Sources), Anton Gottschaller, who had been a POW at Annecy, wrote the author on 23 March confirming the case and enclosing his own affidavit and a map of the area, including the grave sites. See below, Chapter 14.

38 BA-MA, RW 2/v. 89, pp. 40–41.

39 *Deutsche Justiz*, 1939, p. 1611; see also Chapter 2.

40 BA-MA, RW 2/v. 89, p. 96.

41 Ibid., 44, pp. 27–28; 79, pp. 48–49. In a letter to the author, 20 April 1978, Reimann wrote: "I was operated on at the Anzio bridgehead because of my wound. . . . In the hospital camp Oran I made my first complaint concerning my treatment as a medical orderly upon falling into American hands. In this camp I also met noncommissioned officer Klug, who upon captivity had been bandaged by an American medical orderly and then transported. . . . After three months' captivity in Oran I was transferred with other POWs to the United States. I was taken to Camp Clark in Missouri. After some time they realized I was a medical orderly and so I was employed in the camp's hospital. . . . I had been working for about two months when I was suddenly called to headquarters, where I was interrogated about my complaint by Captain Hutchin. Fourteen days later I was transferred to another camp where I had to work with the farmers in the corn and potato harvest." Willi Reimann made a similar statement for the television special on the *Wehrmacht-Untersuchungsstelle* on 18 March 1983.

42 BA-MA, RW 2/v. 44, p. 29. Again interrogated on 13 October 1944 at Camp Clark, Missouri, Reimann repeated his version of the events but was unable to describe the perpetrators in detail. It is unclear whether further investigations were conducted, since the traces of the Reimann case disappear after a mention on 3 November 1944 in the official records: NA, RG 389, Records of the Office of Provost Marshal General, 330.14, Gen P/W 4.

43 BA-MA, RW 2/v. 34, pp. 2ff. See also Chapter 12.

CHAPTER FIVE

1 Rudolf Albrecht, letter to the author, 28 September 1976.

2 *Vorgelesen, genehmigt, unterschrieben.*

3 Transcript of author's interview with Mackel, 12 November 1975, pp. 7–8.

4 Letter from Steigmeier to the author, 7 April 1978.

5 BA-MA, RW 2/v. 80, p. 115.

6 Ibid., 78, p. 287 (dated 26 May 1944).

7 Ibid., 80, p. 129.

8 Ibid., 79, p. 234. Art. 5 of the Tenth Hague Convention of 1907 provides that hospital ships shall be painted white with a one-and-a-half-meter green band horizontally along the sides. See L. Oppenheim and H. Lauterpacht, *International Law*, 1944 edition, 2:396. Today, this green line has been replaced by large red crosses on the side and on deck. (Art. 43 of the Second Geneva Convention of 1949).

9 See Chapter 24.

10 Letter from Gerhard Wulle to the author, 11 January 1977. Haase reported maltreatment of German POWs in France in 1940. Kircher reported maltreatment in Russia in 1941. Judge Wulle appeared in the televised documentary.

11 Transcript of author's interview with Erich Kuhr, 7 February 1973, pp. 25, 26.

12 BA-MA, RW 2/v. 79, p. 274 (typical admonition on a deposition).

13 This formula can be read in many of the protocols: BA-MA, RW 2/v. 52, 56, 62, 134, etc.

14 Mackel interview, p. 7.

15 BA-MA, RW 2/v. 169, p. 139. The examining judge verified the case in a letter to the author, 9 March 1976.

16 Letter to the author from Judge Landwehr, 30 September 1976.

17 BA-MA, RW 2/v. 36, p. 24.

18 See Chapter 16.

19 BA-MA, RW 2/v. 160, pt. 1, pp. 45–46.

20 Ibid., pt. 2, pp. 3ff.

21 Ibid., 169, p. 138.

22 Ibid., 160, pt. 1, pp. 74ff.

23 Ibid., p. 81.

24 Ibid., pp. 71ff.

25 Transcript of author's interview with Waltzog, 29 June 1976, p. 25.

26 Transcript of author's interview with Schattenberg, 20 October 1975, p. 6.

27 Ibid., 235, pp. 130, 138.

28 Ibid., pp. 134, 136.

29 Ibid., pp. 142, 146.

30 Ibid., pp. 155–56.

31 Ibid., p. 157.

32 Ibid., pp. 158, 180.

33 Ibid., pp. 170, 173–74.

34 Ibid., p. 181.

35 Ibid., p. 184.

36 Letter from the *Deutsche Dienststelle* to the author, 26 January 1977.

37 Further probing in the army personnel and court-martial records, BA-ZN, was without results; the name "Donkels" does not appear in the criminal registry, which is, however, very incomplete (letter from the Zentralnachweisstelle to the author, 1 February 1977). There is an interesting postscript, however. In a letter to the author dated 20 March 1982, a former soldier of the German 52d Infantry Division maintained: "In our army unit it was general knowledge that a massacre of wounded German soldiers had taken place at Roslawl," which "must have occurred after the 16th of December 1941, because I remember that on that day the Russians attacked us and we had to retreat. . . . Once I had to return to the area to pick up ammunition. On the way to our unit with some two tons of ammo we passed through Roslawl. The temperature was between −35 and −40. There was no one in the town. In the houses we only found dead German soldiers. In front of some of the houses there were ambulances. The stretchers were hanging out, and there is no doubt that this hospital convoy was attacked either upon arrival or while attempting to evacuate the wounded. They were all massacred there. . . . Apparently they had not all been shot but merely thrown on the snow. We looked all over for survivors but did not find any. I also recall having seen a woman's corpse outside one of the houses. We continued our journey after about half an hour in Roslawl."

CHAPTER SIX

1 BA-MA, H 20/293, pp. 147–48.

2 Ibid., p. 213.

3 BA-MA, RW 2/v. 211, p. 103.

4 Ibid., 195, p. 156. Judge Rudolf Albrecht, who took the sworn deposition of the witness, verified the protocol in a letter to the author dated 28 September 1976. Another witness, Corporal Otto Brentano, gave similar testimony in his deposition of 19 September 1942 (ibid., p. 160).

5 Ibid., 180, pp. 230ff.

6 BA-MA, Tätigkeitsbericht der Abteilung Ic beim RH 20-17, 49 (Geb.) A.K., vol. 18253/4b.

7 BA-MA, RW 2/v. 168, pp. 153ff. In an interview on 19 August 1975 Judge Hans-Georg Jeremias confirmed having taken this deposition and showed me entries in his diary concerning this case. The clerk at the deposition, noncommissioned officer Kempe, also confirmed the case. The medical officer who first found Hans Muth took a picture of him, which was appended to the deposition sent to the Bureau.

8 Ibid., pp. 138–39. Military secrecy forbade revealing the location where the deposition was taken; the protocol notes only "local quarters."

9 Interview with Dr. Emil Stankeit on 31 August 1976, pp. 2 and 3. Dr. Georg Wendler and the medical orderly Mueller were also present at the examination of the bodies. In a letter dated 5 August 1976, Wendler confirmed the results of the investigation as set forth in the deposition of 5 August 1941. Judge Erich Kuhr gave additional information in an interview on 7 February 1976, as did Lieutenant Werner Augustin in a letter of 9 June 1976, and Colonel Ulrich Engelke in letters of 5 and 6 April 1976, with which he also sent two pictures of the victims. The *Deutsche Dienststelle* in Berlin confirmed that the persons reported to have been mutilated near Skomorocchy on or about 26 June 1941 did fall there at that time (letter of 10 March 1976).

10 BA-MA, RW 2/v. 152, pp. 85ff. This witness prefers not to be named. The interrogating judge, Erich Fischer, confirmed the case on 27 September 1976 in a letter to the author.

11 BA-MA, RW 2/v. 41, pp. 214ff. In an interview on 6 October 1975 Taschen confirmed his 1942 observations.

12 BA-MA, H 20/293, p. 161. The Bureau's files contain hundreds of depositions of medical officers, among them Reinhold Mayer, RW 2/v. 166, p. 129; Hans Bock, 195, p. 266; Martin Koslowski, 160, p. 84ff; Herbert Schmitz, 187, p. 287; Arnulf Hammerl, 198, pp. 94ff.

13 BA-MA H 20/293, pp. 215ff.

14 Ibid., pp. 169ff.

15 Ibid., 178, p. 83.

16 Ibid., 206, p. 128. Dr. Mattern gave a sworn deposition before Judge Wilhelm Doms on 15 July 1941 at Gora; he confirmed the content of his 1941 deposition in a letter to the author, 7 December 1976.

17 BA-MA, RW 2/v. 201, p. 96; letter from Dr. K.G. dated 3 March 1978 (the witness prefers not to be named).

18 BA-MA, RW 2/v. 212, p. 44.

19 Ibid., pp. 48ff. There are indications that Dr. Panning himself (who died on 23 March 1944) employed criminal methods in the course of one experiment designed to test captured Soviet dumdum ammunition. Panning published his results in a long article titled "Effect and Proof of Explosive Munition," in *Der Deutsche Militärarzt*, 1942, pp. 20ff. According to Adalbert Rückerl, ed., *NS-Prozesse* (Karlsruhe, 1971), p. 75, there is suspicion that he may have used living Soviet prisoners of war and not corpses for his experiment. The files of the Army Medical Inspector contain numerous reports on experiments with explosive ammunition; all of them, however, were carried out either on inert substances like glass or on living animals: BA-MA, H 20/287, p. 10; H 20/287/1, pp. 22ff., 3ff; H 20/290, pp. 255ff.; H 20/293, p. 235.

20 BA-MA, RW 2/v. 212, p. 49.

21 Ibid.

22 Cf. Dr. Panning's circular letter dated 2 May 1942 to the consulting doctors at the Army High Command Medical Offices: BA-MA, H 20/287, pp. 81ff.

23 BA-MA, H 20/287, pp. 110ff.

24 Ibid., pp. 113ff.

CHAPTER SEVEN

1 PA, VR/KR vol. 82/4, Doc. R 27191.

2 Ibid.; see also Lehmann's letter to the Foreign Office, 26 January 1940, and Goldsche's to the Foreign Office, 26 May 1940.

3 PA, VR/KR vol. 82/4, doc. R 13636.

4 Ibid.

5 See Chapter 18.

6 BA-MA, RW 2/v. 139, p. 27. The Foreign Office used the Bureau's report in its white book "War Crimes of British Forces and of Civilians in Crete," which was published in 1942.

7 Author's interview with Altenburg, 19 June 1976, in particular about the efforts to remove document 109 from the foreign-language edition of the white book.

8 PA, Kult. Pol. Geheim, vol. 50. Cf. depositions of the witnesses Bormann, Saenger, Lange, Marschner, Mauve, Pollei, Olt, Schmidt before military judges Reger, Schattenberg, and Zirner in BA-MA, RW 2/v. 56, pp. 411ff., 419ff., 424ff., and 248ff.

9 PA, Kult, Pol. Geheim, vol. 50.

10 "Since the official investigation of the events at the internment camp of Bereza-Kartuska were not complete at the time of printing, and since sworn witness testimony is not yet available, we publish here this witness report from the pages of the *Posener Tageblatt* of 27 October 1939."

11 PA, Kult. Pol. Geheim, vol. 50. The Italian version, however, includes it.

12 Ibid., telegram dated 6 February 1940. The War Crimes Bureau did not attempt to compute the number of dead and missing, since its task was limited to interrogating the witnesses, but its records suggest that there were between 5,000 and 6,000. See Chapter 13.

13 "L'invasion allemande en Pologne: Documents, temoignages autentifiés et photographiés, recueillis par le Centre d'Information et de Documentation du Gouvernement Polonais," Paris, 1939.

14 PA, Kult. Pol. Geheim, vols. 49–51. Kramarz commented: "Unfortunately, enemy propaganda with respect to alleged German crimes in Poland has considerably anticipated ours, so that we can only speak now of defensive propaganda on our part" (vol. 120).

15 *Dokumente polnischer Grausamkeit*, p. 15. The two white books issued on Poland were not intended exclusively for distribution in neutral countries; on the contrary, they played an important role in justifying Nazi policies in Poland to the Germans themselves. They were necessary as internal propaganda measures, since there had been much indignation on the part of German soldiers and civilians at the way members of the ss and sd and the *Parteibonzen* (party bigwigs, otherwise known as "golden pheasants") behaved. These abuses were supposed to be justified as punishment for Polish crimes on the ethnic Germans of Bromberg and elsewhere.

16 PA, Kult. Pol. Geheim, vol. 51.

17 Ibid., Doc. R 29189/42.

18 PRO, FO 371/28887.

19 PRO, FO 371/43002.

20 PA, Kult. Pol. Geheim, vol. 51.

21 BA-MA, RW 2/v. 177, p. 158. Although the Bureau's files still contain some 400 pictures, probably well over 1,000 have been lost.

22 See Chapters 21–22.

CHAPTER EIGHT

1 Janner, *La puissance protectrice*; Muralt, *Die Schweiz als Schutzmacht*.

2 As reported in a letter of 20 October 1942 from P. Felscher, Swiss diplomat in charge of Protecting Power functions at the Swiss Embassy in Berlin, to A. de Pury at the Swiss Political Department in Bern, BB, 2000 Berlin 3, Classeur 4.

3 See letter from de Pury to Felscher, 4 November 1942, BB, 2200 Berlin 3, Classeur 4.

4 See Chapter 10.

5 BA-MA, RW 2/v. 129, p. 40. Art. 7 of the 1929 Geneva Convention provides: "As soon as possible after their capture, prisoners of war shall be evacuated to depots sufficiently removed from the fighting zone for them to be out of danger." Art. 9, para. 4, provides: "No prisoner may at any time be sent to an area where he would be exposed to the fire of the fighting zone, or be employed to render by his presence certain points immune from bombardment."

6 BB, 2021 (c), Classeur 92.

7 NA, RG 389. Records of the Office of Provost Marshal General, 330.14 Gen P/W, complaints alleging violation of Geneva Convention by American troops in the European Theater of Operations.

8 BA-MA, RW 2/v. 80, p. 144.

9 Ibid., pp. 250ff. The text of the diplomatic note is also found in the Swiss Federal Archive, BB, 2021 (c), Classeur 69. See also PA, VR/KR vol. 82/3; PRO, FO 371/43003, FO 371/50526.

10 PRO, FO 371/50526. RAF headquarters for the Mediterranean telegraphed the Foreign Office: "We have not as yet received detailed replies from our subordinate formations. . . . You will realise that investigations of this nature cannot be undertaken at the expense of more important work and must of necessity take some time."

11 PRO, FO 371/50566.

12 Ibid.

13 Ibid. See also NA, RG 59, Doc. 740.0011 E.W./2-2545. "The War Department has conducted a careful investigation of these alleged attacks and is unable to deny the correctness of the claims. However, the Commanding General, Allied Forces Headquarters, Caserta, Italy, states that because of the nature of these attacks it was virtually impossible to see the Red Cross markings until after the attacks had begun and that the attacks were broken off whenever the markings were seen."

14 BB, 2021 (c) Classeur 66; PRO, FO 371/43002 Document W 15841/106/49.

15 BB, 2021 (c), Classeur 66.

16 BB, 2021 (c), Classeur 51. See Chapter 24.

17 NA, RG 331, U.S. Operational and Occupation Headquarters, USFET S.G.S. 383.6/10, "Treatment of Military POWs held by Allies."

18 BB, 2021 (c), Classeur 66. The inquiry exposed gross negligence on the part of several American soldiers, and court-martial proceedings were recommended.

19 BB, Washington 2200/15, Classeur 11.

20 BA-MA, RW 2/v. 29, p. 5; RW 5/v. 506, p. 14. For more thorough treatment, see International Committee of the Red Cross, *Report of Activities during the Second World War*, 1:412ff.; Kurt Böhme, *Die deutschen Kriegsgefangenen in sowjetischer Hand* (Munich, 1966), in Maschke, *Zur Geschichte*, 7:161ff. See also Chapter 16.

21 BA-MA, RW 5/v. 333, p. 2.

22 Ibid., p. 1. The answer of the German Foreign Office to the ICRC is missing from the records. For Lvov, see Chapter 20.

23 BA-MA, RW 2/v. 29, p. 3. Cf. ICRC *Report of Activities*, 1:413ff.

24 PA, files of the Representative of the German Foreign Office (VAA) in the Reichskommissariat Ukraine, vol. 4, in a letter dated 17 March 1942, no. 6259.

25 ICRC, *Report of Activities*, 2:253–54. Cf. Christian Streit, *Keine Kameraden* (Stuttgart, 1978), pp. 83ff.

CHAPTER NINE

1 Wehrmacht-Auskunftstelle für Kriegsverluste und Kriegsgefangene.

2 BA-MA, RW 2/v. 163, pp. 213ff.

3 Ibid., 57, pp. 159, 179.

4 The remaining Bureau files contain a number of such transcripts involving Polish, French, Yugoslavian, Greek, and Russian prisoners of war: e.g., a judgment against Polish prisoner Jan Laska, delivered by the District Court at Königsberg on 2 March 1942 (BA-MA, RW 2/v. 57, pp. 183–89).

5 Bert V. A. Röling, "Criminal Responsibility for Violations of the Laws of War," *Revue belge de droit international* 12 (1976): 8ff.

6 Both manuals quoted in Hans Frey, *Die disziplinarische und gerichtliche Bestrafung von Kriegsgefangenen* (Vienna, 1948), pp. 102ff.

7 BA-MA, RW 2/v. 49, pp. 3ff.; cf. there the memorandum of the legal department of the Wehrmacht.

8 BA-MA, RW 5/v. 28, pp. 50ff.

9 NA, RG 59, Doc. 740.0016 E.W. 1939/1257; Oppenheim and Lauterpacht, *International Law*, vol. 2, art. 251. See also Röling, "Criminal Responsibility," p. 20.

10 Frey, *Bestrafung von Kriegsgefangenen*, p. 104.

11 Letter to the author, 18 July 1977. Cf. Moltke, *Dokumente*, p. 25.

12 BA-MA, RW 2/v. 57, pp. 3, 93.

13 Ibid., 54, pp. 305ff.

14 Ibid., 57, pp. 19–22, 144.

15 Ibid., p. 199.

16 Ibid., 58, p. 154. Judge Horst Reger took the depositions of a number of survivors of this march: BA-MA, RW 2/v. 56, pp. 37ff., 370ff. Cf. also the "Documentation of Forced Marches" in BA, Ost-Dok, 7, no. 36.

17 BA-MA, RW 2/v. 58, pp. 1–177.

18 Ibid., 57, pp. 319, 197.

19 Ibid., 57.

20 Ibid., 65, pp. 121ff.; PA, Kult. Pol. Geheim, vol. 45 (Report of the Court of the Commanding General of the 2d Flak Corps, 25 September 1940); see also Kult. Pol. Geheim, vol. 40. As in most field courts-martial, the Bureau had no opportunity to supply any documents for the prosecution, but after completion of the proceedings the court sent a transcript to the Bureau for its records. It should be noted that these lynchings were not part of official French policy, whereas in 1944 Martin Bormann sent a circular letter to all Gau-and Kreisleiters to try to induce the lynching of Allied Fliers. No police protection was to be afforded to enemy parachutists. *IMT* Vol. I, p. 261.

21 BA-MA, RW 2/v. 65, pp. 116ff.

22 PA, VR/KR vol. 82/4, R 19256.

23 *Reichsstrafgesetzbuch.* See *Reichsgesetzblatt* 1 (1940): 754.

24 *Ausland-Abwehr* argued similarly in a letter to the War Crimes Bureau dated 21 January 1941 with respect to criminal proceedings against a Major Reverseau on charges of having murdered a German airman: "It is the view of all agencies involved that extradition of French soldiers on the grounds of alleged war crimes is out of the question, because the armistice agreement does not contain such provision and because we do not want to repeat the example of the Western Allies at the end of the last war. The only possibility . . . consists in presenting clear and convincing evidence to the French and demanding that they punish the culprits": PA, VR/KR vol. 82/4.

25 BA-MA, RW 2/v. 27, pp. 6ff.

26 PA, VR/KR vol. 82/4.

27 Ibid., Doc. R 13636.

28 Ibid., Doc. R 15560.

29 Ibid.

30 BA-MA, RW 2/v. 67, pp. 287ff. Cf. the decisions in two *franc-tireur* cases on 31 October 1941: *Entscheidungen des Reichskriegsgerichts und des Wehrmachtdienststrafhofs*, 2 vols. 2 pts. (Berlin 1942), pp. 117ff.

31 Cf. the incomplete records of the case against the French prisoner of war Captain Debilly, 1942–44, BA-MA, RW 36/237.

32 BA-MA, RW 5/v. 28, p. 13.

33 Ibid., pp. 15, 56, 67.

34 PA, VR/KR 26 no. 5, Frankreich, vol. 5.

35 BA-MA, RW 5/v. 28, p. 72.

36 Information of the International Tracing Service in Arolsen in letters dated 10 February and 22 June 1978; letter from Bruchsal Prison, 17 February 1978; letter from ICRC, 7 March 1978.

37 Information from Secretariat d'Etat aux Anciens Combattants, Paris, 6 June 1978.

38 PRO, FO 371/28885, Docs. W 8788, W 8789, W 9613; NA, RG 59, Doc. 740.00116 E.W. 1939/392.

39 BA-MA, RW 2/v. 139, p. 6.

40 PRO, FO 371/28886, Doc. 11959.

41 PA, VR/KR vol. 814; BA-MA, Fremde Heere Ost, H 3/493, H 3/657, pp. 353ff.; see also "Deutsche Greuel in Russland: Gerichtstag in Charkow," Vienna, undated [1945].

42 Gerhard Wagner, *Lagevorträge des Oberbefehlshabers der Kriegsmarine vor Hitler, 1935–1945* (Munich, 1972), p. 557.

43 BA-MA, RW 2/v. 31, pp. 116–70.

44 Ibid., 145–46. For correspondence with *Ausland-Abwehr* and the Wehrmacht operations staff, see RW 2/v. 139, pp. 114ff.

45 BB, 2200 Berlin 3, Classeur 14 bis.

46 NA, RG 59, Doc. 740.00116 E.W. 1939/1257.

47 Ibid., 1939/1380.

48 Letter from Rudolphi to the author, 3 August 1976.

49 It is conceivable that had these pilots been brought before a military court, they would have been convicted of machine-gunning civilians far from any military objectives; conclusive evidence, however, was difficult to obtain, though there are hundreds of reports of such deliberate acts. According to Hitler's order of 21 May 1944, airmen shot down over Germany could be executed without court-martial if they had shot German air crews while they were parachuting to earth; made aerial attacks on German planes and crews that had made emergency landings; attacked railway trains engaged in public transport; made low-level aerial attacks on individual civilians or civilian vehicles. See *IMT*, 9:570; see also Göring interrogation, 9:360–61.

50 NSB, Nuremberg Doc. C-50, Friedman, *Laws of War* 2:1441.

51 On 24 July 1942 Commissar Nedostupow and Sergeant Schweweljow were executed by an Einsatzkommando without trial (BA-MA, RW 2/v. 162, p. 187); in March 1943 eleven persons suspected of being partisans were shot in the village Krassnoje-Snanja (ibid., 201, p. 153).

52 BA-MA, RW 2/v. 212, pp. 72ff.

53 Ibid., 219, pp. 71ff.

54 Ibid., 164, pp. 53ff.

55 Ibid., 162, p. 195; 176, p. 251; 163, p. 225, etc.

56 Ibid., 214, pp. 207ff., 229.

57 Ibid., 205, p. 261.

58 Ibid., 192, p. 112.

59 BA-MA, RW 4/v. 296, pp. 24ff.

60 The *Fremde Heere Ost* was particularly effective in collecting names; it thoroughly investigated the crimes committed by the Soviet Army in East Prussia and in eastern Germany after October 1944 and submitted a list of responsible officers (BA-MA, RH 2/680, pp. 282ff.). See also "War Crimes List No. 1," containing 21 names (BA-MA, RH 2/123 pp. 73ff.).

CHAPTER TEN

1 *IMT*, 7:156, 8:122.

2 *IMT*, 6:399, 411.

3 *IMT*, 15:657.

4 *IMT*, 1:62.

5 *IMT*, 7:585.

6 *IMT*, 11:489, 520.

7 Allied reprisals were also reported: e.g., Private Josef Lengauer, who fled from Russian captivity, described the killing of German prisoners of war following an air attack (BA-MA, RW 2/v. 194, p. 206).

8 *IMT*, 9:362.

9 BA-MA, Tätigkeitsberichte der Abteilung Ic beim 49th Geb. A. K. vol. 18253/4b, pp. 158ff.

10 BA-MA, RW 2/v. 198, p. 62.

11 Transcript of author's interview with Willi Knobloch, 1 July 1976, p. 11. See also Chapter 18.

12 BA-MA, RW 2/v. 187, p. 253.

13 Ibid., 139, pp. 116ff.

14 BA-MA, RW 4/v. 619, pp. 27ff.; *IMT*, 40:61–65, Dönitz Doc. 39, Cf. Dönitz Doc. 41, pp. 66–69: when similar reports of attacks by the Royal Air Force were the subject of discussion at the German Navy High Command in June 1943, "the degree of resentment and indignation among soldiers of all ranks was very great. The idea came up that as a reprisal to prevent the repetition of such events we should similarly attack the shipwrecked of enemy ships. . . . Grand Admiral Dönitz rejected these ideas emphatically."

15 BA-MA, RW 2/v. 40, p. 23; 235, p. 265. Early in 1943 the Bureau compiled a list titled "Attack on German, Italian, and Japanese Hospital Ships," including fifteen attacks on German hospital ships and planes, and eight on Italian hospital ships (BA-MA, RW 2/v. 40, pp. 22ff.; 234, pp.

263ff); a second list cited twenty-four attacks between May 1943 and November 1944 (BA-MA, RW 2/v. 79, pp. 234ff).

16 BA-MA, RW 4/v. 619, p. 23.

17 BA-MA, RW 2/v. 62, pp. 179, 204. The author has spoken with numerous Germans who were in British captivity at the time. It is true that they were tied up for a few hours each day, but they and their guards considered these measures to be a farce, and they were implemented without cruelty. On the German side Hitler's order proved to be unpopular and was carried out only *pro forma*.

18 *Revue Internationale de la Croix Rouge*, November 1947, pp. 863ff. The Geneva Convention of 27 July 1929 prohibits in Art. 2, para. 3, all reprisals on prisoners of war. On the other hand, reprisals on civilians were in conformity with international law provided they did not violate the principle of proportionality (in re List, Nuremberg, Case 7, the "hostage case"). Such reprisals against civilians were prohibited in Art. 33 of the Fourth Geneva Convention of 1949. See Frits Kalshoven, *Belligerent Reprisals* (Leyden, 1971), pp. 178ff.

CHAPTER ELEVEN

1 Statement of 14–15 January 1977 during the symposium at the University of Göttingen (see Note on the Sources); Alfons Waltzog was among the participants.

2 The author's study of the records of the German Foreign Office (PA) did not reveal the existence of any such protests transmitted by the Protecting Power, nor did a search of the Protecting Power Papers, which—unlike the German records—are complete.

3 Without exception, all the German military judges interviewed by the author claimed not to have known about exterminations at any of the concentration camps until after the end of the war. A few admitted hearing rumors of executions on the Eastern Front but claimed that they had been unable to obtain corroborative evidence.

4 *IMT*, 10:536–37. Karl Hofmann, member of the Bureau from 1940 to 1944, remembers that Hitler's Order No. 1 "was posted in every office, and it was taken seriously" (transcript of author's interview with Hofmann, 5 May 1976, p. 4).

5 *IMT*, 29:145, Nuremberg Doc. PS-1919. See also Raul Hilberg, *The Destruction of the European Jews* (Chicago, 1961), p. 648.

6 Reichsstatthalter and Gauleiter of Vienna, member of the Reichstag, SA Obergruppenfuehrer, leader of the Hitler Youth.

7 Sarah Gordon, *Hitler, the Germans, and the Jewish Question* (Princeton, N.J.), p. 140; John Toland, *Adolf Hitler*, p. 1016.

8 Gordon, *Hitler*, p. 140; Toland, *Adolf Hitler*, p. 1038.

9 *IMT*, 17:172–73.

10 *IMT*, 17:181.

11 *IMT*, 20:506.

12 *IMT*, 21:533.

13 Gordon, *Hitler*, p. 140; Toland, *Adolf Hitler*, p. 1188.

14 BA-MA, RW 2/v. 50, pp. 4ff. See also PRO, FO 371/36547, Doc. W 12851.

15 BA-MA, RW 2/v. 50, pp. 4, 9. Art. 23 of the Hague Regulations prohibits killing or wounding "an enemy who, having laid down his arms, or having no longer means of defense, has surrendered at discretion."

16 BA-MA, RW 2/v. 50, pp. 8, 11.

17 Ibid., pp. 27–28.

18 PA, VR/KR vol. 22, General.

19 Ibid.

20 PRO, FO 371/43002, Doc. W 15894.

21 Geneva Convention for the Amelioration of the Conditions of the Wounded and Sick in the Armies in the Field; Geneva Convention Relative to the Treatment of Prisoners of War. See Schindler and Toman, *The Laws of Armed Conflict*.

22 BA-MA, RW 2/v. 709, pp. 53ff.

23 Ibid., pp. 50ff. The paragraph provides: "The pilot, mechanics, and wireless telegraph operators [of an aircraft used as a means of medical transport] shall be sent back, on condition that they shall be employed until the close of hostilities in the medical service only."

24 BA-MA, RW 4/v. 709, p. 54.

25 NA, RG 59, Doc. 711.62114/1-145, incoming telegram, Bern, 1 January 1945.

26 See Dwight Eisenhower, *Crusade in Europe* (New York, 1948), pp. 253ff.

27 See, e.g., Alexander McKee, *Caen: Anvil of Victory* (London, 1964), esp. chap. 13; pp. 203ff.: "No prisoners are taken that day on either side"; also Cornelius Ryan, *The Longest Day* (London, 1963), pp. 190ff.

28 BB, 2200 Berlin 3, Classeur 14 bis; same in Bern 2021 (E), Classeur 37.

29 Ibid.

30 Ibid.

31 BA-MA, RW 4/v. 709, p. 89. (Von Kluge was later dismissed for complicity in the plot to assassinate Hitler on 20 July 1944; he committed suicide on 18 August 1944.)

32 Ibid., p. 86.

33 BB, 2200 Berlin 3, Classeur 14 bis; 2021 (E), Classeur 37.

34 BB, Bern 2021 (e), Classeur 37.

35 BA-MA, RW 4/v. 709, pp. 66–67.

36 BB, 2200 Berlin 3, Classeur 65.

37 BA-MA, RW 4/v. 765, p. 32.

38 During the investigation the special unit Solar reported that on 30 December 1944 First

Mark as Uncited

Lieutenant Ziemann . . . found the corpses of 14 German infantrymen near Steinbrunn: "All dead lay with their arms raised in a position which clearly indicated that they had surrendered; neither weapons nor belts were found near the bodies. All had been killed at close range by a shot in the head. . . . Surgeon-major Dr. Poszich examined the corpses and determined that all shots had been fired at close range" (BA-MA, RW 4/v. 765, p. 31). An American report from Technical Intelligence Branch, Intelligence Div. ASF, WD, contains the summary of a statement of Sergeant Max Cohen, 21st Armored Infantry Battalion of the 11th Armored Division, which may confirm those observations of German Lieutenant Ziemann, since it describes events occurring in roughly the same area at about the same time: "On about 27 December 1944 while engaging in combat in northern Luxembourg, Source received an order that he was not to take prisoners. In a period of three or four days Source saw one group of about 20 German prisoners 'machine gunned,' two groups of about 15 to 20 'machine gunned' and one group of about 10 'machine gunned.' . . . Source said that the Major who was Battalion Commander was present when the group of more than 20 German prisoners was killed. After the Germans were searched, Source reports, they were lined up and then 'machine gunned.' Source said that a 'grease gun' or M 3 was used. The name of the town (a small one) that they were near cannot be recalled by Source, but said it was about 30 to 40 miles southwest of Morehet": NA, RG 331, Operational and Occupation Headquarters, USFET S.G.S., 383.6/10, "Treatment of Military POWs Held by Allies." See also "Summary of Reports of Investigations Pursuant to Direction of the Theater Commander, dated 18 July 1945, in Compliance with the Provisions of the Geneva Prisoner of War Convention by United States Forces" (NA, RG 331).

39 BA-MA, RW 4/v. 765, pp. 26–27, 29.

40 BB, 2200 Berlin 3, Classeur 14 bis.

41 See James Weingartner, *Crossroads of Death: The Story of The Malmedy Massacre and Trial* (Berkeley, 1979). Dietrich Ziemssen, *Der Malmedy Prozess* (Munich, 1952), pp. 16ff. (Ziemssen described the events to the author in an interview, 11 June 1972); Rudolf Aschenauer, *Um Recht und Wahrheit im Malmedy Fall* (Nuremberg, 1950); Aschenauer, *Der Malmedy Fall: 7 Jahre nach dem Urteil* (Munich, 1953), pp. 12ff. Lucius Clay, *Decision in Germany* (New York, 1950), p. 253.

42 The Malmédy trials were the subject of an inquiry by a special committee appointed by War Minister Kenneth Royall and headed by Judge Gorden B. Simpson of the Texas Supreme Court. See ed. U.S. Information Services Division, Office of the U.S. High Commissioner for Germany, *Ein Dokumentarischer Bericht* (Munich, 1951), esp. Handy's statement, pp. 28–31.

CHAPTER TWELVE

1 See Chapter 1.

2 BA-MA, RW 4/v. 298, p. 9.

3 Ibid., p. 45.

4 Ibid., p. 46.

5 Fleet Admiral 1933 and Reichskommissar in the Prize Court until his dismissal in 1943 because of his anti-Nazi attitude, Gladisch was very close to such Hitler opponents as Admiral

Wilhelm Canaris and General Henning von Tresckow (van Roon, "Graf Moltke," pp. 14, 40ff.). He belonged to the board of trustees [*Kuratorium*] of the Institut für ausländisches Recht und Völkerrecht der Kaiser-Wilhelm Gesellschaft in Berlin, Germany's most prestigious academy of international law, and the predecessor of today's Max Planck Institut für ausländisches öffentliches Recht und Völkerrecht in Heidelberg. It was Admiral Gladisch who brought Count Helmuth James von Moltke into the legal department of the Wehrmacht. See the Gladisch legacy at the Institute for Military Research in Freiburg, Nachlass Gladisch, Militärgeschichtliches Forschungsamt, Freiburg (Marinearchiv: 7742/3, Teil I), III M 501/1. Cf. also Walter Baum, "Marine, Nationalsozialismus und Widerstand," *VfZ* 11 (1963): 16, 29; Moltke, *Documente*, pp. 24ff., 174ff.

6 BA-MA, RW 2/v. 26, p. 4.

7 Ibid., pp. 14–16.

8 Art. 2 provides: "The inhabitants of a territory which has not been occupied, who, on the approach of the enemy spontaneously take up arms to resist the invading troops without having had time to organize themselves in accordance with Article 1, shall be regarded as belligerents if they carry arms openly and if they respect the laws and customs of war."

9 PA, VR/KR vol. 82/4. See van Roon, *Moltke*, pp. 174ff.

10 BA-MA, RW 2/v. 34, p. 3.

11 Ibid., p. 7.

CHAPTER THIRTEEN

1 Transcript of author's interview with Schattenberg, 20 October 1975, p. 1.

2 BA-MA, RW 2/v. 51, pp. 51–52 (taken from Schattenberg's report of 14 September 1939). An extensive postwar investigation by a team of researchers from the Bundesarchiv-Koblenz comprises over 400 affidavits and 6,000 pages of depositions (BA, Ost-Dok. 7).

3 BA-MA, RW 2/v. 51, pp. 56–57.

4 Ibid., p. 65. The evangelical pastor of Schwedenhoehe, Paul Gerhard Lassahn, had been arrested on 25 August and survived his deportation. His wife and four children, who sought shelter with the parents of their Polish cook, were discovered and put against the wall to be executed; an officer prevented the shooting. See the Verschlepptenkartei, BA, Ost-Dok. 7.

5 BA-MA, RW 2/v. 51, pp. 63–64.

6 Ibid., pp. 258ff.

7 Ibid., pp. 1ff.

8 Documents in Waltzog's private papers.

9 BA-MA, RW 2/v. 52, pp. 23ff.; transcript of author's interview with Reger, 10 May 1976, p. 8 (Reger, who was president of the Association of Ex-Military Judges after the war, also made a statement on his investigations in Poland for the television documentary). Other judges included Bockisch, Boetticher, Heinemann, Hurtig, Kleiss, Peltzer, von Ramdohr, Richter, Schöne,

Zirner, and Zornig. I have questioned Boetticher, von Ramdohr, Reger, Schattenberg, Schölz, and Zornig, as well as a number of judges subsequently assigned to investigations in Poland: Franz, Kandt, Kleint, Mackel, and Wodtke.

10 An extensive scholarly manuscript, "Documentation on the Deportation of the Germans from Posen and Pomerelia in September 1939," can be consulted in the archives at Koblenz ("Dokumentation der Verschleppungsmarsche," BA, Ost-Dok. 7), which attempts to reconstruct the whole complex. It shows that long before the outbreak of the war Polish authorities had prepared lists of persons to be arrested, comprising the entire German intelligentsia in both western provinces. Those arrested (without any warrant) were deported on foot to eastern Poland. Treatment by the Polish guards and civilians was inhuman: whoever could not continue was beaten or shot to death. Some groups were nearly annihilated; others were liberated in September at Lowitsch, Kutno, Bereza-Kartuska, Brest-Litovsk, and Warsaw after the fall of the city to the Germans. The routes of the various marching columns (up to 300 kilometers) are indicated on a map, which also shows where the executions took place. The documentation mentions 1,131 towns and villages in Posen and Pomeralia from which Germans were deported; they are compiled by district, and the names of men, women, and children deported and/or killed are collected in separate lists for every town. Every person has a catalogue card containing name, age, profession, description of arrest and deportation, and sources; the card catalogue comprises about 4,500 persons, of whom it was established that 1,794 perished, but the documentary evidence (parts of which were collected long after the events) is incomplete; it is estimated that as many as 10,000 persons were deported and at least 2,200 persons perished. Additional deportations took place in other parts of Poland (more than 600 persons from Lodz alone), including central Poland and Galicia.

11 Cf. ibid., no. 12, BA, Ost-Dok. 7.

12 BA-MA, RW 2/v. 52, pp. 17ff.

13 Ibid., 56, pp. 80ff.

14 Ibid., 52, p. 146. In a letter to the author, 5 March 1978, Hoffmann added that he continued looking for graves after giving his deposition and found among others the graves of the families Fuchs and Kadolowski; he made a statement on these families for the televised documentary.

15 BA-MA, RW 2/v. 52, p. 209. See no. 11 in the "Dokumentation der Verschleppungsmarsche," BA, Ost-Dok. 7.

16 BA-MA, RW 2/v. 56, pp. 92ff. Cf. the deposition of fifteen-year-old student Georg Malinowski before Judge Reger, ibid., pp. 438ff.

17 Ibid., pp. 158ff. Cf. the deposition of widow Martha Resmer, ibid., pp. 163ff.; letter to the author from Judge Zornig, 18 March 1978.

18 See text of a speech by Johannes Goldsche, "Violations of International Law by Our Enemies in Land Warfare in the Present War," delivered on 28 January 1941 before the German Society for Military Science and Politics: BA-MA, RW 2/v. 30, p. 8.

19 BA-MA, RW 2/v. 56, pp. 31ff., 301ff., 310ff., 332ff., 386ff., 446ff., 455ff., 508ff., etc. Similar evidence was also obtained by Judges Schattenberg and Zirner: ibid., 51–56.

20 Ibid., 55, p. 118.

21 Ibid., p. 119.

22 Ibid., pp. 58–59.

23 Ibid., pp. 92ff.; cf. ibid., pp. 110, 139, 154.

24 Ibid., 56, pp. 7ff.; letter to the author from Judge Bockisch, 25 April 1978.

25 Notes from the diary of Horst Reger; transcript of author's interview with Wilken von Ramdohr, 17 April 1976, p. 6.

26 BA-MA, RW 2/v. 53, pp. 99ff.; transcript of author's interview with Udo Ritgen (subsequently General of the Armed Forces, Federal Republic of Germany), 28 June 1976, p. 1; transcript of author's interview with Otto Mackel (subsequently Public Prosecutor, Federal Republic of Germany), 12 November 1975, p. 6. The clerk of the military court, then Corporal Josef Czaplewski (who subsequently took the name Schapner), also remembered the case and confirmed the authenticity of his signature (letter to the author, 28 November 1975).

27 BA-MA, RW 2/v. 54, pp. 72ff. In an interview with the author, 1 September 1976, John Freyend confirmed the accuracy of his 1939 deposition and added further details. There are numerous similar reports. A more serious case involved the deposition of medical officer Siegfried Grosskopf before Judge Kleint on 27 January 1940 concerning the autopsy of the body of a tortured and mutilated German soldier; in an interview on 20 April 1976 Judge Kleint confirmed the authenticity of the deposition.

28 Pospieszalski, *The 58,000 Volksdeutsche*, pp. 76, 51.

29 Louis De Jong, *The German Fifth Column in the Second World War* (New York, 1956), p. 57.

30 See Richard Breyer, Wolfgang Kohte, and Gotthold Rhose, introduction to Peter Aurich, *Der Deutsch-Polnische September 1939* (Munich, 1969), p. 11.

31 Thirty military and civilian judges took the depositions of other witnesses concerning crimes committed against members of the German armed forces. These depositions have not been taken into account in estimating the number of victims among the ethnic Germans.

32 Much material on German crimes during the occupation of Poland was published both during and after the war, in addition to the documentation provided by the Nuremberg trials. Among the leading publications in Poland is the documentation of Czeslaw Madajczyk, *Polityka III Rzeszy w okupowanej Polsce* (The policies of the Third Reich in occupied Poland), 3 vols. (Warsaw, 1970). Another important postwar study is Szymon Datner, Janusz Gumbowski, and Kazimierz Lesczynski, *War Crimes in Poland* (Warsaw, 1962). During the war the Polish Ministry of Information, part of the Polish government-in-exile in London, published a 586-page documentation entitled *The New German Order in Poland*, London 1942. Shortly after the war the Polish Central Commission for Investigation of German Crimes in Poland published the multivolume *German Crimes in Poland* (Warsaw, 1946–47). See also Jan Gross, *Polish Society under German Occupation* (Princeton, N.J., 1979); Martin Broszat, *Nationalsozialistische Polenpolitik 1939–1945* (Frankfurt, 1965).

33 The original of this letter is lost, but there is a carbon copy among the papers of Alfons Waltzog.

34 *IMT*, 35:91ff. at 93, Doc. 421-D. But see Chapter 2 for examples of other courts-martial and death sentences that were carried out.

35 Affidavit of General Otto von Knobelsdorff at Zuffenhausen, 1 June 1946, Peace Palace, IMT Doc. 712.

36 Ulrich von Hassell, *Vom anderen Deutschland* (Frankfurt, 1964), p. 92.

37 Helmut Krausnick: "Hitler und die Morde in Polen," *VfZ*, 1963, p. 204.

38 IMT Doc. 3011, Peace Palace.

CHAPTER FOURTEEN

1 PA, Kult. Pol. Geheim, vol. 41. See the reports of the Sonderkolonne Schnock van Gorhom-Kropf on a special mission in Zeeland, p. 1.

2 PA, Kult. Pol. Geheim, vol. 45: Summary of material collected for the white book, p. 1.

3 Minor instances of plundering were reported in Breskens, Biervliet, Aardenburg, Schoondijke, and Oostburg.

4 PA, Kult. Pol. Geheim, vol. 45.

5 BA-MA, RW 2/v. 68, pp. 61, 67 (translation from Dutch by Walter Rabus).

6 Author's interview with Waltzog, 29 June 1976.

7 BA-MA, RW 2/v. 63, p. 69.

8 Ibid., pp. 70ff.

9 Ibid., p. 114.

10 Ibid., p. 125.

11 Belgium capitulated on 28 May 1940.

12 BA-MA, RW 2/v. 64, pp. 63ff. See also German Foreign Office, "Documents of British-French Cruelty" (*Dokumente britisch-französischer Grausamkeit*), which, however, contains witness testimony that was not given under oath; and BA-MA, RW 2/v. 64, pp. 47ff.

13 BA-MA, RW 2/v. 64, pp. 160ff.; see also RW 36/433, p. 35.

14 PA, Kult. Pol. Geheim, vol. 60. See also s.v. "Abbeville" in Henri Coston, *Dictionnaire de la politique française*, p. 11.

15 The files are very incomplete in this regard. Former military judge Heinz Schmidt sent to the author on 6 October 1976 copies of several depositions he took on 23 June 1940. In the relevant files of the Wehrmacht operations staff, BA-MA, RW 4/v. 318, pp. 165ff., the complete investigation of the Abbeville case is found in the files of the commander-in-chief for Belgium and northern France. A war crimes trial of French Lieutenant René Caron and Sergeant Emile Mollet was held by the Germans at Amiens; it ended on 17 January 1942 with death sentences: BA-MA, RW 36/434, pp. 3ff.; RW 36/436, pp. 30ff. Cf. Maurits van Gijsegen, *Het Bloedbad van Abbeville* (Antwerp, 1942).

16 BA-MA, RW 2/v. 61, pp. 46ff. For the full text, see BA-MA, RW 36/433, pp. 7ff.

17 BA-MA, RW 2/v. 62, pp. 71ff.

18 Ibid., 31, pp. 116ff.

19 Ibid., 66, p. 118. Gaudé was subsequently killed in combat on 23 September 1942.

20 Ibid., pp. 118–19.

21 Facsimile of the order in ibid., 65, p. 248.

22 Cf. court-martial proceedings against French civilians, Chapter 9.

23 BA-MA, RW 2/v. 65, pp. 205ff.

24 Ibid., pp. 211ff.

25 Ibid., 66, p. 106. Wiegand fell in combat on 27 September 1944 near Boxtel, Holland.

26 Ibid., p. 108.

27 PA, VR/KR vol. 82/4.

28 See Chapter 4 regarding the intercession of the ICRC.

29 BA-MA, RW 2/v. 72, pp. 12ff., 15ff.

30 Letters of Gottschaller to the author, 22 March 1983, 8 and 14 October 1984, including maps showing the locations of the mass graves. After the war Gottschaller established a complete list of names and addresses of the victims, contacted their families, and assisted in efforts to have the bodies transferred to Germany. His papers are in the Bayerische Hauptstaatsarchiv in Munich, Abteilung V, Nachlasse und Sammlungen, classified under "Nachlass Gottschaller."

31 ICRC, *Report of Activities*, 1:523.

CHAPTER FIFTEEN

1 I. McD. G. Stewart, *The Struggle for Crete* (London, 1966), p. 475.

2 BA-MA, RW 2/v. 138, pp. 80ff.

3 See Chapter 23.

4 BA-MA, RW 2/v. 146.

5 Ibid., 134, pp. 42ff.; author's interview with Schölz, 11 May 1976.

6 BA-MA, RW 2/v. 135, pp. 22–27. Judge Rüdel's letter to the author of 17 September 1976 confirmed this report.

7 A member of the salvage corps, Alfred Steeb, was employed with four others in the area of Castelli. On 24 May 1941 he found some thirty-five corpses in the vineyards north of the road from Malemes to Castelli: "On a corpse that also had a shot through the head and in the chest I saw that the genitals had been amputated. I consider it out of the question that the lack of genitals could have any other explanation but deliberate mutilation. It was no longer possible to determine whether the mutilation took place when the victim was still alive." Corporal Steeb, a medical student, gave his deposition before Judge Rüdel on 30 May 1941: BA-MA, RW 2/v. 146, p. 130.

8 Ibid., 139, pp. 82ff. Following up on Unger's report, the Bureau endeavored to take the depositions of Kurtz and Greve. On 19 July 1941, however, Hofmann noted that Kurtz had died in the military hospital in Marienfelde. Greve, who had lost an arm, did make a sworn statement: BA-MA, RW 2/v. 139, p. 85.

9 See the discussion of the forensic examination of eye injuries in Chapter 6.

10 BA-MA, RW 2/v. 146, p. 137.

11 Ibid., p. 185. Cf. John H. Spencer, *Battle for Crete* (London, 1962), p. 248: "Isolated Germans who were taken prisoner occasionally met with fairly barbarous treatment beyond the usages of war from Cretan village irregulars."

12 BA-MA, RW 2/v. 146, p. 96.

13 PRO, FO 371/28885, Docs. W 8791, W 9613.

14 BA-MA, RW 2/v. 138, p. 200. This deposition was taken on 25 August 1941, more than a month after Judge Rüdel's report had expressed a positive attitude toward the British troops.

15 BA-MA, RW 2/v. 146, p. 46.

16 Ibid., pp. 71ff.

17 Ibid., pp. 79ff.

18 Ibid., p. 87.

19 Ibid., 135, p. 23.

20 Michael Llewellyn Smith, *The Great Island: A Study of Crete* (London, 1961), p. 163; Spencer, *Battle for Crete*; Stewart, *Struggle for Crete*, pp. 488ff.

CHAPTER SIXTEEN

1 "Wir müssen von dem Standpunkt des soldatischen Kameradentums abrücken. Der Kommunist ist vorher kein Kamerad und nachher kein Kamerad. Es handelt sich um einen Vernichtungskampf": speech to the commanders-in-chief and chiefs-of-staff of the Eastern Armies on 30 March 1941. See also Streit, *Keine Kameraden*; Omer Bartov, *Eastern Front, 1941–1945* (London, 1986); G. K. Zhukov, *The Memoirs of Marshal Zhukov* (London, 1971).

2 See Chapter 8.

3 Cf. telegram dated 8 July 1941 to the High Command of the 6th Army: "According to a report of the 3rd Army Corps, 150 German soldiers of the 25th Infantry Division who had been captured by the Russians were murdered on 30 June 1941" (Armored Group 1, Ic, BA-MA, Daily Reports, RH 20-6/515, 516, p. 155). See also morning report of 4 July 1941 to the High Command of the 17th Army: "Eighty members of our 295th Division, who had been left behind wounded at Dabrowka (south of Rawa Ruska) were murdered by Russian soldiers of the 41st and 159th Divisions. Evidence follows" (ibid., p. 386); morning report of 28 June 1941: "Battalion 36 ordered the shooting of all German prisoners. Other German prisoners were killed at Rawa Ruska. Evidence follows" (BA-MA, RH 20-6/513, p. 143; RH 20-17/277.

4 BA-MA, RW 2/v. 176, pp. 113–14, 116; letter of Franz Kröning, 23 May 1978. Kröning gave the

author an album containing eight pictures of the massacre at Broniki (interview, 18 June 1979). He also described the events at Broniki in the televised documentary.

5 BA-MA, RW 2/v. 176, p. 124. In a letter to the author, 13 March 1978, the witness confirmed his deposition.

6 BA-MA, RW 2/v. 176, pp. 119, 161–62. Jäger and Metzger confirmed the events in letters to the author of 21 February 1978 and 2 March 1978; Metzger also described his experiences for the televised documentary.

7 BA-MA, RW 2/v. 176, p. 154. According to the central card register of the Wehrmacht personnel office in Berlin, Heiss returned to the Eastern Front, was again taken prisoner, and never returned to Germany; presumably he died in a POW camp.

8 BA-MA, RW 2/v. 176, pp. 120ff., 161ff.; ibid., 152, pp. 2ff.; numerous photographs in ibid., 153, pp. 37ff. In BA there is also a black and white film, "Soviet Massacres," which shows some four to five minutes on Broniki; the film was used in the televised documentary.

9 The names of Soviet prisoners of war who gave testimony before German military judges are in the Bureau's files but are sometimes deleted here in order to protect them from possible reprisals should they or their families still live in the Soviet Union.

10 BA-MA, RW 2/v. 147–241 (95 volumes containing 100 to 500 pages each).

11 See Böhme, *Die deutschen Kriegsgefangenen in sowjetischer Hand*, p. 49. Of the 3,155,000 Germans who were at one time or another in Soviet POW camps, an estimated 1,110,000, or about 35.2 percent, perished. According to Böhme (p. 110), the death rate declined over the years: in 1941–42 it was 90–95 percent; 1943, 60–70 percent; 1944, 30–40 percent; after 1945, 20–25 percent. It is estimated that of 5.7 million Soviet prisoners of war in German camps, some 3.3 million, or 57.8 percent, perished; see H. A. Jacobsen, "Kommissarbefehl und Massenexekution sowjetischer Krigsgefangener," in H. Buchheim et al. *Anatomie des SS-Staates*, 2:197. See also Streit, *Keine Kameraden*, p. 10; and Alfred Streim, *Sowjetische Gefangene im Hitlers Vernichtungskrieg* (Heidelberg, 1982).

12 BA-MA, RW 2/v. 152, p. 10; ibid., 155, pp. 301ff. (author's translation from the Russian).

13 Ibid., 153, p. 12; ibid., 157, p. 44.

14 PA, VR/KR, vol. 81-1.

15 BA-MA, RW 2/v. 151, p. 216. Cf. diary of Lieutenant Bonschenko: PA, VR/KR, vol. 81-1.

16 BA-MA, RW 2/v. 161, pp. 230–31.

17 Ibid., 220, p. 322.

18 Ibid., 165, pp. 16–17.

19 Ibid., 158, p. 266. Cf. message from Moscow Radio: ibid., 151, p. 9.

20 Ibid., 160, pt. 1, p. 45.

21 Ibid., 220, pp. 261–62.

22 Testimony of Soviet prisoner of war J.: ibid., 158, p. 188. Cf. similar cases, ibid., 162, p. 103; 192, p. 102.

23 Testimony of Soviet prisoner of war A.: ibid., 161, p. 251. Cf. testimony of a regimental commissar, ibid., 157, pp. 56–57. See also a captured Soviet order: "It is forbidden to liquidate German soldiers and officers who voluntarily desert" (ibid., 160, pt. 1, p. 20).

24 Captured report of scouting patrol 36-K, dated 4 February 1942, of the 636th Regiment, ibid., 153, p. 5. See also captured diary entry in ibid., 161, pp. 230–31; testimony of prisoner of war J.J. (ibid., 153, p. 7); testimony of German Corporal J.S., who escaped Russian captivity (ibid., 220, pp. 172–73); testimony of prisoner of war R. (ibid., 221, pp. 43–44).

25 Intercepted radio message, ibid., 164, p. 38.

26 Ibid., 216, p. 194.

27 Captured document, ibid., 165, pp. 16–17. Cf. similar orders and statements in ibid., 191, p. 316; 165, p. 124; 160, pt. 2, p. 3.

28 Ibid., 264, p. 37. Reported reply given by the Russian Lieutenant Ivanov to Russian prisoner of war D. Cf. intercepted radio message, ibid., 160, pt. 2, pp. 3–4.

29 Captured report of 78th Division intelligence, ibid., 164, p. 160; cf. testimony of Soviet prisoner of war A.P., ibid., 218, pp. 26–27.

30 Testimony of Soviet prisoner of war S., ibid., 162, p. 147.

31 Testimony of Soviet prisoner of war Lieutenant P.S., ibid., 175, p. 114 (*politruk* = political officer or commissar).

32 BA-MA, RW 2/v. 168, p. 146.

33 Testimony of Soviet prisoner of war F., ibid., 161, p. 221.

34 Ibid., p. 141. Cf. testimony of Corporal Franz Kuhn, who escaped from Soviet captivity: ibid., 203, pp. 130–31.

35 Ibid., 150, p. 10.

36 Testimony of Soviet prisoner of war, ibid., 161, p. 226.

37 Ibid., 158, p. 255.

38 Author's translation from the Russian. PA, Kult. Pol. Geheim, vol. 127, records of the Foreign Office representative at 16th Army High Command, Alfred Frauenfeld. During an interview on 18 August 1976, Frauenfeld confirmed having seen many such leaflets.

39 PA, VR/KR vol. 81-5.

40 This may have been interpreted as encouragement to kill POWs.

41 Author's translation from the Russian. PA, Kult. Pol. Geheim, vol. 148, files of Foreign Office representative Heinrich von zur Mühlen. The same text is found in Ilya Ehrenburg's book *Vojna* (The war) (Moscow, 1942–43), 2:22–23, and in an article in the *Krasnaja Swesda*.

42 Nuremberg Doc. USSR-356, cited in *IMT* 19:203, 412, 473, 595; BA-MA, RW 2/v. 158, p. 27. The Soviet prosecution at Nuremberg introduced this document to show that it subscribed to the Hague Regulations on Land Warfare (*IMT* 36:322–27). See also W. Ratza, *Die deutschen Kriegsgefangenen in der Sowjetunion*, in Maschke, *Zur Geschichte*, 4:277–80.

43 BA-MA, RW 2/v. 158, p. 40 (translated from the German).

44 Ibid., pp. 37–39.

45 Ibid., 151, p. 6. Cf. similar order no. 0086 of the staff of the Coastal Army, Sevastopol, dated 2 December 1941: ibid., 158, pp. 312–13.

46 Ibid., 151, p. 3.

47 Ibid., 162, p. 101; cf. similar orders of Marshal Boris Shaposhnikov and Colonel A. N. Kravchenko, ibid., 29, pp. 6–7.

48 Ibid., 164, pp. 38–39; cf. intercepted radio messages in ibid., 158, p. 283.

49 Ibid., 29, p. 3; cf. order of commander of 6th Infantry Corps, Major General Alexejev: ibid., 158, p. 123. This document was used by the prosecution in the trial against Field Marshal Erich von Manstein: PRO, WO 235/594.

50 BA-MA, RW 2/v. 158, p. 81.

51 Ibid., p. 256.

52 Ibid., 193, p. 213.

53 Ibid., 162, pp. 185–86. Both Nedostupov and the sergeant were executed on 24 July 1942 by an *Einsatzkommando*.

54 Ibid., p. 101. Cf. similar testimony by Red Army soldier I.A., in ibid., 158, p. 286.

55 Ibid., 215, p. 7.

56 Ibid., 506, p. 16.

57 Ibid., p. 60.

58 Ibid., 158, p. 81.

59 On the German side, Hitler openly condoned crimes committed by the ss on the Polish civilian population and Polish prisoners of war. The attempt of the Wehrmacht courts to punish ss soldiers for murders of Polish Jews resulted in its losing jurisdiction over the ss and police.

60 BA-MA, RW 2/v. 151, p. 12.

61 Author's translation from the Russian. PA, Kult. Pol. Geheim, vol. 127, records of the representative of the Foreign Office at the High Command of the 16th Army, Alfred Frauenfeld.

62 BA-MA, RW 2/v. 151, p. 10.

63 Ibid., 158, p. 146. Cf. report dated 6 January 1942, ibid., p. 88.

64 Ibid., 163, p. 234.

65 Ibid., 157, p. 57.

66 Ibid., 161, p. 265.

67 Ibid., 164, p. 27.

68 Ibid., 163, p. 290.

69 Ibid., 158, p. 7.

70 Ibid., p. 8.

71 Ibid., p. 82; cf. a similar report by the High Command of the 1st Armored Army, ibid., 58, p. 80.

72 Ibid., 161, p. 24.

73 Ibid., 162, p. 71. Cf. testimony of Corporal Otto Schmied, a German who escaped from Soviet capture, in ibid., 203, p. 31.

74 Ibid., 162, p. 213. Cf. report dated 18 June 1944 from Department IIb of *Fremde Heere Ost*, "Treatment of German Prisoners of War in the Soviet Union": "Soviet prisoners of war refer again and again to a Stalin order which allegedly prohibits the killing of German prisoners of war and provides for humane treatment. At this office we have the text of Order 001 of the People's Commissioner for Defense, dated 2 January 1943, which deals with the treatment of prisoners of war from the moment of transport behind the lines, and which appears to be of general application in the Soviet Union. This order, however, does not contain a prohibition of execution. Two captured orders—of the 8th Corps, dated 6 December 1943, and the 226th Infantry Division, dated 2 November 1943—specifically prohibit execution, ill-treatment, and plundering. It is probable that these orders have been given on the basis of higher authority, eventually even a Stalin order" (BA-MA, RH 2/682, p. 2).

75 BA-MA, RW 2/v. 158, p. 82. The name of the lieutenant has been deleted.

76 J. V. Stalin, *Works*, ed. Robert McNeal (Stanford, Calif., 1967).

77 Author's interview with Hentig, 31 August 1976; PA, Kult. Pol. Geheim, vol. 140.

78 BA-MA, RW 2/v. 156, p. iii.

79 J. V. Stalin, *Works*, 2:30, 35. A German translation made in 1942 has survived in the records of the Reichsleiter Rosenberg, Hauptabt. IV-Ubersetzungsburo, NA, RG EAP 99/1157, Guides to Ger. Records Microfilmed at Alexandria, Va., No. 28, p. 10, T-454, Roll 13, pp. 0861ff. For the official Soviet postwar German translation, see J. Stalin, *Uber den Grossen Vaterländischen Krieg der Sowjetunion* (Moscow, 1946), pp. 31, 37, 38, 42.

80 PA, VR/KR, no. 22, vol. 82/7; cf. files of the VAA at the Reichskommissariat Ukraine, vol. 4.

81 BA-MA, RW 2/v. 208, p. 12.

82 Ibid., p. 13.

83 Ibid., 147, pp. 3–6.

84 *IMT*, 7:366, Nuremberg Docs. USSR-351, 884-PS.

85 BA-MA, RW 2/v. 150, pp. 4, 11.

86 Winston Churchill, *The Second World War: The Closing of the Ring* (London, 1951), 5:361.

87 Milovan Djilas, *Wartime* (London, 1977), p. 435.

88 A. de Zayas, *Nemesis at Potsdam* (Lincoln, 1988) pp. 61–69.

89 A. Solzhenitsyn, *The Gulag Archipelago*, vol. 1, p. 21.

CHAPTER SEVENTEEEN

1 BA-MA, RW 2/v. 150, pp. 108–17. The fifteen-minute black and white film "Soviet Massacres" in the Bundesarchive in Koblenz contains about three minutes on Feodosia, also used in the televised documentary on the Wehrmacht-Untersuchungsstelle.

2 Ibid., 182, pp. 93ff.

3 For instance, pertinent VAA files have survived in the records of the German Foreign Office, notably those of Werner Otto von Hentig, liaison officer at the High Command of the 11th Army, who on 23 February 1942 forwarded copies of the Feodosia documentation to the information department of the German Foreign Office, including the depositions of a German Army doctor, Rudolf Burkhardt, of a Soviet doctor named Dimitrijew, and of a Soviet laborer named Bursud. PA, Kult. Pol. Geheim, vol. 141; author's interview with Hentig, 31 August 1976.

4 BA-MA, RW 2/v. 208, pp. 31, 30.

5 BA-MA, AOK 11/RH 20/XI/348.

6 BA-MA, RW 2/v. 152, pp. 217ff. In an interview on 1 July 1976, Wilhelm Weber, retired justice of the Supreme Court of the Federal Republic of Germany (see Chapter 2), confirmed having seen such pictures in his capacity as senior judge of the 11th Army (interview transcript, p. 16); he thought he remembered having copies sent to the International Committee of the Red Cross, but the author has looked in vain for these photographs in the archives of the ICRC in Geneva.

7 BA-MA, RW 2/v. 151, pp. 13ff. Alexander Buldejew, chairman of the Russian-German Committee to Investigate Bolshevik Atrocities (see Chapter 3), wrote in the newspaper "Voice of Crimea" on 4 April 1942 that it was imperative to document all such atrocities committed by the commissars and NKVD. The records of this committee, however, appear to be lost; only a few copies remain in Hentig's private papers (n. 3, above).

8 BA-MA, RW 2/v. 152, pp. 229ff.

9 Ibid., pp. 213ff.

10 Ibid., pp. 215ff. Burkhardt participated in the University of Göttingen symposium, and also appeared in the televised documentary.

11 BA-MA, RW 2/v. 151, pp. 17ff.

12 Ibid., 152, pp. 231ff. Cf. deposition of Private Johann Scheid, who also survived his wounds. Hagemann recalls that "the men were lying in bed and their condition was such that I could take their depositions. They were entirely credible. . . . One of them, Niedermair, was older, about thirty-six years old, and he made a very truthful impression. Today I cannot tell you anymore whether I actually saw their wounds. I seem to remember that their wounds had been dressed and that they had plaster around their necks" (transcript of interview with author, 18 June 1976, p. 5). See also BA-MA, RW 2/v. 156, pp. 40ff.

13 BA-MA, RW 2/v. 152, pp. 236ff. Letters from Diderichs (12 June 1976) and Wilhelm Törber (2 September 1976) confirmed the events described in the deposition. Törber later appeared in the televised documentary.

14 BA-MA, RW 2/v. 157, pp. 306ff.

15 Ibid., 203, pp. 131ff.

16 Ibid., 235, pp. 27ff.

17 The photographer sent the author additional corroborative information on 20 December 1977.

18 Nuremberg Docs., Peace Palace The Hague, (Laternser Papers), Affidavit No. 1613.

19 PRO, WO 235/594.

CHAPTER EIGHTEEN

1 Today Donets, an important industrial center in the Ukrainian Soviet Socialist Republic.

2 The Todt Organization was a special corps of technicians, mostly engineers and communications experts, who followed the troops to perform construction and other technical assignments. It was named after Fritz Todt, general inspector for the road system, who died in an accident in 1942; see Franz Seidler, *Fritz Todt: Baumeister des Dritten Reichs* (Munich, 1987).

3 PA, VR/KR, no. 22, Russia, vol. 2, p. 6.

4 Ibid., p. 7.

5 BA-MA, RW 2/v. 200, pp. 86ff. The text of this deposition was not reproduced in the Bureau's report on Grischino.

6 Ibid., 199, p. 29. This deposition appears as supplement 10 to the Bureau's Grischino report: PA, VR/KR no. 22, Russia, vol. 2.

7 Transcript of author's interview with Willi Knobloch (today a practicing lawyer in West Germany), p. 3.

8 Letter to the author from Block, 27 April 1976.

9 Gerhard Wulle made a statement on Grischino for the television documentary.

10 Supplement 7 to the Grischino report, pp. 13ff. PA, VR/KR vol. 82/7, no. 22, Russia; letter to the author from Gerhard Wulle, 11 January 1977.

11 Supplement 8 to Grischino report, p. 14.

12 Supplement 8a, ibid., p. 15.

13 Knobloch interview, p. 2.

14 Supplement 23 to Grischino report, pp. 23ff.

15 BA-MA, RW 2/v. 220, pp. 344ff. In a letter to the author, 6 January 1977, Friedrich Schümann confirmed the authenticity of the copy of the protocol of Wilhelm Asche. He added that earlier in the war he had been an officer in an artillery unit in the Soviet Union: "I remember that as a lieutenant at the front I myself saw similar things. . . . The members of my battery, who had also seen these things, were profoundly shocked and bitter. Partisans in southern Russia had ambushed a German train with soldiers on home leave. Ten to twelve female members of the Wehrmacht staff had been horribly mutilated."

16 PRO, WO 235/594. On this point the author spoke to the British defense attorneys for Field Marshal von Manstein—with Lord Reginald Paget on 18 November 1980, with H. M. Croome on 16 November 1980—and with one of the prosecutors, Colonel G. I. A. D. Draper, on 17 August and 19 November 1980. See also R. T. Paget, *Manstein* (Wiesbaden, 1952).

CHAPTER NINETEEN

1 BA-MA, RW 2/v. 184, p. 147.

2 Ibid., 153, pp. 281ff. On 26 October 1975 the author interviewed several former members of the Spanish Blue Division in Madrid. M. Sanchez and Enrique Quesada had served fifteen months in the division, from July 1941 until September 1942: they knew of the Casanova deposition and remembered the gruesome murder of the soldiers who had been nailed down with pickaxes; they also confirmed the frequency of Soviet attacks on German hospitals and medical transports. Antonio Cascos cited several Spanish books that describe these atrocities: among them Juan Eugenio Blanco, *Rusia no es cuestión de un día* (Madrid, 1954), pp. 43ff.; Carlos M. Idigoras, *Algunos no hemos muerto* (Madrid, 1960), pp. 272ff.; Fernando Vadillo, *A Orillas del Voljov* (Madrid, 1968), 1:735ff.; Antonio Jose Hernandez Navarro, *Ida y Vuelta* (Madrid, 1955), pp. 215ff.

3 See Chapter 18.

4 *Istoriya Velikoi Otechestvennoi Voiny Sov.-Soyuza* (History of the great patriotic war of the Soviet Union) (Moscow, 1960–64), 3:50ff. Another explanation could be quite simply that those Italian prisoners who were not liquidated did not survive the POW camps of northern and central Russia. It has been estimated that many thousands died of exposure and disease, including pneumonia and tuberculosis. See Alexander Werth, *Russia at War, 1941–1945*, (New York, 1964), p. 507.

5 See Chapter 20.

6 *Frankfurter Allgemeine Zeitung*, 3 February 1987, p. 7: the president of the Italian National Association of Soldiers from the Russian Front, General Giuseppe Joli, commented that in September 1943 Italian soldiers had in fact been interned by the Germans in Lvov but had not been killed; they were subsequently liberated and then newly interned by the Soviet troops that captured Lvov from the Germans. He added, "If there really was a massacre of this kind, then it was perpetrated by the Russians."

7 The author has consulted the relevant records in BA and BA-MA. Further, the archive staffs informed the author in May 1987 that an Italian commission of historians had also searched the archives but could find no evidence of such a massacre.

8 BA-MA, RW 2/v. 160, pt. I, pp. 117ff. The map is attached to the report. See also the investigations of the Department IIb, *Fremde Heere Ost*, BA-MA, H 3/579.1, p. 50; H 3/665, p. 391; H 3/690, pp. 141ff.

9 BA-MA, RW 2/v. 219, p. 103. In a letter to the author, 7 October 1976, Judge Schürmann, who took the deposition, confirmed its authenticity.

10 BA-MA, RW 2/v. 204, pp. 117ff. For the fate of the Russian soldiers of the Vlassov Army, see Nikolai Tolstoy, *Victims of Yalta* (London, 1977).

11 See Chapter 13.

12 See Chapter 14.

13 BA-MA, RW 2/v. 147, p. 9.

14 PA, Kult. Pol. Geheim, vol. 135, files of liaison officer (VAA) Hellenthal. See also the affidavit

of Colonel Hans-Wolfgang Schoch, 16 June 1946, introduced by defense counsel Laternser at Nuremberg on 21 August 1946 (*IMT*, 21:398ff.); and the full text of Schoch's affidavit (IMT Doc. 1689) in the Laternser papers at the Peace Palace in The Hague.

15 PA, Kult. Pol. Geheim, vol. 135.

16 Ibid., testimony of German official Brugmann, dated June 1941.

17 Ibid.

18 BA-MA, RW 2/v. 149, pp. 298ff.

19 BA-MA, Kriegstagebuch, RH 20-17/277, pp. 125, 163. See also the Ic report dated 3 July 1941; also 49 A.K. Tätigkeitsberichte Ic, vol. 18253, p. 100.

20 BA-MA, RW 2/v. 149, pp. 280ff.

21 Ibid., 200, p. 155.

22 BA-MA, War Diary of High Command of 17th Army, vol. 14499/54, p. 137, Ic Report of 1 July 1941.

23 BA-MA, RW 2/v. 182, pp. 156ff.; ibid., 149, pp. 270ff.

24 Ibid., 147, pp. 119ff.

25 Ibid., pp. 400ff.

26 Ibid., pp. 120ff.; ibid., 149, pp. 413ff. Cf. white book of the German Foreign Office, *Bolschewistische Verbrechen gegen Kriegsrecht und Menschlichkeit*, vol. 1 (Berlin, 1941); and BA-MA, RW 2/v. 155, p. 84.

27 Walther von Seydlitz, *Stalingrad—Konflict und Konsequenz* (Oldenburg, 1977), p. 372.

28 Ibid., p. 378.

29 Seydlitz and Holzki were both repatriated in the early 1950s. In a letter to the author, 22 September 1976, Alfred Holzki confirmed the authenticity of a number of other depositions found in the Bureau's files. After the publication of the Seydlitz memoirs in 1977, Holzki similarly confirmed the Alexandrovo events.

30 Transcript of author's interview with Hans Georg Jeremias, 19 August 1975, p. 11.

CHAPTER TWENTY

1 BA-MA, Tätigkeitsberichte der Abteilung Ic beim 49 (Geb.) A.K. vol. 18253/1, p. 65; cf. AOK 17/14499/54, p. 147.

2 BA-MA, RW 2/v. 149, pp. 335ff. See also Ic Tätigkeitsberichte, 49 A.K. 18252/1, pp. 98ff.; 18253/4b, pp. 136ff.

3 BA-MA, Ic Tätigkeitsberichte, 49 A.K. 18253/4b, p. 135.

4 BA-MA, RW 2/v. 166, pp. 16ff.

5 Ibid., 149, pp. 339ff.

6 Ibid., 148, pp. 56ff., 54ff.

7 Ibid., pp. 49ff.; BA-MA, Ic Tätigkeitsberichte, 14499/54, p. 119.

8 BA-MA, RW 2/v. 149, pp. 350ff. The author interviewed Wilhelm Möller on this matter on 20 August 1976 at Lensahn, Schleswig-Holstein.

9 BA-MA, RW 2/v. 148, pp. 63ff.

10 Ibid., 166, pp. 14ff. The witness, deported to Siberia after the war, was able to emigrate to the United States in 1975. In an interview in Philadelphia on 28 December 1977, Fedoruk confirmed the events as described in his deposition and added that he had not been under pressure from the Germans to make any statement.

11 BA-MA, RW 2/v. 149, pp. 342ff. Omelian Matla emigrated to the United States after the war and died in 1968 in New York.

12 Ibid., pp. 355ff. Kazaniwsky emigrated to the United States after the war. On 11 October 1954 in New York he testified before a subcommittee of the House Select Committee on Communist Aggression. The text of his statement is reproduced in the committee's hearings, *Communist Takeover and Occupation of Poland*, House of Representatives, 83rd Congress (Washington, D.C.), 1954, pp. 110–14; he also published memoirs in 1975. The author interviewed Kazaniwsky in Philadelphia in December 1976 and again in December 1977, and he testified before the cameras for the 1983 television documentary.

13 BA-MA, RW 2/v. 149, p. 346.

14 Ibid., p. 347.

15 Ibid., p. 348.

16 Ibid., pp. 375ff.

17 Ibid., 147, pp. 109ff.

18 Ibid., 155, pp. 22ff.; PRO FO 371/30915, C. 3827.

19 Ibid., 149, pp. 373ff.

20 PRO, FO 371/26758.

21 PRO, FO 371/26756, C 8191; FO 371/26755, C 7890.

22 Letter from Sir Frank Roberts to the author, 20 December 1976.

23 *IMT*, 1:47.

24 *IMT*, 7:490ff.

25 PA, Inland IIg, vol. 431: Russia, SD-Einsatzgruppen, pp. 29ff.; NS, Nuremberg Doc. NO-2651, pp. 2, 11. In the BA film archive the 16-mm black and white film "Soviet Massacres" and a newsreel both show the corpses of Ukrainians in the Lvov prisons and the pogromlike disorders and beatings of Jews by Ukrainian civilians. Photographs in BA-MA, Tätigkeitsbericht der Abteilung Ic der 49 Geb. A.K., vol. 182537/4b, pp. 114ff.

26 NSB, Nuremberg Trial, Case no. 9, protocol of 18 October 1947, p. 957.

27 NSB, Nuremberg doc. NO-3644, p. 4.

28 IMT Doc. 1604 (Laternser Papers), Peace Palace.

29 Ibid., IMT Docs. 1604, 1606. See also the affidavit of General Wolf Ewerts, no. 1605. Cf. statement of ministerial director Hans Fritzsche of the Reich Ministry of Propaganda on 27 June 1946 at Nuremberg: "Dr. Taubert, who was head of the section dealing with Jewish questions in the propaganda department, told me in 1941 . . . that there had been pogroms during the occupation of Lvov and Kovno, but they were carried out by the local population" (*IMT*, 17:177). The author interviewed Eberhard Taubert at his home in Cologne on 6 October 1975 (he died in December 1976).

30 IMT Doc. 1603, Peace Palace; PRO, WO 235/594. See also Philip Friedman, "Ukrainian-Jewish Relations during the Nazi Occupation," *Yivo Annual of Jewish Social Science* 12 (1958–59):259–96.

31 U.S. Congress, House. Select Committee on Communist Aggression, *Communist Takeover and Occupation of Ukraine*, p. 28.

32 Upon the outbreak of war against the Soviet Union, Oberländer was liaison officer with a battalion that marched into Lvov on 30 June 1941.

33 Hermann Raschhofer, *Der Fall Oberländer* (Tübingen, 1962), p. 1.

34 Joop Zwaart, ed., *Lemberg 1941 und Oberländer: Das Ergebnis einer Untersuchung* (Amstelveen, 1960), p. 31. In a letter to the author, 31 March 1977, Norwegian lawyer Hans Cappelen wrote: "The commission . . . after thorough investigation came to the conclusion that Oberländer had not taken any part in the murders in Lemberg in 1941 . . . it was the NKVD that performed these murders." It should be noted, however, that in spite of its good will, the commission was not properly equipped to carry out a thorough investigation. A civilian or military court or a parliamentary committee can administer the oath and has the necessary machinery to deter and punish perjury; an international commission of individuals, regardless of their integrity, is necessarily less effective in getting at the whole truth. These considerations were shared by Professor Flor Peeters, whom I interviewed in St. Niklaas, near Ghent, Belgium, on 26 and 27 February 1977.

35 Roman Ilnytzkyi, *Deutschland und die Ukraine, 1934–1945* (Munich, 1956–58), 1:268ff., 284ff.

36 *Russischer Kolonialismus in der Ukraine: Berichte und Dokumente*, (Munich, 1962), pp. 129ff.

37 Borys Lewytskyi, "Die Affäre um Dr. Oberländer," *Kultura* (journal of Polish exiles in Paris) 1 (1960): 174; he also focuses on the murder of Lvov professors by the German *Einsatzgruppe* "Galicia." Lewytzkyi wrote to me on 9 March 1977 enclosing a German translation of his Polish article in *Kultura*.

38 Transcript of author's interview with Wilhelm Möller, 20 August 1976, p. 1.

39 Photographs taken immediately after the capture of Lvov show that the prison was still burning. Mrs. Strutynska published her memoirs (in Ukrainian) in Philadelphia in 1952.

40 Transcript of author's interview with Mrs. A.K., 1 April 1977, in Munich, pp. 2–3 (she requested that her name be withheld because of family members still living in the Ukraine). See also *Russischer Kolonialismus in der Ukraine*, pp. 136ff., and Zwart, *Lemberg 1941 und Oberländer*, pp. 42ff.

41 Esp. Nuremberg Trial No. 9: U.S. *v.* Otto Ohlendorf. et al.

CHAPTER TWENTY-ONE

1 Of the 4,143 bodies, 2,914 were identified. They included three generals: B. Bohaterewicz, H. Minkiewicz, M. Smorawinski; one rear admiral: K. Czerkicki; and approximately 100 colonels and lieutenant-colonels, 300 majors, 1,000 captains, and 2,500 lieutenants. See Louis Fitzgibbon, *Katyn* (London, 1975), p. 1.

2 See Zdzislaw Jagodzinski, *The Katyn Bibliography* (London, 1976), including, of course, the standard works by Jozef Mackiewicz, *The Katyn Wood Murders* (London, 1951); Wladyslaw Anders, *Katyn* (Paris, 1946); Janusz Zawodny, *Death in the Forest* (Notre Dame, Ind., 1962); and Count Jozef Czapski, *The Inhuman Land* (London, 1951).

3 U.S. Congress, House. Select Committee to Conduct an Investigation of the Facts, No. 2505, *The Katyn Forest Massacre: Final Report.* Cf. British reports by Sir Owen O'Malley, PRO, FO 371/34577.

4 BA-MA, RW 2/v. 149, p. 124. Merkuloff, who was taken prisoner in Finland, turned out to be a political commissar (see Chapter 16) and may have been killed by the Germans as a result of Hitler's Commissar Order.

5 *Amtliches Material zum Massenmord von Katyn* (Berlin, 1943), p. 25.

6 Ibid., pp. 22ff.

7 See Chapter 3.

8 *Amtliches Material . . . Katyn*, pp. 38ff., 94. Original photographs of the diggings, examinations, autopsies, items found on the bodies, etc., are in the record group of the Army Medical Office, Heeressanitäts-Inspektion, BA-MA, H 20/242.

9 *Amtliches Material . . . Katyn*, pp. 117ff. The original Katyn documents, including reports, identification papers, newspapers, personal items of the Polish officers, etc., have not been found since the war. According to West German archive officials and Z. Jagodzinski of the Polish Library, London (letter to the author, 28 April 1980), the entire documentation was taken by the retreating Germans to Krakau, where it was initially stored; it is probable that the records were lost or destroyed in the maelstrom of the last months of the war.

10 *IMT*, 1:54. See also Introduction.

11 *IMT*, 17:333ff.

12 *IMT*, 17:338ff.

13 *IMT*, 17:345, 350–51.

14 *IMT*, 17:349–61.

15 Fitzgibbon, *Katyn*, pp. 94ff.

16 See Chapter 8.

17 Fitzgibbon, *Katyn*, pp. 81ff. Naville's report is in the Swiss Federal Archives, Bern: BB, Documents of the Grand Conseil de Genève, B.55.11.43, memorandum of 24 September 1946.

18 Nuremberg Documents, The Hague (IMT), Affidavit no. 1204.

19 IMT, 17:274–97, 309. See also Fitzgibbon, *Katyn*, p. 96.

20 U.S. Congress, House. Select Committee to Investigate the Facts, *The Katyn Forest Massacre: Hearings*, pp. 1249–62.

21 Ibid., pp. 1420–70.

22 Ibid., pp. 1597–1602.

23 Ibid., pp. 1602–15, 1617–21, 310–35.

24 Ibid., pp. 1230–46.

25 Ibid., pp. 1497–1505.

26 Ibid., pp. 2–29, 32–74.

27 U.S. Congress, House. Select Committee to Investigate the Facts, *The Katyn Forest Massacre: Final Report*.

28 Louis Fitzgibbon, *Unpitied and Unknown* (London, 1975), p. 439.

29 Ibid., pp. 484–85.

30 Bundesarchiv, *Das Bundesarchiv und seine Bestände* (Boppard, 1977). Katyn is mentioned in the records of the Reichsministerium für Volksaufklärung und Propaganda, of the Reichsjustizministerium, of the personal staff of the Reichsführer-ss (Himmler), of the Generalgouvernement Polen (Hans Frank), etc.

31 BA, Publikationsstelle Berlin-Dahlem, vol. 153/1671.

32 Ibid.

CHAPTER TWENTY-TWO

1 BA-MA, RW 2/v. 149, pp. 275ff.

2 Ibid., 147, p. 102.

3 *Amtliches Material zum Massenmord von Winniza* (Berlin, 1944), p. 105.

4 Ibid., p. 257.

5 Ibid., p. 255.

6 Ibid., p. 253.

7 Ibid., p. 107. The members of the international commission were Drs. Soenen (Ghent), Michailov (Sofia), Pesonen (Helsinki), Duvoir (Paris), Cazzaniga (Milan), Jurak (Zagreb), ter Poorten (Amsterdam), Birkle (Bucharest), Häggquist (Stockholm), Krsek (Bratislava), and Orsos (Budapest). Orsos had also been a member of the Katyn commission, and had testified before the U.S. congressional committee on Katyn (see Chapter 21).

8 PA, files of liaison officer of the German Foreign Office (VAA) at the office of the Reich Commissioner for the Ukraine, vol. 4; PA, VR/KR, vol. 82/7.

9 The author interviewed four members of the German commission: Jungmichel (Göttingen), Timm (Jena, later Marburg), Weyrich (Prague, later Freiburg), and Hausbrandt (Königsberg, later Bolzano). Hausbrandt made a statement before the cameras for the television documentary;

unfortunately, time constraints eliminated important sections of the documentary film, including the Vinnitsa section. Dr. Hausbrandt's statement is on file in the archives of Bastei-Lubbe Verlag.

10 U.S. Congress, House. Select Committee on Communist Aggression, *Hearings*, pp. 1–23.

11 Ibid., pp. 28–29.

12 U.S. Congress, House. Select Committee on Communist Aggression, *Communist Takeover and Occupation of the Ukraine*, p. 26.

13 U.S. Congress, Senate. Judiciary Committee, *The Human Cost of Soviet Communism*, p. 29. See also Robert Conquest, *The Great Terror* (London, 1968).

14 *Russischer Kolonialismus in der Ukraine.*

CHAPTER TWENTY-THREE

1 On 17 March 1941 a British destroyer rescued the German submarine commander Otto Kretschmer and most of his German crew during a heavy sea battle (letter from J. D. Brown, Naval Historical Branch, Ministry of Defense, London, 5 June 1978). Cf. Friedrich Ruge, *Der Seekrieg, 1939–1945* (Stuttgart, 1969), p. 126. The author is grateful to Admiral Ruge, Inspector of the Navy of the Federal Republic of Germany, for informative interviews in 1977–80.

2 *IMT*, 40; Dönitz Doc. 39, p. 65.

3 J. D. Brown wrote the author on 16 June 1978: "I am unable to imagine the SKL's [*Seekriegs-leitung*, Naval War Staff] source for believing that the British Government could justify the shooting of survivors in the water. . . . The Royal Navy was bound by the Hague Convention; instructions to naval personnel on their conduct towards the survivors of enemy warships may have been laid down in the pre-1939 'Fighting Instructions.'"

4 Following the battle in the Bismarck Sea north of New Guinea, the U.S. Navy attacked the Japanese shipwrecked because "Japanese soldiers do not surrender," according to Samuel Eliot Morison, *History of United States Naval Operations in World War II* (Boston, 1950), 6:62: "Planes and PTs went about the sickening business of killing survivors in boats, rafts or wreckage. Fighters mercilessly strafed anything on the surface. On 5 March the two PTs which had sunk *Oigawa Maru* put out to rescue a downed pilot and came on an enemy submarine receiving survivors from three large landing craft. Torpedoes missed as the U-boat crash-dived. The PTs turned their guns on, and hurled depth charges at the three boats—which, with over a hundred men on board, sank. It was a grisly task, but a military necessity, since Japanese soldiers do not surrender and, within swimming distance of shore, they could not be allowed to land and join the Lae garrison." See also Robert Buckley, *At Close Quarters: PT-Boats in the United States Navy* (Washington, D.C., 1962), p. 181. Cf. *Newsweek*, 15 March 1943, p. 18: "On the morning of March 4, the seas north of New Guinea were awash with Jap survivors on rafts and in barges and lifeboats. Squadrons of Allied planes ruthlessly strafed them as they drifted"; *Life*, 22 March 1943, p. 28: "Mopping up begins on March 4 when B-17s and P-38s go out to strafe lifeboats and finish off two destroyers still afloat." See also Jürgen Rohwer and Gerhard Hümmelchen: *Chronik des Seekrieges* (Oldenburg, 1968), p. 335.

5 The Narvik episode was dealt with in the televised documentary.

6 BA-MA, RW 54/40, p. 1. In an interview on 22 June 1974, Helmut Sieber described how he was called upon to carry out the investigations. During the University of Göttingen symposium in 1977 Judge Sieber explained how sworn depositions were obtained and how carefully their statements were compared. A special Narvik dossier, "England A 9," was put together by the Bureau; it has unfortunately been lost, but Judge Sieber had kept a dossier for himself with copies of all the documents, which he allowed me to study. This dossier is now in BA-MA, RW 54/40.

7 BA-MA, RW 54/40, p. 31.

8 BA-MA, RW 2/v. 62, p. 262; author's interview with Captain Böhme, Bremerhaven, 22 May 1976.

9 BA-MA, RW 2/v. 62, pp. 263–64; author's interview with Admiral Wolff, Bremerhaven, 22 May 1976.

10 BA-MA, RW 2/v. 62, pp. 263–64.

11 Ibid., pp. 271–72; author's interviews with Admiral Smidt, 4 May 1974, 22 May 1976, and at the University of Göttingen symposium. Smidt also testified for the television documentary. Korvettenkapitan Smidt became Konteradmiral in 1944 and retired as Vice-Admiral of West Germany's Bundesmarine.

12 BA-MA, RW 2/v. 62, p. 278; author's interview with Wilzius, 22 May 1976.

13 This is partly incorrect. It is true that when the *Giese* was abandoned, there were no other German destroyers in sight; but in a neighboring fjord the crews of the *Georg Thiele*, *Wolfgang Zenker*, *Bernd von Arnim*, and *Hans Luddemann*, which had fired all their ammunition, were attempting to sink their ships.

14 BA-MA, RW 2/v. 62, pp. 279–80; author's interviews with Backus, 4 May 1974, 22 May 1976. Cf. the log of the *Erich Giese*, BA-MA, RM 94/v. M-896/74243: "A number of survivors of the Hunter were still swimming with vests or on rafts. We could rescue 16 men . . . eight of whom died on board from exhaustion."

15 Transcript of author's interview with Linn, 4 May 1974, p. 1. Linn also testified for the television documentary.

16 Transcript of author's interview with Captain Ernst Gunter Kray, pp. 7–15.

17 Among those rescued were Johannes Landfried, Ernst Weinert, and Josef Pütz, whom the author interviewed on 4 May 1974 and 6 May 1978. See rescue report of the *Foxhound* in PRO, ADM 199, vol. 473, pp. 169ff.

18 PRO, ADM 199, vol. 473, pp. 169ff. The *Cossack* was already notorious for its capture of the German steamer *Altmark* on 16 February 1940 in Norwegian territorial waters. For the German side, see Strupp-Schlochauer, *Wörterbuch des Völkerrechts*, 1:35. For the British side, see C. H. M. Waldock, "The Release of the Altmark's Prisoners," *British Yearbook of International Law* 24 (1947): 216–38; and W. R. Bisschop, "The Altmark" in *Transactions of the Grötius Society* 26 (1941): 67–82. Cf. also *IMT*, 3:279ff.; 40:59ff., Dönitz Doc. 37.

19 PRO, ADM 199, vol. 473, p. 191.

20 The original log went down with the ship, but Smidt and his officers reconstructed it shortly after reaching shore at Narvik: BA-MA, log of the *Erich Giese*, RM 94/v. M-896/74243, p. 77.

21 BA-MA, RW 2/v. 63, pp. 273ff.; letter to the author from Felix Reich, 28 June 1976.

22 Fritz Otto Busch, "Kommodore Bonte und seine Zerstörer" *Die Kriegsmarine*, 20 May 1940, p. 13.

23 BA-MA, RW 2/v. 30, pp. 29ff.

24 Ibid., 31, pp. 158ff.; cf. *IMT*, 40:61–65, document Dönitz-39.

25 The *Paraskevi* case was dealt with in the televised documentary, Judge Prechtel making a long statement.

26 BA-MA, RW 2/v. 62, pp. 79–83.

27 Ibid., p. 83.

28 BA-MA, RW 4/v. 619, pp. 71ff.

29 NA, RG 59, 868.857/70. The British government issued a dementi but at the same time endeavored to investigate the case. Unfortunately, Foreign Office documents C7275/C7281/C8424/ C8495/C8931/1582/43 were destroyed by the Foreign Office after the war, so that it is impossible to determine the results (letter to the author from British Foreign and Commonwealth Office, 26 November 1976).

30 PRO, ADM 199/1151, HMS *Rorqual*, Report of Proceedings, p. 164. A letter addressed to the captain of the *Rorqual* in care of the British Ministry of Defense has remained unanswered.

31 J. D. Brown, letter to the author, 31 July 1978: "The incident described . . . agrees in most respects with the Greek deposition, with the exception of the alleged machine-gunning of the Germans; the number of Germans aboard the caïque is not of great relevance. There is no doubt at all as to the fact that the submarine involved was the *Rorqual*—doubt must remain as to what in fact happened until the surviving Greeks and British submarine officers have been interviewed." The log of the German submarine U-852 under Captain Heinz Eck, which sank the *Peleus* (see this chapter, below), did not mention the shooting of shipwrecked either.

32 See Chapter 1.

33 Letter to the author from Georg Prechtel, 26 July 1978.

34 Daniel Davin, *Crete* (Wellington, N.Z., 1953), p. 487; Stewart, *Struggle for Crete*, pp. 281, 476.

35 BA-MA, RW 2/v. 62, pp. 300–301. In a letter to the author, 25 April 1978, Walter Segel wrote: "Now as ever I stand by my word and today I can eliminate a former doubt. It was the caïque number S-103 and not 107." In an interview on 25 February 1979 he explained how the invasion had been planned and why it failed. He also provided a number of photographs of the caïque S-103 and others showing British planes attacking survivors in the morning of 21 May 1940. After reaching Milos on 21 May, Segel joined the parachutists and four hours later landed in Crete (see Chapter 15). He also appeared on the televised documentary. Alan Clark described this sea battle in *The Fall of Crete* (London, 1962), p. 114: "A wild melee followed with the English destroyers ramming one after another of the caïques, sinking [them] by gunfire . . . and threshing this way

and that in water crowded with drowning soldiers and enemy crews who were clinging to rafts and pieces of wreckage."

36 BA-MA, RW 2/v. 135, pp. 162–63; letter to the author from Oskar von Jagwitz, 28 April 1978.

37 BA-MA, RW 2/v. 62, pp. 302–3; letter to the author from Roland Rüdel, 17 September 1976.

38 BA-MA, RW 2/v. 62, pp. 289–90; author's interview with Joachim Schölz, 11 May 1976.

39 BA-MA, RW 2/v. 134, pp. 192–93.

40 Ibid., pp. 195–96.

41 Ibid., pp. 198–99.

42 Ibid., pp. 231ff.

43 PRO, ADM 199/414, pp. 267ff.

44 BA-MA, RW 2/v. 138, p. 330; letter to the author from Wilhelm Landwehr, 30 September 1976.

45 BA-MA, RW 2/v. 138, p. 337. See also reports on the sinking of the *Yoannis* and *Varvara*, ibid., 139, pp. 77–78.

46 Ibid., 62, pp. 92–93. Buchholz perished in an accident at the Cognac airport on 5 March 1943.

47 Ibid., pp. 90–91; letter to the author from Hugo Lemser, 5 May 1978.

48 BA-MA, RW 2/v. 79, p. 113; on 12 May 1978 Schiedlauske confirmed his 1944 deposition.

49 BA-MA, RW 2/v. 79, p. 114.

50 PRO, FO 371/36546, W 8521.

51 Ibid., W 7934.

52 Ibid.

53 The attack was described to the author by Richard Lenz and Wolfgang Schwender of the U-852 on 11 November 1975. In the *Peleus* trial, Lenz was condemned to life and Schwender to fifteen years' imprisonment. One of the witnesses at the trial was Hans Cierniak, whom the author interviewed on 25 August 1974.

54 The incomplete files of the Bureau do not contain any mention either of Eck's actions on 13 March 1944 or of the British attack on the U-852 crew on 3 May 1944.

55 U-847, 848, 429, and 850: John Cameron, ed., *The Peleus Trial* (London, 1948), pp. 25, 49.

56 *IMT*, 40:51, *Dönitz* Doc. 36.

57 Execution by firing squad took place on 30 November 1945.

58 Cameron, *Peleus Trial*, p. 136. On 22 June 1974 the author discussed the Eck defense with Judge Helmut Sieber, who carried out the Narvik investigations for the War Crimes Bureau. After the war Sieber was the only active navy judge in Hamburg, and in this capacity he organized the defense of Eck and his officers. Because of his experience with the Narvik case, he thought that mentioning the shooting of German shipwrecked by British destroyers would lead to milder sentences. The defense attorneys approached Rear-Admiral Karl Smidt, former commander of the *Erich Giese*, but the court declined to call Smidt to testify; in an interview on 4 May 1974 Smidt commented, "The British made it clear that they were not interested in any statement from

me." In an interview on 23 May 1974 Hans Meckel (special adviser to the defense) confirmed this and added that hundreds of German sailors offered to testify that they had also been shot at in the water by Allied planes and ships. Cf. *IMT*, 40:52. In a request for clemency the attorneys for August Hoffmann specifically mentioned that he had been gravely wounded by strafing from British planes while he was trying to save himself and another wounded sailor, Corporal Damm (PRO, WO 235/604). The request for clemency was denied, and Hoffmann literally limped to his execution (information from Meckel).

CHAPTER TWENTY-FOUR

1 War Diary of the Navy War Office, pt. C, vol. 8, 1941 (17 July 1941); *IMT*, 40:50–51.

2 BA-MA, RW 2/v. 234, pp. 17–38, 39ff. In an interview on 17 August 1976 the chief medical officer of the *Alexander von Humboldt* confirmed the authenticity of the 1941 report.

3 The Geneva Convention for the Amelioration of the Condition of the Wounded in Armies in the Field of 22 August 1864 was supplemented on 20 October 1868 by additional articles providing immunity to hospital ships (not in force) extending in the Third Hague Convention of 29 July 1899. Most important in regard to hospital ships is the Tenth Hague Convention for the Adaptation to Maritime Warfare of the Principles of the Geneva Convention (1899/1907). Art. 1 provides: "Military hospital ships, that is to say, ships constructed or assigned by states specially and solely with a view to assisting the wounded, sick, and shipwrecked, the names of which have been communicated to the belligerent powers at the commencement or during the course of hostilities, and in any case before they are employed, shall be respected, and cannot be captured while hostilities last. These ships, moreover, are not on the same footing as warships as regards their stay in a neutral port." Art. 4 provides in part: "The governments undertake not to use these ships for any military purpose." The general observance of these rules in many wars since 1868 renders them part of customary international law. See "Customary International Law" in Bernhardt, *Encyclopedia of Public International Law*, vol. 7.

4 BA-MA, RW 2/v. 31, pp. 37–38. It has been the practice of all belligerents to employ as hospital ships those best suited to the area of operation; obviously, they should not be so large that they cannot enter small ports, a fact that influenced the size of hospital ships used in the English Channel. But the British viewed any small ship with distrust at the time of the projected German invasion of the British Isles (Sealion).

5 PRO, FO 371/43003, doc. W 1667; BA-MA, RW 2/v. 31, p. 37.

6 After repeated protests from the German government, the British agreed in February of 1945 to release the *Freiburg*, which had been detained at Alexandria, and to accept it as a hospital ship. The records of the Bureau do not indicate whether the *Freiburg* was in fact released.

7 BA-MA, RW 2/v. 40, pp. 21–22; 235, pp. 63–64. This list also includes three bombardments by Russian forces. Several attacks were excusable on the grounds that the hospital ships were anchored in port near legitimate military objectives.

8 Ibid., 79, pp. 235–36. This list includes four Soviet attacks.

9 Ibid., 78, pp. 164ff. Cf. log of the German Naval Command in Italy (vol. 28), BA-MA, RM 36

v.M/635/45012, p. 1037: at 12:12 hours the *Erlangen* radioed, "sos, enemy bombers are attacking us"; 12.35 hours, "Thus far four wounded, continue voyage"; 12.45 hours, "We are level with Cape Messo, new attack by fighter bombers. One hit, *Erlangen* on fire, must strand 6 sm sos Levante. Wounded will be disembarked. Monitoring service indicated initial report about a 'big steamer'; another transmission reports the steamer as hospital ship *Erlangen*. In spite of this the station on land orders the plane to attack the ship." Cf. also log of the German Naval Command in Italy (vol. 29) for 16 June 1944, RM 36 v.M/635/45013, and log of the 7th *Sicherungsdivision*, RM 67 v.M/1021/81157–58.

10 BA-MA, RW 2/v. 79, pp. 18ff. For pictures of the damaged hospital ships, see Rudolf Schmidt and Arnold Kludas, *Die deutschen Lazarettschiffe im zweiten Weltkrieg* (Stuttgart, 1978), *Erlangen* on p. 73, *Freiburg* on p. 82.

11 PRO, FO 371/43003, W 16667, W 16698; BB, 2200 London 55, Classeur 11, and 2021 (E) Classeur 11.

12 The *Tübingen* sinking played a small role in the defense of Admiral Dönitz at Nuremberg: *IMT*, 13:540. The author thanks Professors H. Schadewaldt and J. Rohwer for information regarding the attacks on the *Freiburg*, *Erlangen*, and *Tübingen*.

13 PRO, FO 371/42995.

14 PA, Papers of the German Legation in Bern, Protecting Power.

15 BB, 2021 (c), Classeur 50; PA, Papers of the German Legation in Bern.

16 BB, 2021 (c) Classeur 51. See also PRO, FO 371/42995.

17 PRO, AIR 8/827-03071.

18 BB, 2200 London 55, Classeur 11.

19 PRO, AIR 8/827-03071.

20 BA-MA, RW 2/v. 31, pp. 12–13; PA, Papers of the German Legation in Bern, doc. D 5463.

21 BA-MA, RW 2/v. 31, pp. 18–21, 27; Franz Nadenau, the examining judge, verified the depositions on 8 and 16 July 1976.

22 BA-MA, RW 2/v. 31, p. 19.

23 Ibid., p. 27.

24 Captain Hermichen, who had received copies of these pictures, gave them to the author during an interview, 18 August 1976.

25 BA-MA, RW 2/v. 31, pp. 5–16.

26 Art. 5 of the Tenth Hague Convention for the Adaptation to Maritime Warfare of the Principles of the Geneva Convention of 18 October 1907, provides: "Military hospital ships shall be distinguished by being painted white outside with a horizontal band of green about a meter and a half in breadth. . . . All hospital ships shall make themselves known by hoisting, with their national flag, the white flag with a red cross provided by the Geneva Convention."

27 BB, 2200 London 55, Classeur 11; PA, Papers of the German Legation in Bern.

28 BA-MA, RW 2/v. 31, p. 37. The other dead and missing were Lieutenant Rindfuss, radioman Marx, and engineman Harkt (letter to the author from Captain Hermichen, 29 August 1976).

29 Letter from J. Mossot to Sir Patrick Dean, 16 March 1945, PRO, FO 371/50572.

30 Transcript of author's interview with Captain Hermichen, 18 August 1976, p. 11.

31 BA-MA, RW 2/v. 31, pp. 37–38.

32 See Sir John Slessor's correspondence in the file "Bombing—Avoidance of Attack on Hospital etc. Ships and Trains," PRO, AIR 23/820.

The archival material used in this study, originating in the government offices of several countries, has made it possible to compare various approaches to the same specific event and thus to arrive at an informed opinion on the credibility and reliability of the documents under investigation. The Bibliography lists the files consulted under the locations where they are housed. This note specifies some of them a bit further and points up their significance.

World War I Sources

Because the bulk of the Prussian Army files were destroyed in the Allied bombardment of Potsdam and Berlin in 1945, only 11 volumes remain of the files of the Prussian Bureau of Investigation: one on reported violations of the laws of war by British troops; one containing a "black list" of 39 English officers and soldiers who allegedly committed crimes against members of the German Army; and nine on similar offenses committed by French soldiers and civilians, including a list of some 400 accused persons. These volumes are housed at the Bundesarchiv-Militärarchiv in Freiburg, West Germany, PH 2/25–35.

Also surviving are numerous memoranda and the white books or white papers of the German Foreign Office, which were either drafted by the Prussian bureau or put together on the basis of its documentation. They include "Belgium: Louvain"; "Memorandum on Belgian *Franc-tireur* Warfare"; "Memorandum on the Killing of the Crew of a German Submarine by the Commander of the British Cruiser *Baralong*, 1915"; and "Memorandum on the Misuse of Enemy Hospital Ships." All these may be consulted *inter alia* in the Niedersächsische Staats bibliothek (State Library of Lower Saxony) in Göttingen, and at the Bayrisches Hauptstaatsarchiv in Munich in the collection "Kriegsrechtsverletzungen," MKr. 142628.

After the war, much of this material was evaluated by a special commission of the German parliament and published in the five-volume *Völkerrecht im Weltkrieg* (Berlin, 1927), edited by Reichsminister Johannes Bell, one of the signers of the Versailles Treaty.

World War II German Sources

It may be estimated that the files of the War Crimes Bureau originally contained records of some 10,000 cases or complexes, of which perhaps 4,000 have survived. The Bureau gave each investigated case a reference number, and all documents relevant to that investigation bear the same number. From 1940 to 1945 the sequence started over each January, with the year added to the reference number: e.g., U-2338.40 is the 2,338th case in 1940.

About half of the existing files are the original documents; the rest are either certified copies or wartime photocopies. Where both originals and certified copies are on hand, comparison shows that they are identical. Investigations were frequently accompanied by photographic evidence: envelopes originally containing pictures or negatives are attached to many files, but most of these are empty; only about 400 photos are still available.

Some 40 of the 226 volumes of War Crimes Bureau records deal with the treatment of German prisoners of war in North Africa, England, and the United States. Because a major scholarly work has already been published on this subject—*Zur Geschichte der deutschen Kriegsgefangenen des Zweiten Weltkrieges*, 22 volumes, edited by Erich Maschke (Bielefeld, 1962–75)—these files are dealt with only marginally in the present study, which concentrates on events that occurred on or near the field of battle. The Bureau's records were not available to the Maschke commission, but although a detailed study of them might yield valuable information in individual cases, in general they supplement and confirm Maschke's definitive work.

Among important original files missing from the records of the War Crimes Bureau are all special compilations dealing with the major investigations *inter alia* at Broniki, Feodosia, Grischino, Lvov, and Narvik; the originals of documents from the investigations in Poland and Yugoslavia are also missing, though certified copies remain, and additional copies are to be found in the records of the *Ausland-Abwehr* (intelligence) bureau, the Army Medical Office, the Foreign Office, and the Wehrmacht operations staff. The records of these agencies also provide additional information on a number of cases, as well as numerous captured enemy documents.

The records of the Army Medical Office at the Army High Command (*Heeres-Sanität-sinspekteur*) also include some correspondence of Bureau officials with the adviser on forensic medicine, and copies of the witness depositions on alleged mutilations that were submitted to the department of forensic medicine for verification.

The records of the *Fremde Heere Ost* contain captured Soviet Army orders, propaganda leaflets, and personal diaries, (together with their translation), as well as the transcription of intercepted radio messages and statements of Soviet prisoners of war.

Descriptions of enemy violations found in official war diaries of the various German divisions, in particular the reports of the military intelligence departments, (Ic), also help to complete the picture given in the records of the Bureau; for example, the war diaries of the 6th, 11th, and 17th German Armies were helpful in the discussion of the Lvov and Feodosia investigations. But since the focus of this study is on the work of the Bureau rather than on the military events themselves, the war diaries were used only marginally. They are a source that remains largely unexhausted and that future researchers may do well to consult.

Two record groups in the political archives of the German Foreign Office contain copies of depositions and captured enemy documents in the original: *Völkerrecht/Kriegsrecht* and *Kult. Pol. Geheim*. The library of the German Foreign Office contains a fairly complete collection of German white books on questions of violations of the laws of war by enemy powers, including the following:

1 *Dokumente polnischer Grausamkeit* (Documents of Polish cruelty), Berlin, 1940.

2 *Die polnischen Greueltaten an den Volksdeutschen in Polen* (Polish atrocities against the ethnic Germans in Poland), Berlin, 1940.

3 *Dokumente britisch-französischer Grausamkeit* (Documents of British-French cruelty), Berlin, 1940.

4 *Frankreichs völkerrechtswidrige Kriegführung* (France's illegal warfare), Berlin, 1940–41.

5 *Dokumente britischer Barbarei* (Documents of British barbarism), Berlin, 1941.

6 *Bolschewistische Verbrechen gegen Kriegsrecht und Menschlichkeit* (Bolshevik crimes against the laws of war and against humanity), 3 vols., Berlin, 1941–43.

7 *Völkerrechtsverletzungen der britischen Streitkräfte und der Zivilbevölkerung auf Kreta* (Violations of international law by the British Navy and the civilian population of Crete), Berlin, 1942.

8 *Amtliches Material zum Massenmord von Katyn* (Official papers on the mass murder at Katyn), Berlin, 1943.

9 *Dokumente über die Alleinschuld Englands am Bombenkrieg gegen die Zivilbevölkerung* (Documents on the sole guilt of England for the air bombardment against civilians), Berlin, 1943.

10 *Der anglo-amerikanische Bombenkrieg* (The Anglo-American air war), Berlin, 1944.

11 *Amtliches Material zum Massenmord von Winniza* (Official papers on the mass murder at Vinnitsa), Berlin, 1944.

Particularly revealing are the notes and internal correspondence relating to the production and publication of the white books (Record Group *Kult. Pol. Geheim*). The records of the liaison officers (VAA) between the Foreign Office and various army headquarters and those of the Reichskommissariat Ukraine help to complete the War Crimes Bureau's documentation.

The personnel files of Johannes Goldsche and some of his associates are to be found at the Bundesarchiv-Zentralnachweisstelle in Kornelimunster; there too one can consult the records of proceedings of German military trials of Polish prisoners of war and courts-martial of German soldiers, trial records that provide further information on the military judges who performed the investigations for the War Crimes Bureau. Unfortunately, the existing legal files of the German Army and Air Force are very sparse; those of the German Navy have been largely preserved, however, and assist the analysis of the methods of German military justice.

World War II Non-German Sources

The Federal Archive at Bern contains the extensive records of the activity of the Swiss government as Protecting Power: both diplomatic notes of the German Foreign Office against the governments of Great Britain and the United States, and official American and British protests that were subsequently submitted to the War Crimes Bureau for investigation.

In London's Public Record Office the records of several British investigations generated by German accusations may be consulted for the sake of comparison. The correspondence with respect to the sinking of the hospital ship *Tübingen* is quite extensive, but thus far the "Court of Enquiry" records have not been released. The British Foreign Office index lists five documents relating to the *Osia Paraskevi* case, but a letter of 26 November 1976 from the Foreign and Commonwealth Office confirms that these documents were destroyed several years ago. Logs of British submarines and destroyers, however, are available and were consulted.

Washington's National Archives preserve the records of some investigations of alleged air attacks on German hospitals and red cross transports. Another case, for which no official German protest has been found, concerns the death by asphyxiation of 143 German prisoners of war in transit between POW camps in France (Record Group 331). General Eisenhower ordered a full investigation, invited the Swiss Protecting Power to designate a participating official, and informed the German High Command of the steps being taken.

Postwar Research

My study of the War Crimes Bureau's files and other relevant records has led me into several projects. In addition to interviewing over 300 judges, victims, and witnesses and engaging in considerable correspondence with those persons and representatives of various governmental offices and archives in several countries, I have participated in the following events:

On 14–15 January 1977 I chaired a two-day symposium on the subject of the *Wehrmacht-Untersuchungsstelle* at the Institute of International Law of the University of Göttingen; participants (some of whom are specified in the notes) included some thirty experts, among them the director of the German Military Archives in Freiburg, professors of history and of international law, and several military judges together with the witnesses whose depositions had been taken for the Bureau. On 30 November 1978 a second symposium was held at the Institute of International Law of the University of Cologne, chaired by Professor Ignaz Seidl-Hohenveldern.

On 18 and 21 March 1983 a two-part documentary film on the War Crimes Bureau, co-authored and introduced by me, was shown on television channel 1 (ARD/WDR) in the Federal Republic of Germany; again, many of those who appeared in the film are pointed out in the notes.

And in 1984 the fourth, enlarged, edition of this book was published: *Die Wehrmacht-Untersuchungsstelle: Deutsche Ermittlungen über alliierte Völkerrechtsverletzungen im Zweiten Weltkrieg* (Munich: Universitas-Verlag/Langen Müller), incorporating reactions from viewers of the TV documentary. The paperback German edition was published in 1987 by Ullstein, Berlin.

BIBLIOGRAPHY

ARCHIVAL SOURCES: GERMAN

Bundesarchiv/Militärarchiv, Freiburg

Militäruntersuchungsstelle für Verletzungen des Kriegsrechts im Preussischen Kriegsministerium, PH 2/25–35.

High Command of the Wehrmacht
Wehrmacht Rechtsabteilung: Untersuchungsstelle für Verletzungen des Völkerrechts, RW 2/v. 15–241.

OKW/Amt *Ausland-Abwehr* RW 5/v. 3, 28, 333, 506.

Wehrmachtführungsstab, RW 4/v. 268, 296, 298, 299, 318, 319, 320, 619, 709, 765.

Führungsstäbe des OKW, OKW 12, 17, 49, 962, 1895, 2009, 2035, 2039, 2123, RW 44.

Militärbefehlshaber Belgien-Nordfrankreich
RW 36/237, 433, 434, 435, 436.

Army High Command
OKH/GenStdH/Abt. Fremde Heere Ost, RH 2/2499, 2678, 2681–88, 2780–86.

Army Medical Office, H 20/242, 287, 287/1, 288, 290, 293, 496.

Heer
Army High Commands: RH 20-6/489, 513, 515, 516; 11/348; 17/277, 282; 30/50; 170/8, 35.

Armeekorps (Army Corps): Tätigkeitsbericht der Abteilung Ic beim Armeeoberkommando 17, in 49 (Geb.) A.K. vol. 18253/1, 18253/3, 18253/4a, 18253/4b; Abteilung Ic beim Armeeoberkommando 6, in 30 A.K. vol. 17749/2.

Divisionen (Divisions): 170 Inf.Div., vol. 20308; Kriegstagebush Ia (January 1942) 15466/1—Anlagen zun KTB Ia 7–18 January 1942.

Oberkommando der Kriegsmarine
Log of the destroyer *Erich Giese* 1940, RM 94 v. M 896/74243.

Narvik file, RM 54/40.

War Diary of the 7. Sicherungsdivision, RM 67 v.M./1021/81157–58.

War Diary of the Marinekommandos Italien: RM 36 v.M./635/45012, pp. 1033ff.; RM 36 v.M./635/45013, pp. 1053ff.

War Diary of the Seekriegsleitung, Teil C VIII (Völker- und Seekriegsrecht) provisional code, RM 7/188.

War Diary of the Seekriegsleitung of 23 October 1943, RM 7/215.

1. Seekriegsleitung 11 (Völkerrecht), Lazarettschiffe 1943–45, RM 7/v. Cases 726–27.

Bundesarchiv, Koblenz

Ost-Dokumentation: Ost-Dok. 2 no. 8; Ost-Dok. 2 no. 21, no. 22; Ost-Dok. 7.

Reichsjustizministerium, R 22/2913, 2914.

Bundesarchiv-Zentralnachweisstelle, Kornelimünster

Personnel file Goldsche, H 2-8242.

Personnel file Schöne, H 2-8255.

Feldurteile: RHL 3/43, RM 34-C 48061; RM 45 West-G; RM 45 Nord-G, Südost-G, Norwegen-G.

Politisches Archiv des Auswärtigen Amtes, Bonn

Völkerrecht/Kriegsrecht 12 (Kriegsgefangenenabkommen) Band 1, 2.

VR/KR 22 (Verletzungen des Völkerrechts im Krieg): Allgemeines, Band 1–6; England, Band 2–4; Frankreich, Band 1–2; Russland, Band 1–3.

VR/KR 26 no. 5 (Strafverfahren gegen Kriegsgefangene in Deutschland).

VR/KR 26 no. 13b (Erschiessungen).

VR/KR 27 no. 13b (Lagerzwischenfälle).

VR/KR 27 no. 23 (Misshandlungen).

VR/KR 82 no. 4.

Kult. Pol. Geheim: 36, 40, 41, 45, 49–51, 54, 60, 96, 99, 111, 112, 115, 120, 121, 123, 125–27, 132–36, 139–44, 148, 149, 154–56, 159–69, 174.

Deutsche Gesandtschaft, Bern, Schutzmacht Abteilung, Aktengruppe Bern, Lazarettschiffe, Bd. Deutschland 7.

V-Stelle, Bf. 1.

Feindpropaganda, Bd. 7.10.40–19.1.43.

Handakte v. Etzdorf, Bd. 1, 2, 3.

IKRK Berichte.

Inland II g, Bd. 22, 29, 431.

VAA beim R-kom. Ukraine, Bd. 4.

Niedersächsische Staatsbibliothek, Göttingen

Nürnberger-Prozessakten: Serien C, D, NO, NOKW, PS.

Proceedings of the Einsatzgruppen Trial (Case 9).

Proceedings of the OKW-Trial (Case 12).

Denkschriften der Militäruntersuchungsstelle für Verletzungen des Kriegsrechts, u.a. Belgien, Löwen, 1915.

Denkschrift über den belgischen Volkskrieg, 1917.

Denkschrift über den Missbrauch feindlicher Lazarettschiffe, 1916.

Institut für Zeitgeschichte, Munich

Mikrofilms MA 10(4), MA 208, MA 538, MA 646, MA 847.

Privatdruck: Memoiren von Christian Freiherr von Hammerstein, "Mein Leben" ED 84.

Archive of the Marine-Offiziers-Vereinigung, Bad Godesberg

Nachlass des Marineoberstabsrichters Helmut Sieber u.a. Feldurteile von Marine- und Heeresgerichten.

Verteidigungsunterlagen vom Nürnberger Prozess und vom Prozess gegen Kpt.lt. Heinz Eck ("*Peleus*-Prozess").

ARCHIVAL SOURCES: NON-GERMAN

Swiss Federal Archive (Bundesarchiv), Bern

Files of the Eidgenössischen Politischen Departements, Abteilung Fremde Interessen: E Bern 2021 (b) Classeur 21, 22; E Bern 2021 (c) Classeur 32, 39, 45, 50, 51, 66, 69, 88, 92, 93; E Bern 2021 (e) Classeur 11, 37; E 2200 Berlin 3, Classeur 4, 14 bis, 65; E 2200 London 55, Classeur 11, 14; E 2200 Washington 15, Classeur 11.

Files of the Swiss Red Cross, Ostfrontmission 1941–43 J II. 15 1969/7 Classeur 133.

Peace Palace, The Hague

Archives of the Nuremberg International Military Tribunal as entrusted to the Court pursuant to a decision of that Tribunal dated 1 October 1946. Affidavits presented by Hans Laternser for the Defense of OKW: IMT Docs. 501, 507, 509, 712, 1204, 1207, 1490, 1601, 1601b, 1602–6, 1608, 1611, 1612, 1612a, 1613, 1619, 1683, 1690, 1693, 3066, 3100, 3101.

Public Record Office, London

Foreign Office

FO 371/24423, Doc. C 6639, C 11978.

FO 371/26755 Doc. C 7890.

FO 371/26756 Doc C 8191.

FO 371/26758.

FO 371/28885, Doc. W 8788, W 8789, W 8791, W 9613.

FO 371/28886, Doc. W 11959.

FO 371/28887.

FO 371/29487 Doc. N 3823.

FO 371/30915 Doc. C 3837.

FO 371/30921 Doc. C 10825.

FO 371/34380 Doc. C 14890, C 15135, C 14742, C 15145.

FO 371/34572 Doc. C 4828, C 4891, C 4897, C 4908, C 4909, C 4910.

FO 371/34575.

FO 371/34577 Doc. C 5947, C 6160, C 6161.

FO 371/36546 Doc. W 7932, W 7933, W 7934, W 8521.

FO 371/36547 W 11347, W 12851.

FO 371/37008 Doc. N 7517, N 4189, N 5009, N 6627, N 7702.

FO 371/39083 Doc. C 147, A 3.

FO 371/43002 Doc. W 15894, W 15817, W 15841, W 15893, W 16380, W 16405, W 16435, W 16617.

FO 371/43003 Doc. W 16667, W 16698, W 18228, W 16828.

FO 371/42995 Doc. W 17037, W 16770.

FO 371/48834 Doc. N 16482.

FO 371/50526, 50566.

FO 371/50572 Doc. W 3970, W 4052.

War Office

WO 235/589–94 (Manstein); 235/604 (*Peleus*).

Admiralty

ADM 1, vol. 16012, vol. 16183, Doc. W 16690, vol. 18500, vol. 18926, Doc. N.I.6475; ADM 199, vol. 140, 144, 414, 473, 807, 1151, 1197.

Air Ministry

AIR 8/827, AIR 8/1358, AIR 22/81, AIR 23/820, 1601.

Ministry of Information

INF 1/678.

Cabinet Papers
CAB 66/36, W.P. (43) 175.

National Archives, Washington

Modern Military Branch
Microfilm Publication T-77, Rolls R1458–98.

Diplomatic Branch
Protecting Power (Switzerland) U.S. interests: 703.5462; German interests: 705.6254.

Record Group 59, General Records of the Department of State
711.62114/1-145.

711.62114/1-445.

711.62114/504, 479, 387.

711.62114/4-445, 1-2545, 1-2645, 3-2145, 1-1045.

711.62114/6-2945.

711.62114/12-144.

711.62114/12-244.

711.62114/12-1344, 12-1444.

711.62114/12-244, 12-2244.

711.62114/535.

711.62114/2-345.

711.62114/2-3.

740.0011 E.W./1-2645, 2-2545.

740.0016 E.W./1939/566, 1939/1353, 1939/406, 1939/392, 1939/415, 1939/1380, 1939/1257.

740.00116 E.W./1-2245, 2-2245, 2-2545, 2-1645, 4-945, 4-2745, 4-2445.

868.857/70.

Record Group 159, Office of the Inspector General

Record Group 260, Records of United States Occupation Headquarters WW II (OMGUS)
Germany 1945, Doc. 711.62144/4-445, ODI files, Box 25.

Record Group 331, Records of Allied Operational and Occupation Headquarters WW II
SHAEF G-1 Division, 383.6/10 Special Investigation re German Prisoners of War.

Record Group 332, Records of U.S. Theater of War, WW II
Ent. Admin. File ETOUSA, Operations History of the Advance Section Communications Zone,
    Box 174.

Records of the Judge Advocate, Boxes 89, 90, Doc. 383.6.

Record Group 338, U.S. Army Commands, 1942–45

Record Group 389, Records of Office of Provost Marshal
General, 330.14 Gen P/W 4, Complaints alleging violation of Geneva Convention by American
troops in E.T.O.; File 383.6/477, Box 1387, Alleged Employment of German Prisoners of
War in Dangerous Zones.

OMGUS files
Advance Section Communications Zone, Operational History, ETOUSA/ADSEC, CCPWE no. 16.

USFET
Adjutant section, Doc. 311.7; 46-31312.

Department of the Army, Office of the Judge Advocate General, Washington, D.C.

8-3.5 AA European Theater, United States Forces, Office of the Judge Advocate General, History
Branch Office of the Judge Advocate General with the United States Forces European The-
ater 18 July 1942–1 November 1945. Joint Authors 1945. 2 vols. 617 pp. text and appendixes.
Mimeo.

4-2 DA A History of the War Crimes Office, 25 September 1944–30 June 1945. Typescript.

4-2 CA History of Military Training, Judge Advocate General's Department to June 1945 and
Supplement to December 1945. 99 pp. Typescript.

4-2 BA Military Justice, 1 July 1940–31 December 1945. 79 pp. Typescript.

4-2 AA A History of the Judge Advocate General's Department, Legal Work of the War Department 1 July 1940–31 December 1945. 408 pp. Typescript.

PUBLISHED SOURCES

Absolon, Rudolf. *Die Wehrmacht im Dritten Reich: Aufbau, Gliederung, Recht, Verwaltung.* Boppard, 1968.

———. *Das Wehrmachtstrafrecht im 2. Weltkrieg: Sammlung der grundlegenden Gesetze, Verord-
nungen und Erlasse.* Kornelimünster, 1958.

Ahlbrecht, A. "War Reprisals in the War Crimes Trials and the Geneva Conventions." *AJIL* 47
(1953): 590ff.

Akten zur deutschen auswärtigen Politik 1918–1945, Serie D, 1937–41, vol. 13, 1. *Die Kriegsjahre, 23.
Juni bis 14. Sept. 41;* vol. 13, 2, *Die Kriegsjahre, 15 Sept. bis 11. Dez. 41.* Göttingen, 1970.

Akten zur deutschen auswärtigen Politik, 1918–1945, Serie E, 1941–45, vol. 1, *12. Dez. 1941 bis 28. Febr.
1942.* Göttingen, 1969.

American Journal of International Law (AJIL) 10, supp. 1 (1916); 16 (1922): 674ff.

Amtliches Material zum Massenmord von Katyn. Im Auftr. des Auswärtigen Amtes aufgrund
urkundl. Beweismaterials zsgest., bearb. Berlin, 1943.

Amtliches Material zum Massenmord von Winniza im Auftrag des Reichsministers für die besetzten Ostgebiete. Berlin, 1944.

Amtliches Weissbuch über die Kriegsverbrecherprozesse. Reichstagsdrücksache. I. Wahlperiode 1920–24, no. 2584. Berlin, 1928.

Anders, Wladyslaw. *Katyn.* Paris, 1946.

Der anglo-amerikanische Bombenkrieg: Tatsachen und Stimmen. Materialsammlung. Auswartiges Amt. Berlin, 1944.

Ansel, Walter. *Hitler and the Middle Sea.* Durham, N.C., 1972.

Armstrong, J. A. *Soviet Partisans in World War II.* Madison, Wis., 1964.

――――. *Ukrainian Nationalism.* New York, 1955.

Arndt, Adolf. "Heilsames Recht (die Einsatzgruppen-Prozesse)." *Neue Juristische Wochenschrift,* 1964, pp. 1210ff.

Arntz, Helmut. "Die Menschenverluste der beiden Weltkriege." *Universitas* 8 (1953): 703–8.

Artzt, H. "Zur Abgrenzung von Kriegsverbrechen und NS-Verbrechen." In A. Rückerl, ed., *NS-Prozesse.* Karlsruhe, 1971.

Aurich, Peter. *Der Deutsch-Polnische September 1939.* Munich, 1969.

Ausschuss fur Deutsche Einheit. *Wir klagen an!* East Berlin, 1959.

Bader, Karl. "Die deutsche Justiz in Selbstzeugnis. *Juristenzeitung,* 1960, pp. 3ff.

Bailey, Sydney. *Prohibitions and Restraints in War.* Oxford, 1972.

Baird, J. W. *The Mythical World of Nazi War Propaganda, 1939–1945.* Minneapolis, Minn., 1974.

Balfour, Michael. *Propaganda in War.* London, 1979.

Bartov, Omer. *Eastern Front, 1941–1945: German Troops and the Barbarisation of Warfare.* London, 1986.

Bauer, Fritz. *Die Kriegsverbrecher vor Gericht.* Zurich, 1945.

Baum, Walter. "Marine, Nationalsozialismus und Widerstand." *VfZ* 11 (1963).

Baumann, Hans. *Die 35. Infanterie-Division im 2. Weltkrieg, 1939–1945: Die Geschichte einer einsatzbereiten, standhaften und anspruchslosen bad.-wurtt. Infanterie-Division.* Karlsruhe, 1953.

Baumgart, Winfried. "Zur Ansprache Hitlers vor den Führern der Wehrmacht am 22. August 1939: Eine quellenkritische Untersuchung." *VfZ* 16 (1968): 120–49; *VfZ* 19 (1971): 294–304.

Baxter, Richard. "The Cambridge Conference on the Revision of the Law of War." *AJIL* 47 (1953): 702ff.

Bell, Johannes, ed. *Völkerrecht im Weltkrieg: Das Werk des Dritten Untersuchungssausschusses.* Berlin, 1927.

Berber, Friedrich. "Some Thoughts on the Laws of War and the Punishment of War Crimes." In M. K. Nawaz, ed., *Essays on International Law in Honour of Krishna Rao.* Leyden, 1976.

Berghahn, Volker R. *NSDAP und "geistige Fuhrung" der Wehrmacht, 1939–1943. VfZ* 17 (1969): 17–71.

Bernhardt, Rudolf, ed. *Encyclopedia of Public International Law*. Vols. 1–12. Amsterdam, 1981–88.

Bertschy, Ruth. *Die Schutzmacht im Völkerrecht*. Fribourg, 1952.

Besymenski, Lew. *Sonderakte Barbarossa: Dokumentarbericht zur Vorgeschichte des deutschen Überfalls auf die Sowjetunion—aus sowjetischer Sicht*. Stuttgart, 1968.

Betz, Herman Dieter. *Das OKW und seine Haltung zum Landkriegsvölkerrecht im Zweiten Weltkrieg*. Diss. jur. Würzburg, 1970.

Bisschop, W. R. "The *Altmark*." *Transactions of the Grötius Society* 26 (1941): 67–82.

Block, Just. *Die Ausschaltung und Beschränkung der deutschen ordentlichen Militärgerichtsbarkeit während des Zweiten Weltkrieges*. Diss. jur. Würzburg, 1967.

Boberach, Heinz, ed. *Richterbriefe: Dokumente zur Beeinflussung der deutschen Rechtspflege, 1942–1944*. Boppard, 1976.

Boelcke, Willi A., ed. *Wollt Ihr den totalen Krieg? Die geheimen Goebbels-Konferenzen 1939–1943*. Munich (dtv), 1969.

Böhme, Kurt W. "Absicht oder Notstand?" Beiheft *Zur Geschicht der Kriesgefangenen*, als Manuskript gedr. v. Suchdienst des DRK. Bonn, 1963.

————. *Die deutschen Kriegsgefangenen in Französischer Hand*. Vol. 13 of *Zur Geschichte der deutschen Kreigsgefangenen des Zweiten Weltkriegs*, ed. Erich Maschke. Munich, 1966.

————. *Die deutschen Kriegsgefangenen in sowjetischer Hand*. Vol. 7 of *Zur Geschichte der deutschen Kreigsgefangenen des Zweiten Weltkriegs*, ed. Erich Maschke. Munich, 1966.

————. *Gesucht wird*. Munich, 1965.

Bollmus, Reinhard. "Das Amt Rosenberg und seine Gegner: Studien zum Machtkampf im nationalsozialistischen Herrschaftssystem" *(Studien zur Zeitgeschicht I)*. Stuttgart, 1970.

Bolschewistische Verbrechen gegen Kriegsrecht und Menschlichkeit. Dokumente zsgest. vom Auswärtigen Amt. Vols. 1–3. Berlin, 1941–43.

Bösch, Herrmann. *Heeresrichter Karl Sack im Widerstand*. Munich, 1967.

Bösch, William, ed. *Judgment on Nuremberg: American Attitudes toward the Major German War-Crime Trials*. Chapel Hill, N.C., 1970.

Bracher, Karl-Dietrich. *The German Dictatorship*. New York, 1970.

Brauns, Peter. *Der Kriegsbrauch' als völkerrechtliche Haftungsgrundlage*. Göttingen, 1956.

————. "Zur Perversion der Strafjustiz im III. Reich." *VfZ*, 1958, pp. 390ff.

Bräutigam, Otto. *So hat es sich zugetragen: Ein Leben als Soldat und Diplomat*. Würzburg, 1968.

Broszat, Martin. "Hitler und die Genesis der "Endlösung": Aus Anlass der Thesen von David Irving. *VfZ* 25 (1977): 739–75.

————. "Nationalsozialistische Konzentrationslager 1933–1945." In H. Buchheim et al., *Anatomie des SS-Staates* (Munich [dtv], 1967), 2:9–133.

————. *Nationalsozialistische Polenpolitik 1939–1945*. Frankfurt, 1965.

————. "Der Staat Hitlers: Grundlegung und Entwicklung seiner inneren Verfassung." In *Weltgeschichte des 20. Jahrhunderts 9*. Munich, 1969.

————. *Zur Perversion der Strafjustiz im III. Reich.* VfZ, 1958, p. 390.

Bryce, Lord James. *Report of the Committee on Alleged German Outrages.* London, 1915.

Buchbender, Ortwin. *Das tönende Erz: Deutsche Propaganda gegen die Rote Armee im Zweiten Weltkrieg.* Stuttgart, 1978.

Buchbender, Ortwin, and H. Schuh. *Heil Beil! Propaganda im Zweiten Welkrieg.* Stuttgart, 1974.

Bucher, Rudolf. *Zwischen Verrat und Menschlichkeit: Erlebnisse eines Schweizer Arztes an der deutsch-russischen Front 1941/42.* Frauenfeld, 1967.

Buchheim, Hans. "Befehl und Gehorsam." In H. Buchheim et al., *Anatomie des SS-Staates* (Munich, 1967), 1:213–318.

———— et al. *Anatomie des SS-Staates.* Munich, 1967.

Buchheit, Gert. *Ludwig Beck: Ein preussischer General.* Munich, 1964.

Buckley, Christopher. *Greece and Crete.* London, 1952.

Buckley, Robert. *At Close Quarters: PT-Boats in the United States Navy.* Washington, D.C., 1961.

Das Bundesarchiv und seine Bestände. Boppard, 1977.

Busch, Fritz Otto. "Kommodore Bonte und seine Zerstörer." *Die Kriegsmarine,* 20 (May 1940): 6ff.

Buxa, Werner. *Weg und Schicksal der II. Infanterie-Division.* Kiel, 1952.

Cameron, John, ed. *The Peleus Trial.* London, 1948.

Carell, Paul. *Unternehmen Barbarossa: Der Marsch nach Russland.* Berlin, 1963.

Churchill, Winston. *The Second World War: The Closing of the Ring.* Vol. 5. London, 1952.

Clark, Alan. *The Fall of Crete.* London, 1962.

Conquest, Robert. *The Great Terror.* London, 1968.

————. *The Harvest of Sorrow: Soviet Collectivization and the Terror Famine.* New York, 1986.

Conze, Werner. *Die Geschichte der 291. Infanterie-Division 1940–1945.* Bad Nauheim, 1953.

Coston, Henri. *Dictionnaire de la politique française,*

Czapski, Jozef. *The Inhuman Land.* London, 1951.

Dahm, Georg. *Zur Problematik des Völkerstrafrechts.* Göttingen, 1956.

Dahms, Hellmuth Günther. *Geschichte des Zweiten Weltkrieges.* Tübingen, 1965.

Dallin, Alexander. *German Rule in Russia.* London, 1957.

van Dam, H. G., and Ralph Giordano. *KZ-Verbrechen vor deutschen Gerichten: Dokumente aus den Prozessen gegen Sommer (KZ Buchenwald), Sorge, Schubert (KZ Sachsenhausen), Unkelbach (Ghetto in Tschenstochau).* Frankfurt, 1967.

Datner, Szymon. *Crimes against POWs: Responsibility of the Wehrmacht.* Warsaw, 1964.

Datner, Szymon, Janusz Gumkowski, and Kazimierz Lesczynski. *War Crimes in Poland: Genocide 1939–1945.* Warsaw, 1962.

Davin, Daniel. *Crete,* Wellington, N.Z., 1953.

De Jong, Louis. *The German Fifth Column in the Second World War.* New York, 1956.

Deutsche Greuel in Russland: Gerichstag in Charkow. Vienna, 1945.

Der deutsche Imperialismus und der Zweite Weltkrieg, ed. Kommission der Historiker der DDR und der UdSSR. Vols. 1–3. East Berlin, 1960–62.

Deutsche Informationsstelle. *Die Rechtsbrüche der Weltdemokratien 1914–1918.* 5 vols.: Werner Schaeffer, *Krieg gegen Frauen und Kinder*; Arthur Fink, *Britische "Humanitat" gegen Wehrlose*; Arthur Fink, *Kolonialkriegsmethoden in Europa*; Werner Friedrich, *Die Piraten des Weltkrieges*; Gerhard Sachs, *Deutsche als Freiwild.* Stuttgart, 1940.

Deutsche Justiz, 1934 and 1939.

Die deutsche Kriegführung und das Völkerrecht, ed. Kriegsministerium. Berlin, 1919.

Deutschland im Zweiten Weltkrieg, vol. 2, *Vom Überfall auf die Sowjetunion bis zur sowjetischen Gegenoffensive bei Stalingrad (Juni 1941 bis November 1942), von einem Autorenkollektiv unter Leitung von Karl Drechsler.* Cologne, 1975.

Dickens, Peter. *Brennpunkt Erzhafen Narvik.* Stuttgart, 1975.

Djilas, Milovan. *Wartime.* London, 1977.

Documents on British Foreign Policy 1919–1939, 1st ser., vols. 2, 9. London, 1960.

Dokumente britischer Barbarei: Die brit. Kriegführung in den Niederlanden, Belgien, und Frankreich im Mai–Juni 1940. Im Auftrag des Auswärtigen Amtes aufgrund urkundl. Beweismat. zsgest. u. hrsg. Deutschen Informationsstelle. Berlin, 1941.

Dokumente britisch-französischer Grausamkeit: Die britische und französische Kriegführung in den Niederlanden, Belgien, und Nordfrankreich im Mai 1940. Im Auftrag des Auswärtigen Amtes aufgrund urkundl. Beweismat. zsgest., bearb. u. hrsg. Deutschen Informationsstelle. Berlin, 1940.

Dokumente polnischer Grausamkeit. Im Auftrag des Auswärtigen Amtes aufgrund urkundl. Beweismat. zsgest., bearb. u. hrsg. Deutschen Informationsstelle. Berlin, 1940.

Dokumente über die Alleinschuld Englands am Bombenkrieg gegen die Zivilbevölkerung. Berlin, 1943.

Dombrowski, H. *Kriegsstrafrecht.* Berlin, 1942.

Dönitz, Karl. *Zehn Jahre und zwanzig Tage.* Frankfurt am Main, 1967.

Downey, W. G. "The Law of War and Military Necessity." *AJIL* 47 (1953): 251–62.

Draper, G. I. A. D. *The Red Cross Conventions.* London, 1958.

Duhr, P. *Der Lügengeist im Völkergericht.* Munich, 1915.

Dunant, Henri. *Un Souvenir de Solférino.* Geneva, 1862.

Dwinger, Edwin Erich. *Der Tod in Polen.* Jena, 1940.

Ehrenburg, Ilya. *Menschen—Jahre—Leben.* Vols. 1–3. Munich, 1965.

———. *Vojna.* Vols. 1–2. Moscow, 1942–43.

Eisenhower, Dwight. *Crusade in Europe.* New York, 1948.

Entscheidungen des Reichskriegsgerichts und des Wehrmachtdienststrafhofs, 2 vols. Berlin, 1942.

Erdmann, Karl Dietrich. "Die Zeit der Weltkriege." In Bruno Gebhard, *Handbuch der deutschen Geschichte*, 9th ed., vol. 4, ed. Herbert Grundmann. Stuttgart, 1976.

Erickson, J. *The Soviet High Command: A Military Political History, 1918–1941*. London, 1962.

Falk, R. A., G. Kolko, and R. J. Lifteon, eds. *Crimes of War: A Legal, Political Documentary and Psychological Inquiry into the Responsibility of Leaders, Citizens, and Soldiers for Criminal Acts of War*. New York, 1971.

Fall 12: Das Urteil gegen das Oberkommando der Wehrmacht. East Berlin, 1960.

Fall Barbarossa: Dokumente zur Vorbereitung der faschistichen Wehrmacht auf die Aggression gegen die Sowjetunion (1940/41), ed. Erhard Moritz. East Berlin, 1970.

Fest, Joachim C. *Das Geshicht des Dritten Reiches: Profile einer totalitären Herrschaft*. Berlin, 1969.

Fischer, G. *Soviet Opposition to Stalin: A Case Study in World War II*. Cambridge, Mass., 1952.

Fischer, Hubert. *Der deutsche Sanitätsdienst*. Osnabrück, 1982.

Fitzgibbon, Louis. *Katyn*. London, 1975.

———. *Unpitied and Unknown*. London, 1975.

Fleischhacker, Hedwig. Die deutschen Kriegsgefangenen in der Sowjetunion: Der Faktor Hunger, vol. 3, *Zur Geschichte der deutschen Kriegsgefangenen des Zweiten Weltkrieges*, ed. Erich Maschke. Munich, 1965.

Foreign Relations of the United States, 1915, supp., pp. 527ff.; 1916, supp. 1, pp. 79ff.

Forwick, Helmuth. "Zur Behandlung alliierter Kriegsgefangener im Zweiten Weltkrieg: Anweisung des Oberkommandos der Wehrmacht über Besuche ausländischer Kommissionen in Kriegsgefangenenlagern." *Militärgeschichtliche Mitteilungen* 2 (1967): 119–34.

Frey, Hans. *Die disziplinarische und gerichtliche Bestrafung von Kriegsgefangenen*. Vienna, 1948.

Friedman, Philip. "Ukrainian-Jewish Relations during the Nazi Occupation." *Yivo Annual of Jewish Social Science* 12 (1958–59): 259–96.

Friedmann, Leon. *The Laws of War*. Vols. 1–2. New York, 1972.

Garthoff, R. I. *Die Sowjetarmee: Wesen und Lehre*. Cologne, 1955.

Gehlen, R. *Der Dienst: Erinnerungen 1942–1971*. Mainz, 1971.

von Gersdorff, R. C. *Soldat im Untergang*. Frankfurt, 1977.

Geschichte des Grossen Vaterländischen Krieges der Sowjetunion, 1941–1945. 6 vols. Published by the Institute for Marxism-Leninism of the Central Committee of the Communist Party of the Soviet Union. East Berlin, 1962–68.

Glueck, Sheldon. *The Nuremberg Trial and Aggressive War*. New York, 1946.

Goebbels, Joseph. *Tagebücher aus den Jahren 1942–1943, mit anderen Dokumenten*. Ed. Louis P. Lochner. Zurich, 1948.

———. *Tagebücher 1945: Die letzten Aufzeichnungen*. Hamburg, 1977.

Golovine, Nicholas. *The Russian Army in the World War*. New Haven, Conn., 1931.

Gordon, Sarah. *Hitler, the Germans, and the Jewish Question*. Princeton, N.J., 1984.

Görlitz, Walter, ed. *Generalfeldmarschall Keitel—Verbrecher oder Offizier? Erinnerungen, Briefe, und Dokumente des Chef OKW*. Göttingen, 1961.

Göttinger Arbeitskreis. *Dokumente der Menschlichkeit*. Würzburg, 1960.

Grasshoff, Richard. *Belgiens Schuld*. Berlin, 1915.

Greenspan, M. *The Modern Law of Land Warfare*. Berkeley, Calif., 1959.

Greil, Lothar. *Die Wahrheit über Malmedy*. Munich, 1958.

Gribbohm, Günter. "Wehrmachtjustiz im Konflikt." *Deutsche Richterzeitung*, February 1973, pp. 53ff.

———. "Wehrmachtjustiz zwischen Hitler und Heer." *Deutsche Richterzeitung*, May 1972, pp. 157ff.

Grigorenko, P. *Der sowjetische Zusammenbruch 1941*. Frankfurt am Main, 1969.

Groppe, Theodor. *Ein Kampf um Recht und Sitte*. Trier, 1959.

Groscurth, Helmuth. *Tagebücher eines Abwehroffiziers 1938–1940, mit weiteren Dokumenten zur Militäropposition gegen Hitler*, vol. 19, *Quellen und Darstellungen zur Zeitgeschichte*, ed. Helmut Krausnick and Harold C. Deutsch with Hildegard von Kotze. Stuttgart, 1970.

Gross, Jan. *Polish Society under German Occupation*. Princeton, N.J., 1979.

Grötius Society. "Minutes of the Proceedings of the Seventh General Meeting." *Transactions of the Grötius Society* 8 (1923): xixff.

Gruchmann, Lothar. Ausgewählte Dokumente zur deutschen Marinejustiz im Zweiten Weltkrieg." *VfZ* 26 (1978): 433ff.

———. *Justiz in Dritten Reich, 1933–40*. Munich, 1987.

———. *Nationalsozialistische Grossraumordnung: Die Konstruktion einer "deutschen Monroe-Doktrin."* Schriftenreihe der *Vierteljahrshefte für Zeitgeschichte* 4. Stuttgart, 1962.

———. *Der Zweite Weltkrieg: Kriegführung und Politik*. Weltgeschichte des 20. Jahrhunderts 10. Munich, 1967.

Guderian, Heinz. *Erinnerungen eines Soldaten*. Heidelberg, 1951.

Halder, Franz. *Kriegstagebuch: Tägliche Aufzeichnungen des Chefs des Generalstabes des Heeres, 1939–1942*. Vols. 1–3. Published by Arbeitskreis für Wehrforschung, bearb. v. Hans-Adolf Jacobsen and Alfred Philippi. Stuttgart, 1962–64.

Hammerstein, Christian F. von. *Mein Leben: Privatdrück im Institut für Zeitgeschichte*. Munich, n.d.

Hankey, Lord. *Politics, Trials, and Errors*. Oxford, 1950.

Hartl, Hans, and Werner Marx. *50 Jahre sowjetische Deutschlandpolitik*. Boppard, 1967.

Hartleben, Hans. "Die organisierte Entwicklung des Heeres-Sanitätswesens von 1930–43." *Wehrmedizin* 1 (1977): 62.

von Hassell, Ulrich. *Vom Andern Deutschland: Aus den nachgelassenen Tagebüchern 1938–1944*. Frankfurt, 1964.

Heeresverordnungsblatt, Teil C, Blatt 26, p. 310, no. 852.

Heiber, Helmut. *Der Generalplan Ost. VfZ* 6 (1958): 281–325.

——, ed. *Lagebesprechungen im Führerhauptquartier: Protokollfragmente aus Hitlers militärischen Konferenzen 1942–1945.* Munich, 1963.

Henkys, Reinhard. *Die nationalsozialistischen Gewaltverbrechen.* Stuttgart, 1965.

von Hentig, W. O. *Mein Leben eine Dienstreise.* Göttingen, 1962.

Hesse, Erich. *Der sowjetische Partisanenkrieg 1941–1944 im Spiegel deutscher Kampfanweisungen und Befehle.* Studien und Dokumente zur Geschichte des Zweiten Weltkrieges 9. Göttingen, 1969.

Heusinger, Adolf. *Befehl im Widerstreit: Schicksalsstunden der deutschen Armee 1923–1945.* Tübingen, 1950.

Higgins, Margarite: *News Is a Singular Thing.* New York, 1955.

Hilberg, Raul. *The Destruction of the European Jews.* Chicago, 1961.

Hildebrand, Klaus. *Deutsche Aussenpolitik 1933–1945: Kalkül oder Dogma?* Stuttgart, 1971.

Hillgruber, Andreas. "Die 'Endlösung' und das deutsche Ostimperium als Kernstück des rassen-ideologischen Programms des Nationalsozialismus." *VfZ* 20 (1972): 133–53.

——. *Hitlers Strategie: Politic und Kriegführung 1940–1941.* Frankfurt, 1965.

——. "In der Sicht des kritischen Historikers." In *Nie ausser Dienst: Zum 80. Geburtstag von Generalfeldmarschall von Manstein,* pp. 65–83. Cologne, 1967.

——. *Kontinuität und Diskontinuität in der deutschen Aussenpolitik von Bismarck bis Hitler.* Düsseldorf, 1969.

——, ed. *Staatsmänner und Diplomaten bei Hitler: Vertrauliche Aufzeichnungen über Unterredungen mit Vertretern des Auslandes,* vol. 1, *1939–1941;* vol. 2, *1942–1944.* Frankfurt, 1967, 1970.

Hillgruber, Andreas, and Gerhard Hümmelchen. *Chronik des Zweiten Weltkrieges.* Frankfurt, 1966.

Hoffman, Gerhard. *Strafrechtliche Verantwortung im Völkerrecht.* Frankfurt am Main, 1962.

Hoffmann, Peter. *Widerstand, Staatsstreich, Attentat: Der Kampf der Opposition gegen Hitler.* Munich, 1969.

Höhne, Heinz. *Der Orden unter dem Totenkopf: Die Geschichte der SS.* 2 vols. Frankfurt, 1969.

Hubatsch, Walther, ed. *Hitlers Weisungen für die Kriegführung 1939–1945: Dokumente aus dem Oberkommando der Wehrmacht.* Frankfurt, 1962.

——. *61. Infanterie-Division: Kampf und Opfer deutscher Soldaten.* Kiel, 1952.

Hürten, H., and G. Meyer, eds. *Adjutant im Preussischen Kriegsministerium.* Stuttgart, 1977.

Ignatow, P. *Partisanen.* East Berlin, 1958.

Ilnytzkyi, Roman. *Deutschland und die Ukraine, 1934–1945.* Vols. 1–2. Munich, 1956–58.

International Committee of the Red Cross. *Inter Arma Caritas.* Geneva, 1947.

———. *Protocols Additional to the Geneva Conventions of 27 July 1929, 12 August 1949.* Geneva, 1977.

———. *Report of Activities during the Second World War (September 1, 1939, to June 30, 1947).* Vols. 1–3. Geneva, 1948.

———. *Report of General Activities.* Geneva (Yearbook).

———. *Report of the Joint Relief Commission of the International Red Cross, 1941–1946.* Geneva, 1948.

———. *Revue Internationale de la Croix Rouge.* Geneva (Monthly).

International Military Tribunal (*IMT*). 42 vols. Nuremberg, 1947.

Irving, David. *The Destruction of Dresden.* London, 1971.

Istoriya velikoi otechestvennoi voiny Sov.-Soyuza. Moscow, 1960–64.

Jäckel, E. *Hitlers Weltanschauung: Entwurf einer Herrschaft.* Tübingen, 1969.

Jacobsen, H. A. "Kommissarbefehl und Massenexekutionen sowjetischer Kriegsgefangener." In H. Buchheim et al., *Anatomie des SS-Staates,* vol. 2: *Konzentrationslager, Kommissarbefehl, Judenverfolgung,* pp. 163–279. Olten, 1965.

———. *Der Zweite Weltkrieg: Grundzüge der Politik und Strategie in Dokumenten.* Frankfurt, 1965.

Jacobsen, H. A., and Arthur Smith. *World War II: Policy and Strategy.* Santa Barbara, Calif., 1979.

Jagodzinski, Zdzislaw. *The Katyn Bibliography.* London, 1976.

Janner, A. *La puissance protectrice en droit international d'après les expériences faites par la Suisse pendant la seconde guerre mondiale.* Basel, 1948.

Jescheck, H. H. *Die Verantwortlichkeit der Staatsorgane nach Völkerstrafrecht.* Bonn, 1952.

Junod, Marcel. *Kämpfer beiderseits der Front.* Zurich, 1947.

Kalshoven, Frits. *Belligerent Reprisals.* Leiden, 1971.

———. *The Law of Warfare.* Leiden, 1973.

Kardel, Hennecke. *Die Geschichte der 170. Infanterie-Division, 1939–1945.* Bad Nauheim, 1953.

Katyn Memorial Fund Committee. *Via Dolorosa.* Drawings by Stefan Starzynski. London, n.d. [1975].

Kaul, Friedrich Karl. *Geschichte des Reichsgerichts.* East Berlin, 1971.

Keiling, W. *Das deutsche Heer 1939–1945: Gliederung, Einsatz, Stellenbesetzung.* 3 vols. Bad Nauheim, 1956–

Klafkowski, Alfons. *The Nuremberg Principles and the Development of International Law.* Warsaw, 1966.

Klotz, L. L. *De la guerre à la paix.* Paris, 1924.

Knieriem, August von. *Nürnberg: Rechtliche und menschliche Probleme.* Stuttgart, 1953.

Kogon, Eugen. *Der SS-Staat: Das System der deutschen Konzentrationslager.* Munich, 1946.

Kosthorst, Erich. *Die Deutsche Opposition gegen Hitler zwischen Polen- und Frankreichfeldzug.* Bonn, 1954.

Kotsch, Lothar. "Baralong-Fall." In Karl Strupp and Hans-Jürgen Schlochauer, *Wörterbuch des Völkerrechts*, 1:157. Berlin, 1960.

Kranzbühler, Otto. "Nürnberg als Rechtsproblem." In *Festgabe für Erich Kaufmann*. Stuttgart, 1950.

———. *Rückblick auf Nürnberg*. Hamburg, 1949.

Kraus, Herbert. *Der deutsche Richter und das Völkerrecht*. Bonn, 1952.

———. *Gerichtstag in Nürnberg*. Hamburg, 1947.

———. "Vom Recht des Nürnberger Internationalen Militärgerichtsprozesses. In *Festschrift für H. Jahrreiss*, pp. 221ff. Cologne, 1964.

Krausnick, Helmut. "Hitler und die Morde in Polen: Ein Beitrag zum Konflict zwischen Heer und SS um die Verwaltung der besetzten Gebiete." *VfZ* 11 (1963): 196–209.

———. "Judenverfolgung." In H. Buchheim et al., *Anatomie des SS-Staates*, 2:233–366. Munich (dtv), 1967.

———. "Kommissarbefehl und 'Gerichtsbarkeitserlass Barbarossa' in neuer Sicht." *VfZ* 25 (1977): 682–738.

Kriegsministerium. *Militäruntersuchungsstelle für Verletzungen des Kriegsrechts: Belgien; Löwen*. Berlin, 1915.

———. *Militäruntersuchungsstelle für Verletzungen des Kriegsrechts: Denkschrift über den belgischen Volkskrieg, Zusammenfassende Darstellung*. Berlin, 1917.

Kriegstagebuch des Oberkommandos der Wehrmacht (Wehrmachtführungsstab) 1940–1945. Vols. 1–4. Ed. Percy Ernst Schramm, Andreas Hillgrüber, Walter Hubatsch, and H. A. Jacobsen. Frankfurt, 1961–65.

Kuhn, A. *Hitlers aussenpolitisches Programm*. Stuttgart, 1970.

———. "Das nationalsozialistische Deutschland und die Sowjetunion." In M. Funke, ed., *Hitler, Deutschland und die Mächte: Materialien zur Aussenpolitik des Dritten Reiches, Bonner Schriften zur Politik und Zeitgeschichte*, 12: 639–53. Düsseldorf, 1976.

Kühnrich, H. *Der Partisanenkampf in Europa 1939–1945*. East Berlin, 1968.

Kurowski, Frank. *Der Kampf um Kreta*. Herford, 1965.

Lachs, Manfred. *War Crimes: An Attempt to Define the Issues*. London, 1945.

Lasswell, Harold. *Propaganda Technique in World War I*. London, 1927.

Laun, Rudolf. *Haager Landkriegsordnung*. Wolfenbüttel, 1948.

———. *Naturrecht und Völkerrecht*. Göttingen, 1954.

Lauterpacht, Herscht, ed. *Annual Digest and Reports of Public International Law Cases*, pp. 278ff., Case 126. London, 1947.

Lemberg 1941 und Oberländer: Das Ergebnis einer Untersuchung. Amstelveen, 1960.

Levie, Howard. *The Code of International Armed Conflict*. 2 vol. London, 1986.

———. *Prisoners of War in International Armed Conflict*. Washington, D.C., 1978.

————. *Documents on Prisoners of War*. Newport, 1979.

————. *Protection of War Victims: Protocol I to the 1949 Geneva Conventions*. 4 vol. Dobbs Ferry, N.Y., 1979–81.

Lewis, John: *Uncertain Judgment: A Bibliography of War Crimes Trials*. Santa Barbara, Calif., 1979.

Lewytskyi, Borys. "Die Affäre um Dr. Oberländer." *Kultura* (Paris), 1960.

von Lossberg, Bernhard. *Im Wehrmachtführungsstab: Bericht eines Generalstabsoffiziers*. Hamburg, 1949.

Lück, Kurt. *Marsch der Deutschen in Polen*. Berlin, 1940.

Lüdde-Neurath, Walter. *Regierung Dönitz*, 3d ed. Göttingen, 1964.

Luther, Hans. *Der französische Widerstand gegen die deutsche Besatzungsmacht und seine Bekämpfung*. Institut für Besatzungsfragen. Tübingen, 1957.

McChesney, B. "The Altmark Incident and Modern Warfare." *Northwestern University Law Review* 52 (1957): 320–43.

McKee, Alexander. *Caen: Anvil of Victory*. London, 1964.

Mackiewicz, Jozef. *The Katyn Wood Murders*. London, 1951.

Madajczyk, Czeslaw. *Polityka III Rzeszy w okupowanej Polsce (Die Politik des III. Reiches im besetzten Polen)*. Vols. 1–3. Warsaw, 1970.

Mangoldt, H. von. "Das Kriegsverbrechen und seine Verfolgung in Vergangenheit und Gegenwart." In *Jahrbuch für internationales und ausländisches öffentliches Recht*, 1948, pp. 283ff.

Manstein, Erich von. *Verlorene Siege*. Munich, 1979.

Manstein, Rudiger von, and Theodor Fuchs. *Manstein, Soldat im 20. Jahrhundert*. Munich, 1981.

Martin, H.-L. *Unser Mann bei Goebbels: Verbindungsoffizier des Oberkommandos der Wehrmacht beim Reichspropagandaminister 1940–1944*, vol. 49 of *Die Wehrmacht im Kampf*. Neckargemünd, 1973.

Maschke, Erich, ed. *Zur Geschichte der deutschen Kriegsgefangenen des Zweiten Weltkriegs*. 22 vols. Bielefeld, 1962–75.

Mayence, Fernand. *La Légende des franc-tireurs de Louvain*. Louvain, 1928.

"Meldungen aus dem Reich." In *Auswahl aus den geheimen Lageberichten des Sicherheitsdienstes der SS 1939–1944*, ed. Heinz Boberach. Munich (dtv), 1968.

Messerschmidt, Manfred. *Das Deutsche Reich und der Zweite Weltkrieg*, vols. 1–10. Stuttgart, 1979.

————. *Die Wehrmacht im NS-Staat: Zeit der Indoktrination*. Hamburg, 1969.

Messerschmidt, Manfred, and Fritz Wüllner. *Die Wehrmachtsjustiz im Dienste des Nationalsozialismus*. Baden-Baden, 1987.

Meurer, Christian. *Die Haager Friedenskonferenz*. Munich, 1907.

Minear, Richard. *Victors' Justice: The Tokyo War Crimes Trial*. Princeton, N.J., 1971.

Moltke, Freya von, Michael Balfour, and Julian Frisby. *Helmuth James von Moltke, 1907–1945: Anwalt der Zukunft*. Stuttgart, 1975.

Moltke, Helmuth James, Graf von. *Dokumente*. Ed. Ger van Roon. Berlin, 1986.

Mommsen, Hans: "Beamtentum im Dritten Reich: Mit ausgewählten Quellen zur national-sozialistischen Beamtenpolitik" Schriftenreihe der *Vierteljahrshefte für Zeitgeschichte* 15. Stuttgart, 1966.

Morison, S. E. *History of United States Naval Operations in World War II*. Vols. 1–6. Boston, 1950.

Moritz, Günther. *Die Gerichtsbarkeit in besetzten Gebieten: Historische Entwicklung und völkerrechtliche Würdigung*. Tübingen, 1959.

——. *Gerichtsbarkeit in den von Deutschland besetzten Gebieten 1939–1945*. Studien des Instituts für Besatzungsfragen in Tübingen zu der Besetzung im 2. Weltkrieg, no. 7. Tübingen, 1959.

Mosler, H. *Das Völkerrecht in der Praxis der deutschen Gerichte*. Karlsruhe, 1957.

Mühleisen, H. O. *Kreta 1941*. Freiburg, 1968.

Müller, Ingo. *Furchtbare Juristen: Die unbewältigte Vergangenheit unserer Justiz*. Munich, 1987.

Müller, Klaus-Jürgen. *Das Heer und Hitler: Armee und nationalsozialistisches Regime, 1933–1940*. Beitrage zur Militär- und Kriegsgeschichte 10. Stuttgart, 1969.

Müller, N. "Massenverbrechen von Wehrmachtorganen an der sowjetischen Zivilbevölkerung im Sommer/Herbst 1941." *Zeitschrift für Militärgeschichte* 8 (1969): 537–53.

——. *Wehrmacht und Okkupation 1941–1944: Zur Rolle der Wehrmacht und ihrer Führungsorgane im Okkupationsregime des faschistischen deutschen Imperialismus auf sowjetischem Territorium*. East Berlin, 1971.

Mullins, Claude. *The Leipzig Trials*. London, 1921.

von Münch, Ingo. "Llandovery Castle." In Strupp-Schlochauer, *Wörterbuch des Völkerrechts*, 2: 420. Berlin, 1960–62.

Muralt, P. von. *Die Schweiz als Schutzmacht*. Basel, 1947.

Murawski, Erich. *Der deutsche Wehrmachtbericht 1939–1945*. Boppard, 1962.

Nekritsch, A., and P. Grigorenko. *Genickschuss: Die Rote Armee am 22 Juni 1941*, ed. G. Haupt. Vienna, 1969.

O'Connell, Daniel. *The Influence of Law on Sea Power*. Manchester, 1975.

Oppenheim, L., and H. Lauterpacht. *International Law*. 7th ed., Vols. 1–2. London, 1952.

Oszwald, R. P. *Der Streit um den belgischen Franktireurkrieg*. Cologne, 1931.

Paget, R. T. *Manstein: Seine Feldzüge und sein Prozess*. Wiesbaden, 1952.

Panning, Gerhart. "Wirkungsform und Nachweis der sowjetischen Infanteriesprengmunition." *Der Deutsche Militärarzt* 7 (1942): 20ff.

Petersen, Horace C. *Propaganda for War*, Oklahoma City, Okla., 1939.

Petri, Franz, and Peter Schöller. "Zur Bereinigung des Franktireurproblems vom August 1914." *VfZ* 9 (1961): 234–48.

Pfeiler, Wolfgang. "Das Deutschlandbild und die Deutschlandpolitik Josef Stalins." *Deutschland Archiv*, December 1979, pp. 1258–82.

Philippi, Alfred, and Ferdinand Heim. *Der Feldzug gegen Sowjetrussland 1941–1945: Ein operativer Überblick*. Stuttgart, 1962.

Pictet, Jean. *Commentaire: La convention de Genève I*. Geneva, 1952.

——— . *Commentaire: La convention de Genève II*. Geneva, 1959.

——— . *Commentaire: La convention de Genève IV*. Geneva, 1956.

Polish Central Committee for Investigation of German Crimes in Poland. *German Crimes in Poland*. Warsaw, 1946–47.

Polish Government-in-Exile. *L'invasion allemande en Pologne: Documents, temoinages autentifiés et photographiés, recueillis par la Centre d'Information et de Documentation du Government Polonais*. Paris, 1939.

Polish Ministry of Information. *The German New Order in Poland*. London, 1942.

Politisches Handbuch 1938

Die polnischen Greueltaten an den Volksdeutschen in Polen. Im Auftrag des Auswärtigen Amts aufgrund urkundl. Beweismat. zsgest., bearb. und hrsg. Berlin, 1940.

Ponsonby, Arthur. *Falsehood in War-Time*. London, 1928.

Pospieszalski, Karol M. *Sprawa 58000 Volksdeutschow; The Case of 58,000 Volksdeutsche* [Polish and English]. Der Documenta Occupationis, Instytut Zachodni, vol. 7. Poznan, 1959.

Prück, E. *Der Rote Soldat*. Munich, 1961.

Rabus, Walter. "Het onderzoek naar oorlogsmisdrijven." *Militair Rechtelijk Tijdschrift* 76 (1983): 121–32.

——— . "A New Definition of the 'Levée en masse.'" *Netherlands International Law Review* 24 (1977): 232ff.

Raschhofer, Hermann. *Der Fall Oberländer*. Tübingen, 1962.

Ratza, W. *Die deutschen Kriegsgefangenen in der Sowjetunion*. Vol. 4 of Maschke, *Zur Geschichte der deutschen Kriegsgefangenen*.

Le régime des prisonniers de guerre en France et en Allemagne au regard des conventions internationales, 1914–1916. Paris, 1916.

Reile, O. *Geheime Ostfront: Die deutsche Abwehr im Osten, 1921–1945*. Munich, 1961.

Reitlinger, Gerald. *Die Endlösung*. Berlin, 1961.

——— . *Ein Haus auf Sand gebaut: Hitlers Gewaltpolitik in Russland, 1941–1944*. Hamburg, 1962.

Rhodes, A. *Propaganda, the Art of Persuasion: An Allied and Axis Visual Record, 1933–1945*. London, 1975.

Ritter, Gerhard. *Carl Goerdeler und die Deutsche Widerstandsbewegung*. Stuttgart, 1956.

Röder, H. F. *Kriegsvölkerrecht*. Berlin, 1940.

Rohwer, Jürgen. *Die Versenkung der jüdischen Flüchtlingstransporter Struma und Mefkure*. Frankfurt, 1965.

Rohwer, Jürgen, and Gerhard Hümmelchen. *Chronik des Seekriegs*. Oldenburg, 1968.

Röling, Bert V. A. "Criminal Responsibility for Violations of the Laws of War." *Revue belge de droit international* 12 (1976): 8ff.

———. *Einführung in die Wissenschaft von Krieg und Frieden*. Neukirchen, 1970.

———. "The Law of War and the National Jurisdiction since 1945." *Recueil des Cours* 100 (1960): 323ff.

Röling, Bert V. A., and C. R. Rüter, eds. *The Tokyo Judgment*. Vols. 1–2. Amsterdam, 1977.

Roskill, S. W. *The Navy at War*. London, 1960.

———. *The War at Sea, 1939–1945*. London, 1954, 1956, 1960, 1961.

Rückerl, Adalbert, ed. *NS-Prozesse, Nach 25 Jahren Strafverfolgung: Möglichkeiten—Grenzen—Ergebnisse*. Karlsruhe, 1971.

———. *NS-Vernichtungslager im Spiegel deutscher Strafprozesse*. Munich, 1977.

———. *Die Strafverfolgung von NS-Verbrechen 1945–1978*. Heidelberg, 1978.

Ruge, Friedrich. *Scapa Flow*. Hamburg, 1969.

———. *Der Seekrieg 1939–1945*. Stuttgart, 1969.

Runzheimer, Jürgen. "Der Überfall auf den Sender Gleiwitz." *VfZ*, 1962, pp. 408ff.

Russischer Kolonialismus in der Ukraine. Munich, 1967.

Rüter, C. F. *Justiz und NS-Verbrechen*. Amsterdam, 1968.

Ryan, Cornelius. *The Longest Day*. London, 1963.

Sack, John. *Lieutenant Calley: His Own Story*. New York, 1971.

St. Oswald, Lord. "A Pledge to the Living Future." Address at the unveiling of the Katyn Memorial. *Polish Affairs* (London) 98 (1976).

Schall-Riaucour, H. Gräfin. *Aufstand und Gehorsam, Offizierstum und Generalstab im Umbruch: Leben und Wirken von Generaloberst Franz Halder, Generalstabschef 1938–1942*. Wiesbaden, 1972.

Scheel, K. "Der Aufbau der faschistischen PK-Einheiten vor dem Zweiten Weltkrieg." *Zeitschrift für Militärgeschichte* 4 (1965): 444–55.

Scheidl, Franz. *Die Kriegsgefangenschaft von den ältesten Zeiten bis zur Gegenwart: Eine völkerrechtliche Monographie*. Berlin, 1943.

Schenck, Ernst-Günther. *Das menschliche Elend: Eine Pathographie der Kriegs-, Hunger- und politischen Katastrophen Europas*. Herford, 1965.

Schieder, Theodor, ed. *Dokumentation der Vertreibung der Deutschen aus Ost-Mitteleuropa*. Vols. 1–5, supps. 1–3. Bonn, 1953, 1957, 1960, 1961.

Schindler, Dietrich. "Vertretung fremder Interessen durch die Schweiz." *Schweiz. Jahrbuch 1* (1944): 130ff.; 3 (1946): 199ff.

Schindler, Dietrich, and Jiri Toman. *The Laws of Armed Conflict*. Leiden, 1973.

Schmidt, Eberhard. *Gesetz und Richter: Wert und Unwert des Positivismus*. Karlsruhe, 1952.

Schmidt, G. "Die deutsche Justiz und der Nationalsozialismus." In *Deutsche Richterzeitung*, 1969, pp. 248ff.

Schmidt, Rudolf, and Arnold Kludas. *Die deutschen Lazarettschiffe im zweiten Weltkrieg*. Stuttgart, 1978.

Schmidt-Scheeder, G. *Reporter der Hölle: Die Propaganda-Kompanien im Zweiten Weltkrieg, Erlebnis und Dokumentation*. Stuttgart, 1977.

Schöller, Peter. *Der Fall Löwen und das Weissbuch*. Cologne, 1958.

Schorn, Hübert. *Der Richter im Dritten Reich: Geschichte und Dokumente*. Frankfurt am Main, 1959.

Schütze, H. A. *Die Repressalie unter besonderer Berücksichtigung der Kriegsverbrecherprozesse*. Bonn, 1950.

Schwarzenberger, Georg. *International Law and Order*. London, 1971.

Schweling, Otto. *Die deutsche Militärjustiz in der Zeit des Nationalsozialismus*. Marburg, 1978.

Schwinge, Erich. *Bilanz der Kriegsgeneration*. Marburg, 1978.

———. "Die deutsche Militärgerichtsbarkeit im Zweiten Weltkrieg." *Deutsche Richterzeitung*, 1959, pp. 350ff.

Seekriegsrecht im Weltkriege. Berlin, 1916–19.

Seidler, Franz. *Fritz Todt: Baumeister des Dritten Reich*. Munich, 1987.

Seidl-Hohenveldern, Ignaz. *Völkerrecht*. Cologne, 1969.

Seraphim, H. G. *Die deutsch-russischen Beziehungen, 1939–1941*. Hamburg, 1949.

———. "Nachkriegsprozesse und Zeitgeschichtliche Forschung." In *Festschrift für Herbert Kraus*, pp. 436–55. Kitzingen, 1954.

———. "Quellen zur Erforschung der Geschichte des Dritten Reichs." *Europa Archiv* 5 (1950): 3307–10.

von Seydlitz, Walther. *Stalingrad—Konflikt und Konsequenz*. Oldenburg, 1977.

Simpson, Colin. *The Lusitania*. New York, 1972.

Smith, Bradley. *Reaching Judgment at Nuremberg*. London, 1977.

Spencer, John H. *Battle for Crete*. London, 1962.

Spetzler, Eberhard. *Luftkrieg und Menschlichkeit: Die völkerrechtliche Stellung der Zivilpersonen im Luftkrieg*. Göttingen, 1956.

Squires, James D. *British Propaganda at Home and in the United States*. Cambridge, Mass., 1935.

Staff, Ilse: *Justiz im Dritten Reich*. Frankfurt am Main, 1964.

Stalin, J. *Uber den Grossen Väterlandischen Krieg der Sowjetunion*. Moscow, 1946.

———. *Works*, ed. Robert McNeal. Stanford, Calif., 1967.

———. *Werke*. 13 vols. Berlin, 1951–55.

Steenberg, S. *Wlassow: Verräter oder Patriot?* Cologne, 1968.

Steinert, Marlies. *Die 23 Tage der Regierung Dönitz*. Dusseldorf, 1967.

Stewart, I. McD. G. *The Struggle for Crete*. London, 1966.

Streim, Alfred. *Die Behandlung Sowjetischer Kriegsgefangener im Fall Barbarossa*. Heidelberg, 1981.

———. *Sowjetische Gefangene im Hitlers Vernichtungskrieg*. Heidelberg, 1982.

———. "Zum Beispiel: Die Verbrechen der Einsatzgruppe in der Sowjetunion." In A. Rückerl, *NS-Prozesse*, pp. 65–106. Karlsruhe, 1971.

Streit, Christian. *Keine Kameraden: Die Wehrmacht und die sowjetischen Kriegsgefangenen, 1941–1945*. Stuttgart, 1978.

Die Streitkräfte der UdSSR: Ein Abriss ihrer Entwicklung. East Berlin, 1974.

Strik-Strikfeldt, Wilfried. *Gegen Stalin und Hitler: General Wlassow und die russische Freiheitsbewegung*. Mainz, 1970.

Strupp, Karl, and Hans-Jürgen Schlochauer. *Wörterbuch des Völkerrechts*. Vols. 1–3. Berlin, 1960–62.

Stülpnagel, Otto von. *Die Wahrheit über die deutschen Kriegsverbrechen*. Berlin, 1921.

Sulzmann, R. "Die Propaganda als Waffe im Krieg." In *Bilanz des Zweiten Weltkrieges*, pp. 381–402. Oldenburg, 1953.

Taylor, Telford. *Final Report to the Secretary of the Army on the Nuernberg War Crimes Trials under Control Council Law No. 10*, Washington, D.C., 1949.

———. *Nuremberg and Vietnam: An American Tragedy*. Chicago, 1970.

Tessin, G. *Verbände und Truppen der deutschen Wehrmacht und Waffen-SS im Zweiten Weltkrieg, 1939–1945*, vol. 1, *Die Waffengattungen*. Osnabrück, 1977.

Thomas, David. *Crete*. London, 1972.

Thorwald, J. *Die Illusion: Rotarmisten in Hitlers Heeren*. Zurich, 1974.

Tiemann, Reinhard. *Geschichte der 83. Infanterie-Division*. Bad Nauheim, 1960.

von Tippelskirch, Kurt. *Geschichte des Zweiten Weltkrieges*. Bonn, 1959.

Toland, John. *Adolf Hitler*. New York, 1984.

Tolstoy, Nikolai. *Victims of Yalta*. London, 1977.

Toynbee, Arnold. *Survey of International Affairs, 1920–1923*. Oxford, 1925.

Trials of War Criminals before the Nuernberg Military Tribunals under Control Council Law No. 10, Nuernberg October 1946–April 1949. Vols. 1–14. Washington, D.C., 1950–53.

Uhler, O. M. *Dervölkerrechtliche Schutz der Bevölkerung eines besetzten Gebietes gegen Massnahmen der Okkupationsmacht*. Zurich, 1950.

U.N. War Crimes Commission. *History of the United Nations War Crimes Commission and the Development of the Laws of War*. London, 1948.

Unsere Ehre heisst Treue: Kriegstagebuch des Kommandostabes Reichsführer SS. Tätigkeitsberichte der 1. und 2. SS-Inf.-Brigade. der 1. SS-Kav.-Brigade und von Sonderkommandos der SS. Ed. Fritz Baade. Vienna, 1965.

U.S. Congress. House. Select Committee on Communist Aggression. *Communist Takeover and Occupation of Poland, the Ukraine, etc.* 83d Cong., 2d sess., 1954. H. Rept. 2684, pts. 3, 4, 5, 7.

——. House. Select Committee to Conduct an Investigation of the Facts of the Katyn Forest Massacre. *Hearings* and *Final Report.* 82d Cong., 1st sess., 1951.

——. Senate. Judiciary Committee. *The Human Cost of Soviet Communism.* 92d Cong., 1st sess., 1971, S-Doc. 92–36.

U.S. Information Services Division, Office of the U.S. High Commissioner for Germany. *Ein Dokumentarischer Bericht.* Munich, 1951.

Valéry, Jules. *Les crimes de la population belge.* Paris, 1916.

Van Gijsegen, Maurits. *Het Bloedbad van Abbeville.* Antwerp, 1942.

Van Langenhove, Fernand. *Comment nait un cycle de légendes.* Paris, 1917.

Van Roon, Ger. "Graf Moltke als Völkerrechtler im OKW." *VfZ* 18 (1970): 12–61.

——. "Hermann Kaiser und der deutsche Widerstand." *VfZ* 24 (1976): 259–86.

——. *Neuordnung im Widerstand: Der Kreisauer Kreis innerhalb der deutschen Widerstandsbewegung.* Munich, 1967.

Verdross, Alfred, and Bruno Simma. *Universelles Völkerrecht: Theorie und Praxis.* Berlin, 1977.

Die Verfolgung nationalsozialistischer Straftaten im Gebiet der Bundesrepublik Deutschland seit 1945. Published by Budesjustizministerium. Bonn, 1964.

Völkerrechtsverletzungen der britischen Streitkräfte und der Zivilibevölkerung auf Kreta. Berlin, 1942.

Wagner, Elisabeth, ed. *Der Generalquartiermeister: Briefe und Tagebuchaufzeichnungen des Generalquartiermeisters des Heeres, General der Artillerie Eduard Wagner.* Munich, 1963.

Wagner, Gerhard, ed. *Lagevorträge des Oberbefehlshabers der Kriegsmarine vor Hitler, 1939–1945.* Munich, 1972.

Waldock, C. H. M. "The Release of the *Altmark*'s Prisoners." *British Yearbook of International Law* 24 (1947): 216–38.

Waltzog, Alfons. *Recht der Landkriegführung.* Berlin, 1942.

Warlimont, W. *Im Hauptquartier der deutschen Wehrmacht, 1939–1945: Grundlagen, Formen, Gestalten.* Frankfurt am Main, 1963.

von Wedel, H. *Die Propagandatruppen der deutschen Wehrmacht: Die Wehrmacht im Kampf.* Vol. 34. Neckargemünd, 1962.

"Wehrgesetz of 21 May 1935." *Reichgesetzblatt* 1, p. 609.

Weingartner, James. *Crossroads of Death: The Story of the Malmédy Massacre and Trial.* Berkeley, Calif., 1979.

Weinkauff, Hermann. *Die deutsche Justiz und der Nationalsozialismus.* Stuttgart, 1968.

Werth, Alexander. *Russia at War, 1941–1945.* New York, 1964.

Wilkens, Erwin. *NS-Verbrechen, Strafjustiz, und deutsche Selbstbesinnung.* Berlin, 1964.

Wolfe, Robert, ed. *Captured German and Related Records: A National Archives Conference*. Athens, Ohio, 1974.

Wolff, Helmut. *Die deutschen Kriegsgefangenen in britischer Hand*. Vol. 11/2 of Erich Maschke, ed., *Zur Geschichte der deutschen Kriegsgefangenen*. Munich, 1974.

Wright, Quincy. *A Study of War*. Chicago, 1967.

Zawodny, Janusz. *Death in the Forest: The Story of the Katyn Forest Massacre*. Notre Dame, Ind., 1962.

Zayas, Alfred de. *Die Anglo-Amerikaner und die Vertreibung der Deutschen*. 7th rev. ed. Berlin, 1988.

————. *Anmerkungen zur Vertreibung*. 2d rev. ed. Stuttgart, 1987.

————. "Amnesty Clause," "Civilian Population," "Combatants," "European Recovery Program," "Forced Resettlement," "London Naval Conference," "Open Towns," "Population: Expulsion and Transfer," "Repatriation," "Ships in Distress," "United Nations Relief and Rehabilitation Activities." In R. Bernhardt, ed., *Encyclopedia of Public International Law*. Amsterdam, 1981–89.

————. *Nemesis at Potsdam*. 3d ed., rev. Lincoln, Neb., 1988.

Zhukov, G. K. *The Memoirs of Marshal Zhukov*. London, 1971.

Ziemssen, Dietrich. *Der Malmedy Prozess*. Munich, 1952.

Zwaart, Joop, ed. *Lemberg 1941 und Oberländer: Das Ergebnis einer Untersuchung*. Amstelveen, 1960.

Zwehl, F. von. *Die Versenkung der Llandovery Castle*. N.p., 1921.

Pelzer, Sergeant Major, 67
Pendelbury (British captain), 34
Pesonen, Dr., 316
Pétain, Philippe, 98
Petsamo, Gulf, 261
Picker, Egbert, 223
Picot, Albert, 232
Piest, Judge, 257
Pihido, Fedir, 242
Pilichiewicz, Josef, 218
Piraeus, 254
Pisarek, Ludwig, 220
Pitea (German hospital ship), 261
Pless (Poland), 132, 139
Podwisskoje, 105
Pogegen, 102
Pola, 86, 263
Poland, 92ff, 129ff
Polish West Institute, 139
Popov Army, 106
Posen. *See* Poznan
Pospieszalski, Karol, 139
Poszich, Surgeon-General, 298
Pothmann (German soldier), 18
Potapov, M. I., 169
Poznan, xvi, 18, 29, 129ff, 300; Himmler's
   speech in, 110
Prasses (Crete), 161
Prechtel, Georg, 251
Premm, Martin, 160
Prisoners of War: asphyxiation of, 86, 328;
   repatriation of, 43f, 114ff; Romanian, 167,
   187; shackling of, 43f, 83, 108, 296; trials of,
   90ff
Prisons. *See names:* Lvov, Vinnitsa
Propaganda, xv, 87, 104, 168ff
Protecting Power, 3, 28, 44ff, 80, 82ff, 90,
   109, 116, 258, 277, 296, 327
Protest notes. *See* Diplomatic protests
Provost Marshal General (U.S.), 46
Prussian Bureau on War Crimes, xiv, 5, 9, 14,
   103, 121f, 325
Publikationsstelle Berlin Dahlem, 239
Pütz, Josef, 318

Quast, Wanda, 137
Quesada, Enrique, 311

Quidde, Günther, 265

Raczynski, Edward, 221
Radianska Ukraina, 224
Radio and wireless messages, 53, 166
Radke, Georg, 181
Rakocy, Sigmund, 93
Ramdohr, Wilken von, 136f
Rasch, Otto, 222
Ratin, Jakov, 103
Rawa Ruska (Soviet Union), 304
Red Cross: German, 10; International Com-
   mittee of the, 9, 14, 43, 88, 108, 132, 153, 229,
   232, 309; nurses, 189f; Polish, 229ff, 233f;
   Soviet, 88; Ukrainian, 221
Red cross markings, 50, 84f, 257, 291
Reddemann (sailor), 249
Red Star (Soviet newspaper), 168
Reger, Horst, 17, 21, 133ff, 299
Reich, Felix, 250
Reichardt, Günther, 68
Reichskriegsgericht, 18
Reimann, Willi, 45, 286
Reims, 4, 6
Reineke, Judge, 161
Repatriation of POWs, 43f, 114ff
Reprisals, 94, 105ff, 122, 154, 161, 222, 259, 295
Rethymon, 158
Retzlaw, Reinhard, 99
Rhode (German POW), 93
Ribbentrop, Joachim von, 81
Riep, Karl, 255
Rimscha (German Foreign Office official), 35
Ritz, Hans, 99
Ritgen, Udo, 138f
Rjassny, 166
Roberts, Frank, 221
Roddewig, W., 158
Roediger, Conrad, 77, 97, 114
Romanian POWs, 167, 187
Roncq, 146
Roosevelt, President Franklin, 11
Rorqual (British submarine), 253
Rose, Werner, 308
Roslawl, 61ff, 288
Rostin, Ernst, 71
Rouen, 146